THE CRIMINAL LAW REVOLUTION AND ITS AFTERMATH

1960-1974

THE CRIMINAL LAW REVOLUTION AND ITS AFTERMATH

1960-1974

By the Editors of
The Criminal Law Reporter

Published 1975 by
THE BUREAU OF NATIONAL AFFAIRS, INC.
WASHINGTON, D.C.

Printed in the United States of America
International Standard Book Number: 0-87179-139-0
Library of Congress Catalog Card Number: 74-24949

Introduction

Meteorologists need but glance at a wind-measuring device to discern the point at which a gale becomes a hurricane. No such simple calculation is available to measure the point at which the "winds of change" in the criminal law passed from evolution to revolution. Certainly the process of evolution quickened in the second and third decades of the twentieth century. As American society became increasingly mobile and urban and the legislation generated by the Sixteenth and Nineteenth Amendments thrust major new law enforcement responsibilities upon the Federal Government, questions concerning the procedural rights of criminal defendants came under closer and more frequent scrutiny by the U.S. Supreme Court. In 1914, the Court first held, in Weeks v. U.S., 232 U.S. 383, that evidence seized in violation of the Fourth Amendment could not be used against a defendant in a federal prosecution. In the 1930s, beginning with Brown v. Mississippi, 297 U.S. 278, the Court first began to examine state interrogation practices for violations of the Fourteenth Amendment Due Process Clause. In 1949, in Wolf v. Colorado, 338 U.S. 23, the Court indicated that the right to privacy embodied in the Fourth Amendment protected against intrusions by state, as well as federal, law enforcement authorities. But not until 1961, in Mapp v. Ohio, 367 U.S. 643, did the Court put to use the instrument that transformed the accelerating evolution of criminal law into a revolution: extension to the states of federal constitutional guarantees—as defined by federal standards—through the Fourteenth Amendment's Due Process Clause. Thereafter, through the 1968–69 Term, with the Fourteenth Amendment as a lever, nearly all the guarantees of the Fourth, Fifth, Sixth, and Eighth Amendments were made binding upon the states.

At the same time, numerous U.S. Supreme Court decisions were strengthening these guarantees. The Court's extension of the mantle of federal protections to persons accused in state criminal proceedings and its bolstering of these protections brought about dramatic changes in the criminal law. Some of these changes can be seen in a brief review of the decisions applying the various Bill of Rights safeguards to state criminal proceedings and of landmark decisions strengthening these safeguards.

The Court extended the various Bill of Rights guarantees to the states in piecemeal fashion. Although the "incorporation" theory espoused by Mr. Justice Black—that the Due Process Clause of the Fourteenth Amendment makes the Bill of Rights applicable in toto to the states—was nearly fulfilled as a practical matter during the 1960s, it has never commanded a majority vote on the Court. The Mapp majority simply asserted that Wolf v. Colorado, 338 U.S. 23, had stood for the proposition "that the right to privacy embodied in the Fourth Amendment is enforceable against the States" and, if the rule were to have any vitality, the exclusion of state-obtained evidence in violation of it was necessary.

If the criminal law revolution began with Mapp v. Ohio, it ended, with a flourish, on June 23, 1969. On that date, the last day of the "Warren Court" era, the Double Jeopardy Clause became the last Bill of Rights provision that the Court has applied to the states.

Fourth Amendment Exclusionary Rule

Mapp required of the states an exclusionary rule that most of them had already adopted. But its announcement that the Fourth Amendment exclusionary rule applied to the states assured that thereafter, each time the federal constitutional prohibition against illegal arrests, searches, and seizures was strengthened or expanded, state as well as federal law enforcement practices would be affected. And much new Fourth Amendment law was written by the Court during the 1960s. Electronic eavesdropping, involving increasingly sophisticated evidence-gathering techniques, was dramatically affected by several decisions, beginning with Berger v. New York, 388 U.S. 41. Striking down New York's electronic eavesdropping statute, the Court drastically stiffened probable-cause requirements for electronic eavesdropping. The next Term, in U.S. v. Katz, 389 U.S. 347, the Court erased the distinction between trespassory and nontrespassory electronic bugs. The Katz decision's impact carried far beyond electronic surveillance cases. In Katz, the Court formulated the "reasonable expectation of privacy" test to replace the property law concept of trespass to determine whether a governmental seizure or intrusion, by whatever means, comes under the Fourth Amendment.

Older and more commonplace government search and seizure techniques were also profoundly affected during this decade. Several decisions, most notably Aguilar v. Texas, 380 U.S. 400, and Spinelli v. U.S., 393 U.S. 410, refined, clarified, and made more stringent the "probable cause" test which all full searches and seizures, with or without warrant, must satisfy. And in 1969, a potential landmark, Davis v. Mississippi, 394 U.S. 721, made clear that the practice of "investigatory arrest"—detention without probable cause—violates the Fourth Amendment's proscription against unreasonable searches and seizures. But the considerable effect of these decisions was probably surpassed by the Court's drastic narrowing, in Chimel v. California, 395 U.S. 752, of the permissible area that may be covered by a warrantless search incident to arrest. The previous Term, however, the Court had taken special note of the rapidly unfolding on-the-street situations that frequently confront patrolmen. In Terry v. Ohio, 392 U.S. 1, it approved protective "stop and frisk" techniques by officers with reason to suspect dangerous criminal activity but no probable cause to arrest or search more fully.

Cruel and Unusual Punishment

The Term after Mapp was decided, the Eighth Amendment's cruel-and-unusual-punishment clause was applied to the states through the Due Process Clause. Holding in Robinson v. California, 370 U.S. 660, that California could not convict a man of addiction to narcotics, the Robinson majority stated "that a state law which imprisons a person thus afflicted as a criminal even though he has never touched any narcotic drug within the State or been guilty of any irregular behavior there, inflicts a cruel and unusual punishment in violation of the Fourteenth Amendment."

No startling changes were to result immediately from Robinson, although a minority of the Court in Powell v. Texas, 392 U.S. 514, was willing to hold that chronic alcoholics cannot be jailed for being drunk in public. But the cruel-and-unusual-punishment clause was applied to the States with the greatest effect 10 years later, in Furman v. Georgia, 408 U.S. 238, when the Court attempted to face squarely the question of the constitutionality of the death penalty. And other state prisoners besides those on death row have benefited from numerous lower federal court decisions condemning certain prison practices as cruel and unusual punishment.

Right to Counsel; Self-Incrimination

Perhaps the most dramatic decision announcing the application of a Bill of Rights guarantee to the states was Gideon v. Wainwright, 372 U.S. 335, in which the Court held that state defendants in noncapital cases are entitled to the assistance of counsel at trial as a matter of right. Its immediate practical effect, like Mapp's, was limited somewhat by the fact that many of the states already provided indigent criminal defendants with some form of legal assistance. But Gideon, in announcing that a state defendant's right to counsel was identical to a federal defendant's under the Sixth Amendment, opened the door for a host of other landmark decisions that greatly expanded an accused's right to legal assistance and compelled many changes in police practices.

It took the application of the Fifth Amendment privilege against self-incrimination to the states in Malloy v. Hogan, 378 U.S. 1, and the extension of the right to counsel to the interrogation room in Escobedo v. Illinois, 378 U.S. 478, to set the stage for the most controversial broadside of the criminal law revolution—Miranda v. Arizona, 384 U.S. 436.

Escobedo, announced the Term following Gideon, held specifically that interrogating policemen who refused to honor an in-custody suspect's request to consult his attorney denied the suspect his right to counsel under Gideon. The suspect's stationhouse interrogation, a majority of the Court emphasized, was clearly a critical stage of the proceedings against him—the process had shifted from the investigatory stage to the accusatory. The "critical stage" concept was the conceptual foundation for subsequent extensions of the right to counsel to other phases of the criminal justice process.

But it remained for Miranda to splice the right to counsel and the privilege against self-incrimination and fashion a procedure requiring police-provided pre-interrogation warnings designed to protect both of these rights from the moment a suspect is taken into custody.

U.S. v. Wade, 388 U.S. 218, extended the right to counsel to defendants in police-conducted lineups on the ground that such lineups were a critical stage of the proceedings. The right to counsel at the time of sentencing—even where sentencing occurs long after trial, at a probation-revocation hearing—was announced in Mempa v. Rhay, 389 U.S. 128. And a state prisoner's right to obtain at least some expert assistance in preparing a federal habeas corpus petition—even if he could do no better than a jailhouse lawyer—was established by Johnson v. Avery, 393 U.S. 483.

The Court held in Garrity v. New Jersey, 385 U.S. 493, that the privilege against self-incrimination forbade the prosecution of police officers who had given incriminating testimony under pain of losing their jobs for refusing to answer the questions that led to their self-incrimination. Also entitled to the privilege of the Fifth Amendment, under Spevack v. Klein, 385 U.S. 511, was a New York attorney who was disbarred for his refusal to produce records and to testify before a state judicial inquiry into unethical practices. The next Term the Court extended the privilege even further into the realm of public employment when it held in Gardner v. Broderick, 392 U.S. 390, that public officials could not be discharged for refusing to surrender the privilege.

The privilege was also expanded at the expense of federal marijuana and wagering tax laws that require individuals operating on the shady side of the law to choose between risking self-incrimination by compliance or prosecution for noncompliance.

Immunity From Prosecution

Malloy v. Hogan has other claims to fame besides its partnership with Gideon in paving the way for Miranda. The day Malloy was announced, the Court, in Murphy v. Waterfront Commission, 378 U.S. 52, overruled previous precedents and held that a state witness granted immunity from state prosecution is likewise protected against incrimination under federal law, and that a federal witness granted immunity is similarly protected from incrimination under state law. In the 1964-65 Term the Court, in Griffin v. California, 380 U.S. 609, held unconstitutional the prosecutorial practice of commenting upon a defendant's failure to explain evidence within his knowledge, as well as the judicial practice of instructing the jury that such silence may be evidence of guilt.

Right of Confrontation

In the years following Gideon, other Sixth Amendment fair-trial guarantees were applied, one by one, to the states. The right to confront witnesses was afforded state criminal defendants in Pointer v. Texas, 380 U.S. 400. Specifically, the Court held that introducing the preliminary-hearing testimony of a complaining witness who did not testify at trial, and who was not subject to cross-examination at the hearing, violated the defendant's right to confrontation.

Pointer subsequently gave birth to two powerful progeny—Barber v. Page, 390 U.S. 719, and Bruton v. U.S., 391 U.S. 123. Barber held that a defendant was denied his right of confrontation by the state's failure to attempt to obtain the presence of a codefendant, who was in federal custody in another state, before introducing prejudicial testimony that the codefendant had given at a preliminary hearing.

Bruton held that a federal robbery defendant's right of confrontation was violated by the use at his joint trial of a nontestifying codefendant's confession that implicated the defendant. Jury instructions that the confession was admissible only against the person who made it could not undo the damage its admission caused the defendant, the Court held.

In view of the practice, common in both state and federal courts, of jointly trying codefendants, Bruton generated much appellate litigation, and many conviction reversals, in the year after it was announced. However, its impact was subsequently limited by Harrington v. California, 393 U.S. 250, in which the Court held that the harmless-error criteria of Chapman v. California, 386 U.S. 18, applied to Bruton violations.

Right to Speedy Trial

The 1966-67 Term saw both the right to a speedy trial and the right to compulsory production of favorable witnesses made available to state defendants. Klopfer v. North Carolina, 386 U.S. 213, held that the speedy-trial right was a bar to a North Carolina procedure under which the state could, over defense objection, *nolle prosequi* a prosecution "with leave" to reinstate it without further order.

Federal prisoners against whom state charges were pending were assured of their right to a speedy state trial. Next Term the Court held, in Smith v. Hooey, 393 U.S. 374, 4 CrL 3077, that such a prisoner is entitled on demand to action by the state directed toward obtaining his relief from federal custody for the purpose of trial.

Production of Witnesses

The Sixth Amendment right of a defendant to compulsory process for obtaining witnesses in his favor was first applied to the states in a decision striking down a Texas statute that rendered persons charged as accomplices, principals, or accessories in the same crime incompetent to testify on each other's behalf. Washington v. Texas, 388 U.S. 14.

Right to Jury Trial

The right to jury trial on charges involving "serious" offenses was announced in Duncan v. Louisiana, 391 U.S. 145. Duncan held that a person who faced up to two years' incarceration was entitled to a jury trial; the Court subsequently held in Bloom v. Illinois, 391 U.S. 194, that serious contempts also carried with them the right to a jury trial.

Double Jeopardy

The last of the Bill of Rights protections to be afforded state defendants was the Fifth Amendment's prohibition against double jeopardy, announced in Benton v. Maryland, 395 U.S. 784, the very last decision of the Warren Court.

The Aftermath

The change in Chief Justices at the end of the 1960s was symbolic, for in two respects the criminal law revolution wrought by the Warren Court was over. No more Bill of Rights protections have been applied to the states through the Fourteenth Amendment; indeed, few remain to be so applied. Also, whereas virtually every Term in the 1960s had brought further expansion of constitutional protections for the accused, this was not to be so in the years that followed. However, the impact of the Court on the criminal justice system has not subsided in the least. On one front, the Court has consolidated some of the gains made in the 1960s with respect to the rights of the accused. On the other hand, in some areas, particularly with respect to searches and seizures and the privilege against self-incrimination, the Court has engaged in what might be termed a counterrevolution—or at least a process of retrenchment. But beyond this, the Court has also brought about fundamental societal changes in entirely new areas--such as capital punishment, practices in the corrections system generally, and in such areas of controversial activity as obscenity, abortion, and the use of vagrancy and loitering statutes to keep "undesirables" off the streets.

The 1969–70 and 1970–71 Terms found defendants gaining a few added protections. The doctrine of collateral estoppel was incorporated into the Fifth Amendment's Double Jeopardy Clause. The sanction of the Speedy Trial Clause—loss of authority to prosecute—was extended to benefit prisoners incarcerated in one jurisdiction who have been denied prompt trial on outstanding charges in another jurisdiction.

The "proof beyond a reasonable doubt" standard was elevated to constitutional stature, but on such critical issues as the binding effect of guilty pleas, the balance was struck in favor of governmental interest. Furthermore, it became apparent that the permanence of a least one major component of the revolution was far from assured. The revolution gained much of its impact from the fact that, at the same time the Court was applying federal constitutional limitations to the states, it was also greatly strengthening and extending them. While there were no hints that these limitations would be lifted from state prosecutions, it became an open question whether the Court would weaken or further extend them.

In 1971, a 5-to-4 majority cut down on the exclusionary rule of Miranda v. Arizona (itself a 5-to-4 decision) by holding that it is inapplicable to impeachment use of an in-custody statement obtained without adherence to Miranda's guidelines, but which is found to satisfy "legal standards of trustworthiness." More important, perhaps, than the actual effect of this decision was the majority's unwillingness to feel bound by language in Miranda "not at all necessary to the Court's holding."

Fundamental Fourth Amendment questions were raised but left unresolved in the 1970–71 Term. While at least a strong minority appeared to favor strengthening the warrent requirement, three Justices expressed reservations about the Fourth Amendment exclusionary rule.

The 1971–72 Term made it clear, however, that the "Burger Court" is no less "activist" than was the "Warren Court"—and no less controversial. Besides handing down several decisions that required or portended fundamental changes in the day-to-day administration of criminal justice, it attempted to answer fundamental social and constitutional questions, such as the constitutionality and underlying morality of capital punishment in a modern society, and the limits on the executive branch's power to gather information that it deems necessary for the Nation's security or welfare.

Not all of the Court's answers to the controversial, headline-generating questions were clear; the Court divided sharply on the death penalty. Although the result of the Court's decision in Furman v. Georgia was to spare the hundreds of state prisoners then on death row, a close reading of the 10 opinions in that case, particularly the opinions of the two "swing" Justices, revealed that capital punishment was not necessarily a thing of the past. While sharp divisions also characterized almost every case involving First, Fourth, or Fifth Amendment questions, the Justices were virtually unanimous in announcing several decisions that were to have a more fundamental day-to-day effect on the criminal justice system than the more publicized cases. No criminal defendant, however petty the charge against him, was to go to trial facing possible incarceration unless given the assistance of an attorney. Each state parolee facing revocation was held entitled, under the Fourteenth Amendment, to comprehensive procedural safeguards. The Court also sounded a clear warning that the typical American vagrancy ordinance, serving any kind of police or community purpose that can be helped along by rounding up and arresting "street people," could no longer constitutionally be enforced.

The 1972–73 Term was most notable for two sets of decisions that went beyond constitutional standards applicable to the criminal justice system to the more basic question of governmental authority to regulate certain widespread but controversial activities.

Probably no controversy since the Dred Scott case presented the Court with deeper philosophical and social issues than the abortion cases. The Court responded by sharply curtailing the power of the states to interfere in the decision of a pregnant woman and her physician to terminate a pregnancy by abortion.

The state and federal governments obtained more leeway, however, in their efforts to regulate the sale, transportation, and exhibition of allegedly obscene materials. Although four Justices protested that it was simply impossible to formulate constitutional obscenity guidelines, the Court, in seven opinions in the 1972–73 Term and two more opinions the following year, offered comprehensive guidance that ranged from a new definition of obscenity to procedures that must be followed in obscenity seizures and prosecutions.

In the 1973–74 Term, the Court again resolved a controversy which had implications for American society and institutions beyond the criminal justice system itself. In announcing on behalf of a unanimous Court that the Constitution required President Nixon to yield key tapes for use in the Watergate coverup trial, the Chief Justice both reaffirmed the Court's historic role as ultimate interpreter of the Constitution and subordinated to the need for valid evidence in a criminal prosecution the right of the executive branch to keep confidential its actions and deliberations—at least absent the need to protect military and diplomatic secrets.

The Court's willingness in the past three Terms to entertain new or long-ignored challenges to institutions and social concepts might support the argument that the criminal law revolution has not ended, but continues along different lines. The Court's decisions on corrections matters furnish another example of its willingness to bring about fundamental changes.

However, the revolution is clearly over with respect to pretrial police and prosecutorial practices. In fact, on Fourth Amendment questions, a counterrevolution of sorts has been underway for the past two Terms. Federal court of appeals decisions carrying out, in the context of state and municipal police practices, what these courts had taken to be a mandate for strengthening Fourth Amendment practices have been consistently reversed. The Court has been faced with the choice, foretold by Mr. Justice Harlan in Chimel v. California, between long-standing Fourth Amendment practices and "state concerns long recognized to be consonant with the Fourteenth Amendment before Mapp * * * came on the books * * *." The Court has been resolving this dilemma in favor of law enforcement interests, and as a result, the Fourth Amendment warrant requirement has been weakened considerably. Moreover, a majority dictum in U.S. v. Calandra, 414 U.S. 338, has made it clear that the exclusionary rule itself is not immune from reconsideration.

This is only a brief outline of the rapid and continuing changes wrought by the Supreme Court during the criminal law revolution and its aftermath. In the pages that follow is a Term-by-Term recounting of the last nine years of the Warren Court and the first five Terms of the Burger Court—years of changes and controversy for the criminal law.

THE CRIMINAL LAW REVOLUTION AND ITS AFTERMATH was edited and primarily written by Anthony E. Scudellari, former Managing Editor of *The Criminal Law Reporter,* and John G. Miles, Jr., Managing Editor of *The Criminal Law Reporter* since 1969. Also contributing were Richard E. Crouch and George F. Knight.

Table of Contents

1960–1961 Term

Although illegally obtained evidence had been inadmissible in federal prosecutions for nearly half a century, since Weeks v. U.S., 232 U.S. 383, the states had not been compelled to follow this exclusionary rule. This, despite the fact that Wolf v. Colorado, 338 U.S. 25 (1949) had subjected the states to the rule against arbitrary intrusion by the police —the essence of the Fourth Amendment. But in Wolf, the Court had declined to take the step of enforcing this constitutional protection by banning the illegal evidence.

SEARCH AND SEIZURE

Mapp v. Ohio, 367 U.S. 643

The 1960–61 Term saw the U.S. Supreme Court take this step. Writing for the majority, Mr. Justice Clark considered, and found wanting, the current validity of the factual grounds upon which Wolf's nonexclusionary rule was based. "The Court in Wolf first stated that '(t)he contrariety of views of the States' on the adoption of the exclusionary rule of Weeks was 'particularly impressive' (at p. 29); and, in this connection, that it could not 'brush aside the experience of States which deem the incidence of such conduct by the police too slight to call for a deterrent remedy * * * by overriding the (States') relevant rules of evidence.' At pp. 31–32. While in 1949, prior to the Wolf case, almost two thirds of the States were opposed to the use of the exclusionary rule, now, despite the Wolf case, more than half of those since passing upon it, by their own legislative or judicial decision, have wholly or partly adopted or adhered to the Weeks rule. See Elkins v. United States, 364 U.S. 206, Appendix, pp. 224–232. Significantly, among those now following the rule is California which, according to its highest court, was 'compelled to reach that conclusion because other remedies have completely failed to secure compliance with the constitutional provisions * * *,' People v. Cahan, 44 Cal. 2d 434, 445, 282 P.2d 905, 911 (1955). In connection with this California case, we note that the second basis elaborated in Wolf in support of its failure to enforce the exclusionary doctrine against the States was that 'other means of protection' have been afforded 'the right to privacy.' 338 U.S., at 30. The experience of California that such other remedies have been worthless and futile is buttressed by the experience of other States. The obvious futility of relegating the Fourth Amendment to the protection of other remedies has, moreover, been recognized by this Court since Wolf. See Irvine v. California, 347 U.S. 128, 137 (1954). * * *

"It therefore, plainly appears that the factual considerations supporting the failure of the Wolf Court to include the Weeks exclusionary rule when it recognized the enforceability of the right to privacy against the States in 1949 while not basically relevant to the constitutional consideration, could not, in any analysis, now be deemed controlling. * * *

"The ignoble short cut to conviction left open to the State tends to destroy the entire system of constitutional restraints on which the liberties of the people rest. Having once recognized that the right to privacy embodied in the Fourth Amendment is enforceable against the States and that the right to be secure against rude invasions of privacy by state officers is, therefore, constitutional in origin we can no longer permit that right to remain an empty promise."

Mr. Justice Black, who wrote a separate concurring opinion, was "still not persuaded that the Fourth Amendment, standing alone, would be enough to bar the introduction into evidence against an accused of papers and effects seized from him in violation of its commands." However, "reflection on the problem * * * in light of cases coming before the Court since Wolf," led him "to conclude that when the Fourth Amendment's ban against unreasonable searches and seizures is considered together with the Fifth Amendment's ban against compelled self-incrimination, a constitutional basis emerges which not only justifies, but actually requires the exclusionary rule."

Also separately concurring, Mr. Justice Douglas asserted that "once evidence, inadmissible in a federal court, is admissible in a state court a 'double standard' exists which leads to 'working arrangements' that undercut federal policy and reduce some aspects of law enforcement to shabby business."

The dissenters, Justices Harlan, Frankfurter, and Whittaker, were of the view that "the Wolf rule represents sounder constitutional doctrine than the new rule which now replaces it." In overruling Wolf, the majority has "forgotten the sense of judicial restraint which, with due regard for stare decisis, is one element that should enter into deciding whether a past decision of this Court should be overruled."

Pugach v. Dollinger, 365 U.S. 458

Curiously, a few months before Mapp was decided, the Court handed down a short per curiam opinion that seemed to embody a rather different philosophy. Defendants in a New York state-court criminal trial were not

1

entitled to a federal district court injunction against the prosecutor's threatened use of wiretap evidence obtained under New York law but in violation of the Federal Communications Act.

Silverman v. U.S., 365 U.S. 505

Two decades ago, in Goldman v. U.S., 316 U.S. 129, the Supreme Court held that the Fourth Amendment did not bar the use of a detectaphone placed against the wall of an office adjoining the suspect's. In the 1960–61 Term, however, the Court distinguished — but did not overrule —Goldman, and declared that a federal court should not admit evidence police obtained by a listening device employing a spike antenna driven into a suspect's party wall from an adjoining building and making contact with a sound-conducting heating duct. Mr. Justice Stewart, speaking for the Court, pointed out that, in Goldman, there had been no actual physical invasion of the premises. "Here by contrast the officers overheard the petitioners' conversations only by usurping part of the petitioners' house or office —a heating system which was an integral part of the premises occupied by the petitioners, a usurpation that was effected without their knowledge and without their consent. In these circumstances we need not pause to consider whether or not there was a technical trespass under the local property law relating to party walls. Inherent Fourth Amendment rights are not inevitably measurable in terms of ancient niceties of tort or real property law."

However, the Court rejected the contention that Section 605 of the Communications Act was violated by the use of the spike antenna to overhear the suspect's telephone conversations. "While it is true that much of what the officers heard consisted of the [suspect's] share of telephone conversations, we cannot say that the officers intercepted these conversations within the meaning of the statute."

Concurring separately, Mr. Justice Douglas would not limit the Fourth Amendment "by nice distinctions depending on the kind of electronic equipment employed."

Chapman v. U.S., 365 U.S. 610

Two additional search-and-seizure problems were disposed of. The Court declared that the Fourth Amendment bars the use, in a federal bootlegging prosecution, of evidence obtained by federal officers summoned by state police to assist in the search of a rented home that state police and the landlord had entered without a warrant after the landlord detected the odor of whiskey mash emanating from the premises.

Wilson v. Schnettler, 365 U.S. 381

And, it was held that a federal district court, in the absence of any showing that federal proceedings had been taken against a state-court defendant, had no jurisdiction either to enjoin federal narcotics agents from testifying at the state prosecution concerning evidence uncovered when they arrested and searched the defendant without a warrant, or to enjoin the use of such evidence which, the state court had found, had been obtained through a search incident to a lawful arrest.

DISCOVERY AND DISCLOSURE

Campbell v. U.S., 365 U.S. 85

The Supreme Court divided 5–4 in reversing a federal district court's ruling that an FBI agent's interview report did not qualify as a "statement" of a witness to be impeached, subject to discovery under the Jencks Act, 18 U.S.C. 3500. The majority based its reversal on the district court's refusal to ascertain the nature of the report, to summon the agent on its own motion, or to require the government to produce him, and then asking him to examine the report and state whether it represented his statement.

For the majority, Mr. Justice Brennan asserted that the government's primary responsibility in a criminal case was to see that justice was done, rather than merely to win the case. He then pointed out that the government had several advantages over the defense, since it not only knew the contents of the agent's report but also had him in its employ and could readily ascertain the facts from him. Moreover, to allow the witness himself to inspect the paper created the "obvious hazard that his self-interest might defeat the statutory design of requiring the government to produce papers which are 'statements' within the statute."

Justices Frankfurter, Clark, Harlan, and Whittaker dissented in part. In their view, the majority decision placed the trial judge "in the position of a voluntary defender for defendants already adequately represented." Nevertheless, they concurred in remand of the case for further consideration as to whether the agent's report on its face actually met the requirements of the statute.

Clancy v. U.S., 365 U.S. 312

The Court also decided that the Jencks Act entitled federal criminal defendants to the production of memoranda that a government agent-witness, after interviewing them had prepared and based in part on notes and interpretations of other agents.

HABEAS CORPUS

Carbo v. U.S., 364 U.S. 611

Broad scope was accorded the federal habeas corpus statute, 28 U.S.C. 2241, when the Court held that a federal district court was authorized to issue a writ of habeas corpus ad prosequendum requiring the production of a state prisoner, then confined beyond the court's territorial jurisdiction, for the trial of an offense allegedly committed within its jurisdiction.

Smith v. Bennett, 365 U.S. 708

In 1958, in Burns v. Ohio, 360 U.S. 252, the Supreme Court held that a state could not constitutionally require an indigent defendant in a criminal case to pay a filing fee before permitting him to file a motion for leave to appeal in one of its courts. That decision was predicated upon an earlier holding, Griffin v. Illinois, 351 U.S. 12, that such a defendant was entitled to a transcript of the record of his trial or an adequate substitute therefor, when needed to effectively prosecute his appeal. In the 1960–61 Term, the Court went one step further and unanimously held that the Federal Constitution's Equal Protection Clause precludes a state from requiring an indigent convicted prisoner to pay a filing fee as a condition precedent to an application for state court habeas corpus.

Bushnell v. Ellis, 366 U.S. 418

Also the Texas Court of Criminal Appeals was told that it must accord a hearing on the habeas corpus petition of a young indigent noncapital felong defendant who was tried without counsel and convicted after the court failed to exclude an alleged involuntary written confession and allegedly failed to limit the jury's consideration of evidence of a prior conviction for another offense.

APPEALS

Lott v. U.S., 367 U.S. 421

An analysis of the Federal Rules of Criminal Procedure convinced five Justices that an appeal from a federal conviction taken within 10 days after the entry of an order denying a motion in arrest of judgment, which motion was filed within 10 days after entry of judgment, was timely under FRCrP 37(a)(2) even though the motion was filed within five days after judgment but more than five days after acceptance of a nolo contendere plea. Decisive of the issue was the majority's determination that the judgment of conviction and sentence, not the tender and acceptance of a nolo contendere plea, constituted the "determination of guilt" from which FRCrP 34's time limit for motion in arrest of judgment is calculated.

Dissenting, Mr. Justice Clark, joined by Justices Frankfurter, Harlan, and Stewart, stated that "acceptance of such a plea is a 'determination of guilt' and * * * today's decision is not only contrary to prior cases, but is also out of tune with the long accepted practice of both federal and state courts."

INTERROGATION AND CONFESSIONS

Rogers v. Richmond, 365 U.S. 534

Two Connecticut murder convictions, based upon challenged confessions, were upset. In the first, Connecticut was told that its courts cannot predicate a determination of the voluntariness of a police-extracted confession merely on a finding that the police method used had no tendency to produce an untruthful confession. Writing for a unanimous Court, Mr. Justice Frankfurter asserted that the Fourteenth Amendment bars such confessions not because they "are unlikely to be true, but because the methods used to extract them offend

an underlying principle in the enforcement of our criminal law: that ours is an accusatorial and not an inquisitorial system —a system in which the state must establish guilt by evidence independently and freely secured and may not by coercion prove its charge against an accused out of his own mouth."

Culombe v. Connecticut, 367 U.S. 568

A second invalidated Connecticut conviction was based on a confession extracted from a mental defective after prolonged pre-arraignment interrogation by police.

Reck v. Pate, 367 U.S. 433

Also held invalid by the Court was an Illinois murder conviction based on the use of confessions obtained by police from a 19-year-old of subnormal intelligence who was detained incommunicado for eight days and during that time interrogated for prolonged periods despite an illness that required hospitalization.

Coppola v. U.S., 365 U.S. 762

However, a federal bank-robbery defendant did not fare as well. In a seven-line per curiam opinion, the Supreme Court affirmed a Second Circuit decision that the defendant was not entitled to the suppression of a pre-arraignment confession elicited by federal agents during his 29-hour detention by New York police officers who had arrested him for the crime of bank robbery.

To Mr. Justice Douglas, the lone dissenter, it was "plain" that the prolonged detention was an "unnecessary delay" within the meaning of FRCrP 5(a).

SENTENCING

Greene v. U.S., 365 U.S. 301

Also before the Court was a case involving the scope of FRCrP 32(a). This Rule, which had its genesis in the old common-law right of allocution, explicitly affords a criminal defendant two rights before sentence is imposed: "to make a statement in his own behalf," and "to present any information in mitigation of punishment." Eight of the Justices rejected the government's contention that merely affording a defendant's counsel the opportunity to speak satisfies the rule. "The most persuasive counsel may not be able to apeak for a defendant as the defendant might, with halting eloquence, speak for himself." Mr. Justice Stewart merely thought this the better practice, to be applied prospectively.

Nevertheless, on the basis of the record before them, Justices Frankfurter, Clark, Harlan, and Whittaker held that Rule 32(a) was not violated by a federal district court's failure to use a defendant's name when phrasing the presentencing question, "Did you want to say something?" which was answered by defense counsel rather than by defendant. "We do not read the record before us to have denied the defendant the opportunity to which Rule 32(a) entitled him. The single pertinent sentence —the trial judge's question 'Did you want to say something?' —may well have been directed to the defendant and not to his counsel. A record, certainly this record, unlike a play is unaccompanied with stage directions which may tell the significant cast of the eye or the nod of the head. It may well be that the defendant himself was recognized and sufficiently apprised of his right to speak and chose to exercise this right through his counsel. Especially is this conclusion warranted by the fact that the defendant has raised this claim seven years after the occurrence. The defendant has failed to meet his burden of showing that he was not accorded the personal right which Rule 32(a) guarantees, and we therefore find that his sentence was not illegal."

However, in the future sentencing courts should "as a matter of good judicial administration, unambiguously address themselves to the defendant."

Mr. Justice Black wrote a dissenting opinion in which the Chief Justice and Justices Douglas and Brennan concurred. In their view, the record clearly shows that the defendant was denied an opportunity to speak before sentence was imposed upon him.

PRIVACY

Poe v. Ullman, 367 U.S. 497

The Court divided sharply when it rejected an opportunity to pass on the constitutionality of Connecticut statutes which, as construed by the Connecticut Supreme Court of Errors, prohibit the use of contraceptive devices and the giving of medical advice in the use of such devices.

Mr. Justice Frankfurter, who announced the judgment of the Court, was joined in his opinion by the Chief Justice and Justices Clark and Whittaker. As they saw it, Connecticut's undeviating policy of nullifying its anticontraceptive laws since they were first passed in 1879 required the dismissal of state declaratory judgment suits attacking such enactments as unconstitutional. The State's nullification, they reasoned, deprives the controversy of that immediacy that is an indispensable condition to constitutional adjudication. In this view, they were supported by Mr. Justice Brennan, who concurred separately.

The four dissenters believed that the case presented a substantial controversy and that the constitutional question should have been reached and decided; in addition, Justices Harlan and Douglas would have declared the laws unconstitutional. The Douglas-Harlan view finally prevailed when the statute was struck down 5 years later in Griswold v. Connecticut, 381 U.S. 479.

RIGHT TO COUNSEL

In three opinions involving the right to counsel, the Supreme Court held:

Ferguson v. Georgia, 365 U.S. 570

A Georgia murder conviction was rendered invalid under the Fourteenth Amendment by the trial court's refusal to allow defense counsel to question the defendant, whom Georgia law declare incompetent as a defense witness, while he was making an unsworn statement permitted in lieu of sworn testimony.

Reynolds v. Cochran, 365 U.S. 525

The Florida Supreme Court must give a state prisoner a hearing on his habeas corpus petition alleging that he was deprived of due process by the trial judge's refusal to grant his motion for a continuance in order that he might have the assistance of counsel he had retained in a second offender prosecution brought after he had served sentence under both earlier convictions, even though he admitted, after his continuance was denied, that he had been convicted of the first felony.

McNeal v. Culver, 365 U.S. 109

An indigent, ignorant, and mentally ill Florida defendant, convicted in a noncapital case involving numerous "highly complex legal questions," was entitled to a hearing on his habeas corpus petition alleging that his due process rights were violated by the trial court's rejection of his request for court-appointed counsel.

CIVIL RIGHTS

Monroe v. Pape, 365 U.S. 167

Mr. Justice Frankfurter was the lone dissenter to a decision that accorded the protection of R.S. 1979, 42 U.S.C. 1983, to a Negro family who complained that Chicago police officers, early in the morning and without a warrant, broke into their home; searched it; arrested the husband on "open charges"; and held him incommunicado and without arraignment while they questioned him for 10 hours. All this was said to be done "under color of" Illinois law, although the State had no statute, custom, or usage authorizing any of it. The defending police officers argued that a state remedy was available for the full redress of the family's grievances.

The majority, through Mr. Justice Douglas, said that R.S. 1979 was intended not only to provide a remedy where state law was inadequate, but to provide a federal remedy even though the state remedy, adequate in theory, was unavailable in practice.

1961–1962 Term

CRUEL AND UNUSUAL PUNISHMENT

Robinson v. California, 370 U.S. 660

In a new approach to the Eighth Amendment's ban on "cruel and inhuman punishments," the Supreme Court declared that sickness may not be made a crime, nor may sick people be punished for being sick. Since narcotics addiction is a sickness, a state cannot make it a punishable offense any more that it could put a man in jail "for the 'crime' of having a common cold."

Only Mr. Justice Clark and Mr. Justice White voted to uphold the conviction. Mr. Justice Stewart, who wrote the majority opinion, said "It is unlikely that any State at this moment in history would attempt to make it a criminal offense for a person to be mentally ill, or a leper, or to be afficted with a veneral disease. A state might determine that the general health and welfare required that the victims of these and other human afflictions be dealt with by compulsory treatment, involving quarantine, confinement, or sequestration. But, in the light of contemporary human knowledge, a law which made a criminal offense of such a disease would doubtless be universally thought to be an infliction of cruel and unusual punishment in violation of the Eighth and Fourteenth Amendments. See Francis v. Resweber, 329 U.S. 459.

"We cannot but consider the statute before us as of the same category. In this Court counsel for the State recognized that narcotic addiction is an illness. Indeed, it is apparently an illness which may be contracted innocently or involuntarily. We hold that a state law which imprisons a person thus afflicted as a criminal even though he has never touched any narcotic drug within the State or been guilty of any irregular behavior there, inflicts a cruel and unusual punishment in violation of the Fourteenth Amendment."

Mr. Justice Harlan was "not prepared to hold that on the present state of medical knowledge it is completely irrational and hence unconstitutional for a State to conclude that narcotics addiction is something other than an illness nor that it amounts to cruel and unusual punishment for the State to subject narcotics addicts to its criminal law." However, he agreed that the application of the California statute was unconstitutional in this case.

Dissenting, Mr. Justice Clark felt that California's "enlightened program" relative to narcotics addicts — including both the criminal and civil provisions — "is inherently one of treatment and lies well within the power of a State."

Also dissenting, Mr. Justice White was not at all ready to place the use of narcotics beyond the reach of state criminal laws. He did not consider the defendant's conviction to be a punishment for having an illness or for simply being in some status or condition, but rather a conviction for the regular, repeated unlawful use of narcotics immediately prior to his arrest.

APPEALS

DiBella v. U.S., 369 U.S. 121

The Supreme Court resolved an inter-circuit conflict respecting the appealability of pre-indictment orders suppressing evidence. With the exception of orders suppressing evidence in narcotics cases, an order entered either by the district of trial or the district of seizure, granting or denying a pre-indictment motion to suppress evidence, is interlocutory and not appealable.

Mr. Justice Frankfurter, for a unanimous Court, asserted that such an order does not fall within any class of independent proceedings the Court has otherwise recognized. To so regard such orders, entails serious disruptions to the conduct of criminal trials. In the 1956 Narcotic Control Act, Congress gave the government the right to appeal from orders granting pretrial motions to suppress the use of seized narcotics, but Congress has declined to extend this right to all suppression orders even though, since 1956, it has had before it at each session bills to accomplish such as extension.

Coppedge v. U.S., 369 U.S. 438

During the late Fifties the Court vacated and remanded numerous cases in which a U.S. court of appeals applied an erroneous standard in passing on a federal criminal defendant's application to appeal his conviction in forma pauperis. The sole statutory language by which the federal district courts are guided in passing upon such applications is found in Section 1915(a) of the Judicial Code, which provides that an appeal "may not be taken in forma pauperis if the trial court certifies in writing that it is not taken in good faith."

The 1961–62 Term saw the Supreme Court, "impelled by considerations beyond the corners of [Section] 1915" articulate a standard for the guidance of the lower federal courts in passing upon appeals by indigents. It was simply this: A federal criminal defendant who seeks review in forma pauperis demonstrates his "good faith" by raising any issue not frivolous. However, "good faith" must be judged by an objective, not a subjective, standard.

Moreover, "it is the burden of the government, in opposing an attempted criminal appeal in forma pauperis, to show that the appeal is lacking in merit, indeed that it is so lacking in merit that the court would dismiss the case on motion of the government, had the case been docketed and a record been filed by an appellant able to afford the expense of complying with those requirements."

Applying this standard, the Court held that an indigent's claim that the indictment under which he was convicted was procured through the use of perjured testimony requires the allowance of his appeal in forma pauperis.

Concurring, Mr. Justice Stewart and Mr. Justice Brennan offered an alternative solution to the problem — that courts of appeals simply grant applications to appeal from criminal convictions in forma pauperis as a matter of course, and appoint counsel to brief and argue each case on the merits. "The Government would then be free in any case to file before argument a motion to dismiss the appeal as frivolous. * * * In the absence of such a motion an appeal which after argument appeared clearly without merit could be expeditiously disposed of by summary affirmance, in the secure knowledge that all the issues had been fully canvassed. This procedure, it seems, * * * would not only save the time and energy of court and counsel, but would obviate the many difficulties which, as the present case shows, a complicated two-step system is all too likely to produce."

The two dissenters, Mr. Justice Clark and Mr. Justice Harlan, asserted that the majority had, for all practical purposes, repealed Section 1915(a) by placing the burden on the Government to sustain the district court certification rather than on the indigent to overturn it.

INSANITY

Lynch v. Overholser, 369 U.S. 705

With but one dissent, the Court gave a narrow construction to the District of Columbia Code provision (Sec. 24–301(d)), which provides for commitment in a mental hospital of defendants acquitted solely on the ground of insanity. The staute, which was Congress' response to Durham v. U.S., 214 F.2d 862, was enacted to protect the public against the immediate unconditional release of accused persons so acquitted.

As the majority reads the statute, it is applicable "only to a defendant acquitted on the ground of insanity who had affirmatively relied upon a defense of insanity, and not to one * * * who has maintained that he was mentally responsible when the alleged offense was committed. * * *

"To construe Sec. 24–301(d) as requiring a court, without further proceedings, automatically to commit a defendant who, as in the present case, had competently and advisably not tendered a defense of insanity to the crime charged and has not been found incompetent at the time of commitment is out of harmony with the awareness that Congress has otherwise shown for safeguarding those

suspected of mental incapacity against improvident confinement."

Mr. Justice Clark, the lone dissenter, expressed his "regret that the Court has seen fit to repeal the 'plain terms' of this statute and write its own policy into the District's law."

SEARCH AND SEIZURE

Lanza v. N.Y., 370 U.S. 139

In an opinion characterized by the Chief Justice as a departure from the Court's practice of refusing to reach constitutional questions not necessary for decision, the Court upheld the contempt conviction of a New York legislative committed witness who, after being granted immunity, refused to answer the committee's questions, all but two of which were based on New York prison officials' electronic interception of a visitors'-room conversation between the witness and his prisoner brother.

First, the Court gave short shrift to the contention that the interception violated the constitutional guarantee against unreasonable searches and seizures. "To say that a public jail is the equivalent of a man's 'house' or that it is a place where he can claim constitutional immunity from search or seizure of his person, or his effects, is at best a novel argument. * * * Without attempting either to define or to predict the ultimate scope of the Fourth Amendment protection, it is obvious that a jail shares none of the attributes of privacy of a home, an automobile, an office, or a hotel room. In prison, official surveilance has traditionally been the order of the day."

The Court then went on to say that the witness' conviction could be sustained solely on the basis of his refusal to answer the two questions that were not in any way related to the intercepted conversations.

Mr. Justice Brennan, joined by the Chief Justice and Mr. Justice Douglas, protested against the court's "gratuitous exposition of several grave constitutional issues * * * not before us for decision." To them it was apparent that the judgment below can be adequately supported by an independent ground of state law.

FAIR TRIAL —FREE PRESS

Beck v. Washington, 369 U.S. 541

The Court upheld Dave Beck's Washington state court conviction for embezzling union funds.

Beck had argued that the trial judge's failure to admonish the grand jurors to disregard or disbelieve adverse news reports and publicity deprived him of due process. To this, the Court replied that there was no denial of due process in the absence of proof that the grand jury was in fact biased or prejudiced.

Beck had also argued that the same publicity also precluded the selection of a fair petit jury. However, a study of the voir dire convinced the Court "that each juror's qualifications as to impartiality far exceeded the minimum standards this Court established in its earlier cases as well as in Irvin v. Dowd, 366 U.S. 717, 29 LW 4610, on which petitioner depends."

Dissenting, Mr. Justice Black, joined by the Chief Justice, felt that "the failure of the Washington courts to follow their own state law by taking affirmative action to protect the petitioner * * * from being indicted by a biased and prejudiced grand jury was a denial to him of the equal protection of the laws guaranteed by the Fourteenth Amendment."

RIGHT TO COUNSEL

In three opinions involving the right to counsel, the Supreme Court held:

Hamilton v. Alabama, 368 U.S. 52

The failure of an Alabama court to provide counsel before arraignment on a capital charge vitiates the conviction even though the defendant does not demonstrate any disadvantage flowing from the lack of court-appointed counsel at arraignment. In Alabama, arraignment "is a critical stage" in a criminal proceeding;

Carnley v. Cochran, 369 U.S. 506

A Florida trial court's failure to provide counsel for an illiterate defendant charged with a noncapital offense under Florida's complex Child Molester Act violated the Fourteenth Amendment; the defendant's failure to affirmatively request counsel did not constitute a waiver of his right to counsel.

Chewning v. Cunningham, 368 U.S. 443

The Fourteenth Amendment invalidates the Virginia conviction of a prisoner who, while serving his sentence for a third offense, was tried under Virginia's recidivist statute but was denied counsel despite his request therefor.

CONTEMPT

Russell v. U.S., 369 U.S. 749

The government came a cropper in several contempt-of-Congress cases heard by the Court. In its key opinion reversing six of the convictions, the Court by a vote of 5–2, held that an indictment charging a defendant with refusing to answer a committee's questions must state the subject under inquiry as found by the grand jury.

Once again Mr. Justice Stewart wrote the majority opinion: "The very core of criminality under 2 U.S.C. 192 is pertinency to the subject under inquiry of the questions which the defendant refused to answer. What the subject actually was, therefore, is central to every prosecution under the statute. Where guilt depends so crucially upon such a specific identification of fact, our cases have uniformly held that an indictment must do more than simply repeat the language of the criminal statute. * * *

"The vice which inheres in the failure of an indictment under 2 U.S.C. 192 to identify the subject under inquiry is thus the violation of the basic principle 'that the accused must be apprised by the indictment, with reasonable certainty of the nature of the accusation against him, * * * .' A cryptic form of indictment in cases of this kind requires the defendant to go to trial with the chief issue undefined. It enables his conviction to rest on one point and the affirmance of the conviction to rest on another. It gives the prosecution free hand on appeal to fill in the gaps of proof by surmise or conjecture. The Court has had occasion before now to condemn just such a practice in a quite different factual setting. Cole v. Arkansas, 333 U.S. 196, 201–202.

Mr. Justice Douglas concurred, but would go further. To the extent the committee was investigating the press, the indictments violated the First Amendment. "Congress," he said, "has no more authority in the field of the press than it does where the pulpit is involved. * * * I see no justification for the Government investigating the capacities, leanings ideology, qualifications, prejudices or politics of those who collect or write the news."

Mr. Justice Harlan and Mr. Justice Clark dissented. In their view, the majority's decision "bids fair to throw the federal courts back to an era of criminal pleading from which it was thought they had finally emerged."

Three contempt-of-court cases, two of which involved attorneys, were disposed of.

In re McConnell, 370 U.S. 230

A short look at the legislative history of Section 401 of the Federal Criminal Code convinced a 5–2 majority that an attorney's mere courtroom statement of his intention to press a barred line of questioning until the presiding federal district judge had the bailiff stop him did not constitute an obstruction of justice summarily punishable as a contempt.

Writing for the majority, Mr. Justice Black noted that Section 401 is based on an Act that was passed in 1831, 4 Stat. 487, in order to correct serious abuses of the summary contempt power and to limit drastically the broad undefined power of the inferior federal courts. "We cannot agree," he concluded, "that a mere statement by a lawyer of his intention to press his legal contention until the court has the bailiff stop him can amount to an obstructuion of justice that can be punished under limited powers of summary contempt which Congress has granted to the federal courts."

Mr. Justice Harlan and Mr. Justice Stewart dissented.

In re Green, 369 U.S. 689

In the other attorney's case the Court reversed his contempt conviction for advising a union in good faith that violation of an ex parte temporary restraining order against picketing provided a means of testing the state court's jurisdiction of the subject matter.

At the time the ex parte injunction and contempt order issued, an unfair labor practice charge involving the same labor dispute was pending before the National Labor Relations Board. Nevertheless, the trial court imposed sentence without giving the attorney a hearing and an opportunity to establish that it was acting in a field reserved exclusively by Congress for the National Labor Relations Board.

To Mr. Justice Douglas, the Court's spokesman, it was clear that due process had been violated. "The question," he said, "was whether the state court was trenching on the federal domain. The issue thus tendered emphasizes one important function that a hearing performs. It is impossible to determine from this record whether or not the dispute was exclusively within the jurisdiction of the National Labor Relations Board under the principles of San Diego Building Trades Council v. Garmon, 359 U.S. 236, 27 LW 4268, and Amalgamated Association v. Wisconsin Employment Relations Board, 340 U.S. 383. The Ohio court could not know whether it was within bounds in citing a person for contempt for violating the injuncion without such a hearing. For, as Amalgamated Association v. Wisconsin Employment Relations Board held, a state court is without power to hold one in contempt for violating an injunction that the state court had not power to enter by reason of federal preemption. Even if we assume that an ex parte order could properly issue as a matter of state law, it violates the due process requirements of the Fourteenth Amendment to convict a person of a contempt of this nature without a hearing and an opportunity to establish that the state court was acting in a field reserved exclusively by Congress for the federal agency. When an activity is 'arguably' subject to the National Board the States must defer to its 'exclusive competence,' 'if the danger of state interference with national policy is to be averted.' San Diego Building Trades Council v. Garmon, at 245."

Dissenting in part, Mr. Justice Harlan, joined by Mr. Justice Clark, stated that the Court's opinion did not enlighten them "as to why the Mine Workers principle should not obtain in a preemption case."

Wood v. Georgia, 370 U.S. 375

In the remaining contempt case, the Supreme Court had occasion to consider the scope of the constitutional protection to which persons are entitled when the publication of their opinions is alleged to be in conflict with the fair administration of justice in state courts.

Applying the clear and present danger doctrine of Bridges v. California, 314 U.S. 252, the Court reversed a Georgia contempt conviction of a county sheriff who, during a local political campaign and while the county grand jury was in session, published statements criticizing a county judge for charging the grand jury with respect to accusations against Negro political leaders and ordering the grand jury to investigate Negro bloc voting. In absence of any showing that the sheriff's statements actually interfered with the grand jury's deliberations, his conviction, the Court said, violated his constitutionally guaranteed freedom of speech. "Our examination of the content of [the sheriff's] statements and the circumstances under which they were published leads us to conclude that they did not present a danger to the administration of justice that should vitiate his freedom to express his opinions in the manner chosen."

In other opinions, the Court held:

INTERROGATION AND CONFESSIONS

Gallegos v. Colorado, 370 U.S. 49

The Fourteenth Amendment forbids a state to utilize a confession obtained from a fourteen-year-old murder defendant after several days detention during which the police failed to send for his parents, to bring him before juvenile court judge immediately, or to see to it that he had advice of counsel or friends.

SENTENCING

Crabtree v. Boles; Oyler v. Boles, 368 U.S. 448

The presentencing notification of a West Virginia defendant, to which neither he nor his counsel objected, that he was to be immediately sentenced under a habitual offender statute, bars his due process attack on his habitual offender sentence; the selective but nondiscriminatory enforcement of West Virginia's habitual offender statute does not violate the Fourteenth Amendment's Equal Protection Clause.

JURIES

Hoyt v. Florida, 368 U.S. 57

A Florida statute that accepts for jury service only those women who volunteer does not deprive a woman, on trial for murdering her husband, of the equal protection of the law in violation of the Fourteenth Amendment; the Florida jury commissioner's placement on the jury list of less than 5 percent of the women who had volunteered since the enactment of the statute but about 33 percent of the women who had volunteered since 1952, did not constitute arbitrary, systematic exclusion of women, in violation of the defendant's Fourteenth Amendment rights.

GUILTY PLEAS

Machibroda v. U.S., 368 U.S. 487

A federal prisoner was entitled to a hearing on his motion under Section 2255 of the Judicial Code to vacate a 40-year prison sentence based on a guilty plea allegedly induced by the prosecutor's out-of-court promise that the sentence would not exceed 20 years, since the allegation related primarily to purported occurrences upon which the trial record could cast no real light.

1962–1963 Term

Since 1942, when Betts v. Brady, 316 U.S. 455, was decided by a 5–4 majority, the problem of an indigent defendant's federal constitutional right to counsel in a state court had been a continuing source of controversy. In the 1962–63 Term, a unanimous Court laid the problem to rest by reexamining and overruling that decision.

RIGHT TO COUNSEL

Gideon v. Wainwright, 372 U.S. 335

The Fourteenth Amendment, the Court held, requires a state to appoint counsel for indigent defendants in noncapital as well as capital cases.

Accordingly, the Court reversed the conviction of an indigent Florida prisoner who had been denied counsel at his trial for breaking and entering a poolroom with intent to commit a misdemeanor —a felony under Florida law. As if to underscore the high value assigned by the Court to the need for counsel at trial, Gideon when retried, with counsel present, was acquitted.

The Supreme Court said, "In deciding as it did —that 'appointment of counsel is not a fundamental right, essential to a fair trial' —the Court in Betts * * * made an abrupt break with its own well-considered precedents. In returning to these old precedents, sounder we believe than the new, we but restore constitutional principles established to achieve a fair system of justice. Not only these precedents but also reason and reflection require us to recognize that in our adversary system of criminal justice, any person summoned into court, who is too poor to hire a lawyer, cannot be assured a fair trial unless counsel is provided for him."

Mr. Justice Harlan, concurring, agreed with the Court that a state criminal defendant's right to counsel in a noncapital case "should now be expressly recognized as a fundamental right embraced in the Fourteenth Amendment." However, "in what is done today I do not understand the Court to depart from the principles laid down in Palko v. Connecticut, 302 U.S. 319, or to embrace the concept that the Fourteenth Amendment 'incorporates' the Sixth Amendment as such."

Also concurring, Mr. Justice Douglas reiterated his belief that the Fourteenth Amendment protects from infringement by the states the privileges, protections, and safeguards granted by the Bill of Rights. "Rights protected against state invasion by the Due Process Clause of the Fourteenth Amendment are not watered-down versions of what the Bill of Rights guarantees."

Douglas v. California, 372 U.S. 353

In the same vein, and on the same day, the Court by a vote of 6–3, held invalid under the Fourteenth Amendment a California requirement conditioning an indigent defendant's right to court-appointed counsel on an appellate court's determination that assistance of counsel would be helpful.

To Mr. Justice Douglas, the Court's spokesman, it was clear that "there is lacking that equality demanded by the Fourteenth Amendment where the rich man, who appeals of right, enjoys the benefit of counsel's examination into the record, research of the law, and marshaling of arguments on his behalf, while the indigent, already burdened by a preliminary determination that his case is without merit, is forced to shift for himself. The indigent, where the record is unclear or the errors are hidden has only the right to a meaningless ritual, while the rich man has a meaningful appeal."

The dissent argued, "What the Court finds constitutionally offensive in California's procedure bears a striking resemblance to the rules of this Court and many state courts of last resort on petitions for certiorari or for leave to appeal filed by indigent defendants pro se." Also, that "with this new fetish for indigency" the Court has imposed an intolerable burden on California's judicial machinery.

Lane v. Brown, 372 U.S. 477

Also found constitutionally deficient was Indiana's Public Defender Act, which was enacted in 1945, to deal with the problem of providing legal assistance to indigent prisoners in post-conviction proceedings. The statute requires the public defender's approval before an indigent criminal defendant can obtain a free transcript of record that is a prerequisite to perfecting an appeal from a denial of a petition for a writ of error coram nobis.

Mr. Justice Stewart, who wrote the opinion of the Court, found it not without irony, that the constitutional problem stems from legislation "evidently enacted to enlarge [Indiana's] existing system of aid to the indigent." However, he was satisfied that the case was controlled by Griffin v. Illinois, 351 U.S. 12, and its progeny.

APPEALS

Draper v. Washington, 372 U.S. 487

The Court was sharply divided on the constitutional sufficiency of the mere stenographic record of a Washington state trial judge's hearing on a motion by indigent criminal defendants for a trial transcript they had requested for prosecution of an appeal alleging trial errors relating to the admission of testimony and exhibits, perjurious and self-contradictory testimony, and the trial judge's prejudice.

According to the 5–4 majority, such a record does not constitute a "record of sufficient completeness" required by the Fourteenth Amendment for the Washington Supreme Court's proper consideration of the errors assigned. "By allowing the trial court to prevent [defendants] from having stenographic support or its equivalent for presentation of each of their separate contentions to the appellate tribunal, the State * * * has denied them the rights assured them by this Court's decision in Griffin. * * *"

The four dissenters, speaking through Mr. Justice White, were satisfied that the defendants were afforded an adequate appellate review upon a satisfactory record. The majority's contrary ruling, they felt, severely limits the power of the states to avoid undue expense in dealing with criminal trials and places "their appellate processes in an inflexible procedural strait jacket."

Norvell v. Illinois, 373 U.S. 420

However, in applying Griffin to situations where no transcript is available due to the death of the court reporter, a state may deny relief to those who, at the time of the trial, had a lawyer and who presumably had his continuing services for purposes of appeal and yet failed to appeal.

HABEAS CORPUS

Fay v. Noia, 372 U.S. 391

Another landmark, Darr v. Buford, 339 U.S. 200, was also overruled. The Court held that neither a state prisoner's failure to appeal from his murder conviction that admittedly was based solely on a coerced confession nor his failure, if he does appeal, to seek Supreme Court review of an adverse state decision bars federal habeas corpus.

Mr. Justice Brennan, who wrote for a 6–3 majority, gave short shrift to the argument that a state prisoner who forfeits his opportunity to vindicate federal defenses in a state court has been given all the process that is constitutionally due him, and hence is not restrained contrary to the Constitution. This argument, said Mr. Justice Brennan, "wholly misconceives the scope of due process of law, which comprehends not only the right to be heard but also a number of explicit procedural rights —for example, the right not to be convicted upon evidence which includes one's coerced confession — drawn from the Bill of Rights."

He also rejected the contention that the adequate state-ground principle should apply to the federal courts in habeas corpus as well as to the Supreme Court on direct review of state court judgements. "The fatal weakness of this contention is its failure to recognize that the adequate state-ground rule is a function of the limitations of appellate review."

Moreover, he found no merit in the further contention that Section 2254 of the Judicial Code —which requires a state prisoner to exhaust his state remedies as a prerequisite to federal habeas corpus —embodies a doctrine of forfeitures and cuts off relief when there has been a failure to exhaust state remedies no longer available at the time habeas corpus is sought. Section 2254 is limited in its application to failure to exhaust state remedies still open to the habeas applicant at the time he files his federal application.

To the three dissenters, Mr. Justice Harlan, Mr. Justice Clark, and Mr. Justice Stewart, the majority decision was "one of the most disquieting that the Court has rendered in a long time." In their view, the majority has done away entirely with the adequate state-ground rule "in every state case, involving a federal question, in which detention follows from a judgment."

Townsend v. Sain, 372 U.S. 293

Dividing 5–4, the Supreme Court laid down six guidelines for determining when a federal court must grant an evidentiary hearing to a federal habeas corpus applicant. Such a hearing must be granted "If (1) the merits of the factual dispute were not resolved in the state hearing; (2) the state factual determination is not fairly supported by the record as a whole; (3) the fact-finding procedure employed by the state was not adequate to afford a full and fair hearing; (4) there is a substantial allegation of newly discovered evidence; (5) the material facts were not adequately developed at the state court hearing; or [if] (6) for any reason it appears that the state trier of fact did not afford the habeas applicant a full and fair hearing."

Jones v. Cunningham, 371 U.S. 236

Another habeas corpus problem was disposed of when a unanimous Court determined that the placing of a state prisoner on parole under the "custody and control" of the state parole board during the pendency of his federal habeas corpus petition did not render the case moot.

Pointing out that in the United States, as well as in England, the use of habeas corpus has not been restricted to situations in which the applicant is in actual physical custody, the Court concluded that a parolee is "in custody" within the meaning of Section 2241 of the Judicial Code and is therefore entitled to invoke federal habeas corpus jurisdiction. "History, usage, and precedent can leave no doubt that, besides physical imprisonment, there are other restraints on a man's liberty, restraints not shared by the public generally, which have been thought sufficient in the English-speaking world to support the issuance of habeas corpus."

Sanders v. U.S., 373 U.S. 1

In addition to its guideline decisions on habeas corpus by state prisoners, the Court set forth "the standards which should guide a federal court in deciding whether to grant a hearing on a federal prisoner's motion under 28 U.S.C. 2255."

A prompt hearing on the motion is required unless the motion and the files and records of the case implicitly show that the prisoner is entitled to no relief. In addition, the Court formulated basic rules to govern successive applications.

SEARCH AND SEIZURE

The Supreme Court threw considerable light that Term on the scope of Mapp v. Ohio, 367 U.S. 643, and the standards by which state searches and seizures must be evaluated.

Ker v. California, 374 U.S. 23

The Fourth Amendment, the Court declared, is enforceable against the states by the same sanction of exclusion as is used against the federal government by the application of the same constitutional standard prohibiting unreasonable searches and seizures. However, the test is not one of "fundamental" fairness; and the lawfulness of arrests by state officers for state offenses is determined by state law insofar as it does not violate the Federal Constitution.

The opinion reads: "Mapp * * * established no assumption by this Court of supervisory authority over state courts * * * and, consequently, it implied no total obliteration of state laws relating to arrests and searches in favor of federal law. * * * Second, Mapp did not attempt the impossible task of laying down a 'fixed formula' for the application in specific cases of the constitutional prohibition against unlawful searches and seizures."

In the light of these principles, the Court affirmed a California decision that state police officers who had received information that a suspect was selling narcotics from his apartment and who had on one occasion observed a meeting between the suspect and a known narcotics supplier, had reasonable cause to believe that the suspect had committed and was committing a felony and to enter his premises without a warrant and without his permission for the purpose of arresting him, using a key furnished by the apartment manager; and that the officers' search of the apartment after entering, seeing some narcotics in plain view, and arresting the suspect, was incident to a lawful arrest.

Moreover, the Court rejected the contention that the lawfulness of the arrest was vitiated by the officers' failure to demand admittance and explain their purpose before breaking into the apartment.

Concurring separately, Mr. Justice Harlan would judge state searches and seizures "by the more flexible concept of 'fundamental' fairness, or rights 'basic to a free society' embodied in the Due Process Clause of the Fourteenth Amendment." He felt that the Court's further extension of federal power over state criminal cases is uncalled for and unwise.

Concurring in part and dissenting in part, Mr. Justice Brennan, joined by the Chief Justice and Justices Douglas and Goldberg, agreed that the Fourth Amendment is enforceable against the states by the same sanction of exclusion as is used against the federal government by the application of the same constitutional standards. However, they felt that the federal requirement of reasonableness contained in the Fourth Amendment was violated in this case. "Even on the premise that there was probable cause by federal standards for the arrest * * * the [arrest was] nevertheless illegal, because the unannounced intrusion of the arresting officers * * * violated the Fourth Amendment."

Lopez v. U.S., 373 U.S. 427

Search and seizure problems arising out of electronic eavesdropping continued to engage the attention of the Court. In the 1962–63 Term, it had an opportunity to, but did not, overrule On Lee v. U.S., 343 U.S. 747.

Dividing 6–3, the Court declared that an Internal Revenue agent's secret electronic recording of a bribe offer made to him in the defendant's private office was admissible at the bribery trial in which the agent testified.

Although they cited On Lee as authority for this holding, the majority were of the view that the instant case "involves no 'eavesdropping' whatever in any proper sense of that term. The government did not use an electronic device to listen in on conversations it could not otherwise have heard. Instead, the device was used only to obtain the most reliable evidence possible of a conversation in which the government's own agent was a participant and which that agent was fully entitled to disclose. And the device was not planted by means of an unlawful physical invasion of [defendant's premises] under circumstances which would violate the Fourth Amendment. It was carried in and out by an agent who was there with [defendant's] assent, and it neither saw nor heard more than the agent himself."

Moreover, a bribe offer made in private to a federal agent who does not intend to accept is not a constitutionally protected communication.

While concurring with the result reached by the majority, the Chief Justice was of the view that On Lee was wrongfully decided and should not be revitalized.

This view was also shared by Justices Brennan, Douglas, and Goldberg, who dissented. According to the dissenters, there is grave danger of chilling all private, free, and unconstrained communication if secret recordings, turned over to law enforcement officers by one party to a conversation, are competent evidence of any self-incriminating statement the speaker may have made. "In a free society, people ought not to have to watch their every word so carefully."

Cleary v. Golger, 371 U.S. 392

Another search and seizure case involved the propriety of the issuance of a federal injunction barring a New York Harbor Waterfront Commission official from testifying, at state criminal and Waterfront Commission proceedings, as to information he obtained as a witness to but not as a participant in, federal customs officers' interrogation and search that violated Rules 5(a) and 41(a) of the Federal Rules of Criminal Procedure.

Voting 6–3, the Court declared that the injunction should not have been issued.

Wong Sun v. U.S., 371 U.S. 471

The "fruit of the poisonous tree" doctrine was applied to bar the government's use against a suspect of (1) incriminating declarations made by him after narcotics agents had unlawfully entered his bedroom and arrested him and (2) of narcotics subsequently discovered in another's premises as a result of such declarations.

However, the Court concluded the inadmissibility of the narcotics as to the suspect whose declarations led to their discovery, does not bar their admissibility as to his codefendant who was implicated by the person who surrendered them. The exclusion of the narcotics as to the suspect "was required solely by their tainted relationship to information unlawfully obtained * * * and not by any official impropriety connected with their surrender * * *. The seizure of this heroin invaded no right of privacy of persons or premises which would entitle [codefendant] to object to its use at his trial."

Also disposed of in this case was the issue whether a codefendant's out-of-court statements that will not suffice to convict can serve as corroboration of a defendant's confession. The Court held that they cannot.

DOUBLE JEOPARDY

Downum v. U.S., 372 U.S. 734

A 5–4 majority of the Supreme Court reversed a Fifth Circuit decision that a federal criminal defendant charged in a six-count indictment was not placed in double jeopardy by his trial by a new jury two days after the first jury, which had been sworn but had not heard any evidence, was discharged because of the absence of a prosecution witness on whom a subpoena could not be served and who was essential only for two counts that the trial judge refused to dismiss on the defendant's motion.

DISCOVERY

Campbell v. U.S., 373 U.S. 487

Finding itself unable to declare "clearly erroneous" a district court finding that an FBI agent's interview report was "almost ipsissima verba" the story told him by the government witness he had interviewed, the Court, by a 6–3 vote, ruled that the report, although neither approved nor adopted by the witness, was producible under the Jencks Act.

The witness' approval, at the conclusion of the interview, of the agent's oral version the notes upon which he had based his subsequently dictated report was sufficient, in the majority's opinion, to raise the report itself to the status of a written statement by the witness.

Brady v. Maryland, 373 U.S. 83

Maryland's suppression of an accomplice's confession, that he, and not the defendant, strangled the victim during a robbery, the Court held, constituted a denial of due process that entitled the defendant to a new trial on the issue of punishment, but not on the issue of guilt, since the accomplice's confession, as a matter of Maryland law, could not have reduced the defendant's offense below first degree murder; the defendant was not denied equal protection of the laws by the denial of a new trial on the issue of guilt.

INTERROGATION AND CONFESSIONS

Lynum v. Illinois, 372 U.S. 528

A unanimous Court upset the narcotics conviction of an Illinois defendant based on her oral confession made only after the police had told her that state financial aid for her infant children would be cut off, and her children taken from her, if she did not "cooperate." These threats were made while she was encircled in her apartment by three police officers who had arrested her in the hallway.

Pointing out that the defendant had no previous experience with the criminal law, and had no reason not to believe that the police had ample power to carry out their threats, the Court thought it clear that a confession made under such circumstances must be deemed not voluntary, but coerced.

Also rejected was the argument that the conviction did not rest in whole or in any part upon the confession. The admission of a coerced confession, the Court declared, cannot be deemed harmless error.

Haynes v. Washington, 373 U.S. 503

In a similar vein, the Court declared that a Washington burglary defendant was deprived of due process by the state court's admission of confession that he signed only after he had been held incommunicado by the police for 16 hours, during which he was told that he could not call his wife unless he cooperated.

GUILTY PLEAS

White v. Maryland, 373 U.S. 59

The taking of a guilty plea at arraignment on a preliminary hearing of a Maryland first degree murder defendant not represented by counsel, it was decided, vitiates the conviction even though the entry of the plea at that time was not necessary.

1963–1964 Term

Extension of the rights of state criminal defendants under the Fifth and Sixth Amendments highlighted the Supreme Court's decisions in the 1963–64 Term.

INTERROGATION AND CONFESSIONS

Escobedo v. Illinois, 378 U.S. 478

The bridge between Gideon v. Wainwright, 372 U.S. 335, which first made the right to counsel binding on the states in non-capital cases, and Miranda v. Arizona, 384 U.S. 436, which brought that right out of the courtroom and into the interrogation room, was Escobedo v. Illinois.

A five-justice majority of the Court declared that the refusal by Illinois police, during an interrogation process conducted while the suspect was in custody, to grant his request to consult his attorney constituted a denial of his constitutional right to counsel. As stated by Mr. Justice Goldberg, for the majority, the critical question was "whether, under the circumstances, the refusal by the police to honor petitioner's request to consult with his lawyer during the course of an interrogation constitutes a denial of 'the Assistance of Counsel' in violation of the Sixth Amendment to the Constitution as made 'obligatory upon the states by the Fourteenth Amendment,' Gideon v. Wainwright, 372 U.S. 342, and thereby renders inadmissible in the state criminal trial any incriminating statement elicited by the police during the interrogation."

To reach an affirmative answer the Court found it necessary to overrule Crooker v. California, 357 U.S. 433, and Cicenia v. Lagay, 357 U.S. 504, which held that a confession was admissible even though obtained after a suspect had requested the assistance of counsel, and been denied that request.

So long as the investigation had ceased to be a general investigation of an unsolved crime, the majority emphasized, it made no difference that the interrogation was conducted before rather than after indictment. At the time of his arrest, the Court emphasized, and throughout the course of the interrogation, the police had told Escobedo that they had convincing evidence that he had committed the crime.

The Court concluded: "We hold only that when the process shifts from investigatory to accusatory —when its focus is on the accused and its purpose is to elicit a confession —our adversary system begins to operate, and, under the circumstances here, the accused must be permitted to consult with his lawyer."

Mr. Justice Harlan dissented and would have reaffirmed Cicenia v. Lagay, 357 U.S. 504. He thought "the rule announced today is most ill-conceived in that it seriously and unjustifiably fetters perfectly legitimate methods of criminal law enforcement." Mr. Justice Stewart thought that the majority conclusion was supported "by no stronger authority than its own rhetoric," and that the Court had converted "a routine police investigation of an unsolved murder into a distorted analogue of a judicial trial." He, along with Mr. Justice Clark, joined in Mr. Justice White's alarm as to the extraordinary implications emanating from the case. He could "only hope we have completely misunderstood what the Court has said."

The alarm sounded by Mr. Justice White was that Escobedo would cripple law enforcement and make the policeman's task a great deal more difficult, all for unsound, unstated reasons, which can find no home in any of the provisions of the Constitution.

Massiah v. U.S., 377 U.S. 201

A few weeks earlier, the Court had held that incriminating post-indictment statements made by a defendant, while out on bail and in the absence of counsel, to a codefendant and surreptitiously recorded by the police with the assistance of the codefendant could not be used at his trial.

Mr. Justice Stewart, for the majority, emphasized that the Court here dealt not with a state court conviction, but with a federal case, where the specific guarantee of the Sixth Amendment directly applies. He concluded that Massiah was denied the basic protections of that guarantee when there was used against him at his trial evidence of his own incriminating words, which federal agents had deliberately elicited from him after he had been indicted and in the absence of his counsel.

He did not question that it was entirely proper to continue an investigation of the suspected criminal activities of the defendant and his alleged confederates even though an indictment had already been handed down. "All that we hold is that the defendant's own incriminating statement, obtained by federal agents under the circumstances here disclosed, could not constitutionally be used by the prosecution as evidence against him at his trial."

Mr. Justice White again led the dissenters. Dissatisfaction with preventive programs aimed at eliminating crime and profound dispute about whether we should punish, deter, rehabilitate, or cure, he stressed, cannot excuse concealing one of our most menacing problems until the millenium has arrived. "A civilized society must maintain its capacity to discover transgressions of the law and to identify those who flout it. * * * It will just not do to sweep these disagreeable matters under the rug or pretend that they are not there at all."

Mr. Justice White, speaking for himself and Justices Clark and Harlan, found it a rather portentious occasion when a Constitutional rule is established barring the use of evidence which is relevant, reliable and highly probative of the issue which the trial court has before it — whether the accused committed the act with which he is charged.

The given reason for the result here —the admissions were obtained in the absence of counsel —seemed to Mr. Justice White equally pertinent to statements obtained at any time after the right to counsel attaches, whether there has been an indictment or not; they would also be equally pertinent to admissions made prior to arraignment, at least where the defendant has counsel or asked for it, to the fruits of admissions improperly obtained under the new rule, to criminal proceedings in state courts, and to defendants long since convicted upon evidence including such admissions.

Jackson v. Denno, 378 U.S. 368

Not many years ago, in Stein v. New York, 346 U.S. 156, the Court upheld the New York procedure that leaves to the trial jury the factual determination of the voluntariness of a confession. But in the 1963–64 Term, that decision was overruled and the New York procedure was held to contravene the Fourteenth Amendment. The Court just could not convince itself that New York's procedure could do justice to a defendant's rights. "The evidence given the jury inevitably injects irrelevant and impermissible considerations of truthfulness of the confession into the assessment of voluntariness. * * * It cannot be assumed, as the Stein Court did, that the jury reliably found the facts against the accused. This unsound assumption undermines Stein's authority." Moreover, it cannot be assumed that a jury which finds a confession involuntary will be able to disregard it. "The New York procedure poses substantial threats to a defendant's constitutional rights to have an involuntary confession entirely disregarded and to have the coercion issue fairly and reliably determined."

Justices Harlan, Clark, and Stewart dissented on the ground that "even under the broadest view of the restrictive effect of the Fourteenth Amendment, I would not have thought it open to doubt that the states were free to allocate the trial of issues, whether in criminal or civil cases, between judge and jury as they deemed best." Mr. Justice Black was also of the view that Stein was properly decided and should not be overruled.

SELF-INCRIMINATION

Malloy v. Hogan, 378 U.S. 1

Few Justices have lived to see one of their dissents become the "law of the land"; Mr. Justice Black has.

In the 1946–47 Term, Mr. Justice Black was unable to convince a majority that Twining v. New Jersey, 311 U.S. 78, should be overruled. Adamson v. California, 332 U.S. 46. In the 1963–64 Term he did, and the Court held that the states, no more than the United States, can compel incriminatory testimony.

"The marked shift to the federal standard in state cases began," the Court notes, "with Lisenba v. California, 314 U.S. 219, where the Court spoke of accused's 'free choice to admit, to deny, or to refuse to answer.' The shift reflects recognition that the American system of criminal prosecution is accusatorial, not inquisitorial, and the Fifth Amendment privilege is its essential mainstay. Rogers v. Richmond, 365 U.S. 534. Governments, state and federal, are thus constitutionally compelled to establish guilt by evidence independently and freely secured, and may not by coercion prove a charge against an accused out of his own mouth. * * * The Fourteenth Amendment secures against state invasion the same privilege that the Fifth Amendment guarantees against federal infringement — the right of a person to remain silent unless he chooses to speak in the unfettered exercise of his own will and to suffer no penalty for such silence * * * .

"The Court thus has rejected the notion that the Fourteenth Amendment applies to the states only a 'watered-down, subjective version of the Bill of Rights,' Eaton v. Price, 364 U.S. 263, (dissenting opinion). If Cohen v. Herley, 366 U.S. 117, and Adamson, suggest such an application of the privilege against self-incrimination, that suggestion cannot survive recognition of the degree to which the Twining view of the privilege has been eroded. What is accorded is a privilege of refusing to incriminate one's self, and the feared prosecution may be by either federal or state authorities. It would be incongruous to have different standards determine the validity of a claim of privilege based on the same feared prosecution, depending on whether the claim was asserted in a state or federal court."

Mr. Justice Harlan and Mr. Justice Clark dissented because the reasoning behind the Court's decision carries "extremely mischievous if not dangerous consequences for our federal system in the realm of criminal law enforcement."

Mr. Justice Harlan wrote: "I can only read the Court's opinion as accepting in fact what it rejects in theory: the application to the States, via the Fourteenth Amendment, of the forms of federal criminal procedure embodied within the first eight Amendments of the Constitution. While it is true that the Court deals today with only one aspect of state criminal procedure, and rejects the wholesale incorporation" of such federal constitutional requirements, the logical gap between the Court's premises and its novel constitutional conclusion can, I submit, be bridged only by the additional premise that the Due Process Clause of the Fourteenth Amendment is a shorthand directive to this Court to pick and choose among the provisions of the first eight Amendments and apply those chosen, freighted with their entire accompanying body of federal doctrine, to law enforcement in the States. * * *

"About all that the Court offers in explanation of this conclusion is the observation that it would be 'incongruous' if different standards governed the assertion of a privilege to remain silent in state and federal tribunals. Such 'incongruity,' however, is at the heart of our federal system. The powers and responsibilities of the state and federal governments are not congruent; under our Constitution, they are not intended to be."

Murphy v. New York Harbor Waterfront Comm., 378 U.S. 52

On the same day the Court turned to a related issue, whether one jurisdiction within our federal structure may compel a witness, whom it has immunized from prosecution under its laws, to give testimony that might then be used to convict him of a crime against another jurisdiction. The Court held that the constitutional privilege against self-incrimination protects a state witness against incrimination under federal as well as state law and a federal witness against incrimination under state as well as federal law.

This decision required the overruling of U.S. v. Murdock, 284 U.S. 141, where the Court had erroneously misrepresented the settled English rule as being "that a witness is not protected against disclosing offenses in violation of the laws of another country." The English rule was exactly the opposite, as pointed out by the Court of Chancery Appeal in United States v. McRae, L.R., 3 Ch.App. 79. Also overruled was Feldman v. United States, 322 U.S. 487. "In order to implement this constitutional rule and accomodate the interests of state and Federal Governments in investigating and prosecuting crime, the Federal Government must be prohibited from making any such use of [state] compelled testimony and its fruits."

Justices Harlan and Clark, concurring, rejected the majority's thesis that the "separate sovereignty" theory of self-incrimination is historically unfounded. However, they reached the same conclusion as the majority, "based rather on the ground that such a rule is protective of the values which the federal privilege against self-incrimination expresses, without in any way interfering with the independent action of the States and the Federal Government in their respective spheres. Increasing interaction between the state and federal governments speaks strongly against permitting federal officials to make prosecutorial use of testimony which a State has compelled when that same testimony could not constitutionally have been compelled by the Federal Government and then used against the witness."

CONTEMPT

U.S. v. Barnett, 376 U.S. 681

In the Ross Barnett contempt case the Court, by a 5–4 vote, held that neither the Sixth Amendment nor Sections 402 and 3691 of the Judicial Code guarantee a jury trial in a criminal contempt proceeding. Mr. Justice Clark, who delivered the majority opinion, said the constitutional issue was fully reviewed only five years ago in Green v. U.S., 356 U.S. 165, the latest of "a long and unbroken line of decisions involving contempt ranging from misbehavior in court to disobedience of court orders, [which] establish beyond peradventure that criminal contempt charges are not subject to a jury trial as a matter of constitutional right. * * * It has always been the law of the land, both state and federal, that the courts —except where specifically precluded by statute —have the power to proceed summarily in contempt matters."

Mr. Justice Goldberg, joined by the Chief Justice and Mr. Justice Douglas, espoused the view that summary contempt proceedings are restricted to "petty" offenses.

A second dissent, by Mr. Black, who was joined by Mr. Justice Douglas, ridiculed the idea that persons charged with criminal offenses such as criminal contempt are not charged with "crimes." He termed this rationale "a judicial fiction," and urged that it is "high time to wipe out root and branch the judge-invented and judge-maintained notion that judges can try criminal contempt cases without a jury."

Ungar v. Sarafite, 376 U.S. 575

In another contempt case, this time from a state court, the Supreme Court declared that the Due Process Clause does not prevent a judge who cites a witness for criminal contempt from sitting at the subsequent criminal contempt hearing. Dissenting, Justices Douglas, Black, and Goldberg deemed it a "travesty" on American justice to allow a judge who has announced his decision on the issue of guilt prior to the trial to sit in judgment at the trial. "Judges are human; and judges caught up in an altercation with a witness do not have the objectivity to give that person a fair trial."

JURIES

Arnold v. North Carolina, 376 U.S. 773

Racial discrimination in the selection of state juries came under fire. In a per curiam opinion, the Court because of systematic exclusion of Negroes from grand jury duty, reversed a North Carolina murder conviction of two Negroes. The defendants had offered testimony of the local county tax assessor showing that 5,583 white men and 2,499 Negro men were listed for poll tax. The clerk of the trial court testified that he could remember only one Negro serving on a grand jury in his 24 years as clerk. "This testimony," the Court said, "in itself made out a *prima facie* case of the denial of the equal protection which the Constitution guarantees."

Coleman v. Alabama, 377 U.S. 129

In another jury discrimination case, the Court held that the Due Process and Equal Protection Clauses invalidate an Alabama murder conviction of a Negro who had been denied the opportunity to present evidence establishing a systematic exclusion of Negroes from both the indicting grand jury and the convicting petit jury. The Alabama Supreme Court's affirmance on the merits of the denial of a new trial permits the United States Supreme Court to consider the exclusion issue even though it was not raised before trial.

SEARCH AND SEIZURE

Fahy v. Connecticut, 375 U.S. 85

Even though the Connecticut Supreme Court of Errors recognized the applicability of Mapp v. Ohio, 367 U.S. 643, 29 LW 4798, to a Connecticut criminal prosecution that antedated Mapp, the court upheld the conviction "because it found the admission of the unconstitutionally obtained evidence to have been harmless error." The U.S. Supreme Court disagreed, being of the view "that the erroneous admission of this illegally obtained evidence was prejudicial * * * and hence it cannot be called harmless error." Justices Harlan, Clark, Stewart, and White dissented.

Stoner v. California, 376 U.S. 483

A second search and seizure question was disposed of in short order as the Court declared inadmissible evidence obtained by California police in the search of a hotel room without a warrant but with the consent of the desk clerk. "No less than a tenant of a house, or the occupant of a room in a boarding house, McDonald v. U.S., 335 U.S. 451, a guest in a hotel room is entitled to constitutional protection against unreasonable searches and seizures. Johnson v. U.S., 333 U.S. 10. That protection would disappear if it were left to depend upon the unfettered discretion of an employee of the hotel."

Preston v. U.S., 376 U.S. 364

Another facet of the problem —reasonableness of the search —was also examined by the Court. Kentucky police made an arrest on a vagrancy charge and took the car in which the prisoner had been riding to a garage. Later they returned to the garage, forced the trunk open, and removed robbery paraphernalia. This, the Court found, was a search too remote to be incident to an arrest and under Elkins v. U.S., 364 U.S. 206, the evidence obtained could not be used in a federal robbery prosecution.

Rugendorf v. U.S., 376 U.S. 528

In what the dissent called a "Baron Parke approach," the Court ruled that a federal defendant's failure, at his trial, to ask for the name of a police informer in order to defend on the merits bars Supreme Court consideration of the trial court's claimed error in refusing this information. The Court also held that an FBI agent's affidavit that he had reason to believe stolen goods were concealed in a defendant's basement, supported merely by statement of an unidentified informant, was sufficient basis for issuing a warrant to search the basement and evidence seized as a result is admissible in a federal prosecution for receiving stolen goods. Moreover, withholding the informant's identity would not require suppression of the evidence.

The case appeared in quite another light to the dissenters. They cited Roviaro v. U.S., 353 U.S. 53, which held that "where the disclosure of an informer's identity, or of the contents of his communication, is relevant and helpful to the defense of an accused, or is essential to a fair determination of a case, the informer's privilege must give way."

Clinton v. Virginia, 377 U.S. 158

Also found invalid was Virginia's use in a criminal prosecution of evidence obtained by city police officers by means of a spiked microphone stuck into a party wall separating adjoining apartments.

Aguilar v. Texas, 378 U.S. 108

Topping off the Court's review of search and seizure questions, a divided Court applied the same standard for obtaining a search warrant to the states as that applicable to the federal government. The majority, in an opinion written by Mr. Justice Goldberg, ruled that a Texas police officer's affidavit that reliable information from a credible person revealed the presence of narcotics on the defendant's premises did not provide a sufficient basis for a finding of probable cause. A "search warrant should not have been issued * * * and * * * evidence obtained as a result of the search warrant was inadmissible at the [defendant's] trial."

DOUBLE JEOPARDY

U.S. v. Tateo, 377 U.S. 463

The problem of double jeopardy bothered the Court. Mr. Justice Harlan, for the majority, declared that the Fifth Amendment does not bar the retrial of a defendant in a federal criminal proceeding, whose conviction had been vacated in collateral proceedings in which he had urged that his guilty plea had not been voluntary, but had been induced in part by the trial judge's comments on punishment. The dissent took the view that the majority was departing from Downum v. U.S., 372 U.S. 734, 31 LW 4369, and in so doing was substantially weakening the constitutional guarantee against double jeopardy.

1964–1965 Term

In the years, immediately preceding the 1964–65 Term, much of the attention of the Supreme Court had been directed toward the delineation of the rights of the individual accused of crime; not a term had gone by in which the Court has not wrought dramatic changes in our criminal law by stiffening restrictions on police practices and extending the mantle of federal protections to state-accused persons.

However, the nearest thing to a lull in this ongoing criminal law revolution occurred in the 1964–65 Term. That Term's decisions on criminal law and procedure included no "blockbuster" decisions of the Mapp-Gideon-Miranda-Wade calibre. Nevertheless, the Court amply evidenced its continuing concern with the shape of modern criminal law by hammering out its usual large number of criminal decisions, many of them in the search and seizure field, and most of them accompanied by the chorus of dissent that was become a hallmark of Supreme Court criminal rulings.

FAIR TRIAL — FREE PRESS

Estes v. Texas, 381 U.S. 532

With only four Justices willing to rule that the televising of the trial of Billy Sol Estes was a per se denial of the constitutional right to a fair trial, and four justices deploring the practice but unable to see the infringement of any federal right, Mr. Justice Harlan contributed the vote necessary to form a majority by agreeing that the televising violated the Fourteenth Amendment, but limiting the ban at this time to notorious trials. Four Justices, in an opinion by Mr. Justice Clark, while carefully avoiding the enshrinement of Canon 35 in the Fourteenth Amendment, wanted to go nearly the whole hog, ruling TV out of the courts altogether with a reservation that future developments might change the situation. Mr. Justice Harlan's vote thus limits the television ban to present day, notorious trials. As a practical matter, these restrictions would seem to put the quietus on TV in the courts within the foreseeable future, since commercial possibilities are largely limited to notorious trials.

Mr. Justice Clark's opinion stressed that no actual prejudice need be shown, but merely the probability of unfairness —the impact on jurors, the effect on quality of testimony, the difficulty of judicial control, and the adverse effects of TV's scrutiny of the defendant.

Justices Stewart, Black, Brennan, and White thought that present-day TV in the courtroom is an extremely unwise policy, inviting constitutional risks and detracting from the dignity of the proceedings, but could not find any constitutional bar to the practice. The ultimate question, they insisted, is whether or not a fair trial was denied.

RIGHT OF CONFRONTATION

Pointer v. Texas, 380 U.S. 400

In other fair trial rulings, the Court held that the Confrontation Clause of the Sixth Amendment applies to the states and that the same Sixth Amendment standards apply to both the states and the federal government. The Sixth Amendment right to confront witnesses, said the Court in an opinion by Mr. Justice Black, is a fundamental one made obligatory on the states by the Fourteenth. The Court ruled that a Texas court had violated a defendant's right to confrontation by using testimony given by the complaining witness, who had identified the defendant at the time of the preliminary hearing without being subject to cross examination, but was not made available at the trial proper. Concurring in this ruling, Mr. Justice Goldberg expounded the view that the incorporation of the Bill of Rights in the Fourteenth Amendment is the process of extending rights, not simply making rulings as to what is fair or not fair. A right, he asserted, is extended undiluted by case law notions of fairness; therefore, federal and state rights under the Constitution are precisely co-equal.

Douglas v. Alabama, 380 U.S. 415

In a companion case, the Court struck down an Alabama prosecutor's tactic of calling a convicted accomplice of the defendant to the witness stand, securing a refusal to testify, and using the refusal as a springboard to read the accomplice's alleged confession into the record without affording the defendant an opportunity to cross-examine.

Mr. Justice Stewart, concurring, would have pitched both rulings on the Fourteenth Amendment, believing the Sixth unnecessary. Similarly, Mr. Justice Harlan, in his concurrences, saw the specter of the "long-since discredited" absorption doctrine rearing its head; he would have held that the situations called for application of the "concept of ordered liberty" test, not the independent invocation of the Sixth Amendment.

JURIES

Turner v. Louisiana, 379 U.S. 466

Unable to achieve concord on a matter of much less complexity, the Court found a deprival of fair trial in Louisiana's permitting deputy sheriffs who were the state's principal witnesses to take charge of the jury in a case involving the death penalty. The confidence of the jury in the testimony of the deputies, the Court pointed out, was part of a life-and-death decision, even if the jurors never discussed the case with the deputies. Justice Clark, dissenting, found no prejudice to the defendant.

Jenkins v. U.S., 380 U.S. 445

Per curiam, the Court held that a trial judge who told his jury "you have got to reach a decision" when informed that it was deadlocked after two hours of deliberation on supposedly insufficient evidence, had improperly coerced the jurors.

SEARCH AND SEIZURE

Linkletter v. Walker, 381 U.S. 618

The Court handed down a steady stream of search and seizure decisions, not the least of which was the long-awaited ruling on whether Mapp v. Ohio, 367 U.S. 643, could be used retrospectively to vitiate convictions antedating the decision.

Blasting the hopes of untold numbers of state prisoners throughout the land, and resolving the conflicting decisions of lower courts, the Court decided that Mapp's exclusionary rule is not retroactive.

There is in the Constitution, said the Court, neither a compulsion to, nor a prohibition of, retroactivity. As Mr. Justice Cardozo said in Great Northern R. Co. v. Sunburst Oil Co., 287 U.S. 358, the Constitution "has no voice" on the subject. Looking to the basis of the exclusionary rule, Mr. Justice Clark held that since Mapp (which he wrote) was essentially aimed at control of police practices, it has the wrong "nature" for retroactivity. What is more, to apply it retroactively would necessitate the rehearing of numerous old cases. "To thus legitimate such an extraordinary procedural weapon that has no bearing on guilt would seriously disrupt the administration of justice." The cases decided under the defunct rule of Wolf v. Colorado, 338 U.S. 25, he concluded, cannot be "obliterated."

Thus for Fourth Amendment purposes the Court adopted the Austinian rather than the Blackstonian approach. Austin thought that judges had done something more than simply "fail at true discovery" when they decided a case wrongly and later overruled it. He believed that at the very least judges make interstitial law and that their past decisions are not erased, but are existing juridical facts until overruled. Overruling, therefore, would leave undisturbed cases decided in the interim.

The accepted rule, the Court concluded, "is that in appropriate cases the Court may in the interest of justice make the rule prospective," citing as authority Mr. Justice Black's dissent in Mosser v. Darrow, 341 U.S. 267.

In a dissent in which Mr. Justice Douglas joined, Mr. Justice Black insisted that the conviction here was admittedly unconstitutional, and could not see how the petitioner could be "late" when, in Fay v. Noia, 372 U.S. 391, a convict of 18 years was not too late to reap the benefits of a subsequent determination that his conviction was unconstitutional. The promises of Mapp and Noia, he said, are broken.

U.S. v. Ventresca, 380 U.S. 102

Persevering in the attempt to define the undefinable — probable cause —the Court ruled that the belief of a revenue officer, based upon his own knowledge and information from other investigators, that an illegal still was being operated at a certain address justified the issuance of a search warrant. Mr. Justice Goldberg, for the majority, was not dismayed by the use of hearsay evidence in obtaining a warrant nor by the asserted unreasonability of inferences drawn by the police from the facts available. As Mr. Justice Jackson pointed out nearly 20 years ago in U.S. v. Johnson, 333 U.S. 10, the point of the Fourth Amendment is that a magistrate, not the police, must make the probable cause decision. If the facts reasonably support him, the Court said, his decision is not assailable on constitutional grounds. The Chief Justice and Mr. Justice Douglas, disagreeing with the majority's interpretation of the facts, dissented.

Beck v. Ohio, 379 U.S. 89

Underlining the difficulty of the definition of probable cause, the Court, by a 6–3 vote, ruled that an arrest, based on police knowledge of a suspect's numbers connections and "information" from a vague source that he was involved in illegal gambling, was invalid under the Fourth and Fourteenth Amendments. The good faith of the police, the Court said, is not enough where the basis for detention is too scanty, as it was here.

Justices Harlan, Clark, and Black thought that the Court was overlooking established and adequate facts, and, on subjective notions of adequacy, was reaching out to disturb reasonable state findings.

Henry v. Mississippi, 379 U.S. 443

In another search and seizure decision, the same three voices, joined by Mr. Justice Stewart's, were heard in dissent from the proposition that Mississippi's failure to determine a defendant's waiver of objection to illegally seized evidence based on the state's contemporary objection rule requires remand for a waiver decision. Mr. Justice Brennan, writing for the majority, held that the waiver question had to be decided, since the contemporary objection rule is a valid state procedural interest that could establish an "independent and adequate state ground" for decision, avoiding the constitutional issues. That is, if the timely assertion of constitutional claims actually was waived, the constitutional claims may be precluded.

The underlying search-and-seizure claim in the case was that consent by the defendant's wife to search of his car did not cure the constitutional infirmity of the search and resultant seizure of incriminating evidence.

Justices Harlan, Clark, and Stewart feared that the Court was extending the rule of Fay v. Noia, 372 U.S. 391, to direct review. The state ground here —the contemporary objection rule —was clearly adequate, said these three, and the Court's decision severely limits the meaning of the word "adequate." Mr. Justice Black could see no independent and adequate state ground and would have gone directly to the underlying search-and-seizure issue or have simply decided the waiver question. The Mississippi rule, he asserted, cannot shut off the Court; this decision allows the state, on remand, to cure a constitutional deficiency by a form of words.

One 1958 Plymouth Sedan v. Pennsylvania, 380 U.S. 693

In nearly complete agreement, the Court ruled that the Fourth Amendment's exclusionary rule, Mapp v. Ohio, 367 U.S. 643, applies to a state criminal proceeding to forfeit an automobile for transporting bootleg liquor. An automobile is clearly not contraband, said the Court, making alcohol and narcotics cases inapposite. Mr. Justice Black concurred on the ground that Mapp recognizes that the principle involved is the Fifth Amendment's self-incrimination provision, which implements the Fourth Amendment.

Stanford v. Texas, 379 U.S. 476

In total accord, the Court decided that a warrant authorizing seizure of literary material concerning the operations of the Texas Communist Party was a general warrant prohibited by the Fourth and Fourteenth Amendments. The warrants, said Mr. Justice Stewart, had an "indiscriminate sweep."

SELF-INCRIMINATION

Griffin v. California, 380 U.S. 609

A practice sanctioned by the American Bar Association, the American Law Institute, the Uniform Code of Evidence, and the Model Code of Evidence bit the dust with a 6–2 decision that the Fifth Amendment forbids a state prosecutor's comment on failure of a defendant to explain evidence within his knowledge and bars an instruction from the court that such silence may be evidence of guilt. The comment rule, said Mr. Justice Douglas, is a remnant of the inquisitorial system and violates the Fifth Amendment whether it is invoked under a state statute or a state constitution. Assertion of the privilege of silence cannot be made "costly" by allowing the state to make hay of the defendant's silence. This holding broadens the meaning of Malloy v. Hogan, 378

U.S. 1, which applied the self-incrimination clause of the Fifth Amendment to the states.

Mr. Justice Harlan concurred "reluctantly," seeing in the decision more of the "creeping paralysis" of the incorporation doctrine "infecting the federal system."

Justices Stewart and White dissented. To them, the key is the presence or absence of a compulsion to bear witness against oneself. The comment rule, they argued, rather than compelling testimony by assessing a penalty for failure to speak, actually does a silent defendant a good turn by controlling a jury's speculations on his silence —a fact of which the jury is assuredly aware.

The Court expressly reserved decision on whether the accused may demand a jury instruction in a state prosecution that his silence must be disregarded. Federal courts deliver such instructions on request.

FIRST AMENDMENT

Garrison v. Louisiana, 379 U.S. 64

The rule of New York Times Co. v. Sullivan, 376 U.S. 254, was extended to criminal cases by an almost unanimous Court. The "differing history and purposes of criminal libel" have no effect on the constitutional infirmity of criminal convictions based upon defamatory statements about public officials that are either true, though malicious, or false but not knowingly false or reckless, said the majority.

Contrary to the New York Times rule, which immunizes good-faith or truthful criticism of public officials, a Louisiana statute directed punishment for true statements made with "actual malice." Even where the utterance is false, said the Court, "the great principles of the Constitution which secure freedom of expression in this area preclude attaching adverse consequences to any except the knowing or reckless falsehood." Even so, the Court cautioned, the fact that "speech is used as a tool for political ends does not automatically bring it under the protection of the Constitution * * *."

Concurring, Justices Douglas and Black felt that the "gloss which the Court has put on * * * the First Amendment" makes it almost unrecognizable. The guarantee of the First Amendment, they contended, is basic and not subject to judicial dilution through a process of case-by-case "balancing." Mr. Justice Goldberg, concurring, would have ruled flatly that the freedom to criticize public officials is unconditional.

STATUTES

U.S. v. Gainey, 380 U.S. 63

In another criminal decision, the Court ruled, 7–2, that the presumption of guilt created, under Section 5601 of the Internal Revenue Code, by the defendant's unexplained presence at an unregistered still does not violate the Fifth Amendment's Due Process Clause, since the presumption constitutes a rational connection between facts proven and ultimate facts presumed. To the majority, the presumption had "natural probative force."

Although the majority read the defendant's failure to testify out of the case, Mr. Justice Black, in dissent, argued that the presumption forced him either to come forward or incriminate himself, a Fifth Amendment violation.

Singer v. U.S., 380 U.S. 24

In another jury decision, the Court held that Article III, Section 2 of the Constitution and the Sixth Amendment give no absolute right to a jury trial. FRCrP 23 (a)'s conditioning of a defendant's right to waive a jury trial on consent of the government and the court thus does not violate the Constitution. In an opinion by the Chief Justice, the Court pointed out that history does not support the contention that the ability to waive trial by jury is of equal standing with the right to demand a jury trial.

POST-CONVICTION RELIEF

Case v. Nebraska, 381 U.S. 336

In a straw-in-the-wind decision that bode no good for the criminal dockets of those states that afford only cursory post-conviction relief procedures, the Court mooted the question of what post-conviction procedures a state must provide, since Nebraska had happily enacted a post-conviction relief statute after certiorari had been granted.

PRIVACY

Griswold v. Connecticut, 381 U.S. 479

The sharp disagreement that marks the Court's criminal law decisions was perhaps most evident in the Planned Parenthood case, when Connecticut's up-to-now impregnable anti-birth-control statute, under siege since 1942, was flattened by a judicial broadside that involved six amendments to the Constitution.

Seven members of the Court agreed that the statute violated the Fourteenth Amendment, but could not agree on why it did. Mr. Justice Douglas, writing for the Court, held that the statute intruded on a right of privacy emanating from the First, Third, Fourth, Fifth, Ninth, and Fourteenth Amendments. The statute, he said, invaded the zone of privacy set up by these amendments by forbidding the use of contraceptives rather than by regulating their manufacture and sale. Thus the statute "sweeps unnecessarily broadly" and seeks to achieve its goals by means having a maximum destructive impact on the marital relationship.

Unable to perceive the emanations of privacy from the six named amendments, Mr. Justice Harlan believed that the Connecticut law violated "basic values inherent in the concept of ordered liberty" under the Fourteenth Amendment.

Agreeing that the statute succumbs to the Fourteenth Amendment, Justices Goldberg and Brennan and Chief Justice Warren would have stressed the Ninth Amendment. Mr. Justice White, also agreeing that the Fourteenth Amendment was contravened, took a different tack and pointed out that Connecticut can show no justification for attempted interference with the marital relationship. "There is no serious contention," he said, "that Connecticut thinks the use of artificial or external methods of contraception immoral or unwise in itself, or that the anti-use statute is founded upon any policy of promoting population expansion. Rather, the statute is said to serve the state's policy against all forms of promiscuous or illicit sexual relationships, be they premarital or extra-marital, concededly a permissible and legitimate legislative law." The state's ban, he concluded, in no way reinforces a policy of preventing illicit relationships and thus cannot stand.

Despite Mr. Justice Douglas' disclaimer, Justices Black and Stewart, in dissent, saw in the decision the renascence of Lochner v. New York, 198 U.S. 45, and its "long-discredited" progeny. They sounded the tocsin that the Court is abusing its function by sitting as a super legislature. Nor were the dissenters enchanted with what they termed the "recent discovery" of Mr. Justice Goldberg that the Ninth Amendment can be used as well as the Fourteenth to throw into the discard state legislation that violates "fundamental principles of liberty and justice," or is contrary to the traditions and collective conscience of our people."

1965–1966 Term

On a Sunday evening over 40 years ago a Mississippi deputy sheriff tied two naked Negro prisoners to jailhouse chairs and beat them with a metal-studded leather strap and a rope until they confessed to murder, thus triggering, in Brown v. Mississippi, 297 U.S. 278, the long judicial struggle to insure the rights of criminal suspects that reached a climax in the 1965–6.

INTERROGATION AND CONFESSIONS

Miranda v. Arizona, 386 U.S. 436

The Court in Miranda laid down a series of definitive rules to prevent police abuse in stationhouse interrogations. It declared that the Fifth Amendment bars the use of exculpating or inculpating statements that stem from custodial interrogation without procedural safeguards that would secure the privilege against self-incrimination as effectively as the requirement that the accused be advised of his right to remain silent, that any statement made can be used against him, and that he is entitled to the presence of appointed or retained counsel during the interrogation. An accused who wishes to consult with counsel or indicates in any way that he does not wish to be interrogated cannot be further questioned. Any questioning initiated by a law enforcement officer after a person has been taken into custody or otherwise deprived of his freedom of action in any significant way constitutes custodial interrogation. Finally, in recognition of the fact that there are almost always two versions of what happened in the stationhouse, the Court held that the prosecution bears the burden of proving that the accused waived his right to remain silent or his right to counsel.

A 5–4 majority of the Court found these measures necessary to extirpate the compulsion inherent in custodial surroundings. The heart of the holding is that the Fifth and Sixth Amendments reach into the stationhouse and require that the accused be adequately and effectively apprised of his rights and that the exercise of those rights be fully honored by the police. The majority denied that there is any necessity for a "stationhouse lawyer" standing by at all times. What is required is that the accused be informed in clear and unequivocal terms of his rights. Nor did the majority find any weight in the contention that the privilege is waived if the individual answers some questions or gives some information on his own prior to invoking his right to remain silent when interrogated. Rather, the mere fact of lengthy interrogation or incommunicado incarceration

before a statement is made is strong evidence that the accused did not validly waive his rights.

Three dissenters, Justices Harlan, Stewart, and White, characterized the majority view as "voluntariness with a vengeance." The due process test of voluntariness is an adequate tool for coping with confessions. Not only is the majority decision poor constitutional law, the dissenters continued, but it entails harmful consequences for the country at large. "It is no secret that concern has been expressed lest long-range and lasting reforms be frustrated by this Court's too rapid departure from existing constitutional standards."

What is more, they maintained, the majority has not given a definitive answer to problems of stationhouse interrogation, since questions as to whether an interrogee is "in custody" and whether a confession is the "fruit" of a prohibited interrogation are still open.

Mr. Justice Clark, dissenting separately, was unable to join the majority because its opinion goes "too far on too little," while his dissenting brethren "do not go quite far enough." The majority's "strict constitutional specific," he observed, "inserted at the nerve center of crime detection may well kill the patient." Mr. Justice Clark would prefer the "totality of circumstances" rule for determining whether an admission of guilt was involuntary.

Johnson v. New Jersey, 384 U.S. 719

Observers did not have to wait long for the retroactivity shoe to drop. One week after Miranda, the Court announced that the ruling applied only in cases in which the trial began after June 13, 1966. Similarly, the Escobedo rule, 378 U.S. 478, affects only those cases in which the trial began after June 22, 1964.

The Court stressed that the choice between retroactivity and nonretroactivity in no way turns on the value of the constitutional guarantee involved, nor is it automatically determined by the provision of the Constitution upon which the rule in question is based. Rather, retroactivity must be determined in each case by looking to the particular traits of the specific rule in question.

Since the prime purpose of Escobedo and Miranda is to guarantee full effectuation of the privilege against self-incrimination, they encompass situations in which the danger is not necessarily as great as when the accused is subject to an obvious coercion. At the same time, case law on coerced confessions is available for persons whose trials have already been completed. The nonretroactivity of Miranda and Escobedo will not preclude the invocation of safeguards outlined in those cases as part of an involuntariness claim.

Davis v. North Carolina, 384 U.S. 907

As if to hammer this point home, the Court on the same day ruled that a confession extracted from an impoverished, uneducated Negro escapee after he had been held incommunicado for 16 days of intermittent interrogation was involuntary. The fact that he was never effectively apprised of his rights, the Court observed, gives added weight to other circumstances that made his confessions involuntary.

Justices Harlan and Clark, dissenting, taxed the majority with reaching a Fifth Amendment retroactivity result "by reading the Due Process Clause as requiring that heavy weight must be given the failure of the state to afford counsel during interrogation * * * ." This engrafting process, these Justices maintained, makes Miranda and Escobedo standards significant factors in considering voluntariness.

SELF-INCRIMINATION

Tehan v. Shott, 382 U.S. 406

Earlier in the Term, the same criteria that led the Court in Linkletter v. Walker, 381 U.S. 618, not to give Mapp v. Ohio, 367 U.S. 643, a retrospective application impelled a 5–2 majority to the same result with respect to Griffin v. California, 380 U.S. 609. Griffin forbids comment by a state prosecutor or judge on a defendant's failure to testify. As in Mapp, the majority pointed out, Griffin dealt with a doctrine resting on considerations of quite a different order from those underlying other recent constitutional decisions that have been applied retrospectively. It is self-evident that to deny a lawyer's help through the technical intricacies of the criminal trial, Gideon v. Wainwright, 372 U.S. 335, or to deny a full opportunity to appeal a conviction because the accused is poor, Griffin v. Illinois, 351 U.S. 12, is to infect the criminal proceeding with a clear danger of convicting the innocent.

By contrast, the majority said, the Fifth Amendment privilege against self-incrimination is not an adjunct to the ascertainment of truth. Rather, it is a means to preserve the judicial system's integrity. The privilege against self-incrimination, like the guarantees of the Fourth Amendment, stands as a protection of quite different constitutional values —values reflecting the concern of our society for the right of an individual to be let alone. Retroactive application does not further the protection of such values.

Justices Black and Douglas, who dissented in Linkletter, dissented again for substantially the same reasons.

Schmerber v. California, 384 U.S. 757

But a claim of self-incrimination, despite enlargement of rights of the accused, is still no infallible key to the jailhouse door. With four Justices dissenting, Mr. Justice

Brennan, for the majority, adhered to Breithaupt v. Abram, 352 U.S. 432, which held that the prosecution can use as evidence in a drunken driving test the analysis of a blood sample taken without the consent of the accused. In fact, the majority went Breithaupt one better: Such evidence is admissible even though the accused, on advice of counsel, objected to the extraction of his blood.

The majority believed that the Fifth Amendment reaches an accused's "communications," whatever form they might take. But, though the privilege is a bar against compelling communications or "testimony," compulsion that makes a suspect the source of "real or physical" evidence does not violate it. Attaching claims under the Fourth, Sixth, and Fourteenth Amendments, the majority continued, does not help. Removal of a blood sample, ephemeral evidence of intoxication, was both a reasonable and appropriate incident to an arrest.

However, the Court took pains to point out that it was not adopting Professor Wigmore's view that the privilege against self-incrimination is limited to testimonial evidence, i.e., words produced by someone's lips. Two of the dissenters, Justices Black and Douglas, were happy with the rejection of the Wigmore approach, but thought the majority fell into basic error in failing to give the Fifth Amendment protection against compulsory self-incrimination the broad and liberal construction that Counselman v. Hitchcock, 142 U.S. 547, and other opinions have declared it ought to have.

The Chief Justice reiterated his dissent in Breithaupt, and Mr. Justice Fortas thought that "as prosecutor, the state has no right to commit any kind of violence upon the person." The extraction of blood, he concluded, pointing to the Chief Justice's dissent in Breithaupt, is an act of violence.

INSANITY

Baxstrom v. Herold, 383 U.S. 107

The Court achieved virtual unanimity in a belief that there is no conceivable basis for distinguishing the civil insanity commitment of a person who is nearing the end of a penal term from all other civil commitments. A New York statute, said the Chief Justice, under which an insane prisoner is civilly committed, without the de novo review by a jury trial that is available to all others, denied him the equal protection of the laws. Civil commitment beyond the expiration of a prison term, without the de novo review by a jury trial that is available to all others, denied him the equal protection of the laws. Civil commitment beyond the expiration of a prison term, without a judicial determination of dangerous mental illness, such as that afforded to all except those nearing the expiration of a penal sentence, is likewise a denial of the equal protection of the laws.

Pate v. Robinson, 383 U.S. 375

There was, however, no unanimity on a question of competency to stand trial. Mr. Justice Clark, for the majority, held that a trial court's failure to hold a sanity hearing for a murder defendant with a long history of bizarre behavior was a denial of due process. A contention that his failure to demand a hearing constituted a waiver did not recommend itself to the majority. The waiver of a potential incompetent can never be binding. Therefore, the defendant was denied a fair trial and is entitled to a complete new trial, not merely a hearing on his competency at the time of the original trial. The majority agreed that the demeanor of a defendant is relevant, but refused to accept it as dispositive.

To Justices Harlan and Black, the facts did not suggest incompetence with the "force necessary to make out failure of due process in failure to pursue the question." The capacity to consult with one's counsel and understand the proceedings, they pointed out, is not the same as criminal responsibility at the time of the commission of a crime.

RIGHT OF CONFRONTATION

Brookhart v. Janis, 384 U.S. 1

Mr. Justice Black, writing for nearly a unanimous Court, held that denial of the right of cross-examination to a defendant who effectively pleaded nolo contendere but insisted that he was "in no way * * * pleading guilty," violated the Fourteenth Amendment. In the face of this unambiguous assertion, the majority said, counsel and the trial court cannot agree to a trial procedure that denies the right of confrontation and cross-examination.

The narrow question is whether counsel has power to enter a plea which is inconsistent with his client's expressed desire and thereby waive his constitutional rights. There is no such power, the majority concluded.

FAIR TRIAL —FREE PRESS

Sheppard v. Maxwell, 384 U.S. 333

In comparison with the fields of self-incrimination, confessions, and right to counsel, which the Court has crossed and re-crossed in almost every direction, the field of trial publicity was practically virgin land. Reversing the murder conviction of Dr. Sam Sheppard, whose prosecution 14 years ago was attended by the kind of publicity usually associated with Roman carnivals, the Court made it clear that trial judges had a duty not to let publicity get out of hand.

Given the pervasiveness of modern communications and the difficulty of effacing prejudicial publicity from the minds of the jurors, strong measures must be taken to insure that the balance is never weighted against the accused.

"There is nothing that proscribes the press from reporting events that transpire in the courtroom," said Mr. Justice Clark, but where there is a reasonable likelihood that prejudicial news prior to trial will prevent a fair trial, the judge should continue the case until the threat abates, or transfer the case to another county not so permeated with publicity. In addition, the trial judge may

raise sequestration of the jury sua sponte. If publicity during the proceedings threatens the fairness of the trial, a new trial should be ordered.

The cure for prejudicial publicity, the majority said, lies in those remedial measures that will prevent the prejudice at its inception. "The courts must take such steps by rule and regulation that will protect their processes from prejudicial outside interferences." No one under the court's jurisdiction should be permitted to frustrate its function. Collaboration between counsel and press as to information affecting the fairness of a criminal trial is not only subject to regulation, but is highly censurable and worthy of disciplinary measures.

Mr. Justice Black dissented without opinion.

SPEEDY TRIAL —DOUBLE JEOPARDY

U.S. v. Ewell, 383 U.S. 116

The Sixth Amendment right to a speedy trial and the Fifth Amendment's Double Jeopardy Clause got only scant mention in the 1965–6 Term. Mr. Justice White, for a 7–2 majority, said the passage of 19 months between an original arrest and hearings on a second set of indictments did not itself demonstrate a violation of the Sixth Amendment's guarantee of a speedy trial. Moreover, it is well established that the Double Jeopardy Clause does not prevent retrial when a defendant obtains a reversal. This rule "protects the social interest in trying people accused of crime rather than granting them immunization because of legal error at a previous trial, and because it enhances the probability that appellate courts will be vigilant to strike down previous convictions that are tainted with reversible error."

Justices Fortas and Douglas, dissenting, pointed out that this is not merely a re-indictment —new counts were added. Re-indictment, they maintained, should be kept within the limits of the original charge.

CIVIL RIGHTS

U.S. v. Price, 383 U.S. 787; U.S. v. Guest, 383 U.S. 745

The long desuetude of the Civil Rights Acts of 1866 and 1870, now Sections 241 and 242 of the Criminal Code, came to an end in the 1965–6 Term. At the same time, "a majority of the members of the court," as Mr. Justice Harlan pointed out in a concurring and dissenting opinion, "express the view today that Section 5 [of the Fourteenth Amendment] empowers Congress to enact laws punishing all conspiracies to interfere with the exercise of Fourteenth Amendment rights, whether or not state officers * * * are implicated * * * . Viewed in its proper perspective, Section 5 appears as a positive grant of legislative power, authorizing Congress to exercise its discretion in fashioning remedies to achieve civil and political equality for all citizens."

Section 241, the Court ruled, vindicates federally created rights, including those conferred by the Fourteenth Amendment; Section 242 reaches conduct by persons who are not state officials but act in association with them.

Mr. Justice Fortas, writing for a nearly unanimous Court, held that the Mississippians who, under color of law, abducted and murdered civil rights workers Schwerner, Goodman, and Chaney, deprived them of their life and liberty without due process, in violation of Section 242. The Court also ruled that Section 241 reaches a conspiracy to deprive the murdered men of rights and privileges protected by the Fourteenth Amendment, since nothing confines Section 241 to rights conferred by or flowing from the federal government, as distinguished from those secured or confirmed or guaranteed by the Constitution.

It would be strange indeed, said Mr. Justice Fortas, for "this Court to revert to a construction of the Fourteenth Amendment which would once again narrow its historical purpose." The Court, he said, is not at liberty to seek ingenious analytical instruments to exclude the Due Process Clause of the Fourteenth Amendment from the general language of Section 241.

Brown v. Louisiana, 383 U.S. 131

The Justices were unable to agree on a single reason, but five of them were in agreement that a Louisiana breach-of-the-peace conviction of five Negroes, who had peaceably remained in a segregated library they had been told to leave, could not stand.

The prevailing opinion, representing the views of Justices Fortas, Douglas, and the Chief Justice, found not the slightest evidence that would or could sustain the application of the breach-of-the-peace statute to the Negroes. Even if the statute were applicable, "we would have to hold that the statute cannot constitutionally be applied to punish petitioners' actions in the circumstances of this case."

Mr. Justice Brennan didn't see why it was necessary to go beyond Cox v. Louisiana, 379 U.S. 536, in which the Court last Term "declared this statute as construed unconstitutional for overbreadth." Mr. Justice White, casting the final vote for reversal, rested his opinion primarily on the conclusion that the standers-in were making only a normal and authorized use of the public library.

The remaining Justices commented that the majority, or at least a "majority of the majority," were reading the First Amendment as giving "any person or group of persons the constitutional right to go wherever they want, whenever they please, without regard to the rights of private or public property or to state law."

Shuttlesworth v. Birmingham, 382 U.S. 87

The Court had a much easier time, with an assist by an Alabama Court of Appeals construction of the Birmingham loitering and traffic ordinances, striking down the conviction of a Negro civil rights leader for refusing to obey a police officer's order to "move on."

Literally read, the loitering ordinance would make it unlawful for any person to stand or loiter upon any street or sidewalk after having been requested by any police officer to move on. Similarly, a traffic ordinance punishes any refusal to comply with a lawful order, signal, or direction of a police officer. However, the loitering ordinance was restricted by the Alabama courts to situations in which the person ordered to move on was blocking free passage of the public way; the traffic ordinance has been limited by the Alabama courts to orders of police officers directing traffic.

As thus limited, neither statute was deemed unconstitutional by the Supreme Court. However, the Court found evidentiary defects requiring the reversal of both convictions. Under the loitering statute, the trial court made no finding, as it should have, that the loiterer had both created an obstruction and disobeyed a policeman's order to move on. Similarly, there was no evidence whatever that the order was given by a police officer directing traffic.

Mr. Justice Fortas, in his first opinion, thought that the court had not gone far enough. The Court's opinion, he asserted, may be read to imply that if the defendant is now put on trial for a violation of the loitering statutes, as construed, the vice of the present conviction may be eliminated. Rather, he thought, the Court should rule that the ordinance as applied to the facts presented would be unconstitutional "even after the plastic surgery by Alabama's Court of Appeals." The arrest was an incident in the tense racial conflict in Birmingham. While this may explain the arrest, Mr. Justice Fortas said, it adds nothing to its lawfulness. Since there was no basis in the facts for charging that the defendant was blocking free passage on the sidewalk, any attempt to punish him would violate the Fourteenth Amendment.

Georgia v. Rachel, 384 U.S. 780

"A text of exquisite obscurity," the civil rights removal statute, Sections 1443 (1) and (2) of the Judicial Code, got a narrow reading from the Court.

With no dissent, Mr. Justice Stewart held that Section 1443(1) permits removal of state prosecutions based on conduct permissible under "any law providing for specific civil rights stated in terms of racial equality." Under this ruling, sit-in's charged with violating Georgia's anti-trespass statue when they refused to obey orders to leave a restaurant covered by the 1964 Civil Rights Act are entitled to removal under 1443 (1) as well as dismissal of their prosecutions upon showing that their exclusion from such places of public accommodation was based on race.

However, he pointed out that broad contentions under the First Amendment and the Due Process Clause of the Fourteenth Amendment cannot support a valid claim for removal under Section 1443; those guarantees are phrased in terms of general application available to all persons or citizens, rather than in the specific language of racial equality demanded by Section 1443.

Greenwood v. Peacock, 384 U.S. 808

The Court then divided 5–4 in holding that Mississippi's prosecutions of civil rights workers for obstructing public streets while engaged in a Negro voter-registration drive are not removable under Section 1443 (1). This holds true even if they show that they were arrested because they were Negroes, or because they were engaged in helping Negroes assert their rights under federal equal civil rights laws, or that they will be unable to obtain fair trials in state courts. Under a broader interpretation of Section 1443 (1), every criminal case in every court of every state —and on any charge —would be removable to a federal court. Moreover, the majority was of the view that Section 1443 (2) permits removal of state prosecutions only by federal officers and persons assisting such officers in performance of their official duties.

The dissenters, Justices Douglas, Brennan, Fortas, and the Chief Justice, maintained that the critical words of 1443 (1) are "denied or cannot enforce in the courts of judicial tribunals" of the state. Whatever the correctness of the Strauder and Rives cases, 100 U.S. 303; 100 U.S. 313, as to the "cannot enforce" clause, "they have no application whatever to a claim of present denial of equal civil rights."

FIRST AMENDMENT

Ashton v. Kentucky, 384 U.S. 195

Is there a crime of common-law libel? The Court seemed to say: "Now you see it, now you don't."

By agreeing with the dissenters in the Kentucky Court of Appeals that since the English common law of criminal libel is inconsistent with constitutional provisions, and since no Kentucky case has redefined the crime in understandable terms, the elements of the crime are so indefinite and uncertain as to preclude enforcement, the Supreme Court seemed to eviscerate the common-law crime. On the other hand, by indicating the invalidity of an affirmance based on a more limited definition of criminal libel than that employed by the trial judge, the Court may have left the common-law crime with some vitality.

An unconstitutional conviction, Mr. Justice Douglas said, cannot be sustained on appeal by a delimiting construction that eliminates unconstitutional features adopted by the trial court.

Memoirs v. Massachusetts, 383 U.S. 413

If there is any issue that seems to totally defy unanimity and a stable approach, it is obscenity. The Court needed 14 opinions to dispose of three obscenity cases, and decide that "Fanny Hill" is protected by the First Amendment, that a New York conviction for marketing "sadistic [or] masochistic" publications is valid, and that a federal prosecution for advertising and mailing books and magazines that were created and exploited entirely to appeal to prurient interests is not barred by the First Amendment, even though the same material in other contexts might be protected.

The "Fanny Hill" case exhibited the widest divergence of opinions. Justices Brennan and Fortas, and the Chief Justice believed that because the book is not "utterly without social importance" it cannot be suppressed. Justices Black and Douglas concurred on broad First Amendment grounds; Mr. Justice Stewart thought that only hard core pornography could be suppressed.

Dissenting, Mr. Justice Clark considered the book pure eroticism unredeemed by any social importance. Mr. Justice Harlan adhered to the premise set forth in his separate opinion in Roth v. U.S., 354 U.S. 476, that in the area of obscenity the Constitution does not bind the states and the federal government in precisely the same fashion. Mr. Justice White pointed out that one of the basic propositions of Roth was that obscene material is inherently without social value.

Mishkin v. New York, 383 U.S. 502

The court had somewhat less trouble with a conviction for marketing books depicting deviant sexual practices such as flagellation, fetishism, and lesbianism. The marketing of books like "Screaming Flesh," "The Violated Wrestler," and "Stud Broad" was "calculated purveyance of filth."

Ginzburg v. U.S., 383 U.S. 463

The case involving the federal obscenity conviction of the publisher of "Eros" magazine produced the only truly novel point in the obscenity field. While such material might be protected in a "scientific" atomosphere, an advertising campaign pitched to lewdness constituted "pandering."

CONGRESSIONAL IMMUNITY

U.S. v. Johnson, 383 U.S. 169

A government argument that the Constitution's Speech or Debate Clause was meant to prevent only prosecutions based on the content of a congressman's floor speech, but not those founded on the antecedent unlawful conduct of accepting or agreeing to a bribe for making the speech, was rejected by a unanimous Court, two Justices not participating. But in so far as the Speech or Debate Clause forecloses judicial inquiry into the motives behind a congressman's speech, it protected a congressman from a criminal conspiracy prosecution charging him with taking a bribe to make it. The language of the clause, the Court emphasized, is "framed in the broadest terms."

However, the Court left open for consideration the propriety of a prosecution that, though possibly entailing inquiry into legislative acts or motivations, is founded upon a narrowly drawn statute passed by Congress in the exercise of its legislative power and designed to regulate the conduct of its members.

The Chief Justice and Justices Douglas and Brennan would have decided the validity of the conviction under seven substantive counts of conflict of interest.

CONTEMPT

Gojack v. U.S., 384 U.S. 702

The Court found it unnecessary to venture into constitutional areas in order to strike down a contempt conviction for refusing to answer questions put by the House Un-American Activities Committee. The Committee's failure to specify the subject of the inquiry, as required by its rules, and its failure to lawfully delegate to its subcommittee the authority to conduct an investigation into political beliefs or associations in the labor field vitiated the contempt conviction of a union leader who refused to cooperate with the subcommittee.

While concurring in the Court's judgment and opinion, Mr. Justice Black would have preferred to reverse the judgement by holding that the Committee's inquiries amounted to an unconstitutional encroachment on the judicial power, for reasons stated in his dissent in Barenblatt v. U.S., 360 U.S. 109, 135.

DeGregory v. New Hampshire, 383 U.S. 825

More resistance was met to a majority ruling, by Mr. Justice Douglas, that the First Amendment bars the contempt conviction of a witness for refusing to answer the New Hampshire Attorney General's questions about Communist activities of more than 10 years ago. The court detected no overriding and compelling state interest that would warrant intrusion into the realm of political and associational privacy protected by the First Amendment. "The information being sought was historical, not current." To Justices Harlan, Stewart, and White, dissenting, New Hampshire's freedom to investigate the existence or nonexistence of Communist Party subversion, or any other legitimate subject of concern to the state, should not be impeded by forcing the state to produce evidence of the very type to be sought in the course of the inquiry.

Harris v. U.S., 382 U.S. 162

The Court divided narrowly on use of the swift and summary contempt procedure of FRCrP 42(a). Rule 42(a), said a 5–4 majority, is reserved for "exceptional circumstances," and cannot be used against a witness who refused to answer questions before a federal grand jury. In deciding that the witness must be accorded a full public hearing under FRCrP 42(b), the majority overruled Brown v. U.S., 359 U.S. 41.

Swiftness was not a prerequisite of justice here, the majority pointed out, and cases of this kind are foreign to Rule 42(a). The notice and hearing requirements of Rule 42(b) serve important ends and may reveal extenuating circumstances. Rule 42(b) prescribes the "procedural regularity" for all contempts in the federal regime except those unusual situations envisioned by Rule 42(a), where instant action is necessary to protect the judicial institution itself. Justices Stewart, Clark, Harlan, and White, in dissent, thought the reason for overturning Brown too flimsy in light of the Court's responsibility for clear and consistent guides to the federal judiciary. The procedure followed here, the dissenters argued, was at least as fair as a Rule 42(b) proceeding.

Cheff v. Schnackenberg, 384 U.S. 373

In a criminal contempt proceeding, the view of two dissenting Justices that jury trials are constitutionally required in all criminal contempt cases made effective a four-Justice ruling that, in the exercise of the Court's supervisory power, sentences exceeding six months for criminal contempt may not be imposed by federal courts unless a jury trial has been received or waived. Two of the other participating Justices thought that a jury trial is never constitutionally required in criminal contempt cases. Their view created a six-Justice majority for the holding that the Sixth Amendment did not require a jury trial in a criminal contempt proceeding that resulted in a six-month sentence. The case arose out of a corporation officer's refusal to obey a U.S. court of appeals pendente lite order requiring compliance with a Federal Trade Commission cease and desist order.

Shillitani v. U.S., 384 U.S. 364

In a companion case, a clear-cut majority of the Court, Mr. Justice Harlan alone dissenting, limited the civil contempt sentences of contumacious grand jury witnesses to the duration of the grand jury before which they refused to testify. The majority relied on the conditional and remedial nature of automatic "purge" clauses, which were contained in two-year contempt sentences, for its conclusion that the contempt proceedings, considered by the trial and reviewing courts to be criminal, were in fact civil.

Stevens v. Marks, 383 U.S. 234

Again demonstrating its dislike for waiver of constitutional rights the Court held that a New York City policeman who announced his intention to withdraw a waiver of immunity he had earlier signed and was then told that he would be fired if he failed to waive his federally secured right to refuse to answer a grand jury's questions cannot be held in contempt. He was not bound to testify, the majority said, until affirmative steps necessary to confer immunity were taken.

DISCOVERY AND DISCLOSURE

Dennis v. U.S., 384 U.S. 855

Noting the "trend toward disclosure in criminal cases analogous to civil practice," the Court reversed a trial court's refusal to give a conspiracy defendant's counsel access to the grand jury testimony of trial witnesses.

The Court, after finding the "particularized need" required under Pittsburgh Plate Glass Co. v. U.S., 360 U.S. 395, turned its attention to the question whether in camera inspection by trial judges is an appropriate or satisfactory device for meeting discovery needs. Trial judges, the Court said, ought not to be burdened with the task or the responsibility of examining sometimes voluminous grand jury testimony in order to isolate inconsistencies. "The determination of what can be useful to the defense can properly and effectively be made only by an advocate." The trial judge's function in this area is limited to deciding whether a case has been made for production of the desired material and to supervising the discovery process.

On another phase of the case, however, the Court could not reach unanimity. Justices Black and Douglas dissented from a holding that an indictment charging a conspiracy to defraud the United States by causing non-Communist affidavits to be filed with the National Labor Relations Board charged an offense under the general conspiracy statute. By the same 7–2 vote, the Court held that those charged with a conspiracy to evade the non-Communist affidavit requirement of the since-repealed Section 9(h) of the Taft Act cannot attack its constitutionality.

STATUTES

U.S. v. Romano, 382 U.S. 136

The Court used the Fifth Amendment to invalidate a presumption in the Internal Revenue Code that an unexplained presence at the site of an unregistered moonshine still is sufficient evidence to authorize conviction for possession, custody, and control of the still. In the October Term of 1964, said Mr. Justice White for the majority, the Court in U.S. v. Gainey, 380 U.S. 63, 33 LW 4200, upheld a companion provision in the Code. This case, however, is different. There is no indication that Congress intended to make mere presence at the site of illegal activity a crime. Three Justices concurred in the result.

U.S. v. Cook, 384 U.S. 257

Mr. Justice White, again for a unanimous Court, thought it a fair construction of the Criminal Code to say that an individual doing business as a common carrier is a "firm" for purposes of Section 660 of the Code, which punishes embezzlements by employees of any firm engaged in commerce as a common carrier.

Giaccio v. Pennsylvania, 382 U.S. 399

And, unanimous again, the Court held that a Pennsylvania statute authorizing the jury to impose costs on an acquitted misdemeanor defendant and subjecting him to commitment for failure to pay such costs is void for vagueness. Mr. Justice Stewart, concurring, expressed fear that the reasoning of the opinion might be used to

cast "grave constitutional doubt upon the settled practice of many states to leave to the unguided discretion of a jury the nature and degree of punishment to be imposed * * *." Though he held no brief for the wisdom of this practice, Mr. Justice Stewart thought its constitutionality quite a different matter.

APPEALS

Rinaldi v. Yeager, 384 U.S. 305

Along the same lines, the Court was nearly unanimous in holding that the Equal Protection Clause invalidates a New Jersey statute that applies an indigent state prisoner's institutional wages to the payment of the cost of a transcript furnished him for use on an unsuccessful appeal from his conviction, while not requiring reimbursement from indigents not in prison. The Equal Protection Clause, said Mr. Justice Stewart, requires rationality as well as nondiscrimination, and the New Jersey statute is not only discriminatory but imposes a distinction that has no relevance to the purpose for which the classification is made. Frivolity of appeals, he added, is not the question here. Mr. Justice Harlan, dissenting, thought that the "traditional" test of rationality, see McLaughlin v. Florida, 379 U.S. 184, would permit this differentiation.

U.S. v. Blue, 384 U.S. 251

The appealability criteria of the Criminal Appeals Act got exegesis by a unanimous Court. A federal district court's pretrial dismissal of a tax evasion indictment on the ground that the defendant had been compelled to incriminate himself in a civil tax proceeding was held to constitute a decision "sustaining a motion in bar" that entitled the government to a direct appeal to the Supreme Court under the Criminal Appeals Act. On the merits, the Court ruled that use of the illegally seized evidence did not bar the prosecution.

JUVENILES

Kent v. U.S., 383 U.S. 541

Once again divided, the Court held that the District of Columbia's Juvenile Court Act requires the Juvenile Court, in determining the "critically important" question whether to waive its jurisdiction over youthful offenders to release them for trial as adults in the federal district court for capital crimes, to (1) conduct a hearing, (2) to provide counsel with social records and probation or similar reports of the juvenile in question, and (3) to provide a statement of reasons for its ultimate decision. The hearing need not conform to all the requirements of a criminal trial or even of the usual administrative hearing, a five-Justice majority said, but it must measure up to essentials of due process and fair treatment.

1966–1967 Term

SEARCH AND SEIZURE

The Fourth Amendment —upstaged by the Fifth and Sixth in the years since Mapp v. Ohio, 367 U.S. 643, set off a series of revolutionary criminal law decisions by the U.S. Supreme Court —reestablished its right to star status.

Berger v. New York, 388 U.S. 41

The part most pleasing to defense attorneys and civil libertarians was no doubt the role it played in thwarting, if not completely destroying, electronic eavesdropping as a legitimate means of law enforcement. Specifically, the five-justice majority of the Court found only that a New York statute permitting judicially authorized wiretaps and bugs was fatally defective by Fourth Amendment standards. The Court's 5–4 opinion, by Mr. Justice Clark, emphasized that under the New York statute a belief that a particular offense had been or was being committed was not a prerequisite to the issuance of an eavesdropping order. Similarly the property sought, i.e. the conversations, was not required to be particularly described. The statute allowed eavesdropping for a two-month period, which the majority described as the equivalent of a series of intrusions, searches, and seizures pursuant to a single showing of probable cause. A third defect to which the majority addressed itself was that the statute did not call for automatic termination of the eavesdrop once the conversation sought was seized. Nor did it require some showing of special facts to justify unconsented entry.

Mr. Justice Clark did not ignore the "necessity" arguments offered by law enforcement officials in support of their right to use bugs and taps. The President's Crime Commission Report, "The Challenge of Crime in a Free Society," informs "us that the majority of law enforcement officials say" that outlawing electronic eavesdropping will severely cripple crime detection, especially in the detection of organized crime. However, Mr. Justice Clark observed that the majority found no empirical statistics on the efficacy of electronic devices in the fight against organized crime. Indeed, he stressed, there are even figures available in the wiretap category that indicate the contrary.

In any event, "we cannot forget the requirements of the Fourth Amendment in the name of law enforcement. This is no formality that we require today but a fundamental rule that has long been recognized as basic to the privacy of every home in America."

Mr. Justice Clark also noted the argument that neither a warrant nor a statute authorizing eavesdropping can be drawn so as to meet the Fourth Amendment's requirements. But, he continues, "if that be true then the 'fruits' of eavesdropping devices are barred under the Amendment." And, looking at the other side of the coin, he asserted that the Court has in the past under specific conditions and circumstances sustained the use of eavesdropping devices. In particular, his opinion stressed the specificity contained in the wiretap order that was before the court in this Term's Osborn case.

Mr. Justice Douglas concurred, joining the opinion of the Court "because at long last it overrules sub silentio Olmstead v. U.S., 277 U.S. 438, and its offspring and brings wiretapping and other electronic eavesdropping fully within the purview of the Fourth Amendment." But, he would have gone much further than the Court did. "I do not see how any electronic surveillance that collects evidence or provides leads to evidence is or can be constitutional under the Fourth and Fifth Amendments. We could amend the Constitution and so provide —a step that would take us closer to the ideological group we profess to despise. Until the amending process ushers us into that kind of totalitarian regime, I would adhere to the protection of privacy which the Fourth Amendment, fashioned in Congress and submitted to the people, was designed to afford the individual * * * . I would adhere to Mapp v. Ohio, 367 U.S. 643, and apply the exclusionary rule in state as well as federal trials —a rule fashioned out of the Fourth Amendment and constituting a high constitutional barricade against the intrusion of Big Brother into the lives of all of us."

Mr. Justice Stewart, though he concurred in the result, could not be counted among the majority. Rather, he fully agreed with the three dissenters that the New York statute was entirely constitutional. He would have held only that the affidavits on which the judicial order issued in the case was based did not constitute a showing of probable cause adequate to justify it.

Each of the dissenters issued a separate opinion. Mr. Justice White did not consider the case a proper vehicle for resolving the broad constitutional and legislative issues raised by the problem of official use of wiretapping and eavesdropping. He would have held only that electronic surveillance is a reasonable investigative tool to apply in uncovering corruption among high state officials and that New York in this case limited itself to a constitutionally permissible search and seizure in executing the court order. He emphasized that the majority, while not in so many words holding that all wiretapping and eavesdropping are constitutionally impermissible, achieved practically the same result by imposing a series of requirements that will be almost impossible to satisfy.

Mr. Justice Harlan found the majority decision in the mold of those it has rendered in recent years that have more and more taken to the Court sole responsibility for setting the pattern of criminal law enforcement throughout the country. "Despite the fact that the use of electronic eavesdropping devices as instruments of criminal law enforcement is currently being comprehensively addressed by the Congress and various other bodies in the country, the Court has chosen, quite unnecessarily, to decide this case in a manner which will seriously restrict, if not entirely thwart such efforts, and will freeze further progress in this field, except as the Court may itself act or a constitutional amendment may set things right." Mr. Justice Harlan emphasized that electronic eavesdropping, as such or as it was permitted under the New York statute, was not an unreasonable search and seizure.

The third dissenter, Mr. Justice Black, reached the conclusion that the Fourth Amendment itself does not bar the use of eavesdropping evidence in courts. Olmstead is still good law, notwithstanding Mr. Justice Holmes "dirty business" epithet. He disagreed with the majority's basic assumption that the Fourth Amendment bars invasions of privacy rather than merely forbids "unreasonable searches and seizures." Use of privacy as a key word in the Fourth Amendment, he observed, "simply gives this court a useful new tool, * * * both to usurp the policy-making power of the Congress and to hold more state and federal laws unconstitutional when the court entertains a sufficient hostility to them." (Berger v. New York, 1 CrL 3120)

Osborn v. U.S., 385 U.S. 323

Earlier in the term the Court, with only Mr. Justice Douglas dissenting, had found the Fourth Amendment no obstacle to the admission into evidence of a recording of a conversation between a government informer and a defendant. The recording had been made with the authorization of a federal court for the purpose of verifying charges that the defendant was attempting to bribe jurors in an impending case. If a wiretap law can be drafted to meet the specificity requirements laid down in Berger, the district court order in this case is perhaps the likeliest source to which the draftsmen should look.

Mr. Justice Stewart phrased the issue as not the permissibility of indiscriminate use of electronic surveillance devices in law enforcement, but the permissibility of using such a device under the most precise and discriminate circumstances.

He pointed out, and Mr. Justice Clark was to reemphasize it in Berger, that the order issued in this case was based upon a detailed factual affidavit alleging the commission of a specific criminal offense directly and immediately affecting the administration of justice in the federal court. The judges of the court jointly authorized the use of a recording device for the narrow and particularized purpose of ascertaining the truth of the affidavit's allegations. There could, according to Mr. Justice Stewart, hardly be a clearer example of the procedure of antecedent justification before a magistrate that is central to the Fourth Amendment as a precondition of lawful electronic surveillance.

The Court could not accept, either, the defendant's argument that he was entrapped by the government informer who had told him that he knew and was related to a member of the jury panel. At most, Mr. Justice Stewart pointed out, the informer's statement afforded the petitioner "opportunities or facilities" for offering a bribe to the juror —that is a far cry from entrapment.

Mr. Justice Douglas, dissenting, made much the same points that he was to later make in his concurrence in Berger. "A warrant authorizing such devices is no different than the general warrants the Fourth Amendment was intended to prohibit." (Osborn v. U.S., 35 LW 4067)

Hoffa v. U.S., 385 U.S. 293

Government use of an unwired informer passed muster under the Fourth, Fifth and Sixth Amendments in an opinion that led to the ultimate incarceration of James Hoffa. The Fourth Amendment argument was based on the contention that the informer was able to hear the incriminating statements in Hoffa's hotel suite only by reason of the informer's failure to disclose his role. This failure to disclose, the argument ran, vitiated the consent that Hoffa gave to the informer's repeated enteries into the suite and that, therefore, the informer's listening to Hoffa's statements constituted an illegal search for verbal evidence. The Court's opinion, by Mr. Justice Stewart, said that argument misapprehended the fundamental nature and scope of the Fourth Amendment protection — it protects against unwarranted governmental intrusion. Once a person puts something in his filing cabinet, in his desk drawer, or in his pocket, he has the right to know it will be secure from an unreasonable search or an unreasonable seizure.

But, Mr. Justice Stewart observed, here the defendant was not relying on the security of his hotel suite when he made the incriminating statements to the informer or in the informer's presence. Rather, he was relying upon his misplaced confidence that the informer would not reveal his wrongdoing.

"Neither this court nor any member of it has ever expressed the view that the Fourth Amendment protects a wrongdoer's misplaced belief that a person to whom he voluntarily confides his wrongdoing will not reveal it."

Hoffa's claim of Fifth Amendment violation was deemed "without merit." The incriminating conversations with the informer "were wholly voluntary."

Since Hoffa's lawyers used his hotel suite as a place to confer with him and with each other, to interview witnesses, and to plan trial strategy, it was also claimed that the informer's presence in and around the suite violated the Sixth Amendment right to counsel. In rejecting this argument, the Court found it "far from clear to what extent [the informer] was present at conversations or conferences of the petitioner's counsel."

The Court cited both Caldwell v. U.S., 205 F. 2d 879, and Coplon v. U.S. 191 F. 2d 749, as supporting the proposition that a surreptitious invasion by a government agent into the legal camp of the defense may violate the protection of the Sixth Amendment. Both those cases, however, dealt with "government intrusion of the grossest kind." Assuming that both Coplon and Caldwell were rightly decided, Mr. Justice Stewart emphasized, in both cases the government's intrusion upon the defendant's relationship with his lawyer was held to invalidate the trial at which it occurred. Here, the intrusion occurred at a prior trial, not the trial resulting in the conviction reviewed by the Court.

A second Sixth Amendment argument made by Hoffa was also rejected. In effect, he argued that once the government had sufficient ground for taking him into custody and charging him, it could no longer continue to question him without observance of his Sixth Amendment right to counsel. Massiah v. U.S., 377 U.S. 201, 32 LW 4389; and Escobedo v. Illinois, 378 U.S. 478, 32 LW 4605. But, the Court decided, "nothing in Massiah, in Escobedo, or in any other case that has come to our attention, even remotely suggests this novel and paradoxical constitutional doctrine, and we decline to adopt it now. There is no constitutional right to be arrested. The police are not required to guess at their peril the precise moment at which they have probable cause to arrest a suspect, risking a violation of the Fourth Amendment if they act too soon, and violation of the Sixth Amendment if they wait too long."

Finally, the court rejected the contention that the due process clause of the Fifth Amendment was violated. The argument, the court noted, boiled down to a general attack upon the use of a government informer as "a shabby thing in any case."

In so far as this general attack upon the use of informers was based upon historic "notions" of "English-speaking peoples," Mr. Justice Stewart found it "without historical foundation."

The Chief Justice, in dissent, found "the nature of the official practices evidenced here * * * offensive to the fair administration of justice in federal courts." Here the government reached into the jailhouse to employ a man who was himself facing indictments far more serious than the one confronting the man against whom he offered to inform. It employed him not for the purpose of testifying to something that had already happened, but rather for the purpose of infiltration to see if crimes would in the future be committed. The government even assisted him in gaining a position from which he could be a witness to the confidential relationship of attorney and client engaged in the preparation of a criminal defense. And, for the dubious evidence thus obtained, the government paid

an enormous price. Certainly, the Chief Justice observed, if a criminal defendant insinuated his informer into the prosecution's camp in this manner he would be guilty of obstructing justice. He therefore could not agree that what happened in the case is in keeping with the standards of justice in our federal system.

Mr. Justice Clark, joined by Mr. Justice Douglas, would have dismissed the writs of certiorari as improvidently granted. (Hoffa v. U.S., 35 LW 4058)

Lewis v. U.S., 385 U.S. 206

The third of this term's trilogy of informer cases held that a federal narcotics agent did not violate a defendant's Fourth Amendment rights by concealing his identity in order to gain entry to the defendant's home to buy narcotics. A holding that the deceptions of the agent in this case were constitutionally prohibited, the opinion by the Chief Justice explained, would come near to a rule that the use of undercover agents in any manner is virtually unconstitutional per se. The fact that the undercover agent entered the petitioner's home did not compel a different conclusion. When, as here, the opinion pointed out, the home is converted into a commercial center to which outsiders are invited for purposes of transacting unlawful business, that business is entitled to no greater protection than if it were carried on in a store, a garage, a car, or on the street.

Mr. Justice Brennan, with whom Mr. Justice Fortas joined, rested his concurrence solely on the ground that the narcotics defendant's apartment was not an area protected by the Fourth Amendment as related to the transactions in the present case.

Mr. Justice Douglas, dissenting, viewed the case as involving a breach of the privacy of the home by government agent posing in a different role for the purpose of obtaining evidence from the homeowner to convict him of a crime. "Entering another's home in disguise to obtain evidence is a 'search' that should bring into play all the protective features of the Fourth Amendment. When the agent * * * had reason for believing that petitioner possessed narcotics, a search warrant should have been obtained." (Lewis v. U.S., 35 LW 4072)

McCray v. Illinois, 386 U.S. 300

Implicit approval of the use of informants could also be found in this Term's holding that a tip from an informant of known reliability that an accused had narcotics on his person was sufficient to give Illinois police probable cause for a warrantless arrest and search. Though the dissenters took issue with this holding, the majority, in an opinion by Mr. Justice Stewart deemed it worthy only of the comment "that there can be no doubt * * * that there was probable cause to sustain the arrest and incidental search in this case."

The crucial issue to the five-justice majority was the scope of the informant's privilege. The defendant had claimed that the Illinois court had violated the constitution by sustaining prosecution objections, at a suppression hearing, to questions as to the identity of the informant.

The majority cited Roviaro v. U.S., 353 U.S. 53, which gave thorough consideration to an aspect of the informer's privilege. Roviaro involved the informer's privilege, not at a preliminary hearing to determine probable cause for an arrest or search, but at the trial itself where the issue is a fundamental one of innocence or guilt. There the Court observed that if "the disclosure of an informer's identity * * * is relevant and helpful to the defense of an accused, or is essential to a fair-minded determination of a cause, the privilege must give way." But it laid down no fixed rule with respect to disclosure.

Much less has the Court ever approached, the majority emphasized, the formulation of a federal evidentiary rule of compulsory disclosure where the issue is the preliminary one of probable cause, and guilt or innocence is not at stake. "Yet we are now asked to hold that the Constitution somehow compels Illinois to abolish the informer's privilege from its law of evidence, and to require disclosure of the informer's identity in every such preliminary hearing where it appears that the officer made the arrest or search in reliance upon facts supplied by an informer they had reason to trust."

The Chief Justice, Mr. Justice Brennan, Mr. Justice Fortas, and Mr. Justice Douglas dissented. In an opinion by Mr. Justice Douglas, they said the crucial question was the validity of the arrest. Noting the exceptions for arrest for crimes committed in a police officer's presence, of persons fleeing the scene of a crime, and so forth, they noted that "normally an arrest should be made only on a warrant issued by a magistrate on a showing of 'probable cause, supported by oath or affirmation,' as required by the Fourth Amendment." But for the Fourth Amendment, the dissenters declared, states could fashion the rule for arrests that the majority now approved. But they insisted that the requirements of the Fourth Amendment make that conclusion unconstitutional.

The dissenters also noted that "only through the informer's testimony can anyone other than the arresting officers determine 'the pursuasiveness of the facts relied on * * * to show probable cause." Aguilar v. Texas, 378 U.S. 108, 113 (1964)." The majority, the opinion by Mr. Justice Douglas lamented, has left "the Fourth Amendment exclusively in the custody of the police." (McCray v. Illinois, 35 LW 4261)

Warden v. Hayden, 387 U.S. 294

Somewhat offsetting the apparent loss of the right to use electronic eavesdropping devices, was last Term's recognition of a policeman's right to conduct searches for mere evidence. In Gouled v. U.S., 255 U.S. 298, the Court had said that search warrants "may not be used as a means of gaining access to a man's house or office and papers solely for the purpose of making a search to secure evidence to be used against him in a criminal or penal proceeding * * *." Reexamining that proposition, a five-justice majority of the Court now found that Gouled was based upon the dual, related premises that historically the right to search for and seize property depended upon the assertion by the government of a valid claim of superior interest and that it was not enough that the purpose of the search and seizure was to obtain evidence to use in apprehending and convicting criminals. But, the development of search and seizure law since Gouled is replete with examples of the transformation in substantive law brought about through the interaction of the felt need to protect privacy from unreasonable invasions and the flexibility in rule-making made possible by the remedy of exclusion.

The opinion by Mr. Justice Brennan also characterized as discredited the premise in Gouled that the government may not seize evidence simply for the purpose of proving crime. "The requirement that the government assert in addition some property interest in material it seizes has long been a fiction, obscuring the reality that the government has an interest in solving crime."

Consigning Gouled to the growing list of discarded criminal law precedents, Mr. Justice Brennan observed that the survival of the Gouled distinction was attributable more to chance than considered judgment.

As a practical matter, the majority pointed out that the mere evidence limitation has spawned exceptions so numerous and confusion so great that it is questionable whether it affords meaningful protection. But, the opinion continued, if its rejection does enlarge the area of permissible searches, the intrusions are nevertheless made after fulfilling the probable cause and particularity requirements of the Fourth Amendment and after the intervention of a neutral and detached magistrate. The Fourth Amendment allows intrusions upon privacy under these circumstances, and the majority could find no viable reason to distinguish intrusions to secure "mere evidence" from intrusions to secure fruits, instrumentalities, or contraband.

Mr. Justice Black concurred in result.

Mr. Justice Fortas with whom the Chief Justice joined, agreed that the Fourth Amendment should not be held to require exclusion of the evidence here found, clothing, but could not join in the majority's broad repudiation of the so-called "mere evidence" rule. They would have gone no further than to hold that the use of identifying clothing worn in the commission of a crime and seized during "hot pursuit" is within the spirit and intendment of the "hot pursuit" exception to the search warrant requirement. "That is because the clothing is pertinent to identification of the person hotly pursued as being, in fact, the person whose pursuit was justified by connection with the crime. I would frankly place the ruling on that basis. I would not drive an enormous and dangerous hole in the Fourth Amendment to accommodate a specific and, I think, reasonable exception."

The gratuitous striking down of the mere evidence rule, according to Mr. Justice Douglas, "needlessly destroys, root and branch, a basic part of liberty's heritage." He would not permit the police to "rummage around among

* * * personal effects, no matter how formally perfect their authority may appear to be." The constitutional philosophy he thought clear. "The personal effects and possessions of the individual (all contraband and the like excepted) are sacrosanct from prying eyes, from the long arm of the law, from any rummaging by police." (Warden v. Hayden, 35 LW 4493)(Warden v. Hayden, 1 CrL 3059)

Cooper v. California, 386 U.S. 58

Another boon to law enforcement officials was an apparent relaxation of the restriction placed upon searches of automobiles by Preston v. U.S., 376 U.S. 364, 32 LW 4258. Preston involved a warrantless search without a warrant, of an automobile after an accused had been placed under arrest and in custody. Preston had been arrested for vagrancy and the fact that the police had custody of his car was totally unrelated to the vagrancy charge for which he was arrested.

This Term's case involved the search of an automobile a week after the arrest of a California narcotics suspect.

Under a California statute, any officer making an arrest for a narcotics violation is authorized to seize and deliver to the State Division of Narcotics Enforcement any vehicle used to store, conceal, transport, sell or facilitate the possession of narcotics, such vehicle to be held as evidence until the forfeiture has been declared or a release ordered. The majority conceded that "lawful custody of an automobile does not of itself dispense with constitutional requirements of searches thereafter made of it," but emphasized that the reason for and nature of the custody may constitutionally justify the search.

Mr. Justice Black, writing for the five-justice majority, pointed out that the police seized the car because of the crime for which they had arrested the defendant. They seized it to impound it and they had to keep it until forfeiture proceedings were concluded. The forfeiture did not take place until over four months after the car was lawfully seized. "It would be unreasonable to hold that the police, having to retain the car in their garage for such a length of time, had no right, even for their own protection, to search it. It is no answer to say that the police could have obtained a search warrant, for the relevant test is not whether it is reasonable to procure a search warrant, but whether the search was reasonable.' U.S. v. Rabinowitz, 339 U.S. 56, 66."

Mr. Justice Douglas, again dissenting, and this time joined by the Chief Justice, Mr. Justice Brennan and Mr. Justice Fortas, could see only two ways to explain the Court's opinion. "One is that it overrules Preston sub silentio. * * * Unless the search is incident to an arrest, I would insist that the police obtain a warrant to search a man's car just as they must do when they search his home.

"If the present decision does not overrule Preston, it can perhaps be rationalized on one other ground. There is the view that when the Bill of Rights is applied to the state by reason of the Fourteenth Amendment, a watered-down version is used." (Cooper v. California, 35 LW 4209)

Camara v. Municipal Court, 387 U.S. 523
See v. Seattle, 387 U.S. 541

Whatever doubts may remain as to the viability of Preston, none can be entertained as to the demise of Frank v. Maryland, 359 U.S. 360. Specifically overruling Frank, a majority of the Court held that health and fire inspectors are no longer entitled to search a home or business without warrant or consent.

Speaking for a six-justice majority, Mr. Justice White found it anomalous to say that the individual and his private property are fully protected by the Fourth Amendment only when the individual is suspected of criminal behavior. He therefore held that administrative searches are significant intrusions upon the interests protected by the Constitution, that such searches when authorized and conducted without a warrant procedure lack the traditional safeguards mandated by the Fourth Amendment, and that the reasons put forth in Frank v. Maryland for upholding these warrantless searches are insufficient to justify so substantial a weakening of the Fourth Amendment protections.

The majority, however, did not lose sight of the public interest served by such inspections. In light of that public interest, it devised a special probable cause standard. Probable cause to issue a warrant to inspect exists if reasonable legislative or administrative standards for conducting an inspection of the area are satisfied.

Mr. Justice Clark, joined by Mr. Justice Harlan and Mr. Justice Stewart, accused the majority of "jeopardizing * * * the health, welfare, and safety of literally millions of people." At the same time he thought the majority was indulging in pretense. He foresaw box-car warrants that will be identical as to every dwelling in the area, save the street number itself. "I dare say they will be printed up in pads of a thousand or more —with space for the street number to be inserted —and issued by magistrates in broadcast fashion as a matter of course." (Camara v. Municipal Court, 1 CrL 3069)(See v. Seattle, 1 CrL 3074)

IDENTIFICATION —RIGHT TO COUNSEL

U.S. v. Wade, 388 U.S. 218

Closely pressing the Fourth Amendment for top billing this Term was the Sixth. Most controversial of the several Sixth Amendment decisions was the one by which the majority ushered counsel into police line-up identification rooms. According to the majority, since police line-ups constitute a critical stage of the prosecutorial process, the right to counsel attaches at that time.

The majority, in an opinion by Mr. Justice Brennan, first rejected the claim that the line-up in question violated the defendant's privilege against self-incrimination. Citing Schmerber v. California, 384 U.S. 757, the majority had no doubt "that compelling the accused merely to exhibit his person for observation by a prosecution witness prior to trial involves no compulsion of the accused to give evidence having testimonial significance."

The majority however did not find Schmerber equally controlling on the right to counsel issue. In Schmerber, Mr. Justice Brennan emphasized, the Court rested its Sixth Amendment finding on the proposition that "no issue of counsel's ability to assist petitioner in respect of any rights he did possess is presented." In contrast, the majority explained, here it was urged that the assistance of counsel at the line-up was indispensible to protect the accused's most basic right as a criminal defendant —his right to a fair trial at which the witnesses against him might be meaningfully cross-examined.

In recognition of the realities of modern criminal prosecution, the Court noted, the Sixth Amendment guarantee has been construed as applying to "critical" stages of the proceedings. Hence, in addition to counsel's presence at trial, the accused must be guaranteed that he need not stand alone against the state at any stage of the prosecution, formal or informal, in court or out, where counsel's absence might derogate the accused's right to a fair trial.

A confrontation compelled by the state between the accused and the victim or witnesses to a crime to elicit identification evidence is, in the majority's opinion, peculiarly riddled with innumerable dangers and variable factors that might seriously, even crucially, derogate from a fair trial. The grave potential for prejudice, intentional or not, in the pre-trial line-up, which may not be capable of reconstruction at trial, and the possibility that counsel can often avert prejudice and assure a meaningful confrontation led the majority to the conclusion that the post-indictment lineup in this case was a critical stage of the prosecution at which the accused was as much entitled to the aid of counsel as at the trial itself.

Finally the majority addressed itself to the question whether the denial of the accused's motion to strike the courtroom identification by the witnesses required the grant of a new trial at which such evidence would be excluded. The majority decided that the proper test to be applied is that quoted in Wong Sun v. U.S., 371 U.S. 471: "whether, granting establishment of the primary illegality, the evidence to which instant objection is made has been come at by exploitation of that illegality or instead by means sufficiently distinguishable to be purged of the primary taint." McGuire, Evidence of Guilt, 221 (1959).

The Chief Justice and Mr. Justice Douglas agreed with the majority on the Sixth Amendment, but not on the Fifth Amendment, issue. In an opinion by Mr. Justice Douglas, they observed that "compulsory lineup violates the privilege against self-incrimination contained in the Fifth Amendment."

Mr. Justice Fortas, concurring and dissenting, did not think an accused placed in a lineup could be compelled to utter words used in the commission of the crime.

Mr. Justice Black dissented from the court's rejection of the accused's Fifth Amendment contention; agreed with the Court's conclusion as to the denial of his right to counsel; and would have reached a contrary disposition. "The Court remands the case to the district court to consider whether the courtroom identification of [accused] was the fruit of the illegal lineup, and if it were, to grant him a new trial unless the Court concludes that the courtroom identification was harmless error. I would reverse the court of appeals' reversal of * * * conviction but I would not remand for further proceeding since the prosecution not having used the out-of-court line-up identification against [accused] at his trial, I believe the conviction should be affirmed."

Mr. Justice White, with whom Mr. Justice Harlan and Mr. Justice Stewart joined, agreed only that no Fifth Amendment violation had occurred. He doubted that "the Court's new rule, at least absent some clearly defined limits on counsel's role, will measurably contribute to more reliable pre-trial identifications. My fears are that it will have precisely the opposite result. It may well produce fewer convictions, but that is hardly a proper measure of its long-run acceptability. In my view, the state is entitled to investigate and develop its case outside the presence of the defense counsel. This includes the right to have private conversations with identification witnesses, just as defense counsel may have his own consultations with those and other witnesses without having a prosecutor present." (U.S. v. Wade, 1 CrL 3106).

Gilbert v. California, 388 U.S. 263

In the second of the three line-up cases decided last term Mr. Justice Brennan, again speaking for the majority, restated the basic principle announced in Wade and refined it with respect to testimony that is "the direct result of the illegal lineup." As to such identifications, he stressed, only a per se exclusionary rule can be an effective sanction to assure that law enforcement authorities will respect the accused's constitutional right to the presence of his counsel at the critical line-up. The state, he concluded, is therefore not entitled to an opportunity to show that the testimony had an independent source.

The majority also rejected the contention that the Fifth Amendment privilege against self-incrimination was violated by placing the defendant in a line-up and having him repeat phrases used by the person who committed the crime at the time he committed it. (Gilbert v. California, 1 CrL 3094)

Stovall v. Denno, 388 U.S. 293

Finally, in the last of the lineup cases, the Court limited the exclusionary rule to cases involving line-ups held after the June 12th announcement of the decision in Wade. Moreover, the rule was applied to bar relief, in the case before it, to a habeas corpus petitioner who claimed that his conviction resulted from an unlawful line-up held before June 12. (Stovall v. Denno, 1 CrL 3102)

SPEEDY TRIAL

Klopfer v. North Carolina, 386 U.S. 213

The Sixth Amendment right to a speedy trial also received adumbration by the Supreme Court. That right was held a bar to North Carolina's "nolle prosequi with leave" procedure, which can be entered over a defendant's objection and without stated justification and which permits the reinstitution of a prosecution without further order. Noting that under this procedure the prosecution of a criminal charge could be delayed indefinitely, the Court emphasized "the pendency of the indictment may subject [the accused] to public scorn and deprive him of employment, and almost certainly will force curtailment of his speech, associations, and participation in unpopular causes. By indefinitely prolonging this oppression, as well as the 'anxiety and concern accompanying public accusation,' the criminal procedure condoned in this case by the Supreme Court of North Carolina clearly denies the petitioner the right to a speedy trial which we hold is guaranteed him by the Sixth Amendment of the Constitution of the United States." (Klopfer v. North Carolina, 35 LW 4248)

WITNESSES

Washington v. Texas, 388 U.S. 14

Two other Sixth Amendment guarantees also played minor roles last Term. The right of a defendant to compulsory process for obtaining witnesses in his favor was invoked to void a Texas procedural statute that deems persons charged as principals, accomplices, or accessories in the same crime incompetent as witnesses for each other.(Washington v. Texas, 1 CrL 3147)

RIGHT OF CONFRONTATION

Parker v. Gladden, 385 U.S. 363

The right of confrontation was the sword with which the court struck down a conviction by a state jury whose shepherding bailiff had told them "Oh that wicked fellow, he is guilty" and "if there is anything wrong, the Supreme Court will correct it." (Parker v. Gladden, 35 LW 4097)

Equality for indigent appellants was the dominant theme that ran through a quartet of decisions last Term.

APPEALS

Anders v. California, 386 U.S. 738

A California narcotics defendant was held by the majority to have been deprived of his Sixth Amendment right to counsel by a state appellate court's summary dismissal of his appeal after permitting withdrawal of appointed appellate counsel who had informed the court merely that the defendant's appeal was without merit. He had not accompanied his request for withdrawal with a brief referring to anything in the record that might arguably support the indigent's appeal. The majority opinion written by Mr. Justice Clark emphasized that the poor defendant must be given the same opportunity as the rich defendant. To accomplish that end, the Court outlined the following procedure to be followed: "if counsel finds his case to be wholly frivolous, after a conscientious examination of it, he should so advise the court and request permission to withdraw. That request must, however, be accompanied by a brief referring to anything in the record that might arguably support the appeal. A copy of counsel's brief should be furnished the indigent and time allowed him to raise any points that he chooses; the court —not counsel —then proceeds after a full examination of all the proceedings to decide whether the case is wholly frivolous. If it so finds it may grant counsel's request to withdraw and dismiss the appeal insofar as federal requirements are concerned or proceed to a decision on the merits, if state law so requires. On the other hand, if it finds any of the legal points arguable on their merits (and therefore not frivolous) it must, prior to decision afford the indigent the assistance of counsel to argue the appeal."

Mr. Justice Stewart, joined by Mr. Justice Black and Mr. Justice Harlan, in dissent, thought the California procedure free of constitutional error. He could not understand how counsel wishing to withdraw could present arguable issues for a wholly frivolous appeal.

Entsminger v. Iowa, 386 U.S. 748

On the same day, the court held that an Iowa indigent who desired that his assigned attorney perfect a plenary appeal was deprived of the right to effective assistance of counsel by the attorney's decision to use Iowa's truncated "clerk's transcript" method. (Entsminger v. Iowa, 1 CrL 3025)

Long v. Iowa, 385 U.S. 192; Nowakowski v. Maroney, 386 U.S. 542

Two other decisions smoothing the appellate path for indigents held that the Fourteenth Amendment's Equal Protection Clause bars a state from denying to an indigent prisoner a free copy of a readily available transcript of a state habeas corpus proceeding for use on appeal. (Long v. Iowa, 35 LW 4046); and that a Federal district judge's grant of a certificate of probable cause necessary to allow an indigent's appeal from the court's denial of habeas corpus requires a United States Court of Appeals to entertain an in forma pauperis appeal. (Nowakowski v. Maroney, 1 CrL 3001)

Sequels to decisions of the past few terms —echoing, affirming, and explaining principles there enunciated — made up the bulk of this Term's Fifth Amendment decisions.

HARMLESS ERROR

Chapman v. California, 386 U.S. 18

Griffin v. California, 380 U.S. 609, 33 LW 3482 decided in 1965, held that a prosecutor cannot, consistent with the Fifth Amendment, comment upon the failure of a defendant to testify. This Term however, the court made clear that such comment is not per se reversible error. Rather the Court pointed to the federal "harmless error" rule laid down in Fahy v. Conn., 375 U.S. 85, 32 LW 4021, as the type of standard to be used for determining whether constitutional error during a criminal trial constitutes reversible error. In the case before it, the Court did find that a California prosecutor's repeated comments on robbery-murder defendants' failure to testify was not such harmless error; there was a reasonable possibility that such comments might have contributed to the convictions.

The majority opinion in refusing to adopt a rule that all such constitutional errors automatically require a reversal, concluded "that there may be some constitutional errors which in the setting of a particular case are so unimportant and insignificant that they may, consistent with the Federal Constitution, be deemed harmless, not resulting in the automatic reversal of conviction * * * ."

"There is little, if any, difference between our statement in Fahy v. Connecticut about 'whether there is a reasonable possibility that the evidence complained of might have contributed to the conviction' and requiring the beneficiary of a constitutional error to prove beyond a reasonable doubt that the error complained of did not contribute to the verdict obtained. We, therefore, do no more than adhere to the meaning of our Fahy case when we hold, as we now do, that before a Federal Constitutional error can be held harmless, the court must be able to declare a belief that it was harmless beyond a reasonable doubt. While appellate courts do not ordinarily have the original task of applying such a test, it is a familiar standard to all courts, and we believe its adoption will provide a more workable standard, although achieving the same result as that aimed at in our Fahy case."

Mr. Justice Stewart, concurring, pointed to several situations in which he thought the harmless error rule could never apply. Reversal would be mandatory, he contended, if an involuntary confession, even if unnecessary to conviction, was used against the defendant; if there had been a denial of counsel at trial or before trial at a critical stage; if the trial judge had a financial interest in the result; if the defendant was tried in a community exposed to highly adverse publicity; if the jury was instructed as to an unconstitutional presumption; and if the conviction rested on a constitutionally impermissible ground even if a valid alternative was available. Though he concurred in the result, Mr. Justice Stewart also felt that an automatic reversal was required for violations of the Griffin rule. Mr. Justice Harlan, dissenting, would have upheld the harmless error rule followed by the California Supreme Court.

INTERROGATION AND CONFESSIONS

Clewis v. Texas, 386 U.S. 707

As foreshadowed by its opinion in Davis v. North Carolina, 384 U.S. 737, the Supreme Court this Term, in determining the admissibility of a confession used at a trial completed before Miranda v. Arizona, 384 U.S. 436, was decided, included the failure to advise the defendant of his right to appointed counsel as a factor bearing upon the voluntariness of the confession. Using the pre-Miranda totality-of-the-circumstances rule, the court in an opinion by Mr. Justice Fortas found that coercive tactics by Texas police during a prolonged custodial interrogation rendered an uneducated Negro's murder confession inadmissible. (Clewis v. Texas, 1 CrL 3013)

Sims v. Georgia, 385 U.S. 538

A third recent decision of the Court, Jackson v. Denno, 378 U.S. 368, received the unqualified reaffirmation of the Court. Georgia's attempt to distinguish its procedures for conducting hearings on the voluntariness of a confession from the New York procedures condemned in Jackson fell upon deaf ears. (Sims v. Georgia, 35 LW 4174)

SELF-INCRIMINATION

Garrity v. New Jersey, 385 U.S. 493

The constitutional guarantee against self-incrimination was invoked to preclude the admission, during a criminal trial of local police officers, of statements that had been obtained from them under a state statute compelling them either to make such statements or be discharged from their employment. The choice imposed, Mr. Justice Douglas stated for the majority, was one between self-incrimination or job forfeiture. "Coercion that vitiates a confession * * * can be 'mental as well as physical'; 'the blood of the accused is not the only hallmark of an unconstitutional inquisition.'"

The option to lose their means of livelihood or to pay the penalty of self-incrimination is, the majority explained, the antithesis of free choice to speak out or to remain silent.

Policemen, Mr. Justice Douglas observed, like teachers and lawyers, are not relegated to a watered-down version of constitutional rights.

Four Justices dissented. Mr. Justice Harlan, joined by Mr. Justice Clark and Mr. Justice Stewart feared that the majority approach would seriously and quite needlessly hinder the protection of other important public values. The dissenters concluded that the sanction provided by the state was constitutionally permissible. From this they reasoned that the warning given of a possibility of discharge was constitutionally unobjectionable.

Spevack v. Klein, 385 U.S. 511

In a related case, the same majority held that a New York attorney's disbarment, based upon his refusal to testify and to produce financial records before a state judicial inquiry into unethical practices, violated the Fifth Amendment.

Again writing for the majority, Mr. Justice Douglas indicated that "the threat of disbarment and the loss of professional standing, professional reputation and of livelihood are powerful forms of compulsion to make a lawyer relinquish the privilege."

Mr. Justice Fortas, concurring, would distinguish between a lawyer's right to remain silent and that of a public employee who is asked questions specifically, directly, and narrowly relating to the performance of his official duties as distinguished from his beliefs or other matters that are not within the scope of the specific duties which he undertook faithfully to perform as a part of his employment by the state. He emphasized that "this Court has never held, for example, that a policeman may not be discharged for refusal in disciplinary proceedings to testify as to his conduct as a police officer." Citing Garrity, he noted that it is quite a different matter if the state seeks to use the testimony given under this lash in a subsequent criminal proceeding.

Mr. Justice Harlan, again setting forth a dissenting view, objected that the true question presented was "the effectiveness of the privilege against self-incrimination under the Fourteenth Amendment in state disciplinary proceedings against attorneys." Specifically, whether an attorney's disbarment for his failure to provide information relevant to charges of misconduct in carrying on his law practice impermissibly vitiated the protection afforded by the privilege.

Mr. Justice White, in a single dissent to both Garrity and the present case, could see no reason for refusing to permit the state to pursue its valid interest in discharging an employee who refused to cooperate in the state's effort to determine his qualifications for continued employment. Similarly, he saw little theoretical or practical basis in terms of the Fifth Amendment for preventing the disbarment of a lawyer who refuses to talk about the performance of his public duty.

One major Fifth Amendment question, the decision of which was expected this Term, was left undecided by the Court, upon finding that it had improvidently granted certiorari on the question originally. The question left unanswered is whether the double jeopardy provision of the Fifth Amendment is made binding on the states by the Fourteenth Amendment.

DISCOVERY AND DISCLOSURE

Miller v. Pate, 386 U.S. 1

While the Supreme Court during this term failed to clearly delineate the specific contours of a prosecutor's duty to disclose, it did at least set the outermost boundaries. Counsel for an Illinois murder defendant had before trial unsuccessfully sought a court order to obtain a scientific inspection of physical evidence —a pair of men's shorts covered with dark, reddish-brown stains —the prosecution intended to introduce. At trial these shorts had been admitted into evidence and referred to by the witnesses and the prosecutor as stained with the victim's blood. In the course of federal habeas corpus proceedings it was established that the spots on the shorts were not blood, but paint, and that the prosecutor knew, but did not disclose, that the paint had been found on the shorts.

The Supreme Court in reversing the conviction characterized the prosecution's action as a deliberate misrepresentation of the truth and held that the defendant had been denied a fair trial.

Giles v. Maryland, 386 U.S. 66

A second opportunity to clear up this cloudy area was presented on review of Maryland rape convictions. The Court, however, skirted the issue by holding only that the state appellate court's denial of post-conviction relief to the convicted rapists whose counsel had been denied access to police reports containing statements inconsistent with trial testimony of the prosecutrix and to the prosecution's information about her subsequent assertion and withdrawal of rape charges against others and her attempted suicide, and who were prevented from exploring, at the post-conviction hearing, evidence of her mental condition and nymphomania, required a remand for further proceedings.

The Court was sharply divided on the reason for taking the unique action of remanding the case to the Maryland court without directions. Mr. Justice Brennan, joined by the Chief Justice and Mr. Justice Douglas, noted that the Supreme Court had had the opportunity to review two police reports that were not a part of the record. These reports they insisted, indicated further inconsistencies between the prosecutrix' earlier statements to the police and her testimony at trial.

In sending the case back to the state court for adjudication of the constitutional issues, Mr. Justice Brennan observed that "we * * * should not operate on the assumption —especially inappropriate in Maryland's case in light of its demonstrated concern to afford post-conviction relief parralleling that which may be afforded federal courts in habeas corpus proceedings —the state courts would not be concerned to reconsider a case in light of evidence such as we have here, particularly where the result may avoid unnecessary constitutional adjudication and minimize federal-state tensions."

A concurrency by Mr. Justice White focused primarily on the possibility that the state had suppressed evidence of the victim's mental condition, that is, her nymphomania, by the prosecution. Mr. Justice Fortas, concurring, stressed that a criminal trial "is not a game in which the state's function is to outwit and entrap its quarry. * * * If it has in its exclusive possession specific, concrete evidence which is not merely cumulative or embellishing and which may exonerate the defendant or be of material importance to the defense —regardless of whether it relates to testimony which a state has caused to be given at the trial —a state is obliged to bring it to the attention of the court and the defense."

The four dissenters, Mr. Justice Harlan, Mr. Justice Black, Mr. Justice Clark, and Mr. Justice Stewart, did not consider as newly discovered the not-of-record matters deemed critical by the majority. As to the scope of a prosecutor's duty to disclose, they noted that "issues of the obligatory disclosure of information ultimately raised fundamental questions of the proper nature and characteristics of the criminal trial. These questions surely are entirely too important for this Court to implant in our laws by constitutional decree answers which, without full study, might appear warranted in a particular case. There are few areas which call more for prudent experimentation and continuing study. I can find nothing either in the constitution or in this case which would compel, or justify the imposition on the states of the very broad disclosure rule" proposed by Mr. Justice Fortas.

JUVENILES

In re Gault, 387 U.S. 1

Perhaps the most far reaching opinion this Term focused not on a single constitutional right of an accused but upon that bundle of rights that makes up "due process". This bundle, in which the Court included the rights to be given sufficient notice to make preparation of a defense, to be advised of the right to counsel (including assigned counsel) and of the right to remain silent, and to be afforded the right of confrontation and cross-examination, was delivered to juveniles subjected to proceedings that could lead to detention as delinquents.

The majority opinion, by Mr. Justice Fortas, traced the history and development of juvenile procedures and made the beginning sketches of a blueprint for future proceedings.

The highest motives and most enlightened impulses, he pointed out, led to a peculiar system for juveniles unknown to our law in any comparable context. But, he continued, the constitutional and theoretical basis for this peculiar system is, to say the least, debatable. And in practice, the results have not been entirely satisfactory. Juvenile court history, he explained, has again demonstrated that unbridled discretion, however benevolently motivated, is frequently a poor substitute for principle and procedure. With the due process requirements engrafted by the majority upon juvenile proceedings, juvenile courts will become courts first and social agencies second.

However, the Gault decision left unsolved several constitutional issues. It did not deal with the application of constitutional rights to pre- and post-judicial stages, the right of appeal, the right to trial by jury, the right to a defense of insanity, the constitutionality of the transfer of juveniles from one institution to another, or the right to bail and to a speedy public trial.

Mr. Justice Black, in a concurrence, noted that his vote was not to "invalidate this * * * law on the ground that it is 'unfair' but solely on the ground that it violates the Fifth and Sixth Amendments made obligatory on the states by the Fourteenth Amendment." The only relevance to him of the Due Process Clause was that it would, of course, violate due process or the law of the land to enforce a law that collides with the Bill of Rights.

Mr. Justice White in his concurrence disassociated himself from the majority's holding that the privilege against compelled self-incrimination had been violated in the case before the Court. He did, however, agree that the privilege applies at the adjudicatory stage of juvenile court proceedings.

Mr. Justice Harlan would have gone no further, in this case, than to impose the following three procedural requirements: First, timely notice of the nature and terms of any juvenile court proceedings in which a determination affecting the rights or interests of juveniles may be made; second, unequivocal and timely notice that counsel may appear in any such proceeding and that in cases in which a child may be confined in an institution, counsel may, in circumstances of indigency be appointed for them; and third, that a written record or its equivalent be maintained by the juvenile court to permit effective review on appeal in collateral proceedings.

SENTENCING

Specht v. Patterson, 386 U.S. 605

Sex offenders subject to indeterminate sentences were the beneficiaries of a similar holding. A majority concluded that the Colorado Sex Offenders Act, by its failure to provide a convicted sex offender with a Due Process hearing on whether he should be sentenced to an indeterminate sentence rather than to the term prescribed for the offense committed, violated the Fourteenth Amendment. An indeterminate sentence could, according to the majority, be imposed only after a hearing at which the defendant was present with counsel, and was afforded the opportunity to be heard and to offer evidence and to confront and cross-examine witnesses.

Spencer v. Texas, 385 U.S. 554

Habitual offenders did not fare so well. A majority of the court held that the Fourteenth Amendment did not prevent Texas from enforcing its recidivist statute by allegations and in proof of past conviction during the trial.

FIRST AMENDMENT —OBSCENITY

Redrup v. New York, 386 U.S. 767

No further refinement of the standards against which purportedly obscene material must be judged was forthcoming this Term. The Court, finding that state-condemned books and magazines were constitutionally protected reversed several state court judgments without deciding more troublesome questions of scienter, vagueness, and prior restraint. The Court's per curiam opinion laid bare the diversity of views among its members: "Two members of the court have consistently adhered to the view that a state is utterly without power to suppress, control, or punish the distribution of any writings or pictures upon the ground of their 'obscenity.' A third has held to the opinion that a state's power in this area is narrowly limited to a distinct and clearly identifiable class of material. Others have subscribed to a not dissimilar standard, holding that a state may not constitutionally inhibit the distribution of literary material as obscene unless '(a) the dominant theme of the material taken as a whole appeals to a prurient interest in sex; (b) the material is patently offensive because it effronts contemporary community standards relating to the description or representation of sexual matters; and (c) material is utterly without redeeming social value,' emphasizing that the 'three elements must coalesce' and that no such material can 'be proscribed unless it is found to be utterly without redeeming social value.' Memoirs v. Massachusetts, 383 U.S. 413, 418–419. Another Justice has not viewed the 'social value' element as an independent factor in the judgment of obscenity."

Mr. Justice Harlan and Mr. Justice Clark dissented.

JURIES

Whitus v. Georgia, 385 U.S. 545

In a unanimous opinion, the Court, speaking through Mr. Justice Clark, reversed convictions handed down by Georgia juries from which, the Court found, Negroes had been systematically excluded. The opinion stressed Georgia's failure to offer any explanation for the disparity between the percentage of Negroes on the tax digest (27.1) —Georgia's legally required source for names of prospective jurors —and the percentage of Negroes on grand jury venier (9.3) and on petit jury venier (7.8).

STATUTES

U.S. v. Fabrizio, 385 U.S. 263

Finally, this Term, the Supreme Court made it clear that you don't have to be a racketeer to run afoul of the Anti-Racketeering Act. Section 1953 of the Criminal Code was held to prohibit transportation to New York of acknowledgements of the purchase of New Hampshire's sweepstake tickets even though the New Hampshire lottery was state run. The majority could find no reason to exempt from the section's provision those who have no connection with organized crime. The acknowledgements, the majority concluded, were documents "to be used" in the lottery even though they were not necessary to collect the prize.

Mr. Justice Stewart, joined by Mr. Justice Fortas, dissented.

CIVIL RIGHTS

Pierson v. Ray, 386 U.S. 547

Policemen were afforded the defense of good faith and probable cause by the Court's reversal of a Ninth Circuit reading of Monroe v. Pape, 365 U.S. 167, as making a policeman civilly liable for an arrest under a state statute later held invalid.

The majority noted that the defense of good faith and probable cause, available in a common law action for false arrest and imprisonment, is also available in an action under Section 1 of the Civil Rights Act of 1871, 42 USC 1983.

With one Justice dissenting, the Court also ruled that a local police judge who unconstitutionally convicted civil rights "pilgrims" of a breach of the peace was immune from liability under the Civil Rights Act. The majority found few doctrines more solidly established at common law than the immunity of judges from liability for damages for acts committed within their judicial jurisdiction and this immunity, according to the Court, applies even when the judges are accused of acting maliciously and corruptly.

Finally, dealing with the contention that the tort principle of volenti non fit injuria barred the pilgrim's damage action, the Court noted that their deliberate but peaceful exercise of their rights to use "White only" waiting rooms of bus terminals in the expectation of arrest did not constitute a consent when their legal arrest.

Mr. Justice Douglas, dissenting, did not think that all judges, under all circumstances, no matter how outrageous their conduct, should be immune from suit under the Civil Rights Act. "Some state courts have been instruments of suppression of civil rights. Their methods may have changed; the means may have become more subtle; but the wrong to be remedied still exists * * * . What about the judge who conspires with local law enforcement officers to 'railroad' a dissenter? What about the judge who knowingly turns a trial into a 'kangaroo court?' "

Walker v. Birmingham, 388 U.S. 307

By taking their cause to the streets rather than to available state courts, Negro demonstrators, a five-justice majority of the U.S. Supreme Court held, forfeited any First Amendment defense they may have had to a criminal contempt charge. Citing Howat v. Kansas, 258 U.S. 181, Mr. Justice Stewart noted that the defendants failed, before denying an injunction, to seek its dissolution or modification; the ex parte injunction issued by an Alabama Circuit court forbade them to hold public demonstrations in Birmingham without permits.

Each of the three dissenting opinions contended that the fundamental First Amendment questions of the case should not yield to an unconstitutional injunction based on an unconstitutional ordinance.

Loving v. Virginia, 388 U.S. 1

A criminal law vestige of White supremacy was ushered into limbo by the Court. The Fourteenth Amendment, it predictably held, rendered Virginia's antimiscegenation statute unconstitutional. Classifying marriage as one of man's basic civil rights, the Court ruled that the denial of such a right on racial grounds is "directly subversive of the principles of equality at the heart of the Fourteenth Amendment." Mr. Justice Stewart in a concurring opinion observed that the Constitution bars a state from making "the criminality of an act depend upon the race of the actor."

1967–1968 Term

If the rate of falling precedents is a reliable indicator of the pace of the criminal law revolution, the march quickened during the 1967–68 Term. Not only did a generous handful of major criminal law decisions fall before the onrushing wave of constitutional evolution, but bits and pieces of several others were washed away by the Court's rulings under the Sixth and Fourteenth Amendments. Ironically, however, the bellwether opinion this Term was written on a clean slate, as the Court, for the first time in its history, turned its attention to the validity of "stop-and-frisk" under the Fourth Amendment.

SEARCH AND SEIZURE

Terry v. Ohio, 392 U.S. 1, 3 CrL 3149

Taking the first steps on this new ground, the Chief Justice upheld the right of police, on less than probable cause for arrest, to pat down suspicious persons they have reason to believe present a danger to themselves or others. It is, however, a very limited license the Court has granted police. The limits are derived from the Fourth Amendment's general proscription against unreasonable searches and seizures, and countenance a "frisk" or "pat down" only "where a police officer observes unusual conduct which leads him reasonably to conclude in light of his experience that criminal activity may be afoot and that the persons with whom he is dealing may be armed and presently dangerous; where in the course of investigating this behavior he identifies himself as a policeman and makes reasonable inquiries; and where nothing in the initial stages of the encounter serves to dispel his reasonable fear for his own or others' safety." Moreover, in these limited circumstances he is entitled only to conduct a carefully limited search of the outer clothing of such persons in an attempt to discover weapons that might be used to assault him.

The Court flatly rejected the argument that would, by distinguishing a stop from an arrest or seizure and a frisk from a search, make the Fourth Amendment irrelevant. "It must be recognized that whenever a police officer accosts an individual and restrains his freedom to walk away, he has 'seized' that person. And it is nothing less than sheer torture of the English language to suggest that a careful exploration of the outer surfaces of a person's clothing all over his or her body in an attempt to find weapons is not a 'search'." The stop and frisk, the Court made plain, is a serious intrusion upon the sanctity of the person, which may inflict great indignity and arouse strong resentment; it is not to be undertaken lightly.

The majority, though limiting the use of stop and frisk to the protection of the police officer and therefore to the discovery of weapons, did not determine whether evidence other than weapons discovered as the result of such a procedure would be inadmissible. The opinion by the Chief Justice, however, did emphasize that "the exclusionary rule has its limitations * * * as a tool of judicial control." Effective though it may be where obtaining convictions is an important objective of the police, it is "powerless to deter evasions of constitutionally guaranteed rights where the police either have no interest in prosecuting or are willing to forego successful prosecution in the interests of serving some other goal." A rigid and unthinking application of the exclusionary rule, in futile protest against practices that it can never be used to effectively control, the majority pointed out, may exact a high toll in human injury and in the frustration of efforts to prevent crime. Approval of legitimate and restrained investigative conduct undertaken on the basis of ample factual justification should in no way discourage the employment of remedies other than the exclusionary rule to curtail abuses for which that sanction may prove inappropriate.

The standard of reasonableness imposed upon the police officer is not whether he was absolutely certain that the individual was armed, but rather whether a reasonably prudent man in the circumstances would be warranted in the belief that his safety or that of others was in danger. In making that determination, the majority explained, due weight must be given, not to the policeman's inchoate and unparticularized suspicion or "hunch," but to the specific reasonable inferences he is entitled to draw from the facts in light of his experience.

That the stop-and-frisk decision is seminal rather than terminal is evident from the majority's statement that it "need not develop at length in this case, however, the limitations which the Fourth Amendment places upon a protective seizure and search for weapons. These limitations will have to be developed in the concrete factual circumstances of individual cases."

Concurring, Mr. Justice Harlan "would make it perfectly clear that the right to frisk depends upon the reasonableness of a forcible stop to investigate a suspected crime. However, the right to frisk must be immediate and automatic if the reason for the stop is an articulable suspicion of a crime of violence."

Mr. Justice Harlan considered the facts of this case a good example of those needed to support such an articulable suspicion. The officer had no probable cause to arrest the suspicious person for anything, but he had observed circumstances that would reasonably lead an experienced, prudent policeman to suspect that the suspicious person was about to engage in a burglary or robbery. This justifiable suspicion afforded a proper constitutional basis for accosting the suspicious person, restraining his liberty of movement briefly, and addressing questions to him.

Under Mr. Justice Harlan's analysis, the right to interrupt the suspect's freedom of movement and invade his privacy arose only because circumstances warranted forcing an encounter in an effort to prevent or investigate a crime. "Once that forced encounter was justified, however, the officer's right to take suitable measures for his own safety followed automatically."

A concurrence by Mr. Justice White addressed itself to the matter of interrogation during an investigative stop. Circumstances that justify a stop and frisk, he asserted, also permit the person to be briefly detained against his will while pertinent questions are directed to him. "If the investigative stop is sustainable at all, constitutional rights are not necessarily violated if pertinent questions are asked and the person is restrained briefly in the process."

It was a "mystery" to Mr. Justice Douglas, dissenting, how the stop and frisk, conceded by the majority to be a search and seizure, could nevertheless be constitutional by Fourth Amendment standards without probable cause to believe that crime had been committed, was in the process of being committed, or was about to be committed. The majority, he objected, holds that the police have greater authority to make a seizure and conduct a search than a judge has to authorize such action. "We have said precisely the opposite over and over again." In his opinion, "to give the police greater power than a magistrate is to take a long step down the totalitarian path." The choice to take that step, if it must be taken, he declares, should be the deliberate choice of the people by constitutional amendment.

Sibron v. New York and Peters v. New York, 392 U.S. 40, 3 CrL 3160

Two New York cases fell at opposite ends of the "reasonable cause" spectrum delineated in Terry. In the first, the Court, again speaking through the Chief Justice, declared that a suspect's mere act of talking with a number of known narcotics addicts over an eight-hour period no more gives rise to reasonable fear of life or limb on the part of the police officer than it justifies an arrest for committing a crime. But even if it did, the opinion continued, reaching into a suspect's pocket, before he has been patted down, exceeds the limits of the frisk authorized in Terry. The search was not here reasonably limited in scope to the accomplishment of the only goal that might conceivably have justified its inception —the protection of the officer by disarming a potentially dangerous man. Therefore, the majority concluded, narcotics found as the result of this on-the-street encounter were inadmissible.

In the second New York case, a prosecution for possessing burglary tools, the officer had so much probable cause that the majority found it unnecessary to consider the question in terms of stop and frisk. Rather, it concluded that, for purposes of the Fourth Amendment, the search was properly incident to a lawful arrest. Here, the officer had heard strange noises at his door; this apparently led him to believe that someone sought to force entry. When he investigated these noises he saw two men, whom he had never seen before in his 12 years in the building, tiptoeing furtively about the hallway. When he entered the hallway, the men fled down the stairs. In these circumstances, the majority opinion observed, "it is difficult to conceive a stronger grounds for an arrest, short of actual eye-witness observation of criminal activity."

In both cases, the Court found it unnecessary to examine the facial constitutionality of the New York statute authorizing stop and frisk. "We decline * * * to be drawn into what we view as the abstract and unproductive exercise of laying the extraordinarily elastic categories of [the New York statute] next to the categories of the Fourth Amendment in an effort to determine whether the two are in some sense compatible." The question upon review of a state approved search or seizure is not, the majority pointed out, whether the search or seizure was authorized by state law, but rather whether the search was reasonable under the Fourth Amendment. Just as a search authorized by a state law may be unreasonable, so may a search not expressly authorized by state law be justified as a constitutionally reasonable one.

In reaching the merits of the New York narcotics case, the court rejected a claim of mootness based on the completion of service of sentence and disregarded a confession of error by the state. As for the mootness argument, the Court emphasized that St. Pierre v. U.S., 319 U.S. 41, must be read in light of later cases to mean that a criminal case is moot only if it is shown that there is no possibility that any collateral legal consequences may be imposed on the basis of the challenged conviction. To accept the New York prosecutor's belated confession of error, the Court explained, "would be a disservice to the State of New York and an abdication of our obligation to lower courts to decide cases upon proper constitutional grounds in a manner which permits them to conform their future behavior to the demands of the Constitution."

Mr. Justice Douglas, concurring separately in each of the New York cases, first pointed out that "talking with addicts without more rises no higher than suspicion" and "if it is sufficient for a 'seizure' and 'search', then there is no such thing as privacy for this vast group of 'sick' people." Agreeing, in the second case, that the police officer had probable cause to believe that the suspect was on some kind of burglary or housebreaking mission, Mr. Justice Douglas would hold that he had probable cause to seize the suspect and conduct a limited search of his person for weapons.

Mr. Justice Harlan, though concurring in the results, took the majority to task for completely ignoring the facial constitutionality of the New York statute. The State of New York, he argued, has made a deliberate effort to deal with the complex problem of on-the-street police work. Without carte blanche to any particular verbal formulation, the Court should indicate the extent to which that effort has been constitutionally successful. Since the decision in Terry recognizes that a right to stop may be premised on reasonable suspicion (it does not require probable cause), Mr. Justice Harlan observed, the New York formulation is to that extent constitutional.

Mr. Justice Harlan also emphasized again that the right to frisk is automatic when an officer lawfully stops a person suspected of a crime whose nature creates a substantial likelihood that he is armed. But, he did not believe that suspected possession of narcotics falls into this category.

In the suspected burglar case, though Mr. Justice Harlan agreed that the stop and frisk was reasonable, he did not think the officer "had anything close to probable cause to arrest * * * before he recovered the burglar's tools." This case, he asserted, will be the latest in an exceedingly small number of cases in which the Court indicates what suffices for probable cause. "While as the Court noted in Terry, the influence of this Court on police tactics 'in the field' is necessarily limited, the influence of a decision here on hundreds of courts and magistrates who have to decide whether there is probable cause for a real arrest or a full search will be large." Additionally, Mr. Justice Harlan said that, even though the frisk is constitutionally permitted only in order to protect the officer, the state is entitled to use "any other contraband" discovered as the result of a lawful frisk.

Mr. Justice White concurred, not because there was probable cause to arrest, but because there was probable cause to stop the burglary suspect for questioning and thus to frisk him for dangerous weapons. The burglary tools discovered while patting down the suspect, he observed, were properly admitted into evidence.

Mr. Justice Fortas noted his agreement, "without qualification," concerning the standards to be used in determining whether the New York stop and frisk law as applied to particular situations is constitutional. "But I would explicitly reserve the possibility that a statute purporting to authorize a warrantless search might be so extreme as to justify our conclusion that it is unconstitutional 'on its face' regardless of the facts of the particular case. To the extent that the Court's opinion may indicate to the contrary, I disagree." Moreover, in the narcotics case, he found nothing in the record or pertinent principles of law to justify disregard of the confession of error by the New York prosecutor. "I would not discourage admissions of error nor would I disregard them."

Mr. Justice Black dissented from the Court's holding that the narcotics discovered were inadmissible. He thought that there was probable cause for the policeman to believe that when the suspect reached his hand into his coat pocket, he had a dangerous weapon that he might use if it were not taken away from him. This, he emphasized, seems to have been the ground on which the Court of Appeals of New York justified the search. The U.S. Supreme Court, he objected, "is hardly, at this distance from the place and atmosphere of the trial, in a position to overturn the trial and appellate courts on its own independent finding of an unspoken 'premise' of the officer's inner thoughts." Because of Mapp v. Ohio, 367 U.S. 643, he warned, the Court will get for review literally thousands of cases raising similar questions. "If we are setting ourselves meticulously to review all such findings our task will be endless and many will rue the day when Mapp was decided. It is not only wise but imperative that where findings of the facts of reasonableness and probable cause are involved in such state cases, we should not overturn state court findings unless in the most extravagant and egregious errors. It seems fantastic to me to even suggest that this is such a case. I would leave these state court holdings alone."

Wainwright v. New Orleans, 392 U.S. 598, 3 CrL 3197

A resisting-arrest case thought to have presented the question whether police, seeing a pedestrian who fits the description of a person suspected of murder, may accost the pedestrian and stop him was disposed of summarily. The Court after hearing arguments decided, with two Justices dissenting, that its grant of certiorari had been improvident. Concurring in the dismissal of the writ, Mr. Justice Harlan finds the record "too opaque" to permit adjudication of the dispositive federal issue —whether the petitioner used an unreasonable amount of force in resisting an illegal attempt by the police to search his person. Mr. Justice Fortas, along with Mr. Justice Marshall, agreed, and added that they would regret "any inference that might be derived from the opinions of my Brethren that this Court would or should hold that the police may not arrest and seek by reasonable means to identify a pedestrian whom, for adequate cause, they believe to be a suspect in a murder case." Nor did they think the Court should, without careful analysis, endorse the right of a pedestrian, accosted by police because he fits the description of a wanted person, to resist the officer so vigorously that they are bounced from wall to wall physically.

Dissenting, the Chief Justice stressed that if the police really believed the petitioner was the murder suspect, and if they had probable cause to so believe, all they had to do was arrest and book him for the murder. If they did not have such probable cause, they might have used techniques short of arresting him on a trumped up charge of vagrancy to verify their suspicions. Calling for reversal of the judgment upholding the conviction for resisting arrest, the Chief Justice asserted that, if the Louisiana courts had reached the correct conclusion that the peace officers had no authority to search in this case, they might well have concluded that the resistance to that unlawful search was not unlawful.

Also dissenting, Mr. Justice Douglas saw this case as pointing up "vividly the dangers which emanate from the Court's decision in Terry." If this "seizure" was constitutional, he maintained, the sleepless professor who walks in the night to find the relaxation for sleep is easy prey for the police, as are thousands of other innocent Americans raised in the sturdy environment where no policeman can lay a hand on the citizen without probable cause that a crime has been or is about to be committed. "I fear that with Terry and with Wainwright we have forsaken the Western tradition and taken a long step toward the oppressive police practices not only of Communist regimes but of modern Iran, 'democratic' Formosa, and Franco Spain, with whom we are now even more closely allied."

U.S. v. Katz, 389 U.S. 347, 2 CrL 3065

Though a limited laying on of police hands is not inconsistent with the Fourth Amendment, almost any electronic intrusion by the police ear is. Overruling Olmstead v. U.S., 277 U.S. 438, and Goldman v. U.S., 316 U.S. 129, the Court with only Mr. Justice Black dissenting, held that the Fourth Amendment was breached by the FBI's use of a non-penetrating bug to pick up a gambler's end of telephone calls he made from a public telephone booth. Speaking for the seven-Justice majority, Mr. Justice Stewart emphasized that the Fourth Amendment "protects people, not places." What a person knowingly exposes to the public, even in his own home or office, is not a subject of Fourth Amendment protection; but what he seeks to preserve as private, even in an area accessible to the public, may be constitutionally protected.

Accepting the premise that the protection attaches to people, not simply areas, the reach of the Fourth Amendment, he reasoned, cannot turn upon the presence or absence of a physical intrusion into any given enclosure. As for Olmstead and Goldman, Mr. Justice Stewart described them as "so eroded by our subsequent decisions that the 'trespass' doctrine there enunciated can no longer be regarded as controlling."

Citing the restraint exercised by the FBI agents— the booth was bugged for only the brief periods during which the gambler used it —the majority opinion asserted that "this surveillance was so narrowly circumscribed that a duly authorized magistrate properly notified of the need for such investigation, specifically informed of the basis on which it was to proceed, and clearly apprised of the precise intrusion it would entail, could constitutionally have authorized with appropriate safeguards, the very limited search and seizure that the government asserts in fact took place." However, in the absence of prior judicial sanction, the evidence obtained as result of the bugging is inadmissible.

The majority opinion left unanswered the question whether safeguards other than prior authorization by a magistrate would satisfy the Fourth Amendment in a situation involving the national security. Mr. Justice Douglas, with whom Mr. Justice Brennan joined, concurring, answered that question in the negative. "There is, so far as I understand constitutional history, no distinction under the Fourth Amendment between types of crimes." Mr. Justice White, also concurring, disagreed —"We should not require the warrant procedure and the magistrate's judgment if the President of the United States or his chief legal officer, the Attorney General, has considered the requirements of national security and authorized surveillance as reasonable." Mr. Justice Harlan, also concurring, hedged —"It will be time enough to consider any such exceptions when an appropriate occasion presents itself, and I agree with the Court that this is not one."

Mr. Justice Black "would be happy to join the Court's opinion" if he could agree that eavesdropping carried on by electronic means (equivalent to wiretapping) constitutes a "search" or "seizure." But, he did not believe that the words of the Fourth Amendment will bear the meaning given to them by the majority nor that it is the proper role of the Supreme Court to re-write the Amendment in order to bring it into harmony with the times and thus reach a result that many people believe to be desirable.

Lee v. Florida, 392 U.S. 378, 3 CrL 3173

Schwartz v. Texas, 344 U.S. 199, was consigned to the legion of lost precedents by a 6–3 decision that evidence obtained by police officers in violation of Section 605 of the Federal Communications Act cannot be used in a state prosecution. The Court's opinion, by Mr. Justice Stewart, cited the language of the Federal Communications Act, doctrinal symmetry, the imperative of judicial integrity, and the counsel of experience as reasons enough to reach that conclusion.

Section 605 of the Federal Communications Act, he explained, speaks in terms of intercepting and divulging a communication; here divulgence by the state police was conceded. Doctrinal symmetry, in view of the imposition by Mapp v. Ohio, 367 U.S. 643, of the exclusionary rule upon the states in Fourth Amendment cases, requires a like rule with respect to evidence obtained in violation of Section 605. The imperative of judicial integrity requires that no court, state or federal, serve as an accomplice in the willful transgression of the laws of the United States, laws which bind the judges in every state. Finally, the counsel of experience —not a single reported prosecution of a law enforcement officer for violation of Section 605 since the statute was enacted —proves vain the hope expressed in Schwartz that the penal provisions of the Communications Act were sufficient to achieve enforcement of the statutory prohibition in Section 605.

Mr. Justice Black, dissenting, would leave to Congress the amendment of the Communications Act he deems necessary to explicitly prohibit state use of evidence obtained in violation of Section 605. Mr. Justice Harlan, with whom Mr. Justice White joined, dissenting, emphasized the importance of the principle of stare decisis in a case such as this: "Congress has considered the wiretapping problem many times, each time against what it naturally assumed to be a stable background of statute law. To vary that background with the inclinations of members of this Court is to frustrate orderly Congressional consideration of statutory problems. I would therefore adhere to Schwartz."

Roberts v. U.S., 389 U.S. 18, 2 CrL 3006

By per curiam order, the Court held that the government's admission that, after the return of an indictment, agents of the Federal Bureau of Investigation had monitored conversations between a codefendant and his attorney entitled the defendant to an evidentiary hearing to determine if he was prejudiced by the monitoring.

With stop-and-frisk, and electronic eavesdropping dominating the Fourth Amendment cases this Term, several garden-variety search and seizure decisions were handed down almost unnoticed.

Mancusi v. DeForte, 392 U.S. 364, 3 CrL 3193

As the Fourth Amendment's protections against illegal searches and seizures grow, standing to seek suppression of illegally obtained evidence, logically enough, grows apace. By a 6–3 vote, the Court upheld the standing of a union official to seek suppression at a state trial of union documents seized from a union office that he shared with others.

Standing, the opinion by Mr. Justice Harlan emphasized, depends not on a property right in the invaded place but upon whether the area was one in which there was a reasonable expectation of freedom from governmental intrusion. Here, the union official shared a large room with several other officials and spent a considerable amount of time in the office. Moreover he had custody of the papers at the moment of their seizure. The fact that they belonged to the union gave the majority little pause. For example, Mr. Justice Harlan pointed out, state officials might conceivably have seized the papers during a search of the official's home, and in that event he clearly would have standing. Nor did it matter to the majority that the state, at the time of the seizure, possessed a subpoena issued by a district attorney directing the union to produce the documents.

Mr. Justice Black, with whom Mr. Justice Stewart joined, dissenting, challenged the majority's facile assumption that if the union papers had been taken from a desk in an office used exclusively by the official his standing would have been clear. He read the majority view as preparing the way to eliminate entirely the requirement for standing to raise a search and seizure question and to permit a search to be challenged at any time, at any place, and under all circumstances, regardless of the defendant's relationship to the person or place searched or to the things seized. According to Mr. Justice Black, while common-law concepts of property ownership are not controlling, standing does not automatically devolve on anyone legitimately on the premises. Mr. Justice White, also dissenting, thought that although the Fourth Amendment perhaps protects the individual's private desk in a union office shared with others, the protected area does not extend to the door of such an office.

Bumper v. North Carolina, 391 U.S. 543, 3 CrL 3119

With two Justices dissenting, the Court held that a search could not be sustained under the Fourth Amendment on the basis of consent granted only after the state official conducting the search had asserted that he possessed a warrant. The opinion by Mr. Justice Stewart made clear that there can be no valid consent under such circumstances.

The prosecutor's burden of proving that consent was freely and voluntarily given cannot be discharged by showing no more than acquiescence to a claim of lawful authority. A law enforcement officer claiming authority to search a home under a warrant is in effect announcing that the occupant has no right to resist the search. Such a situation, Mr. Justice Stewart insisted, is "instinct with coercion —albeit colorably lawful coercion."

Mr. Justice Black in dissent would not only find, on the record, that consent was freely given but, assuming it was not, that introduction of the evidence found constituted no more than harmless error. Mr. Justice White, also dissenting, would remand for a determination of whether the state did in fact have a valid warrant for the search.

Harris v. U.S., 390 U.S. 234, 2 CrL 3146

By invoking the "in plain view" rule, the Court, in a per curiam opinion, avoided the ticklish problem of deciding whether a police department regulation can authorize the warrantless search of lawfully impounded vehicles. The evidence, according to the Court's opinion, was discovered by a policeman who was rolling up the windows of an impounded vehicle to protect it from rain, and was in plain view.

Mr. Justice Douglas, in a concurrence, "assumes" that the majority opinion means Preston v. U.S., 376 U.S. 364, has survived. Noting the majority's failure to mention Preston, he pointed out that the car was lawfully in police custody, the police were responsible for protecting the car and that, while engaged in the performance of their duty, and not engaged in inventory or other search of the car, came across the incriminating evidence.

Sabbath v. U.S., 391 U.S. 585, 3 CrL 3107

Faced with a non-constitutional arrest problem the Court, over the unexplicated dissent of Mr. Justice Black, held that federal agents were not entitled to make an unannounced entry into a heroin suspect's apartment by opening the closed, but unlocked door. Since the method of entry vitiated the arrest, the opinion by Mr. Justice Marshall pointed out, the evidence seized in the subsequent search incident thereto should not have been admitted at the defendant's trial.

It would be indeed a "grudging application" of Section 3109 of the Criminal Code, the opinion continued, to hold that the use of "force" is an indispensible element under the statute, which permits an officer to break into a house only after notice of his authority and purpose.

An unannounced intrusion into a dwelling, Mr. Justice Marshall reasoned, is no less an unannounced intrusion whether officers break through a door, force open a chain lock on a partially open door, open a locked door by use of a pass key, or, as here, open a closed but unlocked door. The majority specifically disclaims any intent to deal with entries obtained by ruse which have been viewed by some lower courts as not involving a break-in.

SELF-INCRIMINATION

Marchetti v. U.S., 390 U.S. 39, 2 CrL 3102

The Fifth Amendment made a spectacular showing this Term.

Though the Court did not go so far as to hold that the federal wagering tax provisions are as such constitutionally impermissible, it did decide that those who properly assert their constitutional privilege against self-incrimination may not be punished for failure to comply with those provisions.

Critical, the opinion by Mr. Justice Harlan pointed out, was the comprehensive system of federal and state prohibitions against wagering activities. In the face of these, requiring a gambler, on the pain of criminal prosecution, to provide information that, it might reasonably be supposed, would be made available to prosecuting authorities and that would surely provide a significant link in the chain of evidence tending to establish guilt violates the Fifth Amendment. By so holding, the majority overruled U.S. v. Kahriger, 345 U.S. 22, and Lewis v. U.S., 348 U.S. 419.

The issue is not, Mr. Justice Harlan explained, whether the United States may tax activities that a state or Congress has declared unlawful. Rather, the issue is whether the methods employed by Congress in the federal wagering tax statutes are consistent with the limitations created by the privilege against self-incrimination. The question is not whether gamblers hold a right to violate state law, but whether, having done so, they may be compelled to give evidence against themselves. The constitutional privilege "was intended to shield the guilty and imprudent as well as the innocent and foresighted; if such an inference of antecedent choice were alone enough to abrogate the privilege's protection, it would be excluded from the situations in which it has historically been granted, and withheld from those who most require it."

The majority also rejected a suggestion by the United States that, the Court, were it to find the Fifth Amendment applicable, shield the privilege's claimants through the imposition of restrictions upon the use by federal and state authorities of information obtained as a consequence of compliance with the wagering tax requirements. But, the majority observed, the Court cannot know how Congress would assess the competing demands of the federal treasury and of state gambling prohibitions; it is entirely certain that the constitution has entrusted to Congress and not to the Court, the task of striking an appropriate balance among such values.

Other methods, entirely consistent with the constitutional limitations, the opinion continued, exist by which Congress may obtain the information necessary for effective taxation of such activities. "Accordingly, nothing we do today will prevent either the taxation or the regulation by Congress of activities otherwise made unlawful by state or federal statutes."

Grosso v. U.S., 390 U.S. 62, 2 CrL 3108

In this companion case to Marchetti, the Court found in the Fifth Amendment a cloak of protection for a gambler convicted of failure to pay the special excise and occupational taxes on gamblers imposed by Sections 4401 and 4411 of Title 26. And, the Court, in an opinion by Mr. Justice Harlan, was unable to view the gambler's failure to present the Fifth Amendment issue as an effective waiver of the constitutional privilege.

Mr. Justice Brennan, concurring in both cases, emphasized that Congress is nevertheless assuredly "empowered to construct a statutory scheme which either is general enough to avoid conflict with the privilege, or which assures the necessary confidentiality or immunity to overcome the privilege."

Only the Chief Justice dissented. The cure, according to him, is not to strike down the tax provisions in question, but to strike the provision of the Internal Revenue Code that permits disclosure to prosecutors of information required for tax purposes.

Haynes v. U.S., 390 U.S. 85, 2 CrL 3115

For the same reasons found fatal to the gambling tax wagering tax provisions, the Court concluded that a proper claim of the constitutional privilege against self-incrimination also provides a full defense to prosecutions either for failure to register a firearm under Section 5841 of the Internal Revenue Code or for possession of an unregistered firearm under Section 5851. Again, the Chief Justice was the lone dissenter.

Gardner v. Broderick, 392 U.S. 273, 3 CrL 3143

Public officials also obtained enlarged benefits under the privilege against self-incrimination. In 1967, public officials were told that incriminating statements compelled from them by the threat of discharge could not be used against them in a criminal trial, Garrity v. New Jersey, 385 U.S. 493. Last Term they learned that they could not be discharged for refusing to surrender the privilege.

Mr. Justice Fortas emphasized that, had the suspected policeman refused to answer questions "specifically, directly, and narrowly relating to the performance of his official duties, without being required to waive his immunity with respect to the use of his answers or the fruits thereof in a criminal prosecution of himself, * * * the privilege against self-incrimination would not have been a bar to his dismissal." But, the opinion emphasized he was dismissed solely for his refusal to waive the immunity to which he is entitled, if he is required to testify despite his constitutional privilege.

Uniformed Sanitation Men Association, Inc. v. Commissioner, 392 U.S. 280, 3 CrL 3141

A like result was reached with respect to 15 employees of the New York City Department of Sanitation who refused at various stages of an investigation to waive their constitutional right against self-incrimination. Three had refused to sign waivers of immunity before a grand jury while the remaining 12 had refused to answer questions that were put to them by the Commissioner of Investigation and that could have been used against them in the subsequent proceedings.

Mr. Justice Harlan, with whom Mr. Justice Stewart joined, could find no "solidly acceptable course" in these cases other than to concur in the judgements. He did so "with a good deal less reluctance than would otherwise have been the case" because "I find in these opinions a procedural formula whereby for example, public officials may now be discharged and lawyers disciplined for refusing to divulge to appropriate authority information pertinent to the faithful performance of their offices." This, according to Mr. Justice Harlan, is "a welcome breakthrough in what Spevack [v. Klein, 385 U.S. 511] and Garrity [v. New Jersey, 385 U.S. 493] might otherwise have been thought to portend."

George Campbell Painting Corp. v. Reid, 392 U.S. 286, 3 CrL 3140

Though the privilege against self-incrimination has broadened in recent years, the Court was still not willing to extend it to a corporation. It therefore held that a corporation could not invoke the privilege to attack the constitutionality of a New York statute providing that any person who refuses to answer any relevant grand jury questions, and any firm or corporation of which he is a member, officer, or director, shall be disqualified for five years from contracting with any public authority and shall be subject to cancellation of any existing contracts.

Mr. Justice Douglas and Mr. Justice Black dissented. Their dissent emphasized that the corporation involved was a family-held corporation. "What New York could not do directly, it may not do indirectly. Yet penalizing this man's family corporation for his assertion of immunity has precisely that effect."

Simmons v. U.S., 390 U.S. 372, 2 CrL 3153

In the second case, the Court forbad the use at trial of inculpatory testimony given by a defendant in support of his pretrial motion to suppress. To allow such a practice, the six-man majority, speaking through Mr. Justice Harlan, observed, forces a defendant to choose between two fundamental rights —his privilege against self-incrimination and his Fourth Amendment right to contest police seizures of his property.

Mr. Justice Black, joined in dissent by Mr. Justice white, commented that the question "is whether the government is barred from offering a truthful statement made by a defendant at a suppression hearing in order to prevent the defendant from winning an acquittal on the false premise that he is not the owner of the property he has already sworn that he owns."

The Court also held, unanimously, in this case, that the inclusion of the accused's photograph those of several youths shown to the witnesses of a bank robbery did not violate the rules of identification laid down in U.S. v. Wade, 388 U.S. 218, 1 CrL 3106; Stovall v. Denno, 388 U.S. 293, 1 CrL 3102; Gilbert v. California, 388 U.S. 263, 1 CrL 3094.

JOINT TRIAL

Bruton v. U.S., 391 U.S. 123, 3 CrL 3085

Confession cases once again proved a staple of the Supreme Court's diet. During preceding Terms, the Supreme Court paid much attention to establishing procedures assuring that the Fifth and Sixth Amendments were respected in obtaining incriminating statements from a defendant. The 1967–68 Term's major confession decision focused on an entirely different problem —the use at a joint trial of a codefendant's confession inculpating the defendant.

Delli Paoli v. U.S., 352 U.S. 232, established that such a confession could be admitted at a joint trial so long as the jury was specifically instructed that the co-defendant's confession was admissible only against the declarant. In the 1967–68 Term Delli Paoli was over-ruled.

The basic premise of Delli Paoli, the majority opinion by Mr. Justice Brennan pointed out, was that it is reasonably possible for a jury to follow sufficiently clear instructions to disregard the confessor's extrajuridical statement that his codefendant participated with him in committing the crime. But, he emphasized, since Delli Paoli was decided "this Court has effectively repudiated its basic premise." The repudiation, he observed, was not in the context of the admission of a confession inculpating a defendant but in the context of a New York rule that submitted to the jury the question of the voluntariness of the confession itself. Jackson v. Denno, 378 U.S. 368. "Nonetheless the message of Jackson for Delli Paoli was clear." In Jackson, the Court "expressly rejected the proposition that a jury, when determining the confessor's guilt, could be relied on to ignore his confession of guilt should they find the confession involuntary." Significantly, that conclusion in Jackson was supported in part by reliance on the dissenting opinion of Mr. Justice Frankfurter in Delli Paoli.

As was recognized in Jackson, there are some contexts in which the risk that the jury will not or cannot follow instructions is so great and the consequences of failure so vital to the defendant that the practical and human limitations of the jury system cannot be ignored. The unreliability of evidence by an accomplice, given the recognized motivation to shift blame on to others, is intolerably compounded when the alleged accomplice does not testify and cannot be tested by cross-examination. It was against just such threats to a fair trial that the Confrontation Clause was directed. Limiting instructions, Mr. Justice Brennan concluded, cannot be accepted as an adequate substitute for the constitutional right of cross-examination.

In a concurrence, Mr. Justice Stewart pointed out that, quite apart from Jackson v. Denno, the underlying rationale of the Sixth Amendment's Confrontation Clause "precludes reliance upon cautionary instructions when the highly damaging out-of-court statement of a codefendant, who is not subject to cross-examination, is deliberately placed before the jury at a joint trial."

Justices White and Harlan dissented. Mr. Justice White emphasized the practical difficulties of separate trials and their potential unfairness. He was "disappointed" that the Court did not spell out how the federal courts might conduct their business consistent with this overruling of Delli Paoli. "I would suppose that it will be necessary to exclude all extrajudicial confessions unless all portions of them which implicate defendants other than the declarant are effectively deleted. Effective deletion will probably require not only omission of all direct and indirect inculpations of codefendants but also of any statement that could be employed against those defendants once their identity is otherwise established. Of course, the deletion must not be such that it will distort the statements to the substantial prejudice of either the declarant or the government. If deletion is not feasible, then the government will have to choose either not to use the confession at all or to try the defendants separately. As a practical matter, the government might best seek a ruling as to the admissibility and deleteability of the confession at the earliest possible stage of the trial proceedings, thereby avoiding needless expenditure, time, and effort. The failure of the government to adopt and follow proper procedures for insuring that the inadmissible portions of confessions are excluded will be relevant to the question of whether it was harmless error for them to have gotten before the jury. Oral statements, such as that involved in the present case, will present special problems, for there is a risk that the witness in testifying will inadvertently exceed permissible limits. Except for recommending that caution be used with regard to such oral statements, it is difficult to anticipate the issues which will arise in concrete factual situations."

Mr. Justice Harlan noted that he had not abandoned his original disagreement with Jackson v. Denno.

Roberts v. Russell, 392 U.S. 293, 3 CrL 4089

By per curiam order, the Court, with Justices White and Harlan again dissenting, ruled that this holding applied in state prosecutions and was entitled to retroactive application. Even if the impact of retroactivity may be significant, the order explained, the constitutional error presents a serious risk that the issue of guilt or innocence may not have been reliably determined.

INTERROGATION AND CONFESSIONS

Mathis v. U.S., 391 U.S. 1, 3 CrL 3051

Custodial interrogation, the guide to deciding the applicability of Miranda v. Arizona, 384 U.S. 456, the Court made clear this Term means more than custody by interrogators and interrogation by custodians. The failure of an Internal Revenue agent to give the Miranda warnings before questioning a Florida prisoner in connection with a "routine" tax investigation, according to a 5–3 majority of the U.S. Supreme Court, required the reversal of the prisoner's subsequent federal tax evasion conviction.

The government had sought to escape application of Miranda on two grounds: (1) that the questions were asked as part of a routine tax investigation where no criminal proceedings might even be brought, and (2) that the prisoner had not been put in jail by the officer's questioning him, but was there for an entirely separate offense. The majority opinion by Mr. Justice Black regarded these differences as "too minor and shadowy to justify a departure from the well-considered conclusions of Miranda with reference to warnings to be given to a person held in custody."

Dissenting, Mr. Justice White, with whom Mr. Justice Harlan and Mr. Justice Stewart joined, first noted his continuing belief that "the decision in Miranda was an extravagant and unwise interpretation of the Fifth Amendment" and that he would "prefer that Miranda be abandoned." But, he continued, even if he were to agree that Miranda had been correctly decided, he would not join in the majority's unexplained extension of that decision. "Certainly the explanation of the need for warnings given in the Miranda opinion does not cover civil investigations, and the Court's opinion in this case furnishes no additional support." Moreover, he deemed the rationale of Miranda as irrelevant "to inquiries conducted outside the allegedly hostile and forbidding atmosphere surrounding police station interrogation of a criminal suspect." Here, although the prisoner was confined, he was at the time, Mr. Justice White emphasized, in familiar surroundings.

Harrison v. U.S., 392 U.S. 219, 3 CrL 3145

The confession branch of the poisonous tree has grown a new variety of fruit. With three Justice dissenting, the

Court held that, unless the prosecution can prove that a defendant's inculpatory testimony at his prior trial was not induced by the admission of a confession later found to have been illegally obtained, his trial testimony cannot be used against him at retrial.

Mr. Justice Stewart declared that the Court was not questioning the general evidentiary rule that a defendant's testimony at a former trial is admissible against him in later proceedings. Here, however, he explained, the original testimony had been given only after the government had illegally introduced into evidence three confessions, all wrongfully obtained. In such circumstances "the same principle that prohibits the use of confessions so procured also prohibits the use of any testimony impelled thereby —the fruit of the poisonous tree, to invoke a time-worn metaphor."

The question is not whether the petitioner made a knowing decision to testify, but why. If he did so to overcome the impact of confessions illegally obtained and hence improperly introduced, his testimony was tainted by the same illegality that rendered the confessions themselves inadmissible. Moreover, the prosecution bears the burden of proving that the use of the illegally obtained confessions did not in fact impel the challenged testimony. "Having 'released the spring' by using the petitioner's unlawfully obtained confessions against him, the government must show that its illegal action did not induce his testimony."

Mr. Justice Harlan, in dissent, found the situation present no different in principle from the sacrifice of surprise, or the conveyance of important leads to the other side, that may occur because a trial continues even after error has been committed. It is the price, he insisted, that is paid for having a system of justice that requires, generally, full trials before appellate review of points of law. It is a problem that can be avoided, within our system, only by doing "what is done here, namely, reaching the wrong result as between the litigants."

To Mr. Justice White, also dissenting, the majority's view has emanated "from the Court's fuzzy ideology about confessions, an ideology which is difficult to relate to any provision of the Constitution and which excludes from the trial evidence of the highest relevance and probity."

Moreover, he did not think the fruit fell close enough to the poisonous tree to be deemed tainted. "When one deals with the fruits of an illegal search or seizure * * * or with the fruits of an illegal confession * * * the reason for suppression of the original illegal evidence itself is prophylactic —to deter the police from engaging in such conduct in the future by denying them its past benefits * * * since deterrence is the only justification for excluding the original evidence there is no justification for excluding the fruits of such evidence unless suppression of them will also serve the prophylactic end. I deem this the crucial issue, and the proper resolution of it requires a different result from that to which the Court has bulled its way."

Given the Court's current ideology about confessions, Mr. Justice White was willing to concede that there is perhaps some logic on the side of the Court. But common sense and policy, he objected, are squarely opposed.

Mr. Justice Black joined in Mr. Justice White's dissent, stressing that "holdings like this make it far more difficult to protect society 'against those who have made it impossible to live today in safety.' "

Darwin v. Connecticut, 391 U.S. 346, 3 CrL 4074

The same burden of proof was placed on the state with respect to a more common poisoned-fruit situation —the obtaining of a voluntary confession after two involuntary confessions had been elicited. The Court held that prolonged incommunicado detention barred the use of a subsequently obtained confession as well as evidence of a subsequent reenactment of the crime.

Mr. Justice Harlan, concurring in part, espoused the view that, when the prosecution seeks to use a confession uttered after an earlier one not found to be voluntary, it has the burden of proving not only that the latter confession was not itself the product of improper threats or promises or coercive conditions, but also that it was not directly produced by the existence of the earlier confession. This reasoning, was then cited with approval over Mr. Justice Harlan's objection, by the majority in Harrison.

Mr. Justice White dissented.

Greenwald v. Wisconsin, 390 U.S. 519, 3 CrL 4004

By per curiam order, the Court held that a pre-Miranda confession obtained in the absence of counsel from an accused who had stated that he desired counsel, who had been deprived of food, sleep, and medication, and who had not been adequately warned of his constitutional rights, could not be deemed voluntary. Mr. Justice Stewart, joined by Mr. Justice Harlan and Mr. Justice White, dissented.

Georgia v. Sims, 385 U.S. 538, 2 CrL 3073

Also, by per curiam order, the Court without dissent, decided that a confession produced by violence or threats of violence is involuntary and cannot be rendered admissible by subsequent warnings given the accused prior to his confessing. In the case before it, the Court pointed out, the accused had been in continuous custody of the police for over 8 hours, had not been fed, had not been given access to his family, friends, or counsel, and was an illiterate whose mental capacity is decidedly limited. Under such circumstances, the fact that the police may have warned him of his right not to speak can have little significance.

The Court also held, on the basis of Whitus v. Georgia, 385 U.S. 545, that the juries by which the accused was indicted and tried were selected in a manner that did not comport with constitutional requirements.

Brooks v. Florida, 389 U.S. 413, 2 CrL 3074

Faced with a record documenting "a shocking display of barbarism" the Court summarily reversed a Florida riot conviction based upon a prisoner's confession obtained after he had spent 14 days in a 7-foot by 6-foot cell with two other prisoners and had been fed only 4 ounces of soup three times a day.

Johnson v. Massachusetts, 390 U.S. 511, 3 CrL 3001

With three Justices dissenting, the Court dismissed as improvidently granted a writ it had issued to determine whether an injured Massachusetts murder defendant's confession obtained after 8 hours in police custody was involuntary.

The dissenters, in an opinion by Mr. Justice Marshall, joined by the Chief Justice and Mr. Justice Fortas, painted this factual picture. The accused had a sixth grade education and an I.Q. of 86. He was held for over 8 hours prior to confessing and was at no time advised of his right to remain silent or his right to consult with an attorney. At the time of arrest he was bleeding from a cut an inch and a half long on the side of his head. After subsequently examining him, two doctors reported that he suffered from headaches, dizziness, had had a blackout spell in the police station, and had vomited a couple of times. Two weeks after his arrest and confession, he underwent a brain operation for a subdural hematoma. The surgeon who performed the operation testified that the hematoma could have been there anywhere from one to two weeks.

The dissenters are unable to agree with the majority that the record revealing these facts was "insufficient" to permit a resolution of the accused's constitutional claim. Rather, they found it abundantly clear that a confession obtained under such circumstances is involuntary and constitutionally inadmissible against its maker.

HABEAS CORPUS

Peyton v. Rowe, 391 U.S. 54, 3 CrL 3093

Overruling McNally v. Hill, 293 U.S. 131, the Court in an opinion by the Chief Justice, laid the prematurity doctrine to rest in habeas corpus cases. McNally v. Hill had held that the habeas corpus statute does not authorize attacks upon future consecutive sentences. But, the Court this Term concluded, the decision in that case was compelled neither by statute nor by history and "today it represents an indefensible barrier to prompt adjudication of constitutional claims in the federal courts."

To the extent that the rule of McNally postpones plenary consideration of issues by the district courts, the Court held, it undermines the character of the writ of habeas corpus as the instrument for resolving fact issues not adequately developed in the original proceedings. Additionally, McNally was found to be at odds with the purposes of the Great Writ in another respect. Its prematurity rule extends, without practical justification, the time a prisoner entitled to release must remain in custody; he remains in prison until the Court acts.

The Chief Justice asserted that in common understanding custody comprehends the entire duration of imprisonment, even though that duration encompasses sentences imposed upon more than one conviction. Therefore, the prisoner serving consecutive sentences is "in custody" under any one of them for purposes of Section 2241 (c)(3) of the Judicial Code.

Carafas v. La Vallee, 391 U.S. 234, 3 CrL 3060

Not only can a prisoner use the Great Writ to test a sentence he has not yet begun to serve, but the Court held, he can also attack in federal habeas corpus a conviction under which he has completed his sentence prior to the final adjudication of his petition on appeal. Completion of sentence, Mr. Justice Fortas pointed out, does not render the pending habeas corpus petition moot and terminate federal jurisdiction.

Overruling Parker v. Ellis, 362 U.S. 574, the Court emphasized that under the statutory scheme, once federal habeas corpus jurisdiction has attached in the district court, it is not defeated by the release of the prisoner prior to completion of proceedings on such application.

Parker, Mr. Justice Fortas emphasized, simply aggravates the hardships that may result from intolerable delays in affording justice.

Mr. Justice Harlan and Mr. Justice Stewart, who had joined in the Parker decision in 1960, "are now persuaded that what the Court there decided was wrong insofar as it held that even though a man be in custody when he initiates a habeas corpus proceeding, the statutory power of the federal courts to proceed to a final adjudication of his claims depends upon his remaining in custody."

Walker v. Wainwright, 390 U.S. 335, 2 CrL 3150

Earlier in the Term, by per curiam order, the Court had held that an unchallenged consecutive sentence that would not commence until completion of the sentence challenged by habeas corpus was no bar to the habeas corpus proceeding. To hold otherwise in the case before it, the Court emphasized, would mean that a prisoner attacking a life sentence to be followed by a five-year sentence could not attack the life sentence he had begun to serve until after he had finished serving it.

Whitney v. Florida, 389 U.S. 138, 2 CrL 3023

Over a dissent by Mr. Justice Douglas, the majority refused to decide whether a Florida court deprived a prisoner of equal protection and due process of law by summarily dismissing his state collateral attack without conducting an evidentiary hearing.

The majority's dismissal was without prejudice to an application for federal habeas corpus in the appropriate federal court. But, Mr. Justice Douglas contended, "we needlessly burden the federal regime when we do not insist that Florida, which has provided a remedy, have the evidentiary hearing which will determine the nature and extent" of the pretrial publicity claimed to have infected the trial and whether such publicity was trivial or potentially damaging.

Mr. Justice Harlan, with whom Mr. Justice Black joined, also dissented, but for a far different reason. "I can find no sound basis for this Court's not reaching the merits of the question brought here for review, even though I believe that the writ should not have been issued in the first place."

MANDAMUS

Will v. U.S., 389 U.S. 90, 2 CrL 3029

While there may be a place in pretrial criminal procedure for use of the extraordinary writ of mandamus, the Court emphasized this Term that such a writ must at least contain a reasoned justification for its issuance. The opinion by the Chief Justice asserted that, while the Court has never approved the use of mandamus to review an interlocutory procedural order that did not result in the dismissal of the prosecution, the case before it did not require a delineation of the circumstances under which such a use would be appropriate. It is enough, he explained, that "we approach the decision in this case with an awareness of the constitutional precept that a man is entitled to a speedy trial and that he may not be placed twice in jeopardy for the same offense." The peremptory common-law writs are, he continued, among the most potent weapons in the judicial arsenal. They are therefore reserved for really extraordinary causes. "A mandamus from the blue without a rationale is tantamount to an abdication of the very expository and supervisory functions of an appellate court upon which the government rests its attempt to justify the action below." The mandamus in this case had been issued to vacate a portion of a pretrial order in a criminal case.

CAPITAL PUNISHMENT

U.S. v. Jackson, 390 U.S. 570, 3 CrL 3003

The frontal attack on capital punishment as cruel and inhuman under the Eighth Amendment had not yet reached the U.S. Supreme Court. But, limited forays under cover of the Sixth Amendment met with moderate success during the 1967–68 Term. The coup de grace dealt the death penalty provision of the Federal Kidnapping Act by the Court may also have dealt a stunning blow to death penalty laws in numerous states. Mr. Justice Stewart, writing for a six-Justice majority pointed out that the death penalty clause in the Lindbergh Act permits imposition of capital punishment only on defendants who assert their right to be tried by a jury, thus needlessly discouraging them from exercising their right to plead innocent and demand jury trials. By putting the federal kidnapping defendant to this choice, he concluded, the Fifth and Sixth Amendments are violated.

Clearly, Mr. Justice Stewart reasoned, if the provision had no other purpose or effect than to chill the assertion of constitutional rights by penalizing those who choose to exercise them, it would be patently unconstitutional. And, even conceding that limiting the death penalty to cases where the jury recommends it may avoid the more drastic alternative of mandatory capital punishment in every case, such an objective cannot be pursued by means that needlessly chill the exercise of basic constitutional rights. "The question is not whether the chilling effect is 'incidental' rather than intentional; the question is whether that effect is unnecessary and therefore excessive." While the goal of limiting the death penalty to cases in which a jury recommends it is an entirely legitimate one, that goal can be achieved without penalizing those defendants who plead not guilty and demand jury trial.

As an illustration, Mr. Justice Stewart pointed out that in some states the choice between life imprisonment and capital punishment is left to the jury in every case — regardless of how the defendant's guilt has been determined.

The demise of the death penalty does not require an invalidation of the Lindbergh Law in its entirety, Mr. Justice Stewart concluded. "It is clear that the clause authorizing capital punishment is severable from the remainder of the kidnapping statute and that the constitutionality of the clause does not require the defeat of the law as a whole." Prosecutions for violating the Act are not barred, but those convicted cannot be put to death under its authority.

In dissent, Mr. Justice White, with whom Mr. Justice Black joined, emphasized that the case raised no question of the validity of the death penalty per se or of the propriety of jury participation in its imposition, but went only to the confining of the power to impose the death penalty to the jury alone.

Under this rationale, he explained, if the vice of this particular provision is that it interferes with the free choice of the defendant to have his guilt or innocence determined by a jury, the cure is to make sure that the pleas of guilty and waivers of jury trial are carefully examined before they are accepted so that it is clear they have been neither coerced nor encouraged by the vesting of death penalty power in the jury alone.

Witherspoon v. Illinois, 391 U.S. 510, 3 CrL 3107

Equally as abhorrent to a majority of the Court as resting the power to impose death solely in the jury is putting that power in the hands of a jury from which have been excluded all persons expressing general objections to or religious scruples against capital punishment.

Mr. Justice Stewart again wrote for the majority. He emphasized at the outset that the issue was a narrow one not involving "the State's assertion of a right to exclude from the jury in a capital case those who say that they could never vote to impose the death penalty or that they would refuse even to consider its imposition in the case before them."

"A prospective juror cannot be expected to say in advance of trial whether he would in fact vote for the extreme penalty in the case before him. The most that can be demanded of a venireman in this regard is that he be willing to *consider* all of the penalties provided by state law, and that he not be irrevocably committed, before the trial has begun, to vote against the penalty of death regardless of the facts and circumstances that might emerge in the course of the proceedings. If the *voir dire* testimony in a given case indicates that veniremen were excluded on any broader basis than this, the death sentence cannot be carried out even if applicable statutory or case law in the relevant jurisdiction would appear to support only a narrower ground of exclusion. * * *

"We repeat, however, that nothing we say today bears upon the power of a State to execute a defendant sentenced to death by a jury from which the only veniremen who were in fact excluded for cause were those who made unmistakably clear (1) that they would *automatically* vote against the imposition of capital punishment without regard to any evidence that might be developed at the trial of the case before them, or (2) that their attitude toward the death penalty would prevent them from making an impartial decision as to the defendant's *guilt.* Nor does the decision in this case affect the validity of any sentence *other* than one of death. Nor, finally, does today's holding render invalid the *conviction,* as opposed to the *sentence,* in this or any other case."

It is entirely possible, he pointed out, that even a juror who believes that capital punishment should never be imposed and who is irrevocably committed to its abolition could nonetheless subordinate his personal views to what he perceived to be his duty to abide by the oath as a juror and to obey the law of the state. In other words, according to Mr. Justice Stewart, unless a venireman states unambiguously that he would automatically vote against the imposition of capital punishment no matter what the trial might reveal, it simply cannot be assumed that that is his position.

Moreover, the Court's decision went only to the imposition of punishment, not to the determination of guilt. "We simply cannot conclude, either on the basis of the record now before us or as a matter of judicial notice, that the exclusion of jurors opposed to capital punishment results in an unrepresentative jury on the issue of guilt or substantially increases the risk of conviction. In light of the presently available information, we are not prepared to announce a per se constitutional rule requiring the reversal of every conviction returned by a jury selected as this one was." But, he continued, it is self-evident that, in its role as arbiter of the punishment to be imposed this jury fell woefully short of that impartiality to which the accused was entitled under the Sixth and Fourteenth Amendments.

On the other hand, if the state had excluded only those prospective jurors who stated in advance of trial that they would not even consider returning a verdict of death, it could argue that the resulting jury was simply "neutral" with respect to the penalty.

Just as veniremen cannot be excluded for cause on the ground that they hold conscientious or religious scruples against capital punishment, so too they cannot be excluded for cause simply because they indicate that there are some kinds of cases in which they would refuse to recommend capital punishment, Mr. Justice Stewart explained.

Finally, since the jury selection standards condemned undermine the very integrity of the fact-finding process, and, since neither the reliance of law enforcement officials, nor the impact of a retroactive holding on the administration of justice would warrant non-retroactivity, the Court makes its holding "fully retroactive."

Mr. Justice Douglas, in an opinion not specifically labeled a dissent or a concurrence, would clearly have gone much further than the majority. A showing of prejudice with respect to guilt, he declared, should not be required. It must be assumed, he continued, that "in many, if not most, cases of class exclusion on the basis of beliefs or attitudes some prejudice does result and many times will not be subject to precise measurement."

Dissenting, Mr. Justice Black, with whom Mr. Justice Harlan and Mr. Justice White joined, noted that a person who has conscientious or religious scruples against capital punishment "will seldom if ever vote to impose the death penalty." If such persons must be allowed to serve on a jury so that the conscience of the community will be fully represented, so too, the dissenters claimed, under the same rationale, must jurors who have conscientious or religious scruples against not inflicting the death penalty be represented. Both classes of persons, Mr. Justice Black suggested should be excluded.

Mr. Justice White, in a separate dissent, reasoned that, since the majority did not hold that the imposition of the death penalty offends the Eighth Amendment or that the state legislature may not specify only death as the punishment for certain crimes, the analytic basis of the result reached by the Court is infirm.

The Constitution, which bars a legislative determination that everyone indicted should be convicted, and so requires the judgment of a guilt determining body unprejudiced as to the result, speaks, he explained, in entirely different terms to the determination of sentence, even when that sentence is death. If the legislature can impose a particular penalty including death, on all persons convicted of certain crimes, "why, then, should it be disabled from delegating the penalty decision to a group who will impose the death penalty more often than would a group differently chosen?," he asked. To Mr. Justice White the delegation by Illinois, which merely excludes those with doubts about one of the punishments among which the legislature sought to have them choose, seems an entirely reasonable and sensible legislative act.

Mr. Justice White also advised the states of "the ease with which they can adjust to today's decision." Replacing the requirement of unanimous jury verdicts with majority decisions about sentence should, Mr. Justice White observed, achieve roughly the same result reached by the Illinois Legislature through the procedure here condemned.

JURY TRIAL

Duncan v. Louisiana, 391 U.S. 145, 3 CrL 3062

It was not only in capital cases that the Sixth Amendment right to trial by an impartial jury underlay a broadening of constitutional rights. Rather, for the first time, the Court also held that the states, even in certain misdemeanor cases, were bound by the Fourteenth Amendment to recognize the accused's right to a jury trial.

The majority opinion by Mr. Justice White stated: "Because we believe that trial by jury in criminal cases is fundamental to the American scheme of justice, we hold that the Fourteenth Amendment guarantees a right to trial by jury in all criminal cases which —were they to be tried in a federal court —would come within the Sixth Amendment's guarantee." Mr. Justice White noted that the Court has in recent cases applying provisions of the first eight amendments to the states adopted a new approach to the 'incorporation' debate. Earlier the crucial question seems to have been whether a civilized system could be imagined that would not accord the particular protection. Recent cases, on the other hand, have proceeded upon the valid assumption that state criminal processes are not imaginary and theoretical schemes but actual systems bearing virtually every characteristic of the common law system that has been developing contemporaneously in England and in this country. The question thus is whether given this kind of system a particular procedure is fundamental —whether, that is, the procedure is necessary to an Anglo-American regime of ordered liberty. When the inquiry is approached in this way the question whether the states can impose criminal punishment without granting a jury trial appears quite different from the way it appeared in the older cases indicating that states might abolish jury trial. See e.g., Maxwell v. Dow, 176 U.S. 581 (1900). A criminal process that is fair and equitable but uses no juries, Mr. Justice White observed, is easy to imagine. But, no American state has undertaken to construct such a system.

The laws of every state guarantee a jury trial in serious criminal cases; no state has dispensed with it; nor are there are significant movements under way to do so.

In reaching its conclusion, the Court overrules dicta in Maxwell v. Dow, Palko v. Connecticut, 302 U.S. 319, and Snider v. Massachusetts, 291 U.S. 97, all of which asserted that the right to jury trial is not essential to ordered liberty and may be dispensed with by the states.

Mr. Justice White emphasized that the Court was not holding "that every criminal trial —or any particular trial —held before a judge alone is unfair or that a defendant may never be as fairly treated by a judge as he would be by a jury. Thus we hold no constitutional doubts about the practices, common in both federal and state courts, of accepting waivers of jury trial and prosecuting petty crimes without extending a right to jury trial."

The incorporation of the jury trial right might, with the gloss of federal interpretations, require 12-man juries in serious criminal cases, a unanimous verdict before guilt can be found, or the end of procedures by which some state crimes are tried in the first instance without a jury but at the first appellate stage by de novo trial with a jury. But Mr. Justice White observed, "Our decision today" seems very unlikely to "require widespread changes in state criminal processes." First, federal decisions interpreting the Sixth Amendment are always subject to reconsideration, a fact amply demonstrated by the instant decision. In addition, most of the states have provisions for jury trials equal in breadth to the Sixth Amendment, if that Amendment is construed, as it has been, to permit the trial of petty crimes and offenses without a jury.

In this case, the specific question was whether jury trial could be denied on a charge of simple battery, which the Louisiana Legislature has made punishable by imprisonment for two years and a fine.

While the boundaries of petty offense category have been ill-defined, if not ambulatory, the Court pointed out, a crime punishable by two years is, based on past and contemporary standards in this country, a serious crime and not a petty offense.

The argument that the length of the penalty actually imposed, not the length of the sentence authorized, should be the critical factor was rejected. This was the rationale espoused in Cheff v. Schnackenberg, 384 U.S. 373. But, the Court pointed out, that case does not reach the situation where a legislative judgment as to the seriousness of the crime is imbedded in the form of an express authorization to impose a heavy penalty for the crime in question. Cheff involved criminal contempt.

In a concurrence, in which Mr. Justice Douglas joined, Mr. Justice Black re-emphasized that he believes as strongly as ever that the Fourteenth Amendment was intended to make the Bill of Rights applicable to the states. The selective incorporation doctrine, he conceded, can be supported as an alternative, although less historically supportable than complete incorporation. And, most importantly for him, the selective incorporation process has the virtue of having already worked to make most of the Bill of Rights protections applicable to the states.

Mr. Justice Harlan, with whom Mr. Justice Stewart joined, dissenting, replied as much to Mr. Justice Black's concurrence as to the majority, "I believe I am correct in saying that every member of the Court for at least the last 135 years has agreed that our founders did not consider the requirements of the Bill of Rights so fundamental that they should operate directly against the states." And, though a few members of the Court have taken the position that the first section of the Fourteenth Amendment was intended to make the provisions of the first eight amendments applicable to the states, this view has never been "accepted by this Court." While today's Court still remains unwilling to accept the total incorporation view, Mr. Justice Harlan continued, it has compromised "on the ease of the incorporationist position, without its internal logic. It has simply assumed that the question before us is whether the jury trial clause of the Sixth Amendment should be incorporated into the Fourteenth, jot-for-jot and case-for-case, or ignored. Then the Court merely declares that the clause in question is 'in' rather than 'out'."

Even if he could agree that the question is whether the right to jury trial is totally "in" or totally "out," he could find no real reasons for concluding that it should be in. The majority, he concluded, has, quite without reason, chosen to impose upon every state one means of trying criminal cases; it is a good means, but it is not the only fair means and it is not demonstrably better than the alternatives states might devise.

Bloom v. Illinois, 391 U.S. 194, 3 CrL 3077

Serious contempts, no less than other serious crimes, carry with them the right to a jury trial, Mr. Justice White also made clear.

"By deciding to treat criminal contempt like other crimes insofar as the right to jury trial is concerned, we similarly place it under the rule that petty crimes need not be tried to a jury." Again, Mr. Justice White noted that the Court did not have to settle "the exact location of the line between petty offenses and serious crimes" but that "a crime punishable by two years in prison is * * * a serious crime and not a petty offense." And, noting that the contemnor was sentenced to two years, Mr. Justice White reasoned that, when the legislature has not expressed a judgment as to the seriousness of an offense by fixing a maximum penalty, the penalty actually imposed is the best evidence of seriousness.

Mr. Justice Fortas concurred in both Duncan and Bloom, but he rejected the majority's implication that "the tail must go with the hide; that when we hold, influenced by the Sixth Amendment, that 'due process' requires that the states accord the right of jury trial for all but petty offenses, we automatically import all of the ancillary rules which have been or may hereafter be developed incidental to the right to a jury trial in the federal courts." He could see no reason to assume that federal requirements such as unanimous verdicts or a jury of 12 should therefore be imposed upon the states.

Neither logic nor history nor the intent of the draftsmen of the Fourteenth Amendment, he explained, can possibly be said to require that the Sixth Amendment or its jury trial provision be applied to the states together with the total gloss that the Court's decisions have supplied.

To Mr. Justice Harlan, with whom Mr. Justice Stewart joined, the contempt case "completes a remarkable circle. In Duncan, ante, the Court imposed on the States a rule of procedure that was neither shown to be fundamental to procedural fairness nor held to be part of the originally understood content of the Fourteenth Amendment. The sole justification was that the rule was found in the Bill of Rights. The Court now, without stating any additional reasons, imposes on the States a related rule that, as recently as Cheff v. Schnackenberg, supra, the Court

declined to find in the Bill of Rights. That the words of Mr. Justice Holmes, inveighing against a century of 'unconstitutional assumption of [state] powers by the courts of the United States' in derogation of the central premise of our Constitution, should be invoked to support the Court's action here can only be put down to the vagaries of the times."

Dyke v. Taylor Implement Co., Inc., 391 U.S. 126, 3 CrL 3083

The extent to which the Supreme Court clearly will not carry its jury-trial for contemnor rule was indicated by its refusal to find error in trying without a jury contempt defendants who received only 10-day sentences and relatively light fines. From Cheff v. Schnackenberg, Mr. Justice White found it clear that a six-month sentence is short enough to be petty. That holding, he decided, was sufficient for resolution of a case in which the maximum penalty permitted was 10 days in jail and a fine of 50 dollars. The contempt was therefore "a petty offense" and no federal constitutional right to jury trial existed. However, the conviction was reversed on a finding that the admission of evidence obtained by a warrantless search of the alleged contemnors' parked automobile, without showing that the officers had sufficient cause to suspect that the automobile contained such evidence, was reversible error. The contempt conviction was based on the alleged violation of an injunction barring the "inflicting of harm or damage upon the persons or property of (an employer's) employees, customers, visitors or any other persons." The evidence found in the search was an air rifle.

Mr. Justice Black, with whom Mr. Justice Douglas joined, dissented from the Court's holding "that persons charged with so-called 'petty' crimes are not entitled to trial by jury. I am not as sure as the Court seems to be that this classification should be used to deprive a criminal defendant of a jury trial."

DeStefano v. Woods, 392 U.S. 631, 3 CrL 4098

Before the Term ended, the Court held that the states' obligation to afford jury trials in all but petty cases did not apply to trials begun before May 20, 1968, the date of the decisions in Duncan and Bloom.

RIGHT TO COUNSEL

Mempa v. Rhay, 389 U.S. 128, 2 CrL 3023

The dramatic extension of the jury trial requirement to state trial proceedings made pale by comparison the slight extension of the right to counsel in state post-trial proceedings. Unanimously, the Court in an opinion by Mr. Justice Marshall, held that the right to counsel attaches to state probation revocation hearings at which a deferred sentence may be imposed.

Burgett v. Texas, 389 U.S. 109, 2 CrL 3026

The Court also held that unless a prior conviction is obtained at a proceeding that satisfied the requirements of

Gideon v. Wainwright, 372 U.S. 335, it is inadmissible for purposes of increasing sentence under a state habitual offender statute. To hold otherwise, the opinion by Mr. Justice Douglas stated, would erode the basic principle of Gideon. Moreover, the error in admitting such evidence was inherently prejudicial and not rendered "harmless beyond a reasonable doubt" by an instruction to disregard it.

Mr. Justice Harlan, joined by Mr. Justice Black and Mr. Justice White, contended, in dissent, that the right to use a prior conviction in a one stage recidivist trial was established by Spencer v. Texas, 385 U.S. 554. The inadmissibility of the prior conviction for other reasons, he explained, was, at the most a later corrected trial error in the admission of evidence.

In answer to the dissenters, the Chief Justice, concurring, noted the "deviation from settled principles of fairness" represented by Spencer and applauded the "needed limitation on the Spencer rule" represented by the majority opinion.

Wood v. U.S., 389 U.S. 20, 2 CrL 3006

By per curiam order, the Court emphasized that a trial court's failure to adequately explore the possibility that a defendant claiming indigency could only partially pay for trial counsel, as provided in the Criminal Justice Act, cannot be presumed non-prejudicial.

Hackin v. Arizona, 389 U.S. 143, 2 CrL 3036

Irked by his Brethren's refusal to review an Arizona unauthorized-practice-of-law conviction based on a layman's free assistance to an indigent seeking habeas corpus, Mr. Justice Douglas called for a searching examination of the role laymen can and should play in making equality under the law meaningful for the poor.

What the poor need as much as corporate grants, Mr. Justice Douglas observed, is protection before they get into trouble and confront a crisis. Broadly phrased unauthorized-practice-of-law statutes, he explained, could make criminal many of the activities regularly done by social workers who assist the poor in obtaining welfare and who attempt to help them solve domestic problems.

For the majority of indigents, who are not so fortunate to be served by neighborhood legal officers, he concluded, lay assistance may be the only hope for achieving equal justice at this time.

RIGHT OF CONFRONTATION

Barber v. Page, 390 U.S. 719, 3 CrL 3048

Twice the Court turned its attention to the use at trial of evidence developed in pretrial proceedings. In the first, it held that an Oklahoma defendant was denied his right of confrontation by the state's failure to even attempt to obtain the presence of a codefendant, who was in federal custody in Texas, and who had given testimony incriminating to the defendant at a preliminary hearing. At trial, the preliminary hearing testimony was put in

evidence. It mattered not to the Court that the defendant's counsel might have been able to cross-examine the absent witness at the preliminary hearing.

CRUEL AND UNUSUAL PUNISHMENT

Powell v. Texas, 392 U.S. 514, 3 CrL 3177

Though the Eighth Amendment was not reached in either of this Term's cases dealing with capital punishment, it was reached with respect to the much less serious but much more common offense of public drunkenness. Chronic alcoholics, can, a bare majority of the Court held, be sent to jail for being drunk in public.

Announcing the Court's judgment, Mr. Justice Marshall, joined by the Chief Justice, Mr. Justice Black, and Mr. Justice Harlan, declared that the Cruel and Unusual Punishment Clause, as interpreted in Robinson v. California, 370 U.S. 660, did not apply. The chronic alcoholic was convicted, not for being a chronic alcoholic, but for being in public while being drunk on a particular occasion. Though chronic alcoholism is, like drug addiction, a status, see Robinson, public drunkenness is "behavior."

Mr. Justice Marshall commented: "If Leroy Powell cannot be convicted of public intoxication, it is difficult to see how a state can convict an individual for murder, if that individual, while exhibiting normal behavior in all other respects, suffers from a 'compulsion' to kill, which is an 'exceedingly strong influence' but 'not completely overpowering.'"

The current state of medical knowledge, he concluded, does not support the conclusion "that chronic alcoholics in general, and Leroy Powell in particular suffer from such an irresistible compulsion to drink and to get drunk in public that they are utterly unable to control their performance of either or both of these acts and thus cannot be deterred at all from public intoxication."

The swing-man, Mr. Justice White, made for a very shaky majority. The Eighth Amendment would have prohibited Leroy Powell's incarceration, he insisted, had the record supported a finding that Mr. Powell found it impossible to avoid public places when intoxicated.

Apparently, there would be a majority for applying the Eighth Amendment as a bar to punishment of a "skid row bum" who could not, given the compulsion to drink, avoid drinking in public.

Mr. Justice Black, in a separate concurring opinion, joined by Mr. Justice Harlan, maintained that the problem of handling public drunks is not national but local. Local communities should therefore be permitted to control their own peculiarly local affairs under their own local rules.

Mr. Justice Fortas, with whom Mr. Justice Douglas, Mr. Justice Brennan, and Mr. Justice Stewart joined, dissenting, contended that Robinson bars the conviction of any chronic alcoholic for public drunkenness. Admittedly, he observed, the crime of public drunkenness covers more than a mere status. "But the essential constitutional defect here is the same as in Robinson, where in both cases the particular defendant was accused of being in a condition which he had no capacity to change or avoid."

FIRST AMENDMENT

U.S. v. O'Brien; O'Brien v. U.S., 391 U.S. 367, 3 Crl 3099

Rejecting the view that "an apparently limitless variety of conduct can be labeled 'speech' whenever the person engaging in it intends thereby to express an idea," the Court, with only Mr. Justice Douglas dissenting, upheld the validity of a 1965 statute that makes draft-card burning a criminal offense.

Since draft card burning involves communicative and noncommunicative elements, the Chief Justice wrote, "a sufficiently important governmental interest in regulating the non-speech element can justify incidental limitations on First Amendments freedoms." He had no difficulty in finding that the statute was within the constitutional power of the government, that it furthered an important or substantial government interest unrelated to the suppression of free expression, and that the incidental restriction on First Amendment freedom was no greater than is essential to the furtherance of that interest.

The Court also rejected the argument that the statute was enacted for an illicit purpose —to suppress freedom of speech. "It is a familiar principle of constitutional law that this Court will not strike down an otherwise constitutional statute on the basis of an alleged illicit legislative motive."

According to the Chief Justice, the Court was being asked to void a statute, constitutional on its face, on the basis of what fewer than a handful of congressman said about it. But, what motivates one legislator to make a speech about a bill, he observed, is not necessarily what motivates scores of others to enact it, and the stakes are sufficiently high to eschew guess work.

Mr. Justice Douglas, dissenting, asked the Court to go to what he considered the root of the matter — "Whether conscription is possible in the absence of a declaration of war."

U.S. v. Johnson, 390 U.S. 563, 3 CrL 3010

Criminal sanctions for interference with the exercise of the right to equality in public accommodations were grafted upon the Civil Rights Act of 1964 through use of Section 241 of the Criminal Code. Section 241, which provides fine and imprisonment for a conspiracy to injure, oppress, threaten, or intimidate any citizen in the free exercise of enjoyment of any right or privilege secured to him by the Constitution or laws of the United States, or because of his having so exercised the same, was held available for prosecution of "outside hoodlums" who conspired to assault Negroes for exercising their right to equality in public accommodations as guaranteed by Section 201 of the Civil Rights Act.

Mr. Justice Stewart, Mr. Justice Black, and Mr. Justice Harlan dissented on the ground that the exclusive remedy provided by Congress to protect the rights secured by Title 2 of the 1964 Civil Rights Act is injunction.

Cameron v. Johnson, 390 U.S. 611, 3 CrL 3043

Though picketing qua picketing cannot be made a crime, the blocking of the entrance of a public building can and, the Court therefore upheld a Mississippi criminal statute that prohibits pickets from obstructing or interfering with the entrances of public buildings. The majority opinion, by Mr. Justice Brennan, found the statute sufficiently clear and unambiguous to survive charges of vagueness and of overbreadth.

Dissenting, Mr. Justice Fortas, with whom Mr. Justice Douglas concurred, argued that, under Dombrowski v. Pfister, 380 U.S. 479, the pickets, who were seeking a federal injunction against their prosecution under the state statute, should have been granted that injunction. While agreeing with the majority's appraisal of the facial constitutionality of the statute, Mr. Justice Fortas emphasized that the pickets were arrested and prosecuted "without any hope of ultimate success," that there was no evidence their activities "obstructed * * * or reasonably interfered with ingress or egress to and from any * * * courthouse * * *."

Zwickler v. Koota, 389 U.S. 241, 2 CrL 3049

But, Dombrowski v. Pfister, 380 U.S. 479, was not forgotten by the majority this Term. The determination of a state statute's constitutionality would be proper in a federal declaratory judgment suit, the Court ruled, and the addition of a request for an injunction against state prosecution under the statute does not bring the abstention doctrine into play.

The statute under attack was Section 781–B of the New York Penal Code, which makes it a crime to distribute in quantity anonymous political handbills. The basis of the constitutional challenge was not that the statute was void for vagueness, but rather that, though lacking neither clarity nor precision, it was void, under the First Amendment, for overbreadth. In such a case, the opinion by Mr. Justice Brennan explained, to force one who has commenced a federal action to suffer the delay of state court proceedings might itself effect the impermissible chilling of the very constitutional right sought to be protected.

Having decided that the claim of unconstitutionality was a proper matter for declaratory judgment, the question for the Court became whether the addition of a plea for injunctive relief supplied a "special circumstance" prerequisite to application of the doctrine of abstention. Citing Dombrowski v. Pfister, the Court concluded that "the questions of abstention and injunctive relief are not the same."

Ginsberg v. New York, 390 U.S. 629, 3 CrL 3019

The concept of "relative obscenity" —that different standards govern restrictions applicable only to young persons —received the qualified approval of the Court. A New York statute prohibiting the sale to minors under 17 years of age of material "defined to be obscene on the basis of its appeal to them whether or not it would be obscene to adults" was upheld over an argument that "the statute invades the area of freedom of expression constitutionally secured to minors."

Interstate Circuit, Inc. v. Dallas, 390 U.S. 676, 3 CrL 3033

A Dallas ordinance providing for classification of films as "not suitable for young persons" was struck down, however; eight Justices agreed that its failure to sufficiently guide the censor was fatal.

Reed Enterprises v. Clark, 390 U.S. 457, 2 CrL 2499

The Court, by per curiam order, affirmed a decision upholding the federal obscenity statute's venue provisions permitting prosecution in "any district from, through, or into which * * * mail matter moves."

OTHER RULINGS

Smith v. Illinois, 390 U.S. 129, 2 CrL 3100

The constitutional right of an accused to confront the witnesses against him prohibits an informer from hiding behind an alias and refusing to supply his correct address while undergoing cross-examination at trial.

Inre Whittington, 391 U.S. 341, 3 CrL 3092

An Ohio court's lack of opportunity to assess the impact of In re Gault, 387 U.S. 1, 1 CrL 3031, on the procedures used in reaching a pre-Gault determination of delinquency, and its failure to have determined the effect on the delinquency determination of a supervening waiver to an adult court, required remand to the Ohio court for consideration of these questions.

U.S. v. Habig, 390 U.S. 222, 2 CrL 3143

The six-year statute of limitations for tax evasion prosecution runs from the time the defendant filed his return, not from the date the tax returns were due.

U.S. v. Neifert-White Co., 390 U.S. 228, 2 CrL 3145

A storage bin dealer's deliberate exaggeration of the purchase price of storage bins on invoices used by grain growers in application for federal loans that provide 80% of the actual purchase price of such bins constituted a fraudulent attempt to cause the government to pay out money and was prosecutable under the Federal False Claims Act.

Lee v. Washington, 390 U.S. 333, 2 CrL 3149

Alabama statutes providing for racial segregation in state prisons and jails violate the Fourteenth Amendment, and a federal district court's desegregation schedule did not fail to make allowance for the necessities of prison security and discipline.

1968–1969 Term

The criminal law revolution took on a different style during the 1968–69 Term. The Court devoted much of its energy to clarifying, explaining, extending, or restricting its earlier landmark decisions. Although the very last decision of the "Warren era" announced the demise of Palko v. Connecticut, 302 U.S. 319, and the application of the Double Jeopardy Clause to the states, it was not a year characterized by numerous falling precedents or constitutional groundbreaking. It was the year of the "sleeper" — the opinion that claims to do no more than clarify a previous landmark or construe a rule, but which takes on a life of its own.

SEARCH AND SEIZURE

Although the First, Fifth, and Sixth Amendments each provided the basis of decisions with far-reaching implications, the Fourth Amendment, for the third Term in a row, led the fireworks parade. Two search and seizure cases, one a precedent-blasting blockbuster, the other a true "sleeper," to have a profound effect on law enforcement practices.

Chimel v. California, 395 U.S. 752, 5 CrL 3131

Insofar as it stands "for the proposition * * * that a warrantless search incident to a 'lawful arrest' may generally extendthe area that is considered to be in the 'possession' or under the 'control' of the persons arrested," U.S. v. Rabinowitz, 339 U.S. 56, was overruled. Such a search, the Court held, must be limited to the area into which an arrestee might reach to obtain a weapon or destroy evidence.

This result was foreshadowed by several Fourth Amendment cases in recent years, Mr. Justice Stewart, the majority spokesman, thought. He noted the numerous inconsistencies of the Court's previous holdings on the question of the permissible scope of searches incident to arrest. From the time the Court first approved warrantless searches incident to arrest, Weeks v. U.S., 232 U.S. 383, the pendulum has swung back and forth between limited characterizations of such searches, Go-Bart Importing Co. v. U.S., 282 U.S. 344, and U.S. v. Lefkowitz, 255 U.S. 452, to liberal open-ended interpretations in Rabinowitz and in Harris v. U.S., 331 U.S. 145. In Harris, the Court condoned the search of an arrestee's entire four-room apartment, desk drawers and all. In the present case, the California Supreme Court applied Rabinowitz to approve the search of a coin theft suspect's entire house; the police had waited for him to come home

before arresting him. But the Rabinowitz doctrine, "at least in the broad sense in which it was applied by the California courts in this case, can withstand neither historical nor rational analysis." The Court's more recent decisions involving searches incident to arrest, such as Terry v. Ohio, 392 U.S. 1, 3 CrL 3149, Sibron v. New York, 392 U.S. 40, 3 CrL 3160, and Preston v. U.S., 376 U.S. 364, emphasized that searches incident to arrest are justified only by the need to seize weapons or to prevent destruction of evidence.

While it might have been possible to distinguish Harris and Rabinowitz on their facts, "such a distinction," as far as the majority was concerned, "would be highly artificial." Mr. Justice Stewart then proceeded to overrule them both: "No consideration relevant to the Fourth Amendment suggests any point of rational limitation, once the search is allowed to go beyond the area from which the person arrested might obtain weapons or evidentiary items. The only reasoned distinction is one between a search of the person arrested and the area within his reach on the one hand, and more extensive searches on the other."

Concurring in the result, Mr. Justice Harlan stressed the difficulties the incorporation doctrine presents. In doing so, he underscored the potential practical effects of this decision. "We simply do not know the extent to which cities and towns across the Nation are prepared to administer the greatly expanded warrant system which will be required by today's decision; nor can we say with assurance that in each and every local situation the warrant requirement plays an essential role in the protection of those fundamental liberties protected against state infringement by the Fourteenth Amendment." This, he thought, raised the dilemma that he had envisioned in Ker v. California, 374 U.S. 23 —of adversely affecting legitimate state law enforcement concerns or of diluting the Bill of Rights to give the states "at least some elbow room."

Mr. Justice White, joined by Mr. Justice Black, also reviewed the history of searches incident to arrest, but he saw the Court's erratic peregrination across constitutional waters in a different light. Deploring the "remarkable instability in this whole area," Mr. Justice White maintained the Court was here adding to the uncertainty. "The rule which has prevailed, but for very brief or doubtful periods of aberration, is that a search incident to an arrest may extend to those areas under the control of the defendant and where items subject to constitutional seizure may be found. The justification for this rule must, under the language of the Fourth Amendment, lie in the reasonableness of the rule."

This very case, Mr. Justice White argued, presents a perfect example of exigent circumstances making reasonable a search that extends beyond the defendant's immediate reach. Had the police simply arrested the petitioner, taken him from the house, and returned later with a warrant, the petitioner's wife, whom they had no grounds to arrest, would have been able to remove the stolen coins. Furthermore, he added, a defendant's privacy interests are disturbed far less by a search incident to a valid arrest than by the arrest itself.

Even beyond the exigent circumstances argument, however, both Congress and the Court have in the past approved of warrantless searches where a warrant could have been obtained with no danger to either people or evidence.

While he saw nothing in an arrest alone justifying a search broader than that permitted by the majority, "where as here the existence of probable cause is independently established and would justify a warrant for a broader search for evidence," Mr. Justice White would permit the broader search even if the arresting officers were without a warrant; the very fact of their arrest creates "an exigent circumstance justifying police action before evidence can be reviewed." Such a rule, applied in most cases, would not authorize general searches. Warrantless searches authorized by this rule could extend no further than if a warrant had been obtained.

Spinelli v. U.S., 393 U.S. 410, 4 CrL 3083

Scrutiny of search and seizure practices was not limited to warrantless searches. Setting out to "explicate" the principles of Aguilar v. Texas, 378 U.S. 108, the Court by a 5–3 vote —Mr. Justice Marshall did not participate — wound up more or less announcing new probable cause standards for search warrant affidavits in which the affiant had relied upon an informer. But the true significance of these standards was a matter of disagreement among the Justices. According to various opinions, the majority revolutionized the law of probable cause as it relates to search warrants; it simply explicated the law; it merely stressed one side of the law.

Mr. Justice Harlan, who wrote the Court's opinion, found inadequate to furnish probable cause an FBI agent's mere allegation that a "confidential reliable informer" had supplied information that a wagering suspect was conducting gambling operations by means of two telephones whose numbers the informer specified. The informer's tip failed to furnish probable cause for a search warrant even though it was partially corroborated in the affidavit by other allegations based on an independent FBI investigation. The agents' observation contributed no more to probable cause than the fact that the suspect went in and out of the apartment where the telephone numbers supplied by the informer were listed.

According to Mr. Justice Harlan, Aguilar requires a magistrate considering an affidavit in support of an application for a warrant to ask himself, "Can it be fairly said that the tip, even when certain parts of it have been corroborated by independent sources, is as trustworthy as a tip which would pass Aguilar's tests without independent corroboration?" Nothing alleged in this affidavit "would permit the suspicions engendered by the informant's report to ripen into a judgment that a crime was probably being committed."

The majority found the tip itself, measured by this test, inadequate to furnish probable cause. The affiant offered no reason in support of his sworn statement that the informer was "reliable." Perhaps even more important was the affiant's failure to meet Aguilar's other tests; he did not sufficiently state the underlying circumstances from which the informer concluded that the defendant was running a bookmaking operation. "We are not told how the FBI's source received his information —it is not alleged that the informant personally observed Spinelli at work or that he had ever placed a bet with him. However, if the informant came by the information indirectly, he did not explain why his sources were reliable." In the absence of a statement detailing the manner in which the affiant gathered his information, the majority said, it was particularly critical that the informer's tip describe the criminal activity in sufficient detail "so that the magistrate may know that he is relying on something more substantial than a casual rumor circulating in the underworld or an accusation based merely on an individual's general reputation."

The detail provided by the informer in Draper v. U.S., 358 U.S. 307 (1959), was deemed "a suitable benchmark." In that case, the informer did not tell how he came by his information, but he described with minute particularity what the actions of the suspect were going to be and what clothing he would be wearing. A magistrate could reasonably infer the reliable source of such material. In the present case, however, the affidavit supplied no more facts than Spinelli's use of two specified telephones and that these telephones were being used in gambling operations. "This meager report could easily have been obtained from an offhand remark at a neighborhood bar."

To four of the seven other members of the Court who wrote opinions, the majority's opinion meant much more or much less than it stated it meant. To Mr. Justice Black, one of the three dissenters, the Court's holding was revolutionary. He accused the Court of expanding Aguilar "to almost unbelievable proportions" by requiring so much probable cause in support of a search warrant that "the only way to obtain a search warrant is to prove beyond a reasonable doubt that a defendant is guilty."

Far different grounds underlay Mr. Justice Fortas' dissent. He agreed with Mr. Justice Harlan's formulation of the test, but he disagreed with its application in this case. He pointed to the length and detail of this particular affidavit, and expressed the belief that the tip was amply corroborated by the observations of the agents.

Mr. Justice Stewart wrote the briefest yet broadest dissent. He expressed agreement with "substantially the reasons stated by my brothers Black and Fortas."

Mr. Justice White, the swing man, interpreted the majority's opinion narrowly. This case, he thought, confined Draper to its special factual setting. The main point in Draper, he emphasized, "relates to the reliability of the source: Because an informant is right about some things, he is more probably right about other facts, usually the critical unverified facts." Under the Draper approach, a warrant would have been justified here. This case points up the tension between Draper and Aguilar. Pending full-scale reconsideration of Draper on the one hand or of Aguilar and its predecessors on the other, "I join the opinion of the Court and the judgment of reversal, especially since a vote to affirm would produce an equally divided Court."

Davis v. Mississippi, 394 U.S. 721, 5 CrL 3038

In another "sleeper" opinion that could prove to be a blockbuster, the Court served notice that the Fourth Amendment applies to the investigatory arrest stage of a prosecution, and that its proscription against unreasonable seizures is violated by the "investigatory arrest" — detention without probable cause. This warning was sounded in the case of a Mississippi rape suspect who was fingerprinted while detained without probable cause, along with virtually every other young Negro male in the community. The Court, holding that the trustworthiness of fingerprint evidence does not place it beyond the Fourth Amendment's proscription against the use of illegally seized evidence, emphasized that the Amendment is as applicable to the investigatory stage of the case as to any other. "Investigatory seizures would subject unlimited numbers of innocent persons to the harrassment and ignominy incident to or involved in detention. Nothing is more clear than that the Fourth Amendment was meant to prevent wholesale intrusions upon the personal security of our citizenry, whether these intrusions be termed 'arrests' or 'investigatory detentions.' " This had been made clear in the 1967–68 Term in Terry v. Ohio, 392 U.S. 1, 3 CrL 3149.

The Court did acknowledge that fingerprinting — and detention for fingerprinting —may well, because of its nature and reliability, "constitute a much less serious intrusion upon personal security than other types of police searches and detentions." However, in this particular case, the detention of the youth was such that it violated the Fourth Amendment.

Only Mr. Justice Black indicated disagreement with the Court's remarks on investigative arrests. He condemned the decision as "but one more in an everexpanding list of cases in which this Court has been so widely blowing up the Fourth Amendment's scope that its original authors would be hard put to recognize their creation."

Mr. Justice Stewart dissented, but only as to the majority's conclusion that the fingerprints were inadmissible. He argued that fingerprints are not evidence in the conventional sense; they can be identically reproduced and lawfully used in any subsequent trial. Thus, they should not have been held inadmissible at trial even though the detention was improper.

Alderman v. U.S., 394 U.S. 165, 4 CrL 3127

Defendants who have been the objects of illegal electronic surveillance won greatly expanded discovery rights as the Court held that persons who have standing to object to such illegally obtained evidence are entitled to inspect records of the recordings without having the material first screened in camera by the trial judge. The task of winnowing irrelevant material is one that should not be wholly entrusted to the court in the first instance, Mr. Justice White, writing for the majority, stressed. Facts that might appear entirely innocent to a judge might have great meaning for one who knows the more intimate facts of an accused's life. "As the need for adversary inquiry is increased by the complexity of the issues presented for adjudication, and by the consequent inadequacy of ex parte procedures as a means for their accurate resolution, the displacement of well-informed advocacy necessarily becomes less justifiable."

However, the Court's message was not a source of unmixed joy to all defendants seeking suppression of electronic eavesdropping evidence. The majority limited the scope of its discovery holding by stating that a co-defendant or co-conspirator whose Fourth Amendment rights were not violated by illegal eavesdropping, but who might be aggrieved by the introduction of damaging evidence against him obtained as a result of such eavesdropping, does not have standing to object to the use of such evidence against him. However the majority carved out a property-based exception to this no-standing holding. A homeowner has standing to object to unlawfully overheard conversations that took place on his property, regardless of whether he was present or participated in them. Mr. Justice Fortas, joined by Mr. Justice Douglas, dissented from the majority's limitation of standing to those whose privacy rights are violated.

Mr. Justice Harlan thought that the majority unduly restricted itself as to the alternative solutions to the discovery and standing problems raised by this case. "The Court seems to assume that either the traditional standing doctrine is to be expanded or that the traditional doctrine is to be maintained. Again, it is assumed that either an in camera decision is to be made by the judge in every case or that there is to be an automatic turnover of all conversations in every case."

On the question of standing, Mr. Justice Harlan was "in substantial agreement" with the majority's reasons for refusing to expand the traditional doctrine to extend to either a co-defendant or a co-conspirator. However, he did not agree that a homeowner should have standing to object to conversations in his home to which he was not a party. The majority here, Mr. Justice Harlan observed, has granted standing to nonparticipating homeowners and denied it to co-conspirator. and co-defendants on the basis of the theory that one is entitled to object to the "fruits" of police infringement upon his property rights. Such a concept is outdated; "We should reject traditional property concepts entirely and reinterpret standing law in the light of the substantive principles developed in Katz. Standing should be granted to every person who participates in a conversation he legitimately expects will remain private —for it is such persons that Katz protects." However, Mr. Justice Harlan did "not mean to suggest that standing may never be properly granted to permit the vicarious assertion of Fourth Amendment rights."

While he would not permit property owners to challenge conversations in which they were not participants, Mr. Justice Harlan recommended that the Court adopt the government's suggested judicial screening procedure concerning third party conversations.

While agreeing with the majority that, ordinarily, an accused with standing to object should have access to all illegally obtained conversations in which he played a part, the considerations behind this position do not apply to cases involving a defendant charged with spying for a foreign power —and both defendants in Alderman's companion cases were so charged. Such an accused may learn important new information that would hamper the efforts of the government to stifle espionage work. Furthermore, an espionage defendant is much more apt to ignore any protective court order and to turn over new information he has received to those who are not entitled to it. Mr. Justice Harlan found the majority's failure to discuss this aspect of the companion Ivanov and Butemko cases "particularly surprising in light of the reasons it gives for creating an absolute rule in favor of an automatic turnover." For the majority properly realized that in camera inspection may be called for in some situations, and the danger of unauthorized disclosure clearly outweighs the risk of judicial error in determining a conversation's relevance.

Mr. Justice Fortas and Mr. Justice Douglas disagreed with the majority's retention of the traditional standing test. They did not think that the government should, under any circumstances, be permitted to profit from its lawless conduct. They urged adoption of a rule that "any defendant against whom illegally acquired evidence is offered, whether or not it was obtained in violation of his right to privacy, may have the evidence excluded."

Mr. Justice Black also dissented, adhering to his dissent in Katz v. U.S.

Giordano v. U.S., 394 U.S. 310, 4 CrL 4217

The government's swift, anguished reaction to Alderman led the Court to further clarification of that decision. The Court denied the Justice Department's motion for a rehearing as it applied to Ivanov v. U.S. The Court also remanded several cases in light of Alderman. Mr. Justice Stewart, concurring in this per curiam remand, found the government's alarm to be unwarranted.

First, Mr. Justice Stewart said, the Alderman- Butenko-Ivanov opinion means that the only time electronic eavesdropping logs must be turned over to the defense counsel is when the surveillance has been held to have violated the Fourth Amendment. This threshhold determination need not be made in adversary proceedings under full-disclosure conditions.

Furthermore, Ivanov left open the question whether electronic surveillance by the federal government in the conduct of international affairs and the protection of national defense secrets is entitled to an exception. He noted that Mr. Justice White, author of Alderman-Ivanov-Butenko, "has elsewhere [in Katz v. U.S.] made clear his view that such surveillance does not violate the Fourth Amendment, 'if the President * * * or * * * the Attorney General has considered the requirements of national security and authorized electronic surveillance as reasonable.' "

Kaiser v. New York, 394 U.S. 280, 4 CrL 3178

While new ground on the question of bugging was broken in Alderman, the Court also found it necessary to return to two of its earlier electronic eavesdropping landmarks and answer some retroactivity questions.

Katz v. U.S., 389 U.S. 347, 2 CrL 3065, which overruled Olmstead v. U.S., 277 U.S. 438, does not apply retroactively, the Court stated as it held that neither the Fourth and Fourteenth Amendments nor former Section 605 of the Federal Communications Act requires reversal of a New York conviction obtained by a state policeman's non-trespassory wiretapping. The Court added that Berger v. New York, 388 U.S. 41, 1 CrL 3129, invalidated the New York wiretapping Code Section 813–a only to the extent that the statutory provision permitted trespassory wiretapping.

Mr. Justice Harlan, who dissented from the Court's "on its face" approach in Berger, nevertheless thinks that "Berger must be taken as having decided that a warrant issued pursuant to the version of Section 813–a then in effect could not possibly satisfy the requirements of the Fourth Amendment."

Desist v. U.S., 394 U.S. 244, 4 CrL 3167

The Court also refused to interfere with nontrespassory, pre–Katz electronic eavesdropping by warrantless federal agents. Katz does not apply retroactively even to a case that was on direct appeal when announced, and pre–Katz decisions rendered nontrespassory eavesdropping unconstitutional.

The whole question of the "retroactivity" of decisions of constitutional dimension should be rethought, Mr. Justice Harlan urged. The Court's decisions on retroactivity have led to hopeless confusion, he contended. To make his point, he reviewed briefly "the extraordinary collection of rules" created by the Court "to govern the application of" the nonretroactivity principle announced in Linkletter v. Walker, 381 U.S. 618 (1965).

In the classical view of constitutional adjudication, Mr. Justice Harlan reminded the majority, the Court is entitled to decide a constitutional issue only when the facts of a particular case require its resolution. The criminal is released "only because the government has offended constitutional principles in the conduct of his case. And when another similarly situated defendant comes before us, we must grant the same relief or give a principled reason for acting differently." Mr. Justice Harlan concluded that "the only solid disposition of this case lies in vacating the judgment of the court of appeals and in remanding this case to that court for further consideration in light of Katz."

DOUBLE JEOPARDY

Benton v. Maryland, 395 U.S. 784, 5 CrL 3141

The last decision announced by the Court for the 1968–69 Term closed the "Warren era" with a flourish. The Double Jeopardy Clause became the last provision of the Bill of Rights to be applied to the states by the "Warren Court" and Palko v. Connecticut, 302 U.S. 319 (1937), was the last of earlier landmark decisions to fall.

The Double Jeopardy prohibition "represents a fundamental idea in our constitutional heritage," Mr. Justice Marshall wrote for the majority. "Palko represented an approach to basic constitutional rights which this Court's recent decisions have rejected."

Palko rested its denial of the Fifth Amendment right on the ground that only a denial of "fundamental fairness" in the overall circumstances of a conviction would cause a state violation of this Bill of Rights provision to vitiate a conviction. Its roots had long ago been cut away. Only last Term, Mr. Justice Marshall noted, the Court continued to look to specific Bill of Rights guarantees in setting standards of due process. Duncan v. Louisiana, 391 U.S. 145, 3 CrL 3062, held that if a particular Bill of Rights guarantee is "fundamental to the American scheme of justice," it must apply to the states. The same standard that applied in Duncan was applied here. The Fifth Amendment guarantee against double jeopardy, "represents a fundamental ideal in our constitutional heritage."

The Court thus granted relief to a Maryland prisoner who was originally charged with burglary and larceny, and acquitted of the larceny charge. He then successfully appealed his burglary conviction on constitutional grounds, and was reindicted, retried, and convicted on both the burglary and larceny counts.

The majority had more trouble with the contention that, since the petitioner's challenged larceny sentence was to run concurrently with a longer, unchallenged, burglary sentence, there was no justiciable case or controversy. However, the majority held that, although defects in a concurrently-running sentence might be held moot as a rule of judicial convenience, they do not lie outside the jurisdiction of the Court. Adverse collateral effects attach to each separate conviction. And, the Maryland Court of Special Appeals ruled on the merits of the double jeopardy claim.

Mr. Justice White concurred in the extension of the double jeopardy prohibition to the states and with the treatment of the concurrent sentence as no bar to jurisdiction. However, he reasserted the idea of concurrent sentence mootness.

Justices Harlan and Stewart, the two dissenters, considered the majority's bases for finding a justiciable case "the flimsiest of reasons." Restating their repeated opposition to the "incorporation" theory, they thought that the petitioner's retrial for larceny in these circumstances constituted a denial of due process even under Palko. As for the concurrent sentence doctrine, while they agreed with the majority that it is a rule of judicial administration rather than a bar to jurisdiction, they would have applied it here to find the petitioner's claim entirely moot.

North Carolina v. Pearce, 395 U.S. 711, 5 CrL 3119

Federal courts of appeal had divided three ways over the question whether a person who obtains relief from his original conviction can incur a harsher sentence following retrial and a second conviction. Some circuits absolutely prohibited a harsher second sentence; others had permitted this practice only where the trial judge stated justifiable reasons for doing so, and a third school of thought left the matter up to the sentencing judge's discretion. What had divided the circuits also divided the Supreme Court. Unable to announce a majority position on this question, the Court took the middle ground. Justices Douglas and Marshall favored a flat prohibition. But their votes, combined with the votes of four other Justices then sitting, provided a majority for the proposition that, while neither the Equal Protection Clause nor the Double Jeopardy Clause places any absolute restriction upon the length of a sentence imposed upon reconviction, "whenever a judge imposes a more severe sentence upon a defendant after a new trial, the reasons for his doing so must affirmatively appear. Those reasons must be based upon objective information concerning identifiable conduct on the part of the defendant occurring after the time of the original sentencing proceeding. And the factual data upon which the increased sentence is based must be made part of the record, so that the constitutional legitimacy of the increased sentence may be fully reviewed on appeal." Such a sentence cannot be a device to penalize those who choose to exercise the right to appeal.

Mr. Justice White thought that an increased sentence on retrial should be authorized on the basis of "any objective, identifiable factual data not known to the trial judge at the time of the original sentencing proceeding."

The Court did decide unanimously that the Double Jeopardy Clause requires a state to credit a retried and reconvicted prisoner for time spent in prison prior to his successful attack upon his original conviction and sentence.

SELF-INCRIMINATION

Leary v. U.S., 395 U.S. 6, 5 CrL 3053

For the second Term in a row, the Court emasculated sumptuary legislation in the guise of tax laws. Key provisions of the Marijuana Tax Act were rendered virtually useless as devices for the prosecution of transporters and possessors of pot. Vacating the conviction of Dr. Timothy F. Leary, the Court held that the Fifth Amendment privilege against self-incrimination bars conviction for violation of 26 U.S.C. 4741 et seq., which prohibits the transportation of marijuana without paying the federal transfer tax. Also, the presumption raised by 21 U.S.C. 176(a) that a transporter of untaxed marijuana knew of its illegal importation was held to violate the Fifth Amendment's Due Process Clause.

An unregistered transporter of marijuana could not comply with Section 4741's requirements without incriminating himself, the majority held. Mr. Justice Harlan, writing for the majority, was unable to distinguish the statute's incriminating effect from that of the gambling and firearms tax laws rendered impotent in Marchetti v. U.S., 390 U.S. 39, 2 CrL 3102, and its companion cases.

The Marijuana Tax Act's two main sub-parts, Mr. Justice Harlan pointed out, work in tandem. The occupational tax provisions require that one who deals in marijuana must, at the time he pays the tax, register with the Internal Revenue Service. The transfer provisions impose a $1 per ounce tax on transfers to registered dealers and a $100 per ounce tax if the transferee is not registered. Further, they make it unlawful to transfer to a purchaser who hasn't obtained a written order from the Treasury. State and federal law enforcement officials have access to records of these forms, which contain considerable personal information. Thus, a person who is not registered as a dealer in marijuana must, to comply with the transfer provisions, identify himself as one who has violated the occupational registration provisions. Furthermore, he exposes himself to state prosecution for possession; possession or transfer of marijuana is an offense in virtually every state of the Union.

The government's reliance on regulations that, it argued, narrow the scope of the statutes was misplaced. The result of these regulations, the government contended, was to simply prohibit nonregistrants like the petitioner in this case from dealing in marijuana at all. However, the legislative history of the Act reveals that Congress "did intend that a nonregistrant should be able to obtain an order form and pre-pay the transfer tax." The effect of the transfer provision was to force an applicant both to pay a $100 per ounce tax on a transfer and to expose himself to self-incrimination. "In short, we think the conclusion inescapable that the statute was aimed at bringing to light transgressions of the marijuana laws. Hence, * * * we decline to impose use restrictions and are obliged to conclude that a timely and proper assertion of the privilege should have provided a complete defense to prosecution under Section 4744(a)(2)."

Turning to the presumption of knowledge of illegal importation raised by Section 176, the majority found that there was no rational connection between the fact proved —possession of marijuana —and the fact presumed —knowledge that it was illegally imported. The Court was able to imagine five ways in which a possessor might acquire such knowledge, but none of these ways have been satisfactorily shown by the government, or by the legislative history of the statutes, to merit so serious a presumption. This is particularly so in view of the fact that "a not inconsiderable proportion of domestically consumed marijuana appears to have been grown in this country, and that its possessors must be taken to have 'known', if anything, that their marijuana was not illegally imported. In short, it would be no more than speculation were we to say that even as much as a majority of possessors 'knew' the source of their marijuana." Not even "the utmost deference to the congressional determination that this presumption was warranted," Mr. Justice Harlan concluded, could overcome the deficiencies in the foundation of the "knowledge" presumption.

Mr. Justice Black concurred in the reversal of the conviction and both points discussed by the majority, but added that the presumption was an unconstitutional attempt by Congress "to tell a jury it can convict upon" an inference as "forced and baseless" as the one raised by Section 176(a).

Mr. Justice Stewart concurred in the Court's construction of Section 176, but reiterated his earlier stated belief that the "Fifth Amendment guarantee against compulsory self-incrimination was originally intended to do no more than confer a testimonial privilege in a judicial proceeding."

U.S. v. Covington, 395 U.S. 57, 5 CrL 3068

The same day, the Court upheld the dismissal of an indictment charging a defendant with having violated the transfer tax provisions of the Marijuana Tax Act. The defendant's timely assertion of his Fifth Amendment privilege against self-incrimination required the dismissal, Mr. Justice Harlan concluded.

Orozco v. Texas, 394 U.S. 324, 4 CrL 3188

Probably no case has brought more criminal defendants under the shelter of the Self-Incrimination Clause than Miranda v. Arizona, 384 U.S. 436. This Term, the Court sought to resolve two questions concerning the scope and application of that case.

First, the Court held in an opinion by Mr. Justice Black that police questioning of a murder suspect while he was at home in bed was custodial. The defendant was, therefore, entitled to the fourfold Miranda warnings, and testimony concerning his incriminating response to questioning as he lay in bed should not have been admitted at trial.

In response to the state's argument that the Miranda rule should not apply to a suspect questioned in the familiar surroundings of his own bedroom, Mr. Justice Black pointed to the testimony of one of the interrogating officers that the defendant was not free to leave, but was "under arrest" from the moment he gave his name. This, Mr. Justice Black emphasized, constitutes the kind of deprivation of freedom described in Miranda.

Mr. Justice Harlan, one of the three Miranda dissenters, concurred "purely out of respect for stare decisis." Mr. Justice Stewart, joined by Mr. Justice White, said, "It seems to me that those of us who dissented in Miranda * * * remain free not only to express our continuing disagreement with that decision but to oppose any broadening of its impact."

Mr. Justice White contended that the Court was drawing even tighter "the constitutional strait jacket" imposed on law enforcement officials by Miranda. If Miranda is justified at all, Mr. Justice White argued, "it rests on the likelihood that in a sufficient number of cases exposure to stationhouse practices will result in compelled confessions and that additional safeguards should be imposed in all cases to prevent possible erosion of Fifth Amendment values."

The simple rule announced here, extending the necessity for Miranda warnings to all in-custody questioning outside the stationhouse, ignores the purpose of Miranda, Mr. Justice White continued. "The Court wholly ignores the question whether similar hazards exist or even are possible when police arrest and interrogate on the spot, whether it be on the street corner or in the home as in this case."

Jenkins v. Delaware, 395 U.S. 213, 5 CrL 3075

Numerous state and lower federal courts have been plagued with the question whether the Miranda requirements should apply to cases originally tried prior to Miranda, but subsequently retried after Miranda. The Court answered this question in the negative. More than once in Johnson v. New Jersey, 384 U.S. 719, Chief Justice Warren pointed out, the Court stated that Miranda does not apply to "cases" commenced before the Miranda date. Furthermore, it was said in Johnson that only "future defendants" were entitled to Miranda's benefits; a defendant who was originally tried six months prior to Miranda cannot be regarded as a "future defendant" within the meaning of Johnson.

Society's interest in the effective prosecution of criminals was uppermost in the Court's mind. The Chief Justice pointed to the burden that might be imposed upon law enforcement officials who relied in good faith upon a statement that was admissible at the first trial but which, because of the absence of warnings that were not required at the time of interrogation, would be inadmissible at a second trial. Furthermore, an accused who cannot claim Miranda's benefits still has recourse to state and local procedures for determining the voluntariness of his statement.

Ironically, only Mr. Justice Harlan dissented. Noting that he was one of the Miranda dissenters, he nevertheless found himself "in the uncomfortable position of having to dissent from a holding which actually serves to curtail the impact of that decision." Observing that it is "quite impossible to discern in the rationale of Johnson any solid basis for the distinction" between post-Miranda trials and post-Miranda retrials, Mr. Justice Harlan was "left wholly unpersuaded" by the majority's view that the prosecution would bear "an intolerable evidentiary burden" should Miranda be applied to retrials. In reply to the majority's observation that the retroactivity "technique" necessarily entails "incongruities" that must be tolerated, Mr. Justice Harlan said, "But surely it is incumbent upon this Court to endeavor to keep such incongruities to a minimum." To do so, he said, the Court must halt the ad hoc approach "that has so far characterized our decisions in the retroactivity field."

GUILTY PLEAS

Guilty plea procedures —a fermenting area of the criminal law in which the Court had not been conspicuously active in the past —came under scrutiny this Term, federal practice in one case and state procedures in another. While neither opinion appeared earth-shaking on its face, taken together they amount to one of this Term's "sleepers" and could require drastic changes in many states' guilty plea practices.

McCarthy v. U.S., 394 U.S. 459, 5 CrL 3007

The first decision held that a federal district court's failure to comply fully with the inquiry requirements of Rule 11 of the Federal Rules of Criminal Procedure entitled a defendant to the opportunity to enter a new plea at a rehearing. Not only did the Court hold that a defendant whose plea was accepted without complying with Rule 11 is absolutely entitled to an opportunity to enter a new plea, but it also held that Rule 11's detailed instructions must be complied with strictly and literally. This means, Mr. Chief Justice Warren emphasized in his majority opinion, a direct inquiry of the pleader as to whether he understands the nature of the offense charged and a judicial determination that there was a factual basis for the plea. The Court rejected the government's suggestion that only an evidentiary hearing to establish the voluntariness of the plea should be required upon remand.

While the decision rested upon Rule 11, and not upon any constitutional requirement, the majority mentioned that the purpose of the rule was to insure compliance with due process.

Mr. Justice Black was the only Justice not to agree fully with the majority opinion; he based his concurrence "exclusively on the failure of the judge to first address the defendant personally, as required by Rule 11."

Boykin v. Alabama, 395 U.S. 238, 5 CrL 3079

The latent implications of McCarthy for state guilty plea procedures was spelled out by the dissenters in a case that was originally expected to turn on the constitutionality of capital punishment for robbery. The majority opinion, by Mr. Justice Douglas, held that the validity of a state guilty plea cannot be presumed from a silent record. Guilty pleas amount to waivers of several federal constitutional rights, Mr. Justice Douglas pointed out, and a waiver of such rights cannot be presumed from a silent record. He referred to McCarthy's statement that a waiver of rights embodied in guilty pleas must be intentionally relinquished if due process requirements are to be met, and that, "consequently, if a defendant's guilty plea is not equally voluntary and knowing, it has been obtained in violation of due process and is therefore void."

By vacating this judgment on the ground that the record failed to adequately show an intelligent and knowing plea of guilty, Justices Harlan and Black argued in their dissent, "[t]he Court thus in effect fastens upon the States, as a matter of federal constitutional law, the rigid prophylactic requirements of Rule 11 of the Federal Rules of Criminal Procedure."

In view of Halliday v. U.S., 5 CrL 4039, in which McCarthy was held to apply prospectively only, the states are thus bound to even stricter standards than the federal courts, the dissenters maintained.

The potential effect of Boykin and McCarthy upon state guilty plea procedures was underscored by a majority footnote, indicating that only six states currently require that an effective waiver of the right to plead not guilty appear affirmatively in the record.

SPEEDY TRIAL

Smith v. Hooey, 393 U.S. 374, 4 CrL 3077

Incidents of a federal prisoner's second-class citizenship do not extend to his speedy trial rights, the Court made clear as it held unanimously that a federal prisoner who faces criminal charges in a state court is not, by virtue of his incarceration, precluded from asserting his right to a speedy state trial. The state is required to honor his demand for a speedy trial by attempting to obtain his release from federal custody for the purpose of trying him.

Mr. Justice Stewart, for the Court, stressed that the prospect of another trial following the service of his prison sentence can have a depressing effect upon a prisoner, and may adversely affect rehabilitation efforts.

Furthermore, the Court pointed out, defense difficulties created by a long delay are apt to be "markedly increased when the accused is incarcerated in another jurisdiction."

The petitioner in this case had for six years attempted to obtain a speedy trial on a state indictment. Had he been at large, "the state would have been under a constitutional duty to try him." And, had he been a state prisoner during this time, the state's obligation "would have been no less." The fact of his federal incarceration did not relieve the state of its speedy trial responsibilities.

The Court set aside a Texas Supreme Court order refusing to compel speedy trial action by mandamus. The Court left unclear, however, what action it expected of the Texas Supreme Court upon remand.

Mr. Justice Black would have made it absolutely clear that "if a trial is given the case should not be dismissed." Mr. Justice White joined the majority with the understanding that its remand left open the ultimate question whether the state was required to dismiss its proceedings against the petitioner.

Mr. Justice Harlan also expressed the belief that Texas had not automatically forfeited the right to try the prisoner. "If the state still desires to bring him to trial, it should do so forthwith."

FAIR TRIAL

Harrington v. California, 393 U.S. 250, 5 CrL 3089

Bruton v. U.S., 391 U.S. 123, 3 CrL 3085, a blockbuster of the 1967–68 Term, may have been trimmed a bit this Term. Over the contentions of three dissenters that the Court was overruling Chapman v. California, 386 U.S. 18 and undermining Bruton, Mr. Justice Douglas, writing for the majority, held that a Bruton violation could be harmless error under Chapman. And, applying the Chapman test, the majority found that the improper admission of two nontestifying co-defendants' confessions placing a California robbery defendant at the scene of the crime was harmless error. Mr. Justice Douglas pointed out that the defendant himself admitted he was at the scene of the crime. Furthermore, aside from the extrajudicial statements of his co-defendants, the evidence against him was overwhelming. The error "was harmless beyond a reasonable doubt," Mr. Justice Douglas concluded, "unless we adopt the minority view in Chapman * * * that a departure from constitutional procedures should result in an automatic reversal no matter the weight of the evidence." Mr. Justice Douglas concluded that "we do not depart from Chapman nor do we dilute it by inference. We reaffirm it."

Joined by the Chief Justice and Mr. Justice Marshall in dissent, Mr. Justice Brennan maintained that "the Court today overrules Chapman * * *, the very case it purports to apply. Far more fundamentally, it severely undermines many of the Court's most significant decisions in the area of criminal law."

Chapman, Mr. Justice Brennan emphasized, "meant no compromise with the proposition that a conviction cannot constitutionally be based to any extent on constitutional error." The majority, he maintained, shifted the inquiry from whether the error contributed to the conviction to whether the untainted evidence was so "overwhelming" that the correction could withstand the taint. Numerous landmark decisions besides Bruton will be undermined by this groundshifting on harmless error, he maintained.

Frazier v. Cupp, 394 U.S. 731, 5 CrL 3041

Far less controversial among the Justices was the holding that a state murder conviction was not upset by the prosecutor's incidental reference in his opening statement to a confession of a guilty pleading codefendant. The codefendant, when called upon to testify, unexpectedly invoked the Fifth Amendment. Mr. Justice Marshall, whose opinion provoked no dissents, made it clear that jury instructions have not altogether lost their efficacy as remedies for potential Bruton violations. In this case, the judge's explicit instructions to disregard the prosecutor's opening-statement remark was sufficient to save the conviction.

The Court also held that, in this pre-Miranda case, the defendant's mere interruption of his in-custody confession to talk about getting a lawyer was not the same thing as a demand for counsel. He was not entitled, under Escobedo v. Illinois, 378 U.S. 478, to the suppression of his confession.

Also, clothing that was seized from a duffel bag used by the defendant was admissible against the defendant on the basis of consent given by the person who shared its use with the defendant.

The Chief Justice and Mr. Justice Douglas merely noted their concurrence in the result.

Boulden v. Holman, 394 U.S. 478, 5 CrL 3013

While Bruton's impact upon state trial practices may have been softened by the court's "harmless error" ruling in Harrington, the Court made it clear that its rule announced in Witherspoon v. Illinois, 3 CrL 3109, forbidding the exclusion of jurors who have no more than "scruples" against imposing the death penalty, is not to be narrowly construed. The Court unaminously granted relief to an Alabama death row inmate sentenced to death by a jury selected pursuant to a statute authorizing the exclusion of jurors who acknowledge "fixed opinion against capital punishment." The case was remanded for a federal district court determination of the Witherspoon issues. In view of Witherspoon's full retroactive application, the prisoner's failure to raise the juror exclusion issue at the state level did not, of course, constitute a waiver of his right to assert it.

Mr. Justice Stewart, who wrote the Court's opinion, noted that no fewer than 11 veniremen "appear to have been excused for cause simply on the basis of their affirmative answers to the question whether, in the statutory language, they had 'a fixed opinion against' capital punishment." Witherspoon emphasized that the critical issue is not how questions asked of a juror concerning his ability to impose the death penalty appear to courts or commentators, but how they might be understood by the juror. It must be made clear to a prospective juror, the Court emphasized, that he is being asked whether he can "never" impose the death penalty.

While it appeared to the Court that this particular sentence could not stand under Witherspoon, it remanded for a hearing below in view of the fact that the Witherspoon issue was not raised before the case came up for Supreme Court review; "a further hearing directed to the issue might conceivably modify in some fashion the

conclusion so strongly suggested by the record now before us. Further, it is not clear whether the petitioner has exhausted his state remedies with respect to this issue."

Foster v. California, 394 U.S. 440, 5 CrL 3001

The Court provided an example of at least one kind of police lineup predating U.S. v. Wade, 388 U.S. 218, 1 CrL 3106, that failed the due process requirements of Stovall v. Denno, 388 U.S. 293, 1 CrL 3102. Police placed the defendant in two lineups. First, they grouped him with two men much shorter than he was. Only he was wearing clothes similar to those worn by the described robber. The victim was nevertheless unable to positively identify the defendant. Several days later the police constructed another lineup, composed of five men. None of the five except the defendant had been placed in the previous lineup. This time the victim was "convinced" that the defendant was the man. Such a procedure was nothing if not unduly suggestive, Mr. Justice Fortas noted in his majority opinion, and in the "totality of the circumstances" violated due process.

Justices White, Harlan, and Stewart, "unwilling in this case to disagree with the jury on the weight of the evidence, would affirm the judgment."

Mr. Justice Black took issue with the majority's "totality of the circumstances" test. The majority here used this test "to justify its invading the constitutional right of jury trial," he maintained. This test, he continued, has been used to strike down a conviction on the basis of what the Court deems "unfair" rather than strictly on the ground of a constitutional violation. "The Constitution," Mr. Justice Black argued, "does not generally prohibit conduct deemed unfair by the courts."

Mr. Justice Black continued at some length to stress the dangers he saw in the adoption of a "totality of the circumstances" test as a constitutional standard.

JURY TRIAL

Frank v. U.S., 395 U.S. 147, 5 CrL 3069

Contempt cases differ from ordinary prosecutions, the Court held, when it comes to affording an accused his right to a jury trial. "In ordinary prosecution," Mr. Justice Marshall said for the Court, "the severity of the penalty authorized, not the penalty actually imposed, is the relevant criterion." But contempt of court is not an offense that imposes any specific limits on the sentencing court's discretion; Congress "has not categorized contempts as 'serious' or 'petty.' " Thus, "in prosecutions for criminal contempt where no maximum penalty is authorized, the severity of the penalty actually imposed is the best indication of the seriousness of the particular offense." In this particular case, the trial court suspended imposition of sentence upon the contemnor, but placed him on three years' probation. Hence, a jury trial was not required.

Five justices took issue with this position, Mr. Justice Harlan, and Mr. Justice Stewart because they thought the

Court had gone too far, the Chief Justice, Mr. Justice Black, and Mr. Justice Douglas because they thought the Court had not gone far enough. Justices Harlan and Stewart, however, considering themselves bound by Bloom v. Illinois, 391 U.S. 194, 3 CrL 3077 and Cheff v. Schnackenberg, 384 U.S. 373, concurred in the result.

The Chief Justice, joined by Mr. Justice Douglas, accused the Court of making "an unfortunate retreat from our recent decisions enforcing the Constitution's command that those accused of criminal offenses be afforded their fundamental right to a jury trial."

This decision, the dissenters maintained, was particularly unfortunate in the context of these unsettled times. It afforded trigger-happy judges the opportunity "to impose, at will," lengthy terms of probation that seriously curtail the contemnor's freedom. The probation conditions that were imposed in this case illustrate the control that a court can maintain over persons brought before it.

The dissenters also disagreed with the majority's statement that this petitioner's sentence was "within the limits of the Congressional definition of petty offense." The Chief Justice found "every indication that Congress affirmatively determined that probation should not affect its earlier definitions by making probation freely available to virtually all crimes —including most felonies not thereby rendered 'petty' because of probation's imposition." The Court was unjustified, he thought, in placing "unlimited reliance on legislative definitions and 'existing practices in the nation' "; by doing so it was permitting Congress and the states "to rewrite the Sixth Amendment of the Constitution by simply terming 'petty' any offense regardless of the underlying sentence." The purpose of suspending imposition of a sentence and substituting probation is not to lessen the degree of the offense, the dissenters emphasized, but to fashion an individualized attempt at rehabilitation.

Mr. Justice Douglas also joined Mr. Justice Black's dissent. Where punishment of as much as six months can be imposed, Mr. Justice Black said, "I could not classify the offense as 'petty' if that means that people tried for it are to be tried as if we had no Bill of Rights." Furthermore, he saw no basis for distinguishing between a man punished for an offense against the public and one punished for an offense against a court.

FIRST AMENDMENT

The First Amendment made a respectable showing in several widely different areas involving freedom of speech and expression.

Brandenberg v. Ohio, 395 U.S. 444, 5 CrL 3107

Ohio's Criminal Syndicalism statute succumbed to a freedom of speech interpretation far more expansive than that applied in Whitney v. California, 274 U.S. 357, which sustained California's Criminal Syndicalism law in 1927. The Ohio statute was enacted in World War I days; 19 other states adopted similar legislation prohibiting

"advocacy" of "criminal syndicalism." Last term, 42 years later, the Court overruled Whitney.

Ironically, the case before the Court involved the prosecution of a leader of a Ku Klux Klan group that held a rally at which speakers talked of the possible need for "revengence" against Negroes and Jews.

The Court's per curiam opinion emphasized the degree to which these criminal syndicalism statutes have been undercut in recent years; Whitney "has been thoroughly discredited by later decisions. See Dennis v. U.S., 341 U.S. 494." There is no longer any room under the First Amendment for a statute that fails to draw a distinction between mere teaching, or even a statement of the moral necessity of force and violence, and the actual preparation of a group for such action.

Justices Douglas and Black, in separate concurring opinions, made it clear that they had no use for the "clear and present danger" doctrine on which Dennis "purported to rely." Mr. Justice Douglas traced the history of the "clear and present danger" test, noted the criticism that it has incurred, and pointed to the difficulty of distinguishing between mere speech and action.

Stanley v. Georgia, 394 U.S. 557, 5 CrL 3019

The growing concept of a citizen's fundamental right of privacy drew nourishment from the First Amendment this Term. Private possession of obscene material is no longer punishable as a criminal offense. The Court unanimously held that a Georgia statute prohibiting private possession of obscene material violated the First and Fourteenth Amendments, and upset the obscenity conviction of a petitioner whose stag films were seized during the course of a warrant-authorized search for illegal gambling paraphernalia.

True, Mr. Justice Marshall acknowledged in his opinion for the majority, Roth v. U.S., 354 U.S. 476, "does declare, seemingly without qualification, that obscenity is not protected by the First Amendment." However, none of the statements in Roth or the Court's subsequent opinions citing Roth have been made "in the context of a statute punishing mere private possession of obscene material; the cases cited deal for the most part with use of the mails to distribute objectionable material or with some form of public distribution or dissemination."

Thus, Mr. Justice Marshall emphasized, this case cannot be decided upon the basis of Roth. It involves another critical factor —"the right to be free, except in very limited circumstances, from unwarranted government intrusion into one's privacy."

The state claimed it had an interest in protecting the individual's mind from the effects of obscenity. Mr. Justice Marshall answered, "We are not certain that this argument amounts to anything more than the assertion that the State has the right to control the moral content of a person's thoughts."

Justices Stewart, Brennan, and White concurred in the result, but maintained that the Court had the obligation to deal with a threshold question —the alleged illegality of the seizure of the films. These films were illegally seized, the three Justices maintained, and were inadmissible at the obscenity trial.

Shuttlesworth v. Birmingham, 394 U.S. 147, 4 CrL 3141

Civil rights marchers won two victories this Term, one over a Birmingham, Alabama procession permit ordinance that the Court found to be unconstitutional on its face. The ordinance, Mr. Justice Stewart observed in his opinion for the majority, conferred "virtually unbridled and absolute power to prohibit any 'parade, procession,' or 'demonstration' on the city's streets or public ways."

Mr. Justice Stewart acknowledged that the conduct regulated here was not "pure speech" —it did involve the use of public streets over which the municipality had a right to exercise considerable control. But previous decisions have made it clear that picketing and parading may constitute methods of expression protected by the First Amendment.

The Alabama Court of Appeals' attempt to sustain the ordinance by judicially modifying and narrowing its obviously overbroad provisions could not succeed, Mr. Justice Stewart concluded. And the Alabama Supreme Court's "commendable effort" in 1967 to narrow the ordinance's effect to comply with constitutional requirements failed to "restore constitutional validity to a conviction that occurred in 1963 under the ordinance as it was written." The absolute power conferred on city officials by the ordinance as it read at the time of the famous "Good Friday" march compels reversal of the marchers' convictions. Furthermore, the Court pointed out, pre-march efforts to obtain a permit were bluntly refused; the authorities' outright refusal indicates that they felt the ordinance gave them all the power it seemed to give them.

Concurring, Mr. Justice Harlan pointed out that this case presents the difficult question "whether the Fourteenth Amendment ever bars a State from punishing a citizen for marching without a permit which could have been procured if all available remedies had been pursued." An inferior state official's view as to a statute's scope does not mean that the state judiciary will construe it as broadly, Mr. Justice Harlan observed. But, taken in the context of the situation here, the would-be marchers had no opportunity to obtain judicial review. It was almost certain that, had the petitioners attempted to exhaust administrative and judicial remedies, they could not have obtained relief by Good Friday.

Gregory v. Chicago, 394 U.S. 111, 4 CrL 3146

The Court also held that comedian-civil rights leader Dick Gregory's disorderly conviction arising out of his refusal to disperse his peaceful and orderly protest march from Chicago's city hall to and around Mayor Daley's home was so unsupported by the evidence that it violated due process. Gregory was ordered to disperse not because he was violating any law, but because hostile onlookers were working themselves into a state of violence. Furthermore, the trial judge's instructions permitting the jury to rest the disorderly conduct conviction on the marchers' refusal to discontinue conduct protected by the First Amendment violated Stromberg v. California, 283 U.S. 359.

Justices Black and Douglas concurred, but thought this case to be of far greater importance than the majority's treatment of it indicated. There is a critical need, they contended, for some "narrowly drawn law" that can reconcile the right of citizens to propagandize their views and protest through the medium of marches and demonstrations and the interest of government in regulating speech-connected conduct. They pointed out that Gregory was asked, and then ordered, to disband not because of anything he or his followers were doing, but because of the hostile crowd that had gathered about them. In effect, they were arrested for disobeying a law that did not exist until they were commanded to disperse. They were not, at the time the order was given, violating any law whatsoever. "Laws, that is valid laws, are to be made by representatives chosen to make laws for the future, not by police officers whose duty is to enforce laws already enacted and to make arrests only for conduct already made criminal."

Watts v. U.S., 393 U.S. 890, 5 CrL 4024

One form of federal prosecution was also affected by the First Amendment. An excited teenage orator, who told a gathering of young people "discussing" police brutality that, if the Armed Forces "ever make me carry a rifle the first man I want to get in my sights is L.B.J." was unconstitutionally prosecuted under 18 U.S.C. 871(a), which makes it a crime to "knowingly and willfully" threaten the life or safety of the President.

"Certainly the statute under which petitioner was convicted is constitutional on its face" the per curiam opinion observed. But, "the kind of political hyperbole indulged in by the petitioner" was symbolic rather than threatening. The Court agreed with the petitioner "that his offense here was 'a kind of very crude offensive method of stating a political opposition to the President.'"

Concurring, Mr. Justice Douglas, tracing the history of similar statutes, rated what he found to be the present statute's oppressive effect on a par with the effect created by the Alien and Sedition Laws.

Mr. Justice White dissented without opinion, and Mr. Justice Stewart stated that he would deny the petition for certiorari. Justices Fortas and Harlan emphasized that "the Court holds, without hearing, that this statute is constitutional and that it is wrongly applied. Neither of these rulings should be made without hearing, even if we assume that they are correct."

MILITARY AND SELECTIVE SERVICE

In the fifth year of America's large-scale involvement in the Viet Nam War, the Court's 1968–69 Term included five significant cases touching upon the military establishment. Of these, one was a precedent-leveling bombshell in the field of military criminal law. Another seems to have rocked the draft law field with its delayed-fuse impact.

O'Callahan v. Parker, 395 U.S. 258, 5 CrL 3082

The Court here restricted military jurisdiction over servicemen's crimes to those offenses having some significant connection with the military and its operations. Article 1 of the Uniform Code of Military Justice does not give the military services jurisdiction to try an Armed Forces member charged with an offense cognizable in civilian courts, committed off duty and off post, and having no other military significance. This decision toppled a precedent that was at least half a century old — and which, the military unsuccessfully argued, actually dated from time immemorial.

Since the military justice system does not include grand jury indictment and petit jury trial, the Court decided that improper assertion of court-martial jurisdiction over a serviceman's civilian-type offenses unconstitutionally deprives him of these Fifth and Sixth Amendment rights. As the Fifth Amendment includes an express exception from the grand jury requirement for "cases arising in the land and naval forces," the Court's opinion constitutes, for the most part, a limitation of the breadth with which the military can interpret the phrase "arising in."

The Court expressly rejected the argument that the status of the defendant is, as UCMJ Article 1 provides, enough to establish military jurisdiction. The concurrent jurisdiction of both military and local authorities over servicemen's ordinary criminal offenses off base has long been implemented by informal waiver of jurisdiction by one sovereignty or the other, and court-martial trial of such offenses has been frequent. But whether the decision will result in a drastic workload reduction for the armed services' judge advocates remains to be seen.

Noyd v. Bond, 395 U.S. 683, 5 CrL 3113

The Court of Military Appeals' 1966 assertion of its own power to issue extraordinary writs under the All Writs Act, 28 U.S.C. 1651(a) (1964) (U.S. v. Frischholz, 16 U.S.C.M.A. 150, 36 CMR 306; Levy v. Resor, 17 U.S.C.M.A. 135, 37 CMR 399) received the Supreme Court's blessing in the case of conscientious objector Captain Dale E. Noyd, but the effects of this blessing did not filter through to Noyd himself. Since he had not sought habeas corpus from the Court of Military Appeals to secure relief from his allegedly unlawful confinement while his appeal to that court was pending, he had not exhausted his military remedies. For that reason, the Court held, a federal district court had no jurisdiction to entertain his habeas corpus petition.

U.S. v. Augenblick, 393 U.S. 348, 4 CrL 3072

Although the world of military criminal jurisprudence is certainly no longer a watertight compartment, court-martial convictions retain considerable immunity from civilian review. In reinstating the court-martial conviction of a navy officer, the Court turned back an attempt by the U.S. Court of Claims to establish a broad beachhead on the "finality" article, Article 76, of the Uniform Code of Military Justice. The Supreme Court held that the U.S. Court of Claims in a backpay suit cannot review a court-martial conviction in which the claimed errors were not of constitutional magnitude.

Oestereich v. Selective Service Board, 393 U.S. 233, 4 CrL 3043

The Term's "sleepers" included the Court's decision that the Selective Service system cannot administratively deprive registrants of "statutory exemptions" for reasons unrelated to the statutory exemption grant and that Section 10(b)(3) of the Military Selective Service Act of 1967, 35 LW 67, allows registrants before induction (or prosecution) to protect such exemptions by suing in federal courts. The decision has apparently meant a great many things to a great many lower courts, and has been cited by them for a vast range of propositions.

Accepting the Justice Department concession of error on both the jurisdictional and the substantive point, the majority, speaking through Mr. Justice Douglas, held that a local board's conduct is "basically lawless" when it tries to deprive a statutorily exempted registrant of his exemption for conduct unrelated to the merits of granting or continuing the exemption. Sustaining such action, the majority said, "would make the boards freewheeling agencies meting out their brand of justice in a vindictive manner."

Though the 1967 Act was meant to stem the tide of civil litigation over draft classifications and reclassifications, the Court made certain that the flow would continue as far as "statutory exemptions" —as opposed to administrative deferments —are concerned. The majority holds that Section 10(b)(3) could not sustain a "literal reading" that would deprive these registrants of access to the courts for such a reading would clearly conflict with the absolute grant of the exemption by Congress —in this case, a divinity student's exemption under Section 6(g) of the Selective Service Act, 50 U.S.C. App 456(g).

To dissenting Justice Stewart, joined by Justices Brennan and White, a literal reading is not only sustainable, but required. The dissenters could see no possible way around the absolute mandate of Section 10(b)(3) that the courts shall not review draft classifications except in passing on criminal prosecutions for refusal to report for induction.

Clark v. Gabriel, 393 U.S. 256, 5 CrL 4118

If Section 10(b)(3) must be construed to include an exception for "statutory exemptions," it is just as clear to the Court that there can be no pre-induction or pre-prosecution review of a local board's mere denial of a classification. The Court clarified Oestereich on this point by refusing to review the case of a registrant who was denied CO classification. Mr. Justice Douglas, author of the Oestereich opinion, added in a concurrence that he would view differently a case of conscientious objector classification denial that seemed to embody punishment for unpopular speech, rather than simply a view of the evidence differing from the registrant's.

POST-CONVICTION RELIEF

The lot of prisoners seeking post-conviction relief was substantially improved in various ways last Term, by several decisions expanding, in one way or another, the rights of state prisoners seeking federal habeas corpus relief. Two others benefited certain federal prisoners seeking the equivalent of habeas corpus relief under 28 U.S.C. 2255.

Kaufman v. U.S., 394 U.S. 217, 4 CrL 3180

A federal prisoner who seeks relief under Section 2255 has just as much right to raise a Fourth Amendment claim as does a state prisoner seeking federal habeas corpus relief. Resolving a split among the circuits on the question of whether such claims are proper matters for a Section 2255 petition, the Court, in an opinion by Mr. Justice Brennan, pointed out that Section 2255, while revising the procedure by which federal prisoners are to seek post-conviction relief, "did not in any respect cut back the scope of" relief previously available by habeas corpus.

The majority rejected a government contention that the denial of Fourth Amendment protections can be differentiated from denials of other constitutional rights that are subject to collateral attack. The Court refused to distinguish Fourth Amendment rights from other constitutional rights.

Dissenting, Mr. Justice Black disagreed vehemently with the majority's refusal to distinguish illegal search and seizure claims from the assertion of other constitutional rights; "ordinarily the evidence seized can in no way have been rendered untrustworthy by the means of its seizure and indeed often this evidence alone establishes beyond virtually any shadow of doubt that the defendant is guilty."

Justices Harlan and Stewart joined in Mr. Justice Black's dissent, but they disassociated themselves "from any implications * * * that the availability of" Section 2255 relief "turns on a petitioner's assertion that he was in fact innocent or on the substantiality of such an allegation."

Harris v. Nelson, 394 U.S. 286, 4 CrL 3161

The flexibility of habeas corpus was emphasized by the Court in holding that a federal district court has the authority to order discovery by written interrogatories on behalf of a petitioner who establishes a prima facie case for relief even though the discovery procedures of the Federal Rules of Civil Procedure do not themselves apply "completely and automatically" to habeas corpus.

While the nature of habeas corpus makes it ill-suited to the Federal Rules' discovery proceedings, in view of the writ's flexibility and its growth in recent times, a habeas court, may, to make sure that justice is done, "fashion appropriate modes of procedure, by analogy to existing rules or otherwise in conformity with judicial usage."

To Mr. Justice Black, who dissented, the majority appeared to be writing "in effect an advisory opinion directing the trial courts to formulate some kind of new legal system for discovery in this kind of case."

Justices Harlan and White feared that the majority's opinion would set district courts "at large" to fashion ad hoc discovery rules as they saw fit. They agreed "that district courts do have power to require discovery when essential to render a habeas corpus proceeding effective." But they would make it clear that such power is narrow and should be exercised sparingly.

Mr. Justice Stewart, agreeing with most of the majority's opinion, would have affirmed the lower court's ruling for the reasons stated by Mr. Justice Harlan in his dissent in Kaufman.

Rodriquez v. U.S., 395 U.S. 327, 5 CrL 3091

An indigent, unassisted prisoner who seeks postconviction relief under Section 2255 of the Judicial Code for purposes of obtaining the direct appeal he claimed he was wrongfully denied cannot be compelled, before his petition will be considered, to show some likelihood of success by disclosing what errors he would raise on appeal.

Mr. Justice Harlan, while agreeing that this requirement is an improper one, could not go along with the majority's reinstatement of the petitioner's right to appeal without further proceedings below.

U.S. v. Nardello, 393 U.S. 286, 4 CrL 3069

The Court was unanimous in holding that the Travel Act, 18 U.S.C. 1952, which makes it a federal crime to travel in or use facilities of interstate commerce to promote "extortion" in violation of state law, comprehends virtually all extortionate conduct forbidden by state law. It does not matter, the Chief Justice wrote for the Court, whether or not the statute under which the indictment is returned actually denominates the offense charged as extortion.

The Travel Act was calculated to cover a wide range of extortionate activities, regardless of the labels that states give to these activities, the Chief Justice emphasized. The Act was described by the late Robert F. Kennedy, who, as Attorney General proposed its enactment, as an effort to get at the "top men" in large-scale extortion activities.

Gregg v. U.S., 394 U.S. 489, 5 CrL 3016

A judge's statement within minutes after the delivery of a jury's guilty verdict that he had read the five-page presentence did not establish a violation of Rule 32(c), the

Court held unanimously. Furthermore, reading of the presentence report prior to the verdict of guilty would not prejudice defendant's rights. The judge already knew of the information contained in the presentence report; it had been obtained from a psychiatric report admitted into evidence.

The Court did caution that, although the judge may have presentence information at his disposal prior to the verdict, "there is no reason to see the document until the occasion to sentence arises, and under the rule he must not do so."

Williams v. Oklahoma, 395 U.S. 458, 5 CrL 3095

The Fourteenth Amendment was held to require that an indigent appealing as of right from a state conviction for drunk driving is entitled to a free trial transcript. The Court, in a unanimous per curiam opinion, restated its previous admonition that, once a state establishes an avenue of appellate review, it must afford all prospective appellants, solvent and indigent alike, the opportunity to use it.

Indigents seeking habeas corpus relief —state and federal —were major beneficiaries of the Court's decisions.

Johnson v. Avery, 393 U.S. 483, 4 CrL 3115

States that fail to provide prisoners seeking federal habeas corpus relief with adequate outside assistance are just going to have to put up with "jailhouse lawyers" until they otherwise meet the needs of these would-be petitioners, the Court held.

Mr. Justice Fortas who wrote the majority opinion, acknowledged the state's interest in preserving prison discipline. But in this situation, he emphasized, that interest must yield to a prisoner's habeas corpus rights.

The majority opinion did not make it clear whether a state prisoner's access to habeas corpus is constitutionally based, or whether it depends upon the federal habeas corpus statute, 28 U.S.C. 2242. Nor did the Court say whether such assistance of jailhouse lawyers, at least, is available as a matter of right to prisoners who seek state post-conviction remedies.

Mr. Justice Douglas, otherwise joining fully in the majority's opinion, suggested that perhaps the time has come to provide lay assistance to prisoners. Some states, he noted, had provided such assistance by last-year law students.

Justices White and Black dissented, emphasizing the evils that can arise from allowing a jailhouse lawyer to set up business. Such an individual, Mr. Justice White observed, "often succeeds in establishing his own power structure, quite apart from the formal system of warden, guards, and trustees which the prison seeks to maintain."

Also, the jailhouse lawyer feels few of the legal profession's ethical restraints.

Gardner v. California, 395 U.S. 925, 4 CrL 3080

Indigent California prisoners seeking state habeas corpus relief are entitled, under the Fourteenth Amendment, to a free transcript of the original habeas corpus hearing for use in filing a subsequent de novo petition in a California appellate court, a majority of the Court held.

As long as the state provides repeated hearings on post-conviction motions for relief, and "so long as transcripts are available for preparation for appellate hearings in habeas corpus cases," Mr. Justice Douglas, writing for the majority, stated, "they may not be furnished to those who can afford them and denied those who are paupers."

Justices Harlan and Stewart accused the majority of not only misconceiving the nature of California's post-conviction procedures, but of imposing upon the state a financial burden that would not be offset by any appreciable benefit to a petitioner. Mr. Justice Harlan stressed that the petition de novo "is self-contained and independent of the prior proceeding. * * * The applicant is neither required nor requested to assign errors, or refer to testimony, in the prior proceeding."

OTHER RULINGS

Johnson v. Bennett, 393 U.S. 253, 4 CrL 3049

An Eighth Circuit ruling that an Iowa rule shifting the burden of proof in an alibi defense to a defendant was unconstitutional led the Court to vacate a previous, inconsistent, Eighth Circuit decision.

McDonald v. Chicago Board of Election Comrs., 394 U.S. 802, 5 CrL 3045

The Court also held that untried state jail inmates who have not shown that the state denies them the right to vote at polls are not denied equal protection by the state's refusal to allow them absentee ballots while extending the absentee ballot privilege to other classes, including those medically incapacitated.

Berger v. California. 393 U.S. 314, 4 CrL 4146

The exercise of a smidgen of clairvoyance is not too much to expect, the Court suggested, in holding retroactive the confrontation-right expansion wrought by Barber v. Page, 390 U.S. 719, 3 CrL 3048.

Barber's holding, the Court pointed out, was clearly foreshadowed, if not preordained, by Pointer v. Texas, 380 U.S. 400.

Weighing most heavily in favor of retroactive application, the Court asserted, is the significant effect the inability to cross-examine might have had on the "integrity of the fact-finding process." One of the important objects of the right of confrontation is "to guarantee that the fact-finder [has] an adequate opportunity to assess the credibility of witnesses."

1969–1970 Term

The criminal law revolution of the last decade ended with the Warren era. In several key areas, the hand of government was strengthened during the 1969–70 Term. Additional benefits for defendants came almost entirely through application of past landmark decisions to particular fact situations. For the first time in several years, few constitutionally required demands were placed on law enforcement officers. And with only eight Justices sitting for most of the Term, the Court disposed of several potentially momentous cases on less than momentous grounds. However, from the criminal law point of view, the Term was anything but dull. Several decisions — particularly those dealing with challenges to guilty pleas — had a strong impact at the state and lower federal court level. And the military draft, placed in a criminal law context by recalcitrant draftees, furnished new fuel for controversy.

GUILTY PLEAS

A trilogy of decisions made it clear that defendants who entered their guilty pleas with the assistance of competent counsel face a steep uphill fight to obtain even a hearing for their contentions that they were improperly induced to waive their rights by such factors as improperly obtained evidence or fear of harsh sentences. These cases have already had a strong effect on appellate courts' disposition of postconviction efforts to obtain relief from guilty pleas. The number of prisoners challenging guilty pleas has risen sharply in recent years, and roughly 70 to 85 percent of all prosecutions are settled on the basis of guilty pleas.

McMann v. Richardson, 397 U.S. 759, 7 CrL 3055

A prisoner's allegation that his otherwise-properly-accepted guilty pleas was induced by an improperly obtained confession does not entitle him to a habeas corpus hearing on the voluntariness of his plea. No federal relief —not even a habeas corpus hearing — was available to three New York prisoners who not only claimed that their pleas were motivated by involuntary confessions, but pointed out that the admissibility of their confessions would have been determined under a practice later held unconstitutional in Jackson v. Denno, 378 U.S. 368 (1963).

The Court, by a 5–3 vote, reversed an en banc decision of the U.S. Court of Appeals for the Second Circuit, 408 F.2d 1069, 4 CrL 2465 (1969), which also divided sharply over this question. "The core of the Court of Appeals'

holding is the proposition that if in a collateral proceeding a guilty plea is shown to have been triggered by a coerced confession —if there would have been no plea had there been no confession —the plea is vulnerable at least in cases coming from New York where the guilty plea was taken prior to Jackson v. Denno. We are unable to agree with the Court of Appeals on this proposition."

Mr. Justice White, writing for the majority, indicated that the opportunity to make a reasoned choice was the key question in determining the validity of the plea, not whether otherwise competent counsel was mistaken in his assessment of the law and facts. Counsel in this position is often faced with a difficult judgment. It is not the place of the courts to second-guess a defense attorney's advice that a guilty plea was the best way out —even if that advice may have been erroneous, "either under the applicable law or under the law later announced." Such questions as whether certain evidence will be admitted at trial, and whether such evidence, if admitted, will weigh heavily in a determination of guilt, "cannot be answered with certitude; yet a decision to plead guilty must necessarily rest upon counsel's answers, uncertain as they may be. Waiving trial entails the inherent risk that the good-faith evaluations of a reasonably competent attorney will turn out to be mistaken either as to the facts or as to what a court's judgment might be on given facts."

The majority emphasized the critical difference between a conviction following a guilty plea induced by the threat of an involuntary confession and a conviction obtained following a trial marred by the introduction of such a confession. "A conviction after trial in which a coerced confession is introduced rests in part on the coerced confession, a constitutionally unacceptable basis for conviction. It is that conviction and the confession on which it rests which the defendant later attacks in collateral proceedings. The defendant who pleads guilty is in a different posture. He is convicted on his counseled admission in open court that he committed the crime charged against him. The prior confession is not the basis for the judgment, has never been offered in evidence at a trial, and may never be offered in evidence."

The Court noted that it was not deciding whether a federal habeas corpus challenge to a guilty plea conviction is available to a prisoner in a state that permits appeal even after a guilty plea has been accepted, from a pretrial determination that a confession was voluntary.

Justices Brennan, Douglas, and Marshall dissented. Mr. Justice Brennan claimed that "the Court moves yet another step toward the goal of insulating all guilty pleas from subsequent attacks no matter what unconstitutional action of government may have induced a particular plea." The majority was violating "the basic principle applicable to this case enunciated for the Court by Mr. Justice Black" in Herman v. Claudy, 350 U.S. 116 (1956): "a conviction following trial or on a plea of guilty based on a confession extorted by violence or by mental coercion is invalid under the federal Due Process Clause." True, the mere existence of a coerced confession does not by itself invalidate a guilty plea. The defendant "must therefore demonstrate the existence of a sufficient interrelationship or nexus between the plea and the antecedent confession so that the plea may be said to be infected by the state's prior illegality." But here, the majority "abruptly forecloses any inquiry" concerning the impact of that confession.

The mere fact that the coercive pressures compelling the confession ceased prior to entry of the plea should not foreclose such an inquiry, Mr. Justice Brennan said. "In short, the 'abiding impact' of the coerced confession may continue to prejudice a defendant's case or unfairly influence his decisions regarding his legal alternatives."

The majority, Mr. Justice Brennan claimed, attached "talismanic significance to the presence of counsel." Furthermore, these pleas were hardly waivers of known rights in view of the constitutional invalidity of New York's procedure at that time for determining the voluntariness of confessions. To reach the result that it did, he maintained, the majority held Jackson v. Denno "to be only partially retroactive, a wholly novel and unacceptable result."

Brady v. U.S., 397 U.S. 742, 7 CrL 3064

Though unanimous in affirming the conviction of a federal kidnapping defendant whose guilty plea may have been motivated by his desire to avoid the Lindbergh Law death penalty procedure subsequently declared unconstitutional in U.S. v. Jackson, 390 U.S. 570, 3 CrL 3083, the Court divided once more as to just what must be considered in evaluating such a plea.

Although Jackson declared that the death penalty provision's infirmity lay in its "inevitable effect" of discouraging defendants from asserting their right to a trial by jury, Jackson itself disavowed any implication "that every defendant who enters a guilty plea to a charge under the Act does so involuntarily." And in the present case, the defendant was unable to persuade the Court that his fear of the death penalty rendered his plea involuntary. There was no "evidence that Brady was so gripped by fear of the death penalty or hope of leniency that he did not or could not, with the help of counsel, rationally weigh the advantages of going to trial against the advantages of pleading guilty." There was nothing to distinguish him from the defendant who pleads guilty in the hope of a more lenient sentence from the judge or in return for having other charges dropped.

To hold that a plea induced by the hope of a more lenient sentence is involuntary "would require the states and federal government to forbid guilty pleas altogether." This defendant was not subject to undue pressure from counsel, and counsel's failure to anticipate Jackson did not "impugn the truth or reliability of his plea."

Mr. Justice Brennan, speaking for the same Justices who dissented in McMann v. Richardson, found it strange that guilty pleas entered under a statutory scheme struck down precisely because it "needlessly encouraged guilty pleas are to be virtually immune from challenge."

The legal concept of involuntariness, Mr. Justice Brennan noted, "has not been narrowly confined but refers to a surrender of constitutional rights influenced by considerations which the government cannot properly introduce. The critical question which divides the Court is what constitutes an impermissible factor, or, more narrowly in the context of these cases, whether the threat of the imposition of an unconstitutional death penalty is such a factor." And the Court here was departing from a strict concept of voluntariness applied as long ago as Bram v. U.S., 168 U.S. 532 (1897).

Guilty pleas entered under the Lindbergh Law prior to the announcement of Jackson were far different things than negotiated pleas, the dissenters contended. The Lindbergh Law allowed a defendant to assure himself of avoiding the death penalty by pleading guilty. Such inducement in negotiations would render a plea involuntary. There was a clear danger of an innocent man pleading guilty simply to be certain that he would not face the executioner. Furthermore, the defendants in no case could have incurred the death penalty under Jackson.

Parker v. North Carolina, 397 U.S. 790, 7 CrL 3069

A five-Justice majority also held that a North Carolina rape defendant's plea of guilty, which may have been motivated not only by his desire to avoid the death penalty under a state statute that resembled the Lindbergh Law but by a coerced confession as well, was not inherently involuntary. For reasons set out in McMann, the Court also rejected the claim that the plea was involuntary, because induced by a coerced confession, even assuming that it was entered on the erroneous advice of counsel that the confession would be used against him. And the Court did not think that the record revealed an involuntary confession.

Again Justices Brennan, Douglas, and Marshall dissented. Mr. Justice Brennan pointed out that the statute here was virtually indistinguishable from the federal statute struck down in U.S. v. Jackson, which applies retroactively. If fundamental rights were violated by this needless encouragement of guilty pleas, and if Jackson must be applied retroactively, it hardly made sense to Mr. Justice Brennan to dismiss as "too speculative" an inquiry into the difference, for purposes of an attorney's decision to recommend a guilty plea, between a pre-Jackson and post-Jackson procedure.

JURY TRIAL

The Court gave a clearer idea of what constitutes a "serious offense," to which the Sixth Amendment right to jury trial attaches. It now appeared that any defendant who faces a possible penalty of more than six months incarceration is entitled to a jury trial. However, another decision made it clear that the jury need not be composed of 12 people.

Williams v. Florida, 399 U.S. 78, 7 CrL 3143

The 12-man jury is not a constitutional requirement, the Court held, and a six-man jury satisfies the requirements of the Sixth Amendment. Thus, the Court overruled by implication a line of its cases going back to Thompson v. Utah, 170 U.S. 343 (1898).

Examining the debates that led to adoption of the Article III right to jury trial, as well as the Sixth Amendment right, the Court found "absolutely no indication" that the constitutional right to a jury was to be equated with the common law right in all its details.

After sketching briefly the Constitutional Convention debates over what form the jury trial right was to take in Article III, Mr. Justice White observed three significant features concerning the relationship between the common law and constitutional rights to jury trial. First, the framers of the Constitution explicitly decided against including in the Article III right the common law right to be tried by a "jury of the vicinage" (a jury of the neighborhood or county); the compromise word "venue" was substituted. And the vicinage requirement was as much a feature of the common law jury in the Eighteenth Century as was the 12-man requirement. "Second, provisions which would have explicitly tied the 'jury' concept to the 'accustomed requisites' of the time were eliminated." While it was arguable that these "accustomed requisites" were assumed to be included, it was at least as plausible that the deletion was intended to free the constitutional right to jury from these "requisites."

"Finally, contemporary legislative and Constitutional provisions indicate that where Congress wanted to leave no doubt that it was incorporating existing common law features of the jury system, it knew how to use express language to that effect." From all this, Mr. Justice White concluded that there is absolutely no indication that the framers explicitly decided to equate the constitutional and common law characteristics of the jury. "Nothing in this history suggests, then, that we do violence to the letter of the Constitution by turning to other than purely historical considerations to determine which features of the jury system, as it existed at common law, were preserved in the Constitution."

The purposes of the right to a jury trial, Mr. Justice White went on, can be satisfied by a jury of fewer than 12 men. The purpose of a jury trial was to give a criminally accused the right to be tried by his peers —to safeguard him against an overzealous prosecutor or biased or inadequate judge. "Given this purpose the essential feature of a jury obviously lies in the interposition between the accused and his accuser of the common-sense judgment of a group of laymen, and the community participation and shared responsibility which results from that group's determination of guilt or innocence. The performance of this role is not a function of the particular number of the body which makes up the jury. To be sure, the number should probably be large enough to promote group deliberation, free from outside attempts at intimidation, and to provide a fair possibility for obtaining a representative cross section of the community. But we find little reason to think that these goals are in any meaningful sense less likely to be achieved when the jury numbers six, than when it numbers 12 —particularly if the requirement of unanimity is retained. And, certainly the reliability of the jury as a factfinder hardly seems likely to be a function of its size."

The argument that a 12-man jury gives a defendant greater chance to avoid conviction cuts both ways; while one juror out of 12 may want a guilty verdict, a single juror may also prevent an acquittal.

Nor was the Court persuaded by the argument that the 12-man jury is apt to be more representative of the community. Even a 12-man jury is not apt to "insure representation of every distinct voice in the community, particularly given the use of the peremptory challenge."

After discussing some of the considerations for and against the 12-man jury, the majority concluded, "our holding does no more than leave these considerations to Congress and the States, unrestrained by an interpretation of the Sixth Amendment which would forever dictate the precise number which can constitute a jury."

Concurring, Mr. Justice Harlan was willing to allow the states to use a six-man jury, but he did not think that the Sixth Amendment permitted the federal government to do so. Neither the Court's historical analysis nor its policy arguments furnished acceptable reasons "for disregarding history and numerous pronouncements of this Court that have made 'the easy assumption' that the Sixth Amendment's jury was one comprised of 12 individuals."

History should not prevent constitutional guarantees from "adaptation of purpose to contemporary circumstances," Mr. Justice Harlan agreed. But, the right to jury trial "has no enduring meaning apart from its historical form."

In departing from the previous 12-man requirement, on the ground that the purpose of the jury trial is not served by it, "this second justification for cutting the umbilical cord that ties the form of the jury to the past is itself, as I see it, the most compelling reason for maintaining that guarantee in its common-law form. For if 12 jurors are not essential, why are six?"

Mr. Justice Harlan thought that the Court's application of the "incorporation theory" in recent years had led it to the unhappy position in which it found itself here — of abandoning stare decisis and a sound, long-standing federal rule to accommodate the needs of the states. "The internal logic of the selective incorporation doctrine cannot be respected if the Court is both committed to interpreting faithfully the meaning of the federal Bill of Rights and recognizing the governmental diversity that exists in this country." Describing this case as the "first major attempt to wriggle free of that 'strait jacket,'" Mr. Justice Harlan offered a broad review of the incorporation theory.

On another point, a six-justice majority found no self-incrimination threat or due process violation in Florida's requirement that a defendant who intends to present an alibi defense must turn over to the prosecution information as to the place he claims to have been and the names and addresses of alibi witnesses he intends to use. The duty to disclose is reciprocal, the Court noted, and Florida's alibi disclosure requirement helps to avoid a "poker game" approach to the trial.

The Court did not decide the validity of the penalty for a defendant's failure to comply —exclusion of the evidence supporting the alibi. "Whether and to what extent a state can enforce discovery rules against a defendant who fails to comply by excluding relevant, probative evidence is a question raising Sixth Amendment issues which we have no occasion to explore."

Joining fully in the Court's opinion, the Chief Justice saw "an added benefit to the alibi notice rule in that it will serve important functions by way of disposing of cases without trial in appropriate circumstances —a matter of considerable importance when courts, prosecution offices and legal aid and defender agencies are vastly over-worked."

Baldwin v. New York, 399 U.S. 66, 7 CrL 3140

Five Justices agreed on the unconstitutionality of a New York statute denying a jury trial to New York City defendants charged with "misdemeanor" crimes punishable by up to a year in jail. Four of the Justices were of the view that the right to a jury trial attaches to any crime punishable by more than six months in prison, while Justices Black and Douglas argued that the Sixth Amendment's language explicitly requires a jury trial for "all crimes," no matter what the punishment. Thus, the practical effect of this decision would seem to be that any defendant who faces a jail sentence of greater than six months must be given trial.

Dissenting, the Chief Justice pointed out just how "serious" were the offenses for which a federal defendant was punishable at the time the Sixth and Fourteenth Amendments were adopted. And he found nothing in the "serious" crime coverage of either of these amendments "that would require this Court to invalidate the particular New York City trial scheme at issue here."

Mr. Justice Harlan dissented for the same reasons that he stated in Duncan v. Louisiana, 391 U.S. 145, 3 CrL 3065.

RIGHT OF CONFRONTATION

Illinois v. Allen, 397 U.S. 337, 7 CrL 3001

Dealing with trial disruption, an issue that was brought to public attention by the chaotic "Chicago Seven" conspiracy trial, the Supreme Court gave considerable latitude to trial judges who must deal with recalcitrant defendants. A judge faced with a disorderly and disruptive defendant can order him bound and gagged, cite him for criminal contempt, or continue the trial without him until he promises to behave. Specifically, the Court held that the Sixth Amendment right to be present throughout trial was lost by an armed robbery defendant who, after several warnings, continued to act so disruptively that the trial could not proceed with him in the courtroom. The Court reversed a decision by a U.S. court of appeals that not even under these circumstances could a defendant be removed from his own trial. Only Mr. Justice Douglas refrained from joining in the majority's holding, and he did so because he considered this case an inappropriate one for announcing rules that would apply to cases involving political issues.

Writing for the Court, Mr. Justice Black observed that "trial judges confronted with disruptive, contumacious, stubbornly defiant defendants must be given sufficient discretion to meet the circumstances of each case. No one formula for maintaining the appropriate courtroom atmosphere will be best in all situations."

He then went on to discuss each of the three alternatives suggested for dealing with such a defendant, and concluded that removal of the defendant may often be the best way of handling the situation.

There are inherent disadvantages in binding and gagging a defendant. Not only is the use of this technique itself "something of an affront to the very dignity and decorum of judicial proceedings that the judge is seeking to uphold," but it defeats one of the primary purposes behind the right of presence at one's own trial —the opportunity to communicate with counsel. And a contempt citation may have little impact upon a defendant who faces severe punishment if convicted.

"It is not pleasant to hold that the respondent Allen was properly banished from the court for a part of his own trial," Mr. Justice Black observed. "But our courts, palladiums of liberty as they are, cannot be treated disrespectfully with impunity. Nor can the accused be permitted by his disruptive conduct indefinitely to avoid being tried on the charges brought against him. It would degrade our country and our judicial system to permit our courts to be bullied, insulted, and humiliated and their orderly progress thwarted and obstructed by defendants brought before them charged with crimes. As guardians of the public welfare, our state and federal judicial systems strive to administer equal justice to the rich and the poor, the good and the bad, the native and foreign born of every race, nationality and religion. Being manned by humans, the courts are not perfect and are bound to make some errors. But, if our courts are to remain what the Founders intended, the citadels of justice, their proceedings cannot and must not be infected with the sort of scurrilous, abusive language and conduct paraded before the Illinois trial judge in this case."

Concurring, Mr. Justice Brennan observed that "to allow the disruptive activities of a defendant like respondent to prevent his trial is to allow him to profit from his own wrong. The Constitution would protect none of us if it prevented the courts from acting to preserve the very processes which the Constitution itself prescribes."

Mr. Justice Brennan "would add only" that the court should make reasonable efforts to enable an excluded defendant to communicate with his attorney and to keep him apprised of the progress of the trial.

Mr. Justice Douglas had no difficulty "with the basic hypothesis of this decision," but he thought the case of a mentally ill bank robber a poor one to resolve such issues. Furthermore, Mr. Justice Douglas noted that this trial took place 14 years ago, and maintained that the Court was dealing with a stale record.

California v. Green, 399 U.S. 149, 7 CrL 3164

Emphasizing that the Confrontation Clause is not a mere "codification of the hearsay rules," the Court gave its blessing to a California law that permits the use, for purposes of establishing guilt, of a witness' pretrial statements conflicting with his trial testimony. The Confrontation Clause is not violated, the Court held, by a California law that permits the admission of a witness' prior inconsistent statement to prove the truth of the matter asserted therein, whether or not the defense had the opportunity to cross-examine when the original statement was made. Also, a prior statement obtained while the witness was under oath and defense counsel had the opportunity to cross-examine was admissible at trial to prove the truth of the matter asserted therein, whether or not the defense has the opportunity to confront this witness at trial.

In coming to this conclusion, the Court not only reversed the judgment of the California Supreme Court in the case before it, but rejected People v. Johnson, 68 Cal.2d 646, 34 P.2d 111, 4 CrL 3153, in which it had previously denied certiorari. In Johnson, the California Supreme Court held that the Sixth Amendment forbade use of a witness' inconsistent pretrial statements, which were not subject to cross-examination, to show the defendant's guilt.

In the case before the Court, the defendant was accused of selling marijuana to Porter, a 16-year-old, who was the chief prosecution witness at trial. Porter, arrested for possession of marijuana, had told an officer that the defendant had sold him the pot. At the preliminary hearing, where he was cross-examined by defense counsel, Porter again named Green as his supplier. But at trial, he became evasive, claimed he had been "high" at the time he was arrested, and that he didn't know who sold him the marijuana. On cross-examination, pursuant to the

California Penal Code provision, the state was permitted to introduce the preliminary hearing statement for the truth of what Porter had said. Furthermore, the officer to whom Porter made the admission at the time he was arrested was also permitted to testify.

The California Supreme Court was wrong in declaring the statute unconstitutional insofar as it permitted this practice, Mr. Justice White said in his opinion for the majority. This procedure adequately served the purposes of the Confrontation Clause. Confrontation of a hostile witness, Mr. Justice White noted, insures that the witness will give his statements under oath, making clear to him the seriousness of what he says and setting up the perjury penalty as a guard against lies. It forces the witness to submit to cross-examination, and permits the jury to observe the witness' demeanor. All of these protections were present in this case. Even though out-of-court statements may not have been surrounded by any of these protections, once the declarant is present and testifying at trial, his out-of-court statements regain "most of the lost protections. If the witness admits the prior statement is his, or if there is other evidence to show the statement is his, the danger of faulty reproduction is negligible and the jury can be confident that it has before it two conflicting statements by the same witness. Thus, as far as the oath is concerned, the witness must now affirm, deny, or qualify the truth of the prior statement under the penalty of perjury; indeed, the very fact that the prior statement was not given under a similar circumstance may become the witness' explanation for its inaccuracy —an explanation a jury may be expected to understand and take into account in deciding which, if either, of the statements represents the truth.

"Second, the inability to cross-examine the witness at the time he made his prior statement cannot easily be shown to be of crucial significance as long as the defendant is assured of full and effective cross-examination at the time of trial. The most successful cross-examination at the time the prior statement was made could hardly hope to accomplish more than has already been accomplished by the fact that the witness is now telling a different, inconsistent story, and —in this case— one that is favorable to the defendant."

But the Court did not stop there; it went on to say "that Porter's preliminary hearing testimony was admissible as far as the Constitution is concerned wholly apart from the question of whether respondent had an effective opportunity for confrontation at the subsequent trial. For Porter's statement at the preliminary hearing had already been given under circumstances closely approximating those that surround the typical trial. * * * Under these circumstances, Porter's statement would, we think, have been admissible at trial even in Porter's absence if Porter had been actually unavailable, despite good-faith efforts of the State to produce him."

Examining its recent cases dealing with the Confrontation Clause, the Court found nothing in Pointer v. Texas, 380 U.S. 400, Barber v. Page, 390 U.S. 719, 3 CrL 3048, or Bruton v. U.S., 391 U.S. 123, 3 CrL 3085, that compelled a contrary result.

In giving its approval to the use of this California procedure, the Court also noted that the statute represents a minority view among different jurisdictions, but one that is supported by most legal commentators.

Concurring fully, the Chief Justice emphasized "the importance of allowing the States to experiment and innovate, especially in the area of criminal justice."

To Mr. Justice Harlan, concurring, "The precise holding of the Court today is that the Confrontation Clause of the Sixth Amendment does not preclude the introduction of an out-of-court declaration, taken under oath and subject to cross-examination, to prove the truth of the matters asserted therein, when the declarant is available for being a witness at trial."

To Mr. Justice Harlan, the California Supreme Court's contrary holding was "the result of an understandable misconception, as I see things, of numerous decisions of this Court, old and recent, that have indiscriminately equated 'confrontation' with 'cross-examination.'"

This decision reveals the need to take a fresh look at the constitutional concept of "confrontation," Mr. Justice Harlan said, and, in view of the scant evidence of its intended scope, urged two conclusions. "First, the * * * Clause * * * reaches no farther than to require the prosecution to *produce* any *available* witness whose declarations it seeks to use in a criminal trial. Second, even were this conclusion deemed untenable as a matter of Sixth Amendment law, it is surely agreeable to Fourteenth Amendment 'due process,' which, in my view, is the constitutional framework in which state cases of this kind should be judged."

Mr. Justice Brennan was the lone dissenter. Neither the prior extrajudicial statement of a witness who claims at trial to be unable to remember the event, nor a preliminary hearing statement, even when made under oath and subject to cross-examination, can be introduced at trial as substantive evidence "without unconstitutionally restricting the right of the accused to challenge incriminating evidence in the presence of the factfinder who will determine his guilt or innocence."

As far as Mr. Justice Brennan was concerned, Barber v. Page had established that a pretrial statement obtained at a preliminary hearing, with the protections of oath and cross-examination, was indistinguishable for confrontation purposes from an extrajudicial statement.

RIGHT TO COUNSEL

Coleman v. Alabama, 399 U.S. 1, 7 CrL 3121

From seven opinions among the eight Justices who participated emerged the rule that an Alabama preliminary hearing, when it is held, is a "critical stage" of a criminal proceeding, at which counsel is required.

Four other Justices, three of whom also wrote opinions of their own, joined with Mr. Justice Brennan in holding that the Sixth Amendment requires counsel at the Alabama preliminary hearing even though the prosecutor can bypass it by taking his case directly to the grand jury. Also, the defendant does not waive defenses by not presenting them, and no evidence brought out at a preliminary hearing where the petitioner does not have counsel can be used against him at trial.

However, these factors did not mean that the Alabama preliminary hearing was not "a critical stage," Mr. Justice Brennan emphasized. A lawyer's cross-examination of witnesses at such a hearing might well expose fatal weakness in the state's case. His examination of witness might also provide him with a vital impeachment tool for cross-examination at trial, or might help him preserve testimony favorable to the defendant. He can also discover the state's case to a large degree, and he may be able to obtain bail or an earlier psychiatric examination if desirable or necessary.

Mr. Justice Stewart, joined by the Chief Justice in dissent, found no precedent for this holding. The majority is really concerned here with assuring a fair trial, rather than a fair preliminary hearing, he maintained. If this was the case, then Mr. Justice Stewart saw no reason to reverse a conviction following a trial that was not shown to be in any way influenced by anything that happened at the preliminary hearing.

With respect to the majority's remand to the Alabama courts to determine whether denial of counsel at the hearing was harmless error, Mr. Justice Stewart observed, "all I can say is that if the Alabama courts can figure out what they are supposed to do with this case now that it has been remanded to them, their perceptiveness will far exceed mine."

The Chief Justice agreed "that as a matter of sound policy counsel should be made available to all persons subjected to a preliminary hearing and that this should be provided either by statute or by the rulemaking process. However, I cannot accept the notion that the Constitution commands it because it is a 'criminal prosecution.'" The Chief Justice went on to state his disagreement with the position taken by Justices Harlan and White that what the Court said lately "controls over the Constitution." Mr. Justice Harlan disagreed with the majority's reasoning and conclusion but felt compelled by recent Supreme Court case law to concur.

While he expressed his wholehearted agreement with the Court's holding, Mr. Justice Black feared "that the Court's opinion seems at times to proceed on the premise that the constitutional principle ultimately at stake here is not the defendant's right to counsel as guaranteed by the Sixth and Fourteenth Amendments but rather a right to a 'fair trial as conceived by judges.'"

The Court also held that Coleman's 1966 lineup at which counsel was not present did not require reversal of a conviction obtained after in-court identification alone, and not the lineup identification, was used at trial.

FAIR TRIAL

In re Winship, 397 U.S. 358, 7 CrL 3007

The Court made fact out of widely believed fiction this Term by holding that the Constitution compels the "proof beyond a reasonable doubt" standard in criminal trials. In an opinion that five Justices joined, Mr. Justice Brennan wrote that the Due Process Clause requires that a conviction of a criminally accused be based upon proof of guilt beyond a reasonable doubt. Furthermore, the same standard applies to the adjudicatory stage of a juvenile court delinquency proceeding in which a youth was charged with an act that would be a crime if committed by an adult.

Mr. Justice Brennan noted that many Supreme Court opinions "indicate that it has long been assumed that proof of a criminal charge beyond a reasonable doubt is constitutionally required." This standard, he went on, "plays a vital role in the American scheme of criminal procedure." It provides "concrete substance for the presumption of innocence."

Use of the standard is essential to the respect and confidence of the community in the criminal law. To maintain such confidence takes a standard of proof which will not leave people "in doubt whether innocent men are being condemned."

Mr. Justice Harlan, concurring, added that "even though the labels used for alternative standards of proof are vague and not a very sure guide to decision-making, the choice of the standard for a particular variety of adjudication does, I think, reflect a very fundamental assessment of the comparative social costs of erroneous factual determinations."

Turning to the question of the application of this standard to juveniles, the Court stated that the same considerations demanding caution in an adult trial are required at a juvenile proceeding. The majority found nothing to the argument that to apply this standard to juvenile proceedings "would risk destruction of the beneficial aspects of the juvenile process."

Chief Justice Burger and Justices Stewart and Black dissented. The Chief Justice and Mr. Justice Stewart maintained that the majority is pushing juvenile courts one step closer toward becoming full-fledged criminal courts.

Mr. Justice Black based his dissent on the contention that the "proof beyond a reasonable doubt" standard, not present anywhere in the Constitution or the Bill of Rights, should not be read into the Due Process Clause.

SPEEDY TRIAL

Dickey v. Florida, 398 U.S. 30, 7 CrL 3085

Without deciding the retroactivity of Klopfer v. North Carolina, 386 U.S. 213, the Court reversed the armed robbery conviction of a Florida defendant who made repeated but unsuccessful efforts during eight years of federal incarceration to have the state try him on armed robbery charges that had been brought against him.

The Chief Justice, writing for the majority, observed: "The right to a speedy trial is not a theoretical or abstract right but one rooted in hard reality on the need to have charges promptly exposed. If the case for the prosecution calls on the accused to meet charges rather than rest on the infirmities of the prosecution's case, as is the defendant's right, the time to meet them is when the case is fresh. Stale claims have never been favored by the law, and far less so in criminal cases. Although a great many accused persons seek to put off the confrontation as long as possible, the right to a prompt inquiry into criminal charges is fundamental and the duty of the charging authority is to provide a prompt trial. This is brought sharply into focus when, as here, the accused presses for an early confrontation with his accusers and with the state. Crowded dockets, the lack of judges or lawyers, and other factors no doubt make some delays inevitable. Here, however, no valid reason for the delay existed; it was exclusively for the convenience of the state. On this record the delay with its consequent prejudice is intolerable as a matter of fact and impermissible as a matter of law."

Mr. Justice Brennan, joined in a concurring opinion by Mr. Justice Marshall, saw a possible retroactivity question; the prosecution here began seven years before Klopfer was decided. Assuming arguendo that Klopfer is not retroactive, he viewed the question as whether the petitioner's trial was unconstitutionally delayed under due process standards applicable to the states prior to Klopfer.

Mr. Justice Brennan believed that not enough attention was given to defining just what the right to speedy trial means. Accordingly, he suggested that consideration begin with a study of two groups of issues —those concerned with when the right attaches and those concerned with the criteria by which to judge constitutionality of delays to which the right attaches.

Also concurring, Mr. Justice Harlan thought that speedy trial claims such as this one should be judged by principles of procedural fairness as required by the Due Process Clause rather than by "incorporating" the speedy trial provision of the Sixth Amendment into the Fourteenth.

SENTENCING

Williams v. Illinois, 399 U.S. 235, 7 CrL 3185

A state defendant's inability to pay his fine and court costs cannot be permitted to result in his confinement for a longer period than the maximum incarceration period for the offense of which he has been convicted. Such imprisonment, the Court said, violates the Fourteenth Amendment Equal Protection Clause. It constitutes impermissible discrimination between those defendants able to pay and those unable to pay.

"Once the state has defined the outer limits of incarceration necessary to satisfy its penological interest and policies," the Chief Justice reasoned in his opinion for the Court, "it may not then subject a certain class of convicted defendants to a period of imprisonment beyond the statutory maximum solely by reason of their indigency."

The Court emphasized that its holding did not deal with the confinement for nonpayment in the case of alternative punishments such as "$30 or 30 days." Nor was it deciding whether a state can, in other circumstances, hold an indigent accountable for a fine by penal sanction. "We hold only that the Equal Protection Clause of the Fourteenth Amendment requires that the statutory ceiling placed on imprisonment for any substantive offense be the same for all defendants irrespective of their economic status."

Concurring in the result, Mr. Justice Harlan called the majority's equal protection reasoning "a wolf in a sheep's clothing." That rationale, he contended, is no more than a masquerade of a supposedly objective standard for subjective judicial judgment as to what state legislation offends notions of "fundamental fairness." Mr. Justice Harlan would have decided the case on due process grounds.

The Court's equal protection reasoning, if carried to its logical conclusion, he said, would require that the consequences of punishment be comparable for all individuals, forcing the state to "embark on the impossible task of developing a system of individualized fines, such that the total disutility of the entire fine, or the marginal disutility of the last dollar taken, would be the same for all individuals."

From his due process reasoning, Mr. Justice Harlan concluded that when a state declares its penal interest may be satisfied by a fine in combination with a jail term, the administrative inconvenience in a judgment collection procedure "does not as a matter of due process justify sending to jail or extending the jail term of individuals who possess no accumulated assets."

Morris v. Schoonfield, 399 U.S. 508, 7 CrL 3219

In a decision related to Williams v. Illinois, the Court, by per curiam order, vacated the judgment of a federal district court which held that Maryland may constitutionally require that fines be worked out at a fixed rate per day. Maryland had recently passed legislation in this area, and the Court remanded for reconsideration in the light of the intervening legislation and Williams v. Illinois.

Concurring Justices White, Douglas, Brennan, and Marshall maintained that "the same constitutional defect condemned in Williams also inheres in jailing an indigent for failing to make immediate payment of any fine, whether or not the fine is accompanied by a jail term and whether or not the indigent's jail term extends beyond the maximum term that may be imposed on a person willing and able to pay the fine."

These Justices contended that the Constitution prohibits a state from imposing a fine as a sentence and then automatically converting it into a jail term solely because the defendant cannot pay. They believed that Williams does not mean that a state cannot jail a person who has the means but refuses to pay the fine. Nor does it answer the question whether the state's interest in deterring unlawful conduct and "enforcing its penal laws through fines as well as jail sentences will justify imposing an 'equivalent' jail sentence on the indigent who * * * is unable to secure the necessary funds."

DOUBLE JEOPARDY

Ashe v. Swenson, 397 U.S. 436, 7 CrL 3020

A direct consequence of the announcement in Benton v. Maryland, 395 U.S. 784, 5 CrL 3141, that the Double Jeopardy Clause applies to the states, was the Court's holding this Term that the doctrine of collateral estoppel, long an established rule of federal criminal law, "is a part of the Fifth Amendment's guarantee against double jeopardy." Thus, a majority concluded that a Missouri armed robbery defendant should not have been tried for the robbery of one victim in a single, multi-victim, poker game robbery after he had been acquitted on a charge of robbing another victim by a verdict which meant the jury had concluded that he was not one of the robbers.

Twelve years earlier, in Hoag v. New Jersey, 356 U.S. 464, the Court had found no denial of due process in a case that, with a fact situation nearly identical to this one, also involved a first trial and acquittal of robbing one victim and then a second trial for the robbery of another victim. In light of Benton, Mr. Justice Stewart said in his opinion for the majority, the question was no longer one of due process, but collateral estoppel's embodiment in the Double Jeopardy Clause. The longstanding status of collateral estoppel as a federal rule and the extreme importance of the principle it stands for led the Court to formally announce that it has constitutional status. Thus, its applicability must be decided "through an examination of the entire record."

Mr. Justice Stewart found that collateral estoppel obviously applied to the facts of this case. Collateral estoppel, he noted, "means simply that when an issue of ultimate fact once has been determined by a valid and final judgment, that issue cannot again be litigated between the same parties in any future lawsuit."

At this defendant's first trial, "the single rationally conceivable issue in dispute before the jury was whether the petitioner had been one of the robbers. And the jury by its verdict found that he had not. The federal rule of law, therefore, would make a second prosecution for the robbery of [another] wholly impermissible."

The Court went on to explain that "the question is not whether Missouri could validly charge the petitioner with six separate offenses for the robbery of the six poker players. It is not whether he could have received a total of six punishments if he had been convicted in a single trial of robbing the six victims. It is simply whether, after a jury determined by its verdict that the petitioner was not one of the robbers, the State could constitutionally hale him before a new jury to litigate that issue again."

Justices Brennan, Douglas, and Marshall, while agreeing that collateral estoppel is incorporated as a constitutional requirement, maintained that its application was not necessary to a holding that a second prosecution was barred here. The "single transaction" test should be accorded constitutional status, Mr. Justice Brennan said, and both prosecutions here "grew out of one criminal episode."

The "same evidence" test in effect in a majority of American jurisdictions is completely inadequate to protect a defendant's right against double jeopardy, they argued. This test "permits multiple prosecutions where a single transaction is divisible into chronologically discrete crimes." And, "given the tendency of modern criminal legislation to divide the phases of a criminal transaction into numerous separate crimes, the opportunities for multiple prosecutions for an essentially unitary criminal episode are frightening."

In the view of these three Justices, "the Double Jeopardy Clause requires the prosecution, except in most limited circumstances, to join at one trial all the charges against a defendant which grow out of a single criminal act, occurrence, episode, or transaction."

Having acceded to Benton, Mr. Justice Harlan also concurred in this decision. However, he made explicit his understanding that the majority's opinion did not hold that the Double Jeopardy Clause embraced the "same transaction" concept espoused by Mr. Justice Brennan.

Dissenting, the Chief Justice found nothing in the Double Jeopardy Clause to justify the majority's treatment of collateral estoppel.

The majority's decision was, to the Chief Justice, a case of expanding a sound principle beyond the limits or needs of its objectives to produce "a strange mutant." While collateral estoppel ordinarily applies to the same parties on each side of a case, the Chief Justice noted, or to those whose interests are identical with the parties in the initial litigation, the complainant in the second trial here is not the same as the complainant in the first, even though the state was a party in both cases. And, certainly the doctrine would not be applied here to both parties; "if Ashe had been convicted at the first trial, presumably no court would then hold that he was thereby foreclosed from litigating the identification issue at the second trial." And, if the Court was justifying its superimposition of a new brand of collateral estoppel on the "same evidence test," on the grounds of preventing harassment of a defendant, "this case does not remotely suggest harassment of an accused who robbed six victims and the harassment aspect does not rise to constitutional levels."

The majority's analysis of the facts completely disregarded the confusion surrounding the identification issue, the Chief Justice maintained, and it was not clear at all that the defendant's acquittal meant the jury believed he was elsewhere at the time of the robbery. Moreover, Mr. Justice Brennan's "same transaction" approach "like

that taken by the Court totally overlooks the significance of there being six entirely separate charges of robbery against six individuals."

Waller v. Florida, 397 U.S. 387, 7 CrL 3017

The same day that Ashe v. Swenson was announced, the Court unanimously held that, for purposes of prosecuting a defendant for a single act, state and municipal governments are not separate sovereignties. Thus, a civil rights protester who had removed from a public building paintings he found offensive could not be tried by the state for grand larceny after he had already been convicted in municipal court for disturbing the peace and malicious destruction. Both charges, the Chief Justice observed, were based on the same act.

The potential effect of this holding on state and municipal law enforcement was indicated by the Chief Justice's observation that many other states besides Florida have treated municipalities and the state as "separate sovereign entities, each capable of imposing punishment for the same alleged crime." The state-municipalities relationship was simply not analogous to the relationship between the federal government and the state. Thus, Florida's reliance upon Bartkus v. Illinois, 359 U.S. 121, and Abbate v. U.S., 395 U.S. 187, was misplaced. Rather, the state-municipalities relationship is controlled by Grafton v. U.S., 206 U.S. 333, which held that prosecution in a United States court is a bar to a subsequent prosecution by a territorial court, since both are arms of the same sovereign.

Mr. Justice Black joined in the Court's opinion, adhering to the views expressed in his dissenting opinions in Bartkus and Abbate. Mr. Justice Brennan, also concurring, added that "unless this case fell within one of the exceptions to the 'same transaction rule,' that rule applied here."

Price v. Georgia, 398 U.S. 323, 7 CrL 3103

The Court was also unanimous in holding that retrial of a state defendant on a murder charge following his successful appeal from a conviction of the lesser included offense of manslaughter violated the Double Jeopardy Clause despite the fact that his second trial also resulted in a mere manslaughter conviction.

The court thus followed the rationale of Green v. U.S., 355 U.S. 184, which reasoned that a guilty verdict on the lesser included offense constituted an "implicit acquittal" of the greater crime. The fact that on retrial, Green was convicted of the greater charge and Price was not, made no difference. The risk, the Chief Justice said for the Court, was the same, and the Double Jeopardy Clause is written "in terms of potential risk of conviction, not punishment."

The harmless error rule did not apply here. The defendant's ordeal of being charged and subjected to a second first-degree murder trial was "an ordeal not to be viewed lightly." Also, it was impossible to determine whether or not the murder charge induced the jury to settle for a lesser verdict rather than continue to debate the defendant's possible innocence.

Left undecided was the question whether the defendant could be retried once more for manslaughter, which depended on the construction of several Georgia statutes and the power of the state court to fashion remedial orders. Thus, the Court remanded the case to Georgia.

Moon v. Maryland, 398 U.S. 319, 7 CrL 3101

Whether North Carolina v. Pearce, 395 U.S. 711, 5 CrL 3119, applies retroactively remains an unresolved question. The Court decided it had improvidently granted certiorari in a case that presented this issue after the trial judge submitted an affidavit explaining why he had imposed a harsher sentence after the 1968 burglary retrial of a successful appellant. Also, defense counsel had conceded that the imposition of the harsher sentence was not vindictive.

SELF-INCRIMINATION

The scope of the Fifth Amendment privilege against self-incrimination, greatly expanded in recent years, grew no more this Term. Each defendant whose self-incrimination claims were heard on the merits wound up a loser.

Minor v. U.S. and Buie v. U.S., 396 U.S. 87, 6 CrL 3014

Particularly noteworthy, in view of the Court's recent holding in Leary v. U.S., 395 U.S. 6, 5 CrL 3053, was its decision this Term that the protections afforded a marijuana purchaser against the order form requirements of the Marijuana Tax Act, 26 U.S.C. Sec. 4742, are not available to a seller of marijuana. Likewise, the privilege was held unavailable to a seller of narcotics or marijuana under 26 U.S.C. Sec. 4705 (a).

The Court, in an opinion by Mr. Justice White, found "no real and substantial possibility that" an unregistered marijuana purchaser would be willing to comply with the order form requirement of Section 4742, particularly in view of the fact that Leary had relieved him of any duty to pay the transfer tax or secure the incriminating order form. The seller is simply not confronted by the same dilemma that faced a buyer before the announcement of Leary. To avoid the federal penalty for failing to secure the form or pay the tax, a marijuana purchaser was forced to incriminate himself under other laws. However, the buyer does not face the first horn of this dilemma; should he refuse to secure the order form, the option of making a legal sale under federal law is simply foreclosed. In such an event, the seller simply cannot sell at all. There is no real and substantial possibility that a seller will in any way face incrimination "for the simple reason that sellers will seldom, if ever, be confronted with an unregistered purchaser who is willing and able to secure the order form."

For similar reasons, the Court reached the same result concerning a seller of heroin convicted of selling narcotics without the written order required by 26 U.S.C 4705 (a).

The Court rejects this defendant's argument that compliance with the order form provision would have compelled him to give incriminating information that would be readily accessible to any law enforcement agents. This argument, Mr. Justice White said, foundered on reality; there is no substantial possibility that the buyer would or could have secured an order form. Virtually all dealings in heroin are illicit. There are virtually no sales in which any order form can be involved. Once more, "full and literal compliance" with Section 4705 (a) "leaves the seller only one alternative: not to sell."

Justices Douglas and Black dissented as to the marijuana seller. Mr. Justice Douglas claimed that "the government is punishing an individual for failing to do something that the government had made it impossible for him to do — obtain an order form from the prospective purchaser prior to making a sale of heroin."

Turner v. U.S., 396 U.S. 398, 6 CrL 3043

Yet another heroin defendant who tried to cash in on Leary's good luck with marijuana was rebuffed by the Court. Affirming a conviction under 21 U.S.C. 174 for receiving, concealing, and facilitating the transportation and concealment of heroin while knowing that it had been unlawfully imported into the U.S., the Court found nothing wrong with the presumption permitted by Section 174 that a heroin possessor knew of its illegal importation. Mr. Justice White, writing the majority opinion, pointed to the overwhelming evidence that heroin is neither produced domestically nor legally imported. Thus, this presumption was not flawed, as was a similar presumption under 21 U.S.C. Sec. 176a with respect to marijuana.

However, the Court also held that the Section 174 inference is not permissible as to a possessor of cocaine, which is both domestically produced and legally imported in large quantities.

Also, the extreme improbability that a package of heroin would ever be legally stamped was held to permit the presumption that the possessor of a large quantity of heroin violated 26 U.S.C. Sec. 4704 by purchasing it not in or from the original, tax-stamped packages. Further, a large quantity of heroin was involved here; it was unlikely that it could have been obtained other than by illegal purchase. But the same presumption was held improperly applied, either as to purchase or distribution, to a possessor of a small quantity of cocaine. He could either have stolen the cocaine or purchased it from the original package bearing tax stamps. He might have intended it solely for his own use.

Concurring, Mr. Justice Marshall was not convinced that the evidence here established that the defendant purchased the heroin.

Justices Black and Douglas accused the majority of weakening or destroying no fewer than eight procedural safeguards guaranteed by the Bill of Rights. The evidence here, the dissenters said, showed only possession of heroin, and two of the three elements necessary to convict —proof that the heroin was illegally imported, and proof of knowledge of illegal importation —were supported by no evidence.

Bryson v. U.S., 396 U.S. 64, 6 CrL 3008

With Justices Douglas and Black again dissenting, the Court also held that a labor leader prosecuted under Section 1001 for furnishing false information while pretending to comply with the requirements of since-repealed Section 9 (h) of the Taft-Hartley Act could not defend against prosecution for his fraud by challenging the validity of the Section 9 (h) requirement itself, Dennis v. U.S., 384 U.S. 855 (1966).

Kordel v. U.S., 397 U.S. 1, 6 CrL 3059

A corporate officer who ran afoul of the Food and Drug Administration lost out in his claim that the Fifth Amendment prohibits the use in a criminal trial of evidence or leads derived from his answer to government interrogatories in an FDA civil libel. The Court held that this claim was barred by his failure at the civil proceeding to plead the Fifth Amendment or to assert that there was no authorized person who could, without risk of self-incrimination, answer the government's interrogatories.

The Court disagreed with the Sixth Circuit's view that the officer's answers were involuntarily given.

Mr. Justice Stewart, writing for the Court, noted that the government did not act in bad faith in obtaining the incriminating information by means of the civil interrogatories.

The Court also held that the FDA is not required to choose either to forego recommendation of a criminal action once it seeks civil relief or to defer a civil prosecution pending the outcome of a criminal trial.

U.S. v. Knox, 396 U.S. 77, 6 CrL 3005

A gambler who nominally complied with the registration requirements of 26 U.S.C. Sec. 4412, but who provided false information, found himself worse off than the defendant in Marchetti v. U.S., 390 U.S. 39, 2 CrL 3102, who never filed at all. In Marchetti, the Court held that the Fifth Amendment against self-incrimination provided an absolute defense against prosecution for failure to file reports under Section 4412. However, the privilege was held to be no bar to a prosecution under 18 U.S.C. Sec. 1001 for filing false information in their Section 4412 report.

The validity of the government's demand for information is not "an element of a violation of Section 1001," Mr. Justice Harlan noted in his opinion for the majority. However, this petitioner will have the opportunity at trial to contend that he committed his crime under compulsion and is not, therefore, criminally responsible.

Mr. Justice Harlan noted that this defendant was being prosecuted neither on the basis of incriminatory information contained in the forms that he had filed, nor for a failure to supply such information. Rather, "he has taken a course other than the one that the statute was designed to compel, a course that the Fifth Amendment gave him no privilege to take."

Justices Douglas and Black dissented, emphasizing that the petitioner was not aware at the time he filed that he had a self-incrimination defense against prosecution for failure to file.

SEARCH AND SEIZURE

Chambers v. Maroney, 399 U.S. 42, 7 CrL 3133

Few search and seizure issues have been in as great a ferment as the question concerning police authority to make warrantless searches of automobiles. Over the past few years, different Supreme Court decisions alternately seemed to limit and then widen that authority. This Term, the Court explicitly announced that policemen who have probable cause to search a car at the time and place of arrest do not violate the Fourth Amendment by conducting a warrantless search at another time and place several hours after arrest. Given probable cause to search, the Court said in an opinion by Mr. Justice White, "for constitutional purposes, we see no difference between * * * seizing and holding a car before presenting probable cause issues to a magistrate and * * * carrying out an immediate search without a warrant."

The Court explicitly stated that Chimel v. California, 395 U.S. 752, 5 CrL 3131, did not purport to modify or affect the rationale of Carroll v. U.S., 282 U.S. 694, in which the Court explicitly recognized a difference between a search of a building and a search of an easily moved vehicle.

Immobilization of an automobile until a warrant can be obtained is just as great an intrusion upon privacy as a warrantless search, the majority thought.

In the same case, the Court also held that the appearance of a Legal Aid Society attorney to represent the defendant at his second trial, minutes before the trial began, was not so belated that the new attorney's legal assistance was ineffective. Furthermore, the Court held an evidentiary hearing was not necessary to determine the claim of ineffectiveness. The only errors that occurred at the trial, the Court noted, were found to be harmless by the court of appeals. The majority was "not disposed to fashion a per se rule requiring reversal of every conviction following tardy appointment of counsel or to hold that, whenever a habeas corpus petition alleges a belated appointment, an evidentiary hearing must be held to determine whether the defendant has been denied his constitutional right to counsel."

Mr. Justice Stewart stated his adherence to the view that the admission at trial of evidence acquired in alleged violation of Fourth Amendment standards is not of itself sufficient ground for a collateral attack upon an otherwise valid criminal conviction, state or federal.

Mr. Justice Harlan dissented from the Court's approval of the automobile search. He accused the majority of ignoring "the framework of our past decisions circumscribing the scope of permissible search without a warrant." Exceptions to the rule that a search must be made pursuant to a warrant should not be extended beyond "the exigencies of particular situations," Mr. Justice Harlan emphasized. Such exceptions should be no broader than absolutely necessary.

It would be no great inconvenience to anyone concerned if police had to hold an automobile until a warrant could be obtained, Mr. Justice Harlan said. And, the endorsement of a "warrantless invasion of * * * privacy where another course would suffice is simply inconsistent with our repeated stress on the Fourth Amendment's mandate of 'adherence to judicial processes.'"

Also, examining the record of the second trial, Mr. Justice Harlan thought the record showed that the counsel's unfamiliarity with the case did prejudice the defendant.

Vale v. Louisiana, 399 U.S. 30, 7 CrL 3130

The warrantless narcotics search of a defendant's house incident to his arrest on the front steps was a violation of the Fourth Amendment, a majority of the Court held. The Court did not need to reach the unanswered question whether Chimel v. California, 395 U.S. 752, 5 CrL 3131, applies retroactively to hold this pre-Chimel search unlawful. No previous opinion of the Court can sustain the constitutional validity of the search in the case before us.

The Chief Justice and Mr. Justice Black saw nothing unreasonable about this search: the officers had interrupted a narcotics transaction. They had probable cause to believe that narcotics were in the house, and did not know if someone else was in the house watching the arrest.

U.S. v. Van Leeuwen, 397 U.S. 249, 6 CrL 3075

Postal officials who detained a suspicious package for 29 hours while waiting to get a search warrant did not violate the Fourth Amendment by their delay, the Court held. Under the circumstances of this case, it took the officials that long to confirm their suspicions about the package and obtain a warrant. The Court, in a unanimous opinion by Mr. Justice Douglas, carefully explained: "The rule of our decision certainly is not that first class mail can be detained 29 hours after mailing in order to obtain the search warrant needed for its inspection. We only hold that on the facts of this case —the nature of the mailings, their suspicious character, the fact that there were two packages going to separate destinations, the unavoidable delay in contacting the more distant of the two destinations, the distance between Mt. Vernon and Seattle —a 29–hour delay between the mailings and the service of the warrant cannot be said to be unreasonable * * *."

Even though papers that one commits to first class mail are as fully protected by the Fourth Amendment as the papers one leaves at home, first class mail is not beyond the reach of all inspections. Here, the Court held, the conditions for detention and inspection were satisfied.

Colonnade Catering Corp. v. U.S., 397 U.S. 72, 6 CrL 3063

Although U.S. treasury agents are authorized to make a warrantless entry and inspection of a liquor licensee's premises, they cannot do so forcibly —even though a licensee's refusal to allow a warrantless entry is a criminal offense. The imposition of a fine for refusal to permit entry, Mr. Justice Douglas said for the majority, is the only sanction for such refusal, "absent a warrant to break and enter."

The Court said that "Where Congress has authorized inspection but made no rules governing the procedure which inspectors must follow, the Fourth Amendment and its various restrictive rules apply."

Joined by the Chief Justice and Mr. Justice Stewart, Mr. Justice Black maintained that the seizure here violated neither the Fourth Amendment nor any federal statute. He saw "no reason on earth" why the conduct in this case, which was based on the officer's observation of a flagrant violation of federal liquor laws, should be condemned as unreasonable.

While the statutes involved do not in express terms authorize forcible breaking and entry, "it is perfectly clear that they do not in express terms declare such seizure illegal, and in my opinion those provisions impliedly authorize exactly the type of official conduct involved here."

Adding his views separately, but also joined by Justices Black and Stewart, the Chief Justice agreed with the majority that there was no constitutional violation here. The statute authorizes entry of any building "so far as it may be necessary for the purpose of examining said articles or objects." The agents, the Chief Justice maintained, acted explicitly under these statutes. Sellers of liquor keep their supplies under lock and key, and surely entry of such premises is a reasonable means of enforcing the inspection necessary to tax collection.

Morales v. New York, 396 U.S. 102, 6 CrL 3013

A case that could have led to one of the Term's most important criminal law decisions —the legality of the "investigatory arrest" —resulted in no ruling at all as the Court sent it back for factual findings. The New York Court of Appeals had approved in principle an arrest without probable cause. The Supreme Court was not convinced that, on the record before it, there might not have been probable cause anyway, that the detained murder suspect's confrontation with the police was not voluntary, or that the confession he made was not in fact the product of illegal detention.

The Court pointed out that the petitioner did not raise the Fourth Amendment legality-of-arrest issue at trial. Thus, there was no adequate factual record to show what basis the police had for arresting him.

Therefore, the Court did not determine whether the supposed New York rule went substantially beyond the limits on stopping a suspect imposed by Terry v. Ohio, 392 U.S. 1, 3 CrL 3149 (1968).

APPEALS

U.S. v. Sisson, 399 U.S. 267, 7 CrL 3194

Under the Criminal Appeals Act, 18 U.S.C. 3731, the government has no right of appeal from a district court's "arrest of judgment" that was, in effect, an acquittal on the basis of facts developed at trial. As a result of this narrow reading of the Criminal Appeals Act, the Court failed to reach the question whether Congress can draft a nonreligious military draft registrant who objects to the Vietnam War, but not to war in general.

Mr. Justice Harlan, who delivered the opinion of the Court, found three reasons to dismiss the government's appeal, but five of the Justices could agree on but one ground —that the order appealed from was bottomed on factual conclusions not found in the indictment but instead made on the basis of evidence adduced at trial.

Mr. Justice Harlan, describing the Act as "awkward and ancient," noted that "three requirements must be met for this Court to have jurisdiction under this provision." First, the decision of the district court must be one "arresting a judgment of conviction." Second, the arrest of judgment must be for the "insufficiency of the indictment or information." And third, the decision must be "based upon the invalidity or construction of the statute upon which the indictment or information is founded."

"Because the District Court's decision rests on facts not alleged in the indictment but instead inferred by the court from the evidence adduced at trial, we conclude that neither the first nor second requirement is met."

To the dissenter's suggestions "that we are too niggardly in our interpretation of the Criminal Appeals Act," Mr. Justice Harlan replied that the government right to appeal is to be strictly limited, and is not viewed with favor.

The Chief Justice, joined by Justices Douglas and White, stated that "my disagreement with the Court's result and rationale is prompted by a fundamental disagreement with the Court's mode of analysis and its excessive reliance on ancient practices of Common Law England long superseded by Acts of Congress."

The use of the facts in this case, the Chief Justice maintained, undisputed at trial and undisputed now, "was akin to a stipulation of facts by parties in a criminal case." But the Chief Justice's disagreement with the Court went deeper than that; "in my view the Criminal Appeals Act contemplates that an arrest of judgment is appropriate in other than a closed category of cases defined by legal history. Specifically, there is no reason for the Court today to read into that class of cases all of the niceties of what might or might not have been included in the 'judgment roll' at common law. We have outgrown those formalisms."

The Court's reasoning, the Chief Justice added, paid scant attention to the purpose of the Act and the problem that Congress attempted to solve by passing it. To make his point, he, like the majority, traced the legislative history of the Act.

Mr. Justice White, joined by the Chief Justice and Mr. Justice Douglas, argued that "not a single passage in the legislative history indicates congressional awareness that the words it was using had the effect of distinguishing cases where a congressional act was held invalid on its face, from cases where it was invalidated as applied to a sub-class within the Act's intended reach. In both cases, the indictment is 'insufficient' to state a valid offense. In both cases, any 'factual findings' necessary to give the particular defendant the benefit of the constitutional ruling are little more than findings as to the defendant's standing to raise the constitutional issue —they are not findings as to the sufficiency of the evidence to prove the offense alleged in the indictment."

The majority's theory, Mr. Justice White claimed, would, if consistently applied, make no case appealable to the Supreme Court for it is always true that a judge might have sent the case to the jury with instructions to acquit if they found the facts alleged in the indictment, "thus insulating the case from review because of the intervening jury acquittal."

Mr. Justice White found "extremely peculiar the path which the Court follows in reaching its conclusion that we cannot hear this case. The 'motion in arrest' provision is confined to its early common-law sense, although there is absolutely no indication that Congress was using the phrase in that sense, and we have never similarly limited the 'motion in bar' provision to its common-law scope."

Gunn v. University Committee to End the War in Vietnam, 399 U.S. 383, 7 CrL 3219

Texas also found itself unable to appeal from a federal district court order effectively foreclosing prosecution. Six Justices agreed that a three-judge district court's failure to enter any injunctive order after finding that a Texas disturbing-the-peace statute was unconstitutional, coupled with the district court's failure to find that the demonstrators were entitled to injunctive and declaratory relief, barred the state's appeal to the Supreme Court under Section 1253 of the Judicial Code. Although the district court had stated that the plaintiffs were entitled to declaratory judgment, it stayed such a mandate until the Texas legislature would have the opportunity to enact a constitutionally sound disturbing-the-peace statute. Until an injuction is issued, Mr. Justice Stewart explained for the majority, "it is simply not possible to know with any certainty what the court has decided —a state of affairs that is conspicuously evident here." Thus, the appeal was dismissed for lack of jurisdiction.

HABEAS CORPUS

Nelson v. George, 399 U.S. 224, 7 CrL 3182

Peyton v. Rowe, 391 U.S. 54, 3 CrL 3093, does not automatically provide a prisoner in one state with a shortcut means of challenging by federal habeas corpus another state's conviction, the Court indicated. With only Mr. Justice Douglas dissenting, the Court held that a California prisoner under a North Carolina detainer was not entitled to test the validity of his North Carolina sentence in a California federal court until he had first sought a California state court determination as to the effect of the detainer on his parole potential and custodial status. However, once this requirement was satisfied, the California federal court would then have jurisdiction to consider the petitioner's claims with respect to the impact of the detainer.

The Court reserved judgment as to the continuing vitality of Ahrens v. Clark, 335 U.S. 188.

The Court noted that prisoners under federal sentence do not face the dilemma of the petitioner here; they may bring a challenge at any time in the sentencing court, wherever they may be incarcerated. Sound judicial administration, the Chief Justice wrote, called for an amendment to Section 2241, the federal habeas corpus statute, to afford a state prisoner the same opportunity for challenging a conviction as that enjoyed by a federal prisoner.

Justices Harlan and Marshall, concurring, also saw the need for congressional action requested by the majority. In the meantime, they thought it "not inappropriate to leave undisturbed such conflicts as exist" between the various federal courts of appeals on this point.

It is the North Carolina court judgment, not merely the detainer, that the prisoners attack here, Mr. Justice Douglas maintained.

Wade v. Wilson, 396 U.S. 282, 6 CrL 3019

A seven-Justice majority refused to consider a contention of a California prisoner, who had neither sought to borrow the California attorney general's copy of his trial transcript for habeas corpus use nor applied to California's courts to direct someone in possession of a transcript to furnish him a copy, that the California rule of court providing a free transcript only to one of two or more jointly tried defendants not under the death sentence denied him equal protection of the laws, and imposed an unconstitutional burden of his right to seek post-conviction relief.

FIRST AMENDMENT

Schacht v. U.S., 398 U.S. 58, 7 CrL 3093

Both of the First Amendment cases that were decided on their merits in the 1969–70 Term related to antiwar protests. In an opinion which also made the point that late certiorari petitions can be allowed, the Court held that an antiwar-skit performer who wore an Army cap and "blouse" came within the 10 U.S.C. Sec. 772 theatrical exemption from Section 702 of the Criminal Code, which punishes unauthorized use of military uniform.

While the Court, speaking through Mr. Justice Black, had no doubt that Section 702 is constitutional on its face, it found the actor was entitled to Section 722's protection

and that Section 722f, which allows exceptions "only if the portrayal does not tend to discredit" the armed forces, was unconstitutional.

The Court rejected an argument by the Solicitor General that the time limitation of Supreme Court Rule 22(2) is jurisdictional and cannot be waived by the court. Citing Stern and Gressman, Supreme Court Practice (Fourth Ed., 1969), the majority stated that this rule "contains no language which calls for so harsh an interpretation * * *"

Bachellar v. Maryland, 397 U.S. 564, 7 CrL 3051

A group of Maryland antiwar protesters with no theatrical pretensions at all also obtained reversal of their convictions, on the basis of a showing that their convictions might have resulted from a jury charge that allowed a finding of guilt merely because their views on Vietnam were offensive to some onlookers. Mr. Justice Brennan, writing for the Court, observed that, while the convictions could have constitutionally rested on the protesters' blocking a public passageway or refusing to obey police commands, it was equally likely that they were based on the defendant's offensiveness to some members of the crowd they had attracted.

JUVENILES

DeBacker v. Brainard, 396 U.S. 28, 6 CrL 3001

Before it decided, In re Winship, that the "beyond a reasonable doubt" standard of proof applies to juvenile delinquency adjudications involving what would be criminal offenses if committed by adults, the Court dismissed a juvenile case presenting that question.

The dismissed appeal also challenged the constitutionality of a prosecutor's unlimited discretion to try juveniles in a juvenile or adult court, and raised the question whether a juvenile has a right to a jury trial at a delinquency proceeding.

Monks v. New Jersey, 398 U.S. 71, 7 CrL 3097

Over the dissents of Justices Marshall and Douglas, the Court, by a per curiam order, ruled that it had improvidently granted certiorari to review a claim that a juvenile's 1957 murder confession was coerced.

CAPITAL PUNISHMENT

Maxwell v. Bishop, 398 U.S. 262, 7 CrL 3099

A case that might have gone far toward resolving the fate of some 500 prisoners on America's death rows was remanded on the basis of a much narrower finding —that the Arkansas jury selection procedure excluded prospective jurors in violation of Witherspoon v. Illinois, 391 U.S. 510, who oppose capital punishment. The Court reached this conclusion even though the petitioner did not raise the Witherspoon issue until his federal habeas corpus case had reached the Supreme Court. However, the Court simultaneously granted review in two cases potentially presenting the death penalty issues left unresolved in Maxwell.

SELECTIVE SERVICE

Gutknecht v. U.S., 396 U.S. 395, 6 CrL 3023

The use of military conscription as punishment was unanimously disapproved by the Court. The Court, in an opinion by Mr. Justice Douglas, held that there was no congressional authorization in the Military Selective Service Act of 1967, 35 LW 67, for punishing by "delinquency declarations" and accelerated induction, those registrants who violated Selective Service regulations by acts ranging from draft card burning to non-reporting of a new address.

The Selective Service System's delinquency regulations, 32 C.F.R. 1642.4, allowed the local boards to place "delinquents" first in the order of call. Given the great congressional concern, obvious in the legislative history of the Act, for a strictly impartial order of call, the Court found it highly unlikely that Congress would have meant to authorize any such punishments. The Court found no support for the accelerated induction process in those references which the Act does make to "delinquency."

Moreover, the Court emphasized, there exist more orthodox remedies for punishment of those who violate Selective Service regulations. Section 12 of the Act expressly provides for criminal prosecution of those who violate Selective Service laws.

Finally, the Court refused to hold that the registrant's challenge to the delinquency regulations was foreclosed by his failure to take an administrative appeal from the declaration of delinquency. Such failure could not bar his assertion of the regulation's invalidity in his defense to a prosecution for refusing to undergo any induction processing. It is true that administrative remedies have to be exhausted in the appeal of draft classifications, but delinquency orders simply were not classifications. This is true even though the regulations purported to give those declared delinquent a right to appeal the declarations of delinquency.

Of the invalidated delinquency induction scheme, the Court said: "While Section 5(a)(1) provides that 'there shall be no discrimination against any person on account of race or color,' 50 U.S.C. Sec. 455(a)(1), there is no suggestion that as respects other types of discrimination the Selective Service has free-wheeling authority to ride herd on the registrants using immediate induction as a disciplinary or vindictive measure. * * * It is a broad, roving authority, a type of administrative absolutism not congenial to our law-making traditions."

Mr. Justice Harlan, concurring, explained that he saw nothing wrong with the board's placing in class I–A, under the authority of 32 C.F.R. Sec. 1622.10, persons who fail to establish eligibility for another classification, and nothing wrong with the President's promulgating regulations to authorize delinquency induction of those who fail to comply with duty essential to the classification process itself.

Mr. Justice Stewart, concurring, did not reach the question of the delinquency regulations' validity, but emphasized that the conviction was void because the Selective Service System violated its own regulations by failing to give the delinquent his required 30 days to seek a personal appearance and an appeal before it ordered him to report.

Mr. Justice Stewart asserted that the authority to reclassify and accelerate induction by reason of delinquency is justified by a remedial objective. He analogized it to a sentence for civil contempt.

The delinquency regulations purportedly authorized not only accelerated induction of I–A registrants, but also reclassification of those who had deferments or exemptions.

Breen v. Selective Service Local Board No. 16, 396 U.S. 460, 6 CrL 3055

Gutknecht was followed promptly by a decision that this latter form of punishment for "delinquency" was also unauthorized by the 1967 Act.

A majority of the Court, in an opinion by Mr. Justice Black, unhesitatingly extended Gutknecht to the "delinquency" forfeiture of a student's II–S deferment.

The student had been reclassified I–A for failure to possess the draft card that he had publicly surrendered in an antiwar demonstration.

When Congress in the Military Selective Service Act of 1967 took over from the President the business of promulgating standards for student deferments, the majority said, it did not in any way indicate that the deferments could be denied for failure to possess a draft card.

Another important procedural question was resolved by the Court's expressly extending the procedural rule of Oestereich v. Local Board, 393 U.S. 233, 5 CrL 3113, to draft cases involving lost deferments. Oestereich had held that Section 10(b)(3) of the Act did not bar a pre-induction judicial review of local board action depriving a registrant of a statutorily granted "exemption." The Court found that under Section 6(h)(i) of the Act, undergraduate student deferments are also congressionally mandated —even though the President is given the power to regulate the granting of them. And what Congress giveth, only Congress can take away.

Mr. Justice Harlan, concurring, reiterated his concurring sentiments in Oestereich —that the availability of preinduction review should turn, not on what amounts to an advance decision on the merits, but rather on the nature of the challenge being made. A challenge such as that involved here is one of "facial unconstitutionality," and not a challenge to factual and discretionary decision-making peculiarly within the province of a local board.

Mr. Justice Stewart and the Chief Justice concurred only in part. They did not believe the delinquency regulations to be unauthorized by Congress.

Mulloy v. U.S., 398 U.S. 410, 7 CrL 3118

Without answering the big question —currently dividing the circuits —whether reopening of a draft classification after the induction order has been sent is required in conscientious objector "crystallization" cases —the Court lent its unanimous endorsement to a view already adopted by virtually all the Courts of Appeals. A draft board, it was held, must reopen the I–A classification of a registrant who before the induction order presents a prima facie claim for conscientious objector classification based on non-frivolous allegations of fact not conclusively refuted by other information in his file.

In an opinion by Mr. Justice Stewart, the Court held that a local board abused its discretion by refusing to reopen when presented with such a claim —even though the wording of 32 C.F.R. Sec. 1625.2 is that a local board "may" reopen and reconsider a classification upon the presentation of new facts relevant to the classification criteria.

Nor does it make any difference that the local board, without reopening, gave the registrant a "courtesy interview" at which it supposedly considered his conscientious objection claim. This is not the same thing as an actual reopening —as the registrant himself found out when, thinking it had been a reopening, he tried to appeal from the rejection, announced after the interview, of his new application.

Welsh v. U.S., 398 U.S. 333, 7 CrL 3106

Although it cast doubt on the oft-used "personal or moral code" ground for denial of conscientious objector status, the Court did not take the opportunity to reach the issue of possible irreconcilable conflict between the Establishment Clause and the Free Exercise Clause in the law's provisions for conscientious objector exemption in a case involving the "religious" objection problem. The case turned upon the old Universal Military Training and Service Act, and the opinion was essentially an interpretation and application of U.S. v. Seeger, 380 U.S. 163 (1965). Moreover, the Justices were so far from unanimity that what could legitimately be called a majority opinion stood for an extremely narrow proposition.

Mr. Justice Black, joined by Justices Douglas, Brennan, and Marshall, declared that even though a registrant's beliefs were purely ethical and moral in source and content, he was nevertheless a "religious" objector under the Seeger definition of religious objection.

Mr. Justice Harlan, however, called the Seeger opinion dead wrong as an interpretation of congressional intent. Acknowledging his original "mistake" in concurring in Seeger, Mr. Justice Harlan declared that even though

Congress did not intend to exempt objectors who are not "religious" in the traditional sense, the Court could save Section 6(j) of the Universal Military Training and Service Act from fatally conflicting with the Establishment Clause. It was doing this, he said, by reading into the statute the Seeger-type broad definition of religious exemption.

Mr. Justice White, joined in dissent by the Chief Justice and Mr. Justice Stewart, agreed that Congress did not intend the broad definition of religious objection. However, Congress can legitimately exempt religious objectors without running afoul of the Establishment Clause, the dissent maintained. A discrimination which is designed to avoid possible violation of the Free Exercise Clause is certainly a reasonable one, and, furthermore, the preference of religious objectors may be based on a simple value judgment by Congress that forcing them into the military would be impractical from the military's own point of view.

Toussie v. U.S., 397 U.S. 112, 6 CrL 3067

One puzzling aspect of the draft laws was cleared up, to the satisfaction of at least the majority of the Court, by a 5–3 holding that the general five-year limitation of 18 U.S.C. Sec. 3282 bars the prosecution of a 26-year-old for his failure, at age 18, to register for the draft. The offense is not a continuing one, Mr. Justice Black wrote for the majority, but is completed when an 18-year-old fails to register within five days of his eighteenth birthday.

It is true that a Selective Service regulation refers to registration as a continuing duty, the Court acknowledged. But an administrative regulation cannot turn what is clearly a one-time statutory offense into a continuing one. The Court found no language in the draft act that "clearly contemplates a prolonged course of conduct."

Mr. Justice White, joined in his dissent by the Chief Justice and Mr. Justice Harlan, thought it obvious that the duty to register should naturally continue as long as liability to the draft continues —i.e., until age 26. The government should have five years after the registrant reaches that age to prosecute.

The dissenters pointed out that this doubly immunizes the scofflaw who is home free at 23 while all law abiding 23-26 year olds are being inducted. The dissenters also attacked the self-incrimination argument of the registrant, although this argument was not relied upon by the majority. They pointed out that if the failure to register is a continuing offense, the non-registrant is still subject to only one prosecution based on his single uninterrupted course of criminal conduct. Finally, they urged that greater weight should be given to the agency's interpretation of the statute it is charged with carrying out.

1970–1971 Term

The main thrust of the criminal law revolution carried out by the Court in the Sixties may have ended with the advent of the Seventies. But the controversy generated during the 1970–71 Term by the efforts of shifting majorities to extend, limit, or reverse the effects of this revolution matched anything seen or heard during the "Warren Court" era. More often than not, the Court divided sharply in deciding particularly significant cases. Several landmark decisions of the past decade were modified. State criminal defendants' access to the federal courts pending prosecution, expanded considerably in 1965, was narrowed significantly. Miranda's exclusionary rule with respect to custodial statements was loosened. Disagreements among the Justices over fundamental Fourth Amendment questions left that area of the law in a state of flux. And the Court agreed, in the waning days of the Term, to face squarely the constitutionality of capital punishment.

While this Term may have produced few discernible trends, it did portend yet further major changes in the criminal law. The question was not whether the criminal law will continue to change, but what direction the changes will take.

SEARCH AND SEIZURE

A law enforcement official looking for "certainty" in Fourth Amendment law would be sorely disappointed by the Court's decisions during the 1970–71 Term. Criteria announced within the past two years for determining probable cause and reliability of informers and for making warrantless automobile searches, which themselves had had a drastic effect on law enforcement techniques, were so modified this year as to emerge virtually unrecognizable. Further, the Court gave ample warning that no "certainty" with respect to Fourth Amendment case law is in the cards for the near future. Only in voicing dissatisfaction with the present state of Fourth Amendment law were the Justices unanimous.

Mr. Justice Stewart was joined by Justices Douglas, Brennan, and Marshall in suggesting that the Court should take a long, hard look at warrantless entries of dwellings to make arrests.

Mr. Justice White and the Chief Justice, dismayed at the confusion caused by the Court's development of two inconsistent lines of reasoning with respect to the warrant requirement, suggested that one line or another be overruled.

Mr. Justice Harlan attributed present confusion to the application of the Fourth Amendment and its exclusionary rule to the states; he called for overruling Mapp v. Ohio, 367 U.S. 643. The Chief Justice and Justices Black and Blackmun recommended abolishing the exclusionary rule itself.

Coolidge v. New Hampshire, 403 U.S. 443, 9 CrL 3208

Perhaps no other case in Supreme Court history has sparked as thorough a discussion of the Fourth Amendment as did the Coolidge decision in this Term, vacating a 1965 New Hampshire murder conviction based in part on evidence seized from the defendant's car.

Only three Justices indicated disagreement with the Court's holding inadmissible evidence seized under a warrant to search a murder suspect's car issued by the state attorney general, who was actively prosecuting the case. The attorney general was, in effect, a law enforcement officer, and not the "neutral and detached magistrate" required for the issuance of a valid warrant.

Five Justices agreed that the seizure of the car, as it sat parked in front of the suspect's house minutes after the suspect was arrested inside the house, could not be justified under any of the Fourth Amendment's recognized exceptions to the warrant requirement, even though the police had probable cause to believe it contained evidence of the murder and saw it in plain view as they lawfully entered the house. Furthermore, its seizure was not incident to the defendant's arrest.

The Court agreed unanimously, however, that the Fourth Amendment's exclusionary rule did not apply to a rifle — the alleged murder weapon —that the suspect's wife had earlier turned over to police who interviewed her at the house. Her delivery of the rifle, whatever her motive, was the act of a private citizen, and it was a voluntary act.

Beyond these specific holdings, the question of just when the warrant requirement applies to government seizures (including formal arrests) and searches of any kind most sharply divided the Court.

Mr. Justice Stewart believes that a warrantless search or seizure, in whatever form, is presumptively unlawful, and that evidence obtained in this manner must be excluded unless truly exigent circumstances make it much more than just inconvenient to obtain a warrant.

But this view was concurred in by just four Justices with respect to state activity. Mr. Justice Harlan, reiterating and expanding on what he had said in his concurrence in Chimel v. California, 395 U.S. 752, 5 CrL

3131 (1969), agreed that the Fourth Amendment requires this stringent application of the warrant requirement. But he emphasized once more his belief that application of the Fourth amendment and its exclusionary rule to state activity not only is constitutionally unsound, but has seriously impaired the development of sound law enforcement techniques.

Mr. Justice White, speaking for himself and the Chief Justice, spelled out in greater detail what was implicit in his dissent in Chimel and his opinion for the Court in Chambers v. Maroney, 399 U.S. 42, 8 CrL 3133: reasonableness, rather than strict application of the warrant requirement, should be the criterion for a warrantless seizure by police who are lawfully at the place they make the seizure.

The very concept of a judicially fashioned Fourth Amendment exclusionary rule was attacked by Mr. Justice Black, who was joined on this point by the Chief Justice and Mr. Justice Blackmun.

In rejecting the contention that Chambers v. Maroney authorized the kind of warrantless car search made in this case, the majority found none of the justifications present in Maroney or Carroll v. U.S., 267 U.S. 132. This simply was not a case where "it is not practicable to secure a warrant." Rather, this case is controlled by Dyke v. Taylor Implement Mfg. Co., 391 U.S. 216, in which there was not only no probable cause to search a parked automobile, but, as here, no exigent circumstances. The police in the present case would have encountered no inconvenience at all in obtaining a warrant. There was not the slightest danger that the car would be removed.

As for the plain view argument, plain view itself is never, standing alone, enough to justify a warrantless seizure. Police must, of course, be lawfully on the premises. But this is not enough; a discovery of evidence in plain view must be inadvertent, and here, the police had ample opportunity to obtain a valid warrant. "They knew the automobile's exact description and location well in advance; they intended to seize it when they came upon Coolidge's property." Nor, even under pre-Chimel law governing searches incident to arrest, could this seizure of the car be deemed incident to the arrest inside the house.

Mr. Justice White disagreed with the majority both as to the plain view and warrantless automobile search questions. Grafting the "inadvertence" rule onto the plain view doctrine accomplished nothing but the muddying of already-clouded Fourth Amendment waters, he maintained. It protects no right not already protected by the law, and its application would only lead to "undue consequences to what will most often be an unintended mistake or a misapprehension of some of this Court's probable cause decisions, a failing which, I am afraid, we all have." The plain view aspect of the holding, Mr. Justice White said, was limited to the protection offered by the Fourth Amendment to "effects" rather than personal papers or documents. Mr. Justice White discussed each of the various contexts in which he thought this new "plain view" requirement would arise,

and the anomalous consequences that would flow from it in each of these areas. Although he would have upheld this search on the basis of the plain view doctrine, Mr. Justice White also disagreed with the majority's view of the warrant requirement for automobile searches. The majority's apparent distinction between "moving" and "movable" vehicles was "a metaphysical distinction without roots in the common sense standard of reasonableness governing search and seizure cases." Dyke, upon which the majority purports to rely, was decided on the basis of lack of probable cause —had there been probable cause, it would have been decided the other way. The majority's reading of Carroll and Cooper is wrong, he suggested. "I find nothing in the language or the underlying rationale of the line of cases from Carroll to Chambers limiting vehicle searches as the Court now limits them in situations such as the one before us. Although each of those cases may * * * have involved vehicles or vessels in motion prior to their being stopped and searched, each of them approved the search of a vehicle that was no longer moving and, with the occupants in custody, no more likely to move than the unattended but movable vehicle parked on the street or in the driveway of a person's house. In both situations the probability of movement at the instance of family or friends is equally real, and hence the result should be the same whether the car is at rest or in motion when it is discovered."

Concluding, Mr. Justice White suggested that the Court either "overrule our prior cases and treat automobiles precisely as we do houses or apply those cases to readily movable as well as moving vehicles and thus treat searches of automobiles as we do the arrest of a person."

Replying to Mr. Justice White's objections to its interpretation of the automobile and plain view exceptions, Mr. Justice Stewart noted that at the heart of the disagreement was the question of when a warrantless intrusion into a suspect's premises is permissible.

This question, he emphasized, has not been squarely faced by the Court, and the conflicting views represented in his opinion and Mr. Justice White's have been responsible for much of the inconsistency in the Court's holdings with respect to the Fourth Amendment's Warrant Clause. The arguments against the position that a warrantless entry is per se unreasonable, absent special difficulties in obtaining a warrant, lose their force if it is assumed that police must have an arrest warrant for entry in the absence of one of the defined exceptions. "It is clear, then, that the notion that the warrantless entry of a man's house in order to arrest him on probable cause is per se legitimate is in fundamental conflict with the basic principle of Fourth Amendment law that searches and seizures inside a man's house without warrant are per se unreasonable in the absence of some one of a number of well defined exigent circumstances." This conflict, which came to the fore in Chimel's case also arises here, Mr. Justice Stewart noted. "And if Mr. Justice White is correct that it has generally been assumed that the Fourth Amendment is not violated by the warrantless entry of a man's house for purposes of arrest, it might be wise to re-examine the assumption."

To take Mr. Justice White's view would be to simply "read the Fourth Amendment out of the Constitution."

However, it was unnecessary to decide the question here. Mr. Justice White's suggestion that the Court bring "clarity" to Fourth Amendment law by overruling either of these two lines of cases and either treat automobile searches and seizures as per se reasonable on probable cause, or treat them the same as searches of dwellings, was ridiculed by Mr. Justice Stewart. "We are convinced that the result reached in this case is correct, and that the principle it reflects —that the police must obtain a warrant when they intend to seize an object outside the scope of a valid search incident to arrest —can be easily understood and applied by courts and law enforcement officers alike."

Fourth Amendment confusion has been the direct result of the application of the Fourth Amendment and its exclusionary rules to the states, Mr. Justice Harlan maintained in his call to overrule Mapp v. Ohio, 367 U.S. 643. He, too, called for resolution of the tension between the Fourth Amendment's reasonableness requirement and the Warrant Clause. The fragility of the majority with respect to the car search was underscored by Mr. Justice Harlan's fear that to decide otherwise would be to set back the trend of decisions strengthening the Fourth Amendment —decisions that he thought should not be binding on the states.

Mr. Justice Black disagreed with the majority on each of its bases for reversing the conviction. And above all, he disagreed with the concept of the Fourth Amendment exclusionary rule, which, he maintained, was improperly analogized to and derived from the Fifth Amendment's exclusionary rule concerning the privilege against self-incrimination. "Apparently the first suggestion that the Fourth Amendment somehow embodied a rule of evidence came in Justice Bradley's majority opinion in Boyd v. United States, 116 U.S. 616 (1886). * * * It was not until 1914, some twenty-eight years after Boyd and when no member of the Boyd Court remained, that the Court in Weeks v. United States, 232 U.S. 383, stated that the Fourth Amendment itself barred the admission of evidence seized in violation of the Fourth Amendment. The Weeks opinion made no express confession of a break with the past. But if it was merely a proper reading of the Fourth Amendment, it seems strange that it took this Court nearly 125 years to discover the true meaning of those words. The truth is that the source of the exclusionary rule simply cannot be found in the Fourth Amendment."

Agreeing with most of Mr. Justice Black's opinion, the Chief Justice found this case a graphic illustration of "the monstrous price we pay for the Exclusionary Rule in which we seem to have imprisoned ourselves."

U.S. v. Harris, 403 U.S. 573, 9 CrL 3249

If the Court made it harder for law enforcement officials to justify searches and seizures without warrants, it also made it easier to get a warrant. The strict probable cause requirements announced in Spinelli v. U.S., 393 U.S. 410, 4 CrL 3083, were eased somewhat by a five-Justice majority.

Spinelli had held that a mere allegation that an informer was "confidential" and "reliable" was inadequate to establish his reliability for the purposes of determining whether he was a reliable source of information on which probable cause to search or arrest could be based. But now, the Chief Justice, writing for a five-Justice majority, found adequate an affidavit based largely on the hearsay evidence of an informer who was described only as "a prudent person" who had recent "personal knowledge" of the suspect's whiskey sales and who admitted that he himself had made several moonshine purchases from the suspect. "While a bare statement by an affiant that he believed the informant to be truthful would not, in itself, provide a factual basis for crediting the report of an unnamed informant, we conclude that the affidavit in the present case contains an ample factual basis for believing the informant which, when coupled with his own knowledge of the respondent's background, afforded a basis upon which a magistrate could reasonably issue a warrant."

The Chief Justice was particularly impressed with the informer's declaration against penal interest. "People do not lightly admit a crime and place critical evidence in the hands of the police in the form of their own admissions. Admissions of crime, like admissions against proprietary interests, carry their own indicia of credibility —sufficient at least to support finding of probable cause to search. That the informant may be paid or promised a 'break' does not eliminate the residual risk and opprobrium of having admitted criminal conduct."

Furthermore, a majority of the Court specifically held that the affiant's knowledge of the suspect's reputation as a moonshiner was entitled to weight in determining probable cause. Spinelli had held precisely the opposite with respect to a suspected gambler's reputation, and had described reputation evidence as "bald and unilluminating," entitled to no weight whatever in determining probable cause. This aspect of Spinelli was pointedly abandoned. "To the extent that Spinelli prohibits the use of such probative information, it has no support in our prior cases, logic, or experience and we decline to apply it to preclude a magistrate from relying on a law enforcement officer's knowledge of a suspect's reputation."

In addition to the reputation evidence, the description of the informer and a recitation of his declaration against penal interest, the warrant also alleged that the informer had knowledge of a person who had purchased illicit whiskey within the suspect's residence within the past two days, that the illicit whiskey was consumed by purchasers in an out building utilized as a "dance hall," and that the suspect had been seen going to "the other out buildings" about 50 yards from the residence to obtain whiskey for his patrons. This information was detailed and "fresh" enough to furnish present probable cause to search, the majority concluded. Jones v. U.S., 362 U.S. 257, which upheld an affidavit based almost entirely on hearsay evidence, was strongly reaffirmed by the majority.

While only four Justices joined in the Court's opinion in its entirety, Mr. Justice Stewart agreed that the informer's reliability had been established. Mr. Justice White, who cast the "swing" vote in Spinelli, agreed as to the weight to be given the declaration against penal interest, and concluded "that the affidavit, considered as a whole, was sufficient to support the issuance of the warrant." Mr. Justice Black would have gone even further than the majority and overruled Spinelli and Aguilar v. Texas, 378 U.S. 108.

Writing for the four dissenters, Mr. Justice Harlan, author of the opinion for the Court in Spinelli, agreed that the knowledge attributed to the informer, if true, would be sufficient to establish probable cause, and that the agent who obtained the warrant was likely relating truthfully what the informer had told him. But, the affidavit gave insufficient reason to believe that the informer himself was a reliable source. The assertion of his "prudence" was no more than the assertion of "credibility" or "reliability" in Spinelli. And, the reliability of the informer's information could not be established by his claim that he spoke from personal knowledge. "It is not possible to argue that since certain information, if true, would be trustworthy, therefore, it must be true. The possibility remains that the information might have been fabricated. This is why our cases require that there be a reasonable basis for crediting the accuracy of the observation related in the tip."

Mr. Justice Harlan acknowledged that there might be situations in which the informer's accountability to the affiant or extraordinarily detailed description of the suspect's criminal activities might "permissibly lead a magistrate, in an otherwise close case, to credit the accuracy of the account as well. I do not believe, however, that in this instance the relatively meager allegations of this character are, standing alone, enough to satisfy the credibility requirement essential to the sufficiency of this probable cause affidavit. Reading this aspect of the affidavit in a not unduly circumspect manner, the allegations are of a character that would readily occur to a person prone to fabricate."

Furthermore, Mr. Justice Harlan rejected the majority's reliance upon the declaration against penal interest. Not only was its relationship to the hearsay exception for declarations against interest "quite tenuous," it is also highly likely that a police informer's implication of himself in the crime is a true declaration against penal interest; he might well be admitting guilt to get a better deal for himself. Furthermore, such a rule would encourage use of criminal participants as informers rather than ordinary citizens.

Mr. Justice Harlan also strongly disagreed with the majority's view that reputation evidence of the kind present in this case could be considered by the magistrate. Contrary to the majority's contentions, Supreme Court case law has lent no weight to "information" based on unspecified sources that could be mere rumors.

Whiteley v. Warden, 401 U.S. 560, 8 CrL 3171

While U.S. v. Harris might have made it easier to establish probable cause, law officers were put on notice that probable cause can't be electronically manufactured out of thin air. A Wyoming sheriff who obtained an arrest warrant on far less than probable cause didn't create probable cause to arrest the suspect by broadcasting his description across the state, the Court, in a 6–3 opinion, explained.

The sheriff, acting on an anonymous tip, obtained the warrant under then-current Wyoming procedure, with nothing more than a sworn conclusory statement that the defendant, a six-time loser, had committed the offense of burglary at a certain place and time.

True, the arresting officers in this case —two Laramie policemen —acted perfectly reasonably in stopping the suspect and his companion on the basis of the bulletin, Mr. Justice Harlan acknowledged in his opinion for the majority. "Certainly police officers called upon to aid other officers in executing arrest warrants are entitled to assume that the officers requesting aid offered the magistrate the information requisite to support an independent judicial assessment of probable cause. Where, however, the contrary turns out to be true, an otherwise illegal arrest cannot be insulated from challenge by the decision of the instigating officer to rely on fellow officers to make the arrest."

The majority rejected out of hand the state's contention that a warrantless arrest should be governed by less stringent probable cause standards than those governing a magistrate's assessment of an affidavit.

Mr. Justice Black, joined by the Chief Justice, once again maintained that recent Supreme Court decisions have made a "little trial" a prerequisite to the issuance of a search or arrest warrant.

Mr. Justice Black emphasized the setting of this case — a sparsely settled area in which people know one another and the sheriff knew the suspect very well. The burglary here was similar to those which the defendant habitually committed. It was committed just a day after he had been released from the state penitentiary for his most recent offense.

Mr. Justice Blackmun expressed his agreement with "much that is said by Mr. Justice Black."

U.S. v. White, 401 U.S. 745, 9 CrL 3036

The proposition that a warrant need not be obtained in order to electronically eavesdrop on a conversation with the consent of one party to the conversation, approved in On Lee v. U.S., 343 U.S. 747, but cast in doubt by Katz v. U.S., 389 U.S. 347, 2 CrL 3065, was narrowly reaffirmed.

A five-Justice majority held that the Fourth Amendment neither prohibits federal agents' warrantless use of an electronic transmitting device to overhear and record the conversations between a suspect and an informer who voluntarily carried the device, nor bars from evidence the agents' testimony to such conversations, even though the Government did not produce the informer himself at trial. Thus, the U.S. Court of Appeals for the Seventh Circuit was wrong in holding that Katz had overruled On Lee. The Seventh Circuit had been the only federal court of appeals to reach this conclusion. Mr. Justice Black, who cast the fifth vote, stated once more that electronic surveillance is not covered by the Fourth Amendment.

Hoffa v. U.S., 385 U.S. 293, and other "misplaced confidence" cases point the way to the result here, the plurality said. "If the conduct and revelations of an agent operating without electronic equipment do not invade the defendant's constitutionally justifiable expectations of privacy, neither does simultaneous recording of the same conversations made by the agent or by others from transmissions received from the agent to whom the defendant is talking and whose trustworthiness the defendant necessarily risks."

The problem here, Mr. Justice White continued, is not what the defendant's privacy expectations happen to have been, but "what expectations of privacy are constitutionally justifiable."

Mr. Justice Brennan concurred in the result only because the electronic surveillance here was used prior to the announcement of Katz, and he agreed that Katz should not be retroactively applied. Mr. Justice Brennan not only announced his agreement that On Lee should no longer be considered sound law, but went further and concluded "that Lopez v. U.S., 373 U.S. 427 (1963), is also no longer sound law. In other words, it is my view that current Fourth Amendment jurisprudence interposes a warrant requirement not only in cases of third-party electronic monitoring (the situation in On Lee and in this case) but also in cases of electronic recording by a Government agent of face-to-face conversation with a criminal suspect, which was the situation in Lopez."

Mr. Justice Douglas, dissenting, traced the development of electronic eavesdropping law. "The threads of thought running through our recent decisions are that these extensive intrusions into privacy made by electronic surveillance make self-restraint by law enforcement officials an inadequate protection, that the requirement of warrants under the Fourth Amendment is essential to a free society."

Justices Harlan and Marshall also wrote separate dissents.

Also emphasizing "the impact of the practice of third-party bugging" on "individual relationships between citizens in a free society," Mr. Justice Harlan thought that "the stream of current developments in Fourth Amendment law" require that all electronic monitoring be subject to the warrant requirement.

Mr. Justice Harlan specifically noted his disagreement with both Congress and the American Bar Association on the question of consensual surveillance. Mr. Justice Marshall noted his agreement with Justices Harlan and Douglas that all electronic surveillance must be preceded by judicial approval.

Bivens v. Six Unknown Named Agents, 403 U.S. 388, 9 CrL 3195

A Fourth Amendment violation by a federal agent acting under color of his authority gives rise to a federal cause of action for damages, the Court held as it answered the question that it had reserved 25 years ago in Bell v. Hood, 327 U.S. 678. Mr. Justice Brennan, writing for the five-Justice majority, rejected the argument that the rights asserted —primarily rights of privacy —were creations of state law, rather than federal, and that they could be vindicated only by state tort actions in which the agents, if found to have violated the Fourth Amendment, would stand before the state laws merely as private individuals.

This argument, Mr. Justice Brennan said, took an unduly restrictive view of the Fourth Amendment's protection against unreasonable searches and seizures by federal officials.

The Fourth Amendment limits federal power independently of any state law concept; "interests protected by state law regulating trespass and the invasion of privacy, and those protected by the Fourth Amendment's guarantee against unreasonable searches and seizures, may be inconsistent or even hostile."

While the Fourth Amendment "does not in so many words" specifically provide for the remedy of damages in a civil action, federal courts may use any available remedy to make good a wrongful invasion of legal rights. There is "no explicit congressional declaration that persons injured by a federal officer's violation of the Fourth Amendment may not recover money damages from the agents, but must instead be remitted to another remedy, equally effective in the view of Congress. The question is merely whether petitioner, if he can demonstrate an injury consequent upon the violation by federal agents of his Fourth Amendment rights, is entitled to redress his injury through a particular remedial mechanism normally available in the federal courts."

Concurring, Mr. Justice Harlan agreed that the interest claimed by the plaintiff here was a federally protected one, which could be protected by federal courts by entertaining damage suits even in the absence of specific congressional authorization. "Damages as a traditional form of compensation for invasion of a legally protected interest may be entirely appropriate even if no substantial deterrent effects on future official lawlessness might be thought to result."

The Chief Justice dissented from a "holding which judicially creates a damages remedy not provided for by the Constitution and not enacted by Congress. We would more surely preserve the important values of the doctrine of separation of powers —and perhaps get a better result

—by recommending a solution to the Congress as the branch of government in which the Constitution has vested the legislative power."

The Chief Justice also strongly criticized the Fourth Amendment exclusionary rule. But he made it clear that he was not recommending its abandonment. "[U]ntil some meaningful alternative can be developed, * * * to overrule Weeks and Mapp, even assuming the Court was now prepared to take that step, could raise yet new problems. Obviously the public interest would be poorly served if law enforcement officials were suddenly to gain the impression, however erroneous, that all constitutional restraints on police had somehow been removed —that an open season on 'criminals' had been declared."

The Chief Justice concluded that "an entirely different remedy is necessary but it is one that in my view is as much beyond judicial power as the step the Court takes today. Congress should develop an administrative or quasi-judicial remedy against the government itself to afford compensation and restitution for persons whose Fourth Amendment rights have been violated."

Mr. Justice Blackmun also noted his dissent from this act of "judicial legislation."

Williams v. U.S., Elkanich v. U.S., 401 U.S. 646, 9 CrL 3015

The limitations imposed by Chimel v. California, 395 U.S. 752, 5 CrL 3131, on searches incident to arrest apply only to searches conducted after the date that Chimel was announced, the Court held. The purpose of Chimel was not to overcome a defect in the integrity of the fact-finding process, but to vindicate the right of privacy. The Court noted that thus far it has not given retroactive effect to cases expanding Fourth Amendment protection. These cases have presented situations quite different from cases that cast doubt upon some aspect of the fact-finding process. (Williams v. U.S., Elkanich v. U.S., 39 LW 4365)

Mr. Justice White, who announced the judgment of the Court, also declared that for retroactivity purposes, there was no constitutional difference between the applicability of Chimel "to those prior convictions which are here under direct appeal and those involving collateral proceedings."

Justices Harlan and Marshall dissented. Mr. Justice Marshall expressed the belief that constitutional decisions should apply to all convictions not final when the decision is announced.

Hill v. California, 401 U.S. 797, 9 CrL 3052

Relying in part on the non-retroactivity of Chimel v. California, a majority of the Court held that the mistaken 1966 arrest of a man, Miller, fitting the description of Hill, a suspect whom the police had probable cause to arrest, did not render unlawful their contemporaneous search of the suspect's entire apartment. The officers' reasonable mistake as to the identity of the person they were arresting did not invalidate the arrest, even though the arrested person protested and correctly identified himself.

"The upshot was that the officers in good faith believed Miller was Hill and arrested him. They were quite wrong as it turned out, and subjective good-faith belief would not in itself justify either the arrest or the subsequent search. But sufficient probability, not certainty, is the touchstone of reasonableness under the Fourth Amendment and on the record before us the officers' mistake was understandable and the arrest a reasonable response to the situation facing them at the time."

And, given the validity of the arrest, the search, valid under Fourth Amendment law at the time, was also good.

Justices Harlan and Marshall, dissenting, agreed with "the Court's opinion except for its conclusion that the Chimel case is not to be applied to this one." The search incident to Miller's arrest clearly violated limitations subsequently announced in Chimel, and Chimel, the dissenters maintained once more, should apply retroactively.

INTERROGATION

Harris v. New York, 401 U.S. 222, 8 CrL 3139

For the first time since the announcement of Miranda v. Arizona, 384 U.S. 436, the Court contracted rather than expanded Miranda's exclusionary rule. By a 5–4 vote, the Court held that in-custody statements that satisfy legal standards of trustworthiness, even though excluded by Miranda from the prosecution's case in chief, may be used to impeach a testifying defendant's credibility.

Writing for the majority, the Chief Justice acknowledged comments in Miranda indicating that confessions or admissions obtained in violation of its mandate may be inadmissible for any purpose. But "discussion of that issue was not at all necessary to the Court's holding and cannot be regarded as controlling." The majority rejected the idea that allowing impeachment use of voluntary but Miranda-barred confessions would encourage impermissible police conduct. "The impeachment process here undoubtedly provided valuable aid to the jury in assessing petitioner's credibility, and the benefits of this process should not be lost, in our view, because of the speculative possibility that impermissible police conduct will be encouraged thereby. Assuming that the exclusionary rule has a deterrent effect on proscribed police conduct, sufficient deterrence flows when the evidence in question is made unavailable to the prosecution in its case in chief."

Walder v. U.S., 347 U.S. 62 (1954), which several state and federal courts of appeal had considered undermined by Miranda, was not only reaffirmed, but extended. Walder was impeached by use of illegally seized evidence as to collateral matters in his testimony, whereas Harris was impeached with respect to matters bearing directly on his guilt or innocence of the crime charged. "We are not persuaded," the Chief Justice said, that this difference was "a difference in principle."

Mr. Justice Black dissented without opinion. Mr. Justice Brennan, joined by Justices Douglas and Marshall, read Miranda as barring the use of any statements obtained in violation of its guidelines. Mr. Justice Brennan emphasized the differences between Walder and the present case. But beyond this, a defendant's privilege against self-incrimination is clearly violated, Mr. Justice Brennan contended, by use in any way of statements obtained in violation of his privilege. Statements obtained without full compliance with Miranda were flatly barred from any use whatsoever by that decision's declaration that "These statements are incriminating in any meaningful sense of the word and may not be used without the full warnings and effective waiver required for any other statement."

Even though deterrence of improper police practices was only a part of Miranda's objective, "I fear that today's holding will seriously undermine the achievement of that objective. The Court today tells the police that they may freely interrogate an accused incommunicado and without counsel and know that although the statement they obtain in violation of Miranda can't be used on the state's direct case, it may be introduced if the defendant has the temerity to testify in his own defense."

Justices Black, Douglas, and Brennan are the only members of the five-man Miranda majority still on the Court. The three Miranda dissenters who are still on the Court, Justices Harlan, Stewart, and White, join without reservation in the majority's opinion.

SELF-INCRIMINATION

Piccirillo v. New York, 400 U.S. 548, 8 CrL 3081

A question that was being fought out at the lower federal court level —whether the Fifth Amendment requires that a witness who may be compelled to incriminate himself be granted "transactional" or only testimonial "use" immunity —was sidestepped by the Court in a case that at first appeared to squarely present the question.

The Court had granted certiorari to determine whether "transactional" immunity was, in fact, required by the self-incrimination clause, but an intervening New York Court of Appeals decision making clear that New York grand jury witnesses must be given transactional immunity rendered the grant improvident.

Mr. Justice Brennan, dissenting from the dismissal, contended that the record presented an excellent case for resolving the ultimate Fifth Amendment question, as it involved a direct attack on a conviction resulting from the use of compelled testimony rather than a witness' prosecution.

Mr. Justice Brennan also expressed the view that Counselman v. Hitchcock, 142 U.S. 547 (1892), which required the broader immunity, is still good law and has not been undermined by Murphy v. Waterfront Comm., 378 U.S. 52 (1964). Murphy, he maintained, is distinguishable.

Justices Douglas and Marshall, also dissenting, quoted Ullman v. U.S., 350 U.S. 422, to the effect that transactional immunity has become "part of the fabric of our federal constitutional law."

Mr. Justice Black would simply have vacated the judgment and let the New York Court of Appeals reconsider this case in light of its intervening decision making clear the broad scope of New York immunity.

California v. Byers, 402 U.S. 424, 9 CrL 3151

There is no constitutional right to flee the scene of an accident, a majority of the Court observed as it held that California's hit-and-run statute does not violate the Fifth Amendment. The statute requires a motorist involved in an accident to stop and identify himself. This information is neither testimonial nor communicative within the meaning of the Constitution, the majority concluded, and therefore the statute does not violate the Self-Incrimination Clause.

The Chief Justice, writing for himself, Mr. Justice Stewart, Mr. Justice White, and Mr. Justice Black, compared the information the motorist must supply to that which a taxpayer must present when he files his return. In each case there is a possibility of prosecution for offenses disclosed by or derived from the information a person is compelled to supply. But the mere possibility of incrimination is "insufficient to defeat the strong policies in favor of disclosure called for by statutes like the one challenged here."

This statute, unlike those involved in Marchetti v. U.S., 390 U.S. 39, 2 CrL 3102, and its companion cases, is not aimed at a "highly select group inherently suspect of criminal activity," nor does compliance with the statute raise a substantial risk of self-incrimination. Further, the purpose of this statute is not to facilitate criminal convictions but to promote the satisfaction of civil liabilities arising from automobile accidents.

Mr. Justice Harlan concurred in the judgment, but would have held "that the presence of a 'real' and not 'imaginary' risk of self-incrimination is not a sufficient predicate for extending the privilege against self-incrimination of regulatory schemes of the character involved in this case."

If the privilege were to be extended to this case, Mr. Justice Harlan argued, it must potentially be available in every instance where the government relies on self-reporting. And the risks to government efficiency of a "self-executing" claim of the privilege would require, at the very least, the acceptance of a use restriction of unspecified dimensions.

Accordingly, Mr. Justice Harlan said, the Court should expressly limit the Marchetti-Grosso line of cases to the extent that they suggest that the presence of perceivable risks of self-incrimination in and of itself justifies the imposition of a use restriction. But he would not have overruled those cases. They must be taken to stand at least for the proposition that the Fifth Amendment requires some limit on the Government's power to compel information.

Mr. Justice Black, joined by Mr. Justice Douglas and Mr. Justice Brennan in dissent, argued that the Court's decision would practically "wipe out the Fifth Amendment protection against compelled self-incrimination." The majority's suggestion that the defendant's compliance with the statute would not have subjected him to substantial risk of self-incrimination could hardly be taken seriously, he contended. Since the defendant was also charged with a traffic violation, his compliance with the statute would have given the state proof of an essential element of the violation —that he was the driver of the car.

Further, this case cannot be distinguished from the Marchetti-Grosso line of cases. The statute here is also aimed at a group inherently suspect of criminal activities: those involved in accidents involving property damage.

Mr. Justice Brennan, writing for himself, Mr. Justice Douglas, and Mr. Justice Marshall, contended that the Court's opinion here bore little relation to the case before it.

U.S. v. Freed, 401 U.S. 601, 9 CrL 3002

Congress proved successful in its effort to amend the National Firearms Act so as to eliminate the defects found by the Court in Haynes v. U.S., 390 U.S. 85, 2 CrL 3115. The Court held, without dissent, that the present Act does not compel firearms possessors to incriminate themselves. The Act prohibits possession of firearms not registered to the possessor, but requires registration only by the transferor of the weapon and forbids any prosecutorial or investigative use of evidence that he provides in compliance with the Act.

Furthermore, the Court held that proof that the possessor knew the firearm was not registered to him is not required for a valid conviction under the Act.

SELF-INCRIMINATION —RETROACTIVITY

The Court added another refinement to the intricacies of its various retroactivity decisions.

Mackey v. U.S., 401 U.S. 667, 9 CrL 3022

Marchetti v. U.S., 390 U.S. 39, 2 CrL 3102, and Grosso v. U.S., 390 U.S. 62, 2 CrL 3108, which interposed the privilege against self-incrimination as an absolute defense against federal prosecution for failure to register as a gambler and pay the occupational tax, apply only to prosecutions involving use of information obtained from registrants that were begun after the date they were announced.

Like the rule in Chimel, Mr. Justice White wrote in the four-Justice lead opinion, the rule of Marchetti and Grosso does not go to preserving the integrity of the fact-finding process and thus should be denied retroactivity. The registration and tax provisions of the federal law had,

until Marchetti and Grosso were decided, the express approval of the Court.

Mr. Justice Brennan, joined by Mr. Justice Marshall, concurred in the judgment. The question in this case, he said, is what use the government can make of the information supplied by one who complied with the gambling law.

Mr. Justice Douglas, writing in dissent for himself and Mr. Justice Black, said, "I had assumed that all criminal and civil decisions involving constitutional defenses which go in favor of the defendant were necessarily retroactive."

Mr. Justice Harlan, dissenting, disagreed with the majority's approach to retroactivity questions. He maintained that the Court's constitutional decisions in cases on direct review must apply to all such cases.

However, as to cases on collateral review, Mr. Justice Harlan said, a different standard should apply. Since these convictions were otherwise final, they involved more properly a question of the scope of the writ of habeas corpus.

U.S. v. U.S. Coin and Currency, 401 U.S. 715, 9 CrL 3006

In another case involving retroactive application of Marchetti and Grosso, a gambler got back the money that was forfeited, prior to the announcement of Marchetti and Grosso, as a gambling instrumentality. The rationale of Marchetti-Grosso, a majority of the Court said, must apply to forefeitures as well as straight criminal prosecutions. What's more, it must apply retroactively to forfeitures.

The majority opinion by Mr. Justice Harlan saw nothing but sophistry in distinguishing such forfeitures from criminal prosecutions. In form they may be civil actions against the property, he said, but an honest reading of all the forfeiture statutes shows they are really directed only at punishing the criminal activity of the property's owner. The self-incrimination principles of Marchetti-Grosso are so important, and so directly related to the integrity of the fact-finding process that when balanced against the incidental inconvenience retroactivity may cause the Government, they call for retroactive application.

In a special concurrence specifically attacking the dissent, Mr. Justice Brennan set forth the reasons he thought Marchetti and Grosso qualified for retroactivity under the criteria of Stovall v. Denno, 388 U.S. 293, 1 CrL 3102.

A dissent by Mr. Justice White, joined by the Chief Justice and Justices Stewart and Blackmun, pointed out the inconsistency between the Court's decision in this case and its decision in Mackey.

CAPITAL PUNISHMENT

It became apparent in the 1970–71 Term that the Court's answer to the question of the death penalty's constitutionality would soon be forthcoming. Late in the

Term, the Court granted review in four cases in which review was limited to the question whether capital punishment violates the Eighth Amendment prohibition against cruel and unusual punishment.

Only eight weeks before it granted review in these cases, the Court rejected a constitutional assault on state procedures for imposing capital punishment.

McGautha v. California, and Crampton v. Ohio, 402 U.S. 183, 9 CrL 3109

Nothing in the Fourteenth Amendment Due Process Clause forbids a state to give a jury absolute discretion in deciding whether to impose the death penalty, a majority of the Court held in affirming two death sentences, one imposed by a California jury and the other by an Ohio jury. Furthermore, Ohio's single-verdict proceeding, in which the trier of fact in a capital case determines both guilt and punishment in a one-stage trial, does not violate the defendant's Fifth Amendment privilege against self-incrimination.

Speaking for five of the six Justices who constituted the majority, Mr. Justice Harlan traced the history of jury discretion in capital cases. Through the centuries, efforts to establish criteria for imposing the death penalty proved unworkable; juries simply refused to convict defendants in capital cases that were technically within, but clearly inappropriate for, the death penalty. Thus, statutes granting juries absolute discretion to impose the death penalty replaced efforts to define offenses carrying a mandatory death penalty.

At one time or another, Mr. Justice Harlan pointed out, all states except the four that abolished capital punishment in the Nineteenth Century have authorized jury sentencing in capital cases, and none of these statutes has "provided standards for the choice between death and life imprisonment." Subsequent efforts to "draft means of channeling capital sentencing discretion" have proved unsuccessful, and the task of doing so seems to be "beyond present human ability."

Britain's Royal Commission on Capital Punishment, before the death penalty was abolished in England, had also come to this conclusion, and the draftsmen of the Model Penal Code, agreeing that factors entering into a death penalty provision could not be compressed within a formula, set forth criteria that provide no more "than the most minimal control over the sentencing authority's exercise of discretion." In light of all this, "we find it quite impossible to say that committing to the untrammelled discretion of the jury the power to pronounce life or death in capital cases is offensive to anything in the Constitution." The defendant's self-incrimination argument, the majority said, was that determination of guilt and penalty at a single trial unlawfully compels a defendant to be a witness against himself on the guilt issue by requiring him to speak prior to determination of guilt or face death without being heard from. However, the question here is a narrow one: "whether it is consistent with the privilege for the state to provide no means whereby a defendant

wishing to present evidence or testimony on the issue of punishment may limit the force of his evidence (and the state's rebuttal) to that issue. We see nothing in the history, policies, or precedents relating to the privilege which requires such means to be available."

Furthermore, the Court cautioned against too broad an interpretation of the language in Simmons v. U.S., 390 U. S. 377, 2 CrL 3153, stating that it is "intolerable that one constitutional right should have to be surrendered in order to assert another." The Court did not question the "soundness of the result in Simmons," but warned that "to the extent that its rationale was based on a tension between constitutional rights and the policies behind them, the validity of that reasoning must now be regarded as open to question, and it certainly cannot be given the broad thrust which is attributed to it * * * in the present case."

The Court noted that in its trilogy of guilty plea cases last Term, McMann v. Richardson, 397 U.S. 759, 7 CrL 3055, "we held the defendants bound by 'waivers' of rights under the Fifth, Sixth, and Fourteenth Amendments in order to avoid burdens which, it was ultimately determined could not have been constitutionally imposed." The Fifth Amendment interests in the guilty plea cases, the Court said, were far more substantial than those of the defendant in Simmons.

The Court concluded: "The criminal process, like the rest of the legal system, is replete with situations requiring 'the making of difficult judgments' as to which course to follow. McMann v. Richardson, * * *. The threshold question is whether compelling the election impairs to an appreciable extent any of the policies behind the rights involved."

Mr. Justice Black, concurring, found no denial of "rights expressly or impliedly guaranteed by the federal Constitution as written."

Justices Brennan, Douglas, and Marshall disagreed completely with the majority.

On the question of jury discretion, Mr. Justice Brennan maintained that satisfactory standards for determining whether death should be the penalty can be formulated. Here, the states did not even attempt to set standards, Mr. Justice Brennan said.

To suggest that juries will carry out the state's interest in executing some capital offenders but not others if they are not instructed as to what these interests are, is to take a position on the wrong side of the "Looking Glass World," Mr. Justice Brennan maintained.

Examining the somewhat different procedures actually involved in standardless jury discretion in both Ohio and California, Mr. Justice Brennan concluded that these procedures "are inconsistent with the most basic and fundamental principles of due process. But even if I thought these procedures adequate to try a welfare claim —which they are not, Goldberg v. Kelly, 397 U.S. 255 (1970) —I would have little hesitation in finding them inadequate where life itself is at stake. For we have long recognized that the degree of procedural regularity required by the Due Process Clause increases with the importance of the interests at stake."

In an opinion by Mr. Justice Douglas, the three dissenters maintained that Ohio's unitary guilty-punishment trial also fell sadly short of due process standards.

The right of allocution, Mr. Justice Douglas maintained, is a constitutional one, and here the defendant is either compelled to forego it or to incriminate himself by exercising it.

While the Court has history on its side, Mr. Justice Douglas observed, that is all it has. "The vestiges of law enshrined today have roots in barbaric procedures" that have been demonstrably unable to cope with the problem of crime. "Our Federal Bureau of Investigation teaches that brains, not muscle, solve crimes."

SENTENCING —EQUAL PROTECTION

Tate v. Short, 401 U.S. 395, 8 CrL 3151

At the other end of the sentencing spectrum, the Court elevated dicta in Williams v. Illinois, 7 CrL 3185, to law and held that the Equal Protection Clause bars a state from automatically converting a fine to imprisonment for those who are unwilling to pay forthwith, while limiting punishment to the payment of a fine for those who are able to pay.

The court was careful to point out that it was not barring the imprisonment of a defendant who is able but refuses to pay. Nor was it forbidding imprisonment as a method of enforcement when alternative means, such as installment payments, fail despite the defendant's reasonable effort to cooperate.

Mr. Justice Blackmun, concurring, thought that this decision might encourage state and municipal governments to do away with the traffic fine altogether and impose a jail sentence as the only punishment. Such a course would eliminate equal protection problems. "If, as a nation, we ever reach that happy point where we are willing to set our personal convenience to one side and we are really serious about resolving the problems of traffic irresponsibility and the frightful carnage it spews upon our highways, a development of that kind may not be at all undesirable."

GUILTY PLEAS

North Carolina v. Alford, 400 U.S. 25, 8 CrL 3039

The binding effect of a plea bargain, strengthened considerably last Term by Brady v. U.S., 397 U.S. 742, 7 CrL 3064, and its companion cases, was further enhanced this Term. Given the appropriate circumstances, including a strong case against him and advice from his counsel that he plead guilty, not even a defendant's protestations of innocence will be enough to undermine his negotiated plea.

The Court thus reversed a U.S. Court of Appeals decision vacating the plea of a first-degree murder defendant whose case presented these circumstances and

who was motivated to enter his plea, despite his claims of innocence, by the threat of a death sentence. The defendant's steadfastness in claiming innocence was almost matched by his steadfastness in asking to plead guilty.

Noting the division of authority among state and federal courts as to the validity of a guilty plea that is made by a defendant who simultaneously claims innocence "and hence contains only a waiver of trial but no admission of guilt," the Court turned to its prior decisions that "yield relevant principles." Of particular interest was Hudson v. U.S., 272 U.S. 451, in which it was held that a trial court has the authority to impose a prison sentence upon a defendant who has entered a plea of nolo contendere, "a plea by which a defendant does not expressly admit his guilt, but nonetheless waives his right to a trial and authorizes the court for purposes of the case to treat him as if he were guilty * * * Implicity in the nolo contendere cases is a recognition that the Constitution does not bar imposition of a prison sentence upon an accused who is unwilling to admit his guilt but who, faced with grim alternatives, is willing to waive his trial and face the sentence." Nothing in U.S. v. Jackson, 390 U.S. 570, 3 CrL 3003, supports the defendant's contention that his plea was unconstitionally obtained, the majority concluded.

Mr. Justice Brennan, joined in dissent by Justices Douglas and Marshall, adhered to his view that Brady and its companion cases were wrong in holding "that a plea of guilty may validly be induced by an unconstitutional threat to subject the defendant to a risk of death, so long as the plea is entered in open court and the defendant is represented by competent counsel who is aware of the threat, albeit not of its constitutionality. * * * Today the Court makes clear that its previous holding was intended to apply even when the record demonstrates that the actual effect of the unconstitutional threat was to induce a guilty plea from a defendant who was unwilling to admit his guilt."

JUVENILES

McKeiver v. Pennsylvania, 403 U.S. 528, 9 CrL 3234

The Sixth Amendment right to a jury trial is not among the constitutional safeguards that the Due Process Clause requires at a juvenile delinquency adjudication, the Court held.

While the Court has, in recent years, greatly increased the number of constitutional rights that must be afforded youths facing incarceration on delinquency charges, it has "insisted that these successive decisions do not spell the doom of the juvenile court system, or even deprive it of its 'informality, flexibility, or speed,'" Mr. Justice Blackmun noted in his opinion for the Court. In view of this, the Court found particularly instructive the Pennsylvania Supreme Court's majority opinion in one of the two cases under consideration.

The Pennsylvania court had found the juvenile court system less than adequate. But, for the purposes of dealing with youthful offenders, it was deemed superior to the criminal court process. And of all the due process rights that could be applied in juvenile courts, the Pennsylvania Court thought that the right to a jury trial is "the one which would most likely be disruptive of the unique character of the juvenile process." The Court agreed with this conclusion, and with the Pennsylvania court's belief that fairness in delinquency proceedings could be obtained without jury trials.

Imposition of the jury requirement on juvenile courts would not only "tend once again to place the juvenile squarely in the routine of the criminal process," but would seriously discourage state efforts "to experiment and to seek in new and different ways the elusive answers to the problems of the young * * *." Most state courts confronted with the jury trial question after the announcement of In re Gault, 387 U.S. 1, 1 CrL 3031, and Duncan v. Louisiana, 391 U.S. 145, 3 CrL 3062, have not found it required by anything said in Gault or Duncan.

"If the formalities of the criminal adjudicative process are to be superimposed upon the juvenile court system," Mr. Justice Blackmun concluded, "there is little need for its separate existence. Perhaps that ultimate disillusionment will come one day, but for the moment we are disinclined to give impetus to it."

Mr. Justice Harlan, concurring in the result, was not sure that the discrimination between juveniles and adults could really be justified, now that the Supreme Court and other authorities have allowed the juvenile process to become so similar to an adult criminal trial. However, he concurred in the result because he could not accept the holding in Duncan v. Louisiana, 391 U.S. 145, 3 CrL 3062, that the Fourteenth Amendment extends the Sixth Amendment jury trial right to state defendants.

Mr. Justice White concurred on the ground that juvenile proceedings are entirely different from adult prosecutions, and hence the hearings cannot really be considered criminal trials. He emphasized, as did Mr. Justice Blackmun's lead opinion, that if the states think jury trials are necessary, they are perfectly free to adopt this method of handling juvenile cases.

Mr. Justice Brennan also joined the plurality opinion's conclusion that the proceedings in these cases were not criminal prosecutions within the meaning of the Sixth Amendment. He did not think a jury trial is required, so long as there is some means of keeping the juvenile court open to public scrutiny. For this reason, he thought the results of the secret proceedings in the delinquency adjudications of youthful North Carolina Negro demonstrators should be reversed. Counsel here moved for public trial and it was refused.

Justices Douglas, Black, and Marshall maintained that "the guarantees of the Bill of Rights, made applicable to the states by the Fourteenth Amendment, require a jury trial."

RIGHT OF CONFRONTATION

Dutton v. Evans, 300 U.S. 74, 8 CrL 3045

The Sixth Amendment's Confrontation Clause is not coextensive with the hearsay rule, the Court emphasized. Without a majority opinion, but mustering a majority for reversal of a Fifth Circuit decision, the Court decided that a Georgia murder defendant's right of confrontation was not violated by the use against him of a non-testifying declarant's hearsay statement against him. The declarant was allegedly a co-conspirator, and a Georgia statute, as interpreted by the Georgia Supreme Court, allows, as an exception to the hearsay rule, the use of a co-conspirator's declarations made during the "concealment phase" of the conspiracy.

Mr. Justice Stewart, joined in his plurality by the Chief Justice and Justices White and Blackmun, considered the Fifth Circuit's grant of federal habeas relief as a holding that the Georgia rule violated the defendant's Sixth Amendment right because its co-conspirator hearsay exception was broader than the corresponding exception in federal law.

Concurring in the result, Mr. Justice Harlan did not view the problem as one of constitutional confrontation at all. The Confrontation Clause, he maintained, sets up a procedural rule which is simply not a rule of evidence. Federal and state evidentiary rules should be tested only under the Due Process Clauses of the Fifth and Fourteenth Amendments respectively.

Mr. Justice Blackmun and the Chief Justice saw an additional reason for the result: the single sentence attributed in testimony by the declarant about the defendant "was, in my view and in light of the entire record, harmless error, if it was error at all."

Mr. Justice Marshall, writing for the four dissenting Justices, found the majority's result "completely inconsistent" with recent opinions such as Douglas v. Alabama, 380 U.S. 415, and Bruton v. U.S., 391 U.S. 123, 3 CrL 3085.

Nelson v. O'Neil, 402 U.S. 622, 9 CrL 3184

The Court also held that the right of confrontation as interpreted in Bruton was not denied a California robbery defendant whose jointly tried codefendant took the stand after his incriminating statement implicating the defendant was admitted into evidence. The codefendant denied making the statement and then proceeded to testify favorably to the defendant as to the underlying facts.

Bruton, Mr. Justice Stewart observed in the Court's opinion, has never gone beyond a fact situation involving the admission of a statement by a non-testifying codefendant. California v. Green, 399 U.S. 149, 7 CrL 3164, was closer to the situation in this case. "The circumstances of Green are inverted in this case," Mr. Justice Stewart noted. There, the witness affirmed the out-of-court statement, but was unable to testify as to the underlying facts. Here, the witness denied ever making an out-of-court statement, but did testify, at length, and favorably to the defendant, concerning the underlying facts.

Adding another reason for his concurrence —the desirability of making Bruton unavailable to a defendant whose conviction was before Bruton was announced — Mr. Justice Harlan found it "difficult to fathom what public policy is served by opening the already-overcrowded federal courts to claims such as these."

Writing for the four dissenters, Mr. Justice Brennan saw the real question was whether the state, having determined that the extrajudicial statement was available against the defendant, could nevertheless present it to the jury that was to decide the defendant's guilt with the instruction that the jury not consider it against the defendant. Bruton makes clear that it could not, Mr. Justice Brennan maintained.

To Mr. Justice Marshall, the case "dramatically illustrates the need for the adoption of new rules regulating the use of joint trials."

FAIR TRIAL —VENUE

Groppi v. Wisconsin, 400 U.S. 505, 8 CrL 3078

Denial of a justified change of venue is a denial of the Sixth Amendment right to jury trial, a majority of the U.S. Supreme Court reasoned as it voided the conviction of vociferous protester Father James Groppi for resisting arrest. Groppi, who was denied the right to seek a venue change because of a Wisconsin statute prohibiting such relief in misdemeanor cases, was to get a chance to offer evidence in the trial court on the issue of community prejudice.

Mr. Justice Stewart, writing for the majority, started from the previous Term's holding in Baldwin v. New York, 399 U.S. 66, 7 CrL 3140, that misdemeanants facing over six months' possible imprisonment are entitled to a jury trial. The Court's earlier holdings make it clear that that means a trial by a jury free from community prejudice.

While Wisconsin does afford misdemeanants the right to examine and challenge jurors and the right to move before trial for continuances or after trial to set aside a verdict infected with community prejudice, the Court has held that sometimes only a change of venue is constitutionally sufficient to guarantee an impartial jury. Rideau v. Louisiana, 376 U.S. 723.

Mr. Justice Blackmun, joined by the Chief Justice, concurred in the result and in the view that a change of venue in a misdemeanor case is constitutionally required upon a proper showing. But he thought that this case presented a Sixth Amendment question of fair trial. Noting the deficiencies in the informal offer of proof made here, he doubted that the evidence presented on remand would show the kind of pervasive community prejudice that would constitutionally require a venue change.

Mr. Justice Black dissented on the ground that the Constitution itself does not expressly grant the right to a change of venue. The Sixth Amendment right to trial by an impartial jury, he thought, can be protected in many ways, including the remedies Wisconsin law made available in this case, such as voir dire, jury challenges, and discretionary continuances. Rideau, he said, was a case wherein pretrial publicity was so bad that fundamental due process was violated, and in which venue change was provided for by the applicable state statute.

DOUBLE JEOPARDY

U.S. v. Jorn, 400 U.S. 470, 9 CrL 3071

Finding that a trial judge abused his discretion by declaring a mistrial after the jury was empanelled, a divided Court affirmed the defendant's motion to bar his retrial. Mr. Justice Harlan, joined by the Chief Justice, Mr. Justice Douglas, and Mr. Justice Marshall, concluded that a trial judge who, acting without the defendant's consent, aborts the proceedings, deprives the defendant of his right to have his trial completed by a particular tribunal. Therefore, the Double Jeopardy Clause of the Fifth Amendment bars reprosecution.

An examination of the circumstances surrounding the mistrial declaration lead to the conclusion that the trial judge failed to exercise sound discretion to assure that there was a "manifest necessity" for the declaration sua sponte.

The case was not a total loss for the Government, however. The Government, the Court said, could appeal from the second trial court's decision to grant a motion, based upon double jeopardy, to bar the second prosecution providing that the motion was granted before the second jury was empanelled.

Justices Black and Brennan thought that the Court lacked jurisdiction over the appeal; the trial judge's action, they maintained, amounted to an acquittal.

The Chief Justice's concurrence was "not without some reluctance, however, since the case represents a plain frustration of the right to have this case tried * * *."

Mr. Justice Stewart, joined by Mr. Justice White and Mr. Justice Blackmun, dissented.

Gori v. U.S., 367 U.S. 364, established that "the simple phrase 'abuse of discretion' is not in itself enough to resolve double jeopardy questions in cases of this kind," Mr. Justice Stewart said. The real question is whether an abuse of the trial process has prejudiced the accused so greatly as to outweigh society's interest in the punishment of a crime. Going on in this case to hold a trial on the merits "would not violate the constitutional guaranty."

FIRST AMENDMENT

While the person who possesses obscene matter purely for private enjoyment is protected by the First Amendment, distributors who seek both to satisfy his desire and to profit by it are not. This is the net effect of two U.S. Supreme Court decisions concerning pornography suppliers, one an importer and the other a mail-order distributor.

U.S. v. Reidel, 402 U.S. 351, 9 CrL 3103

Two Terms ago, the Court had held that a private citizen has the right to savor obscene materials within the privacy of his home. Stanley v. Georgia, 394 U.S. 557, 5 CrL 3019. But, the Court added this Term, it does not follow that commercial distributors have a First Amendment right to mail the smut to him. The First Amendment, Mr. Justice White wrote for six Justices, does not bar application of 18 U.S.C. Section 1461, which forbids such use of the mails to distributors of obscene materials to willing recipients who state that they are adults. Stanley, the majority emphasized, did not overrule Roth v. U.S., 354 U.S. 476.

The distributor of obscene materials is "in a wholly different position" from the individual who privately enjoys them. "He has no complaints about governmental violations of his private thoughts or fantasies, but stands squarely on a claimed First Amendment right to do business in obscenity and use the mails in the process. But Roth has squarely placed obscenity and its distribution outside the reach of the First Amendment and they remain there today. Stanley did not overrule Roth and we decline to do so now."

Concurring, Mr. Justice Harlan noted that Stanley explicitly reaffirmed Roth. He understood Stanley to rest in relevant part on the proposition that the power which Roth recognized in both state and federal governments to proscribe obscenity as constitutionally unprotected cannot be exercised to the exclusion of other constitutionally protected interests of the individual.

Also concurring, Mr. Justice Marshall noted the danger that obscene materials sent through the mails might fall into the hands of children. "While the record does not reveal that any children actually received appellee's materials, I believe that distributors of purportedly obscene merchandise may be required to take more stringent steps to guard against possible receipt by minors. This case comes to us without the benefit of a full trial, and, on this sparse record, I am not prepared to find that appellee's conduct was not within a constitutionally valid construction of the federal statute."

U.S. v. 37 Photographs, 402 U.S. 363, 9 CrL 3098

The Court also found no First Amendment violation in the enforcement of 19 U.S.C. Section 1305(a), which authorizes customs officials to seize obscene matter imported into the U.S. and subjected to forfeiture proceedings. The statute, the majority noted, can be construed as requiring that the Government institute forfeiture proceedings 14 days after seizure and that such proceedings be completed within 60 days of their pronouncement. Furthermore, to enforce this statue, the Government has authority to seize obscene matter privately possessed at a port of entry into the U.S. by a person who intends it for commercial distribution.

The importer of obscene materials stands on no different footing from one who mails them, the majority held, even though, at the time his materials are taken from him, he does have them in his private possession. A port of entry "is not a traveler's home."

Mr. Justice Harlan, concurring, thought that the question of importation for private use need not be raised here.

Also concurring, Mr. Justice Stewart "would not in this case decide, even by way of dicta, that the Government may lawfully seize literary material intended for the purely private use of the importer. The terms of the statute appear to apply to an American tourist who, after exercising his constitutionally protected liberty to travel abroad, returns home with a single book in his luggage, with no intention of selling it or otherwise using it, except to read it. If the Government can constitutionally take the book away from him as he passes through customs, then I do not understand the meaning of Stanley v. Georgia, 394 U.S. 557."

Dissenting, Mr. Justice Marshall, the author of the Court's opinion in Stanley, maintained that "the Government has ample opportunity to protect its valid interests if and when commercial distribution should take place."

Justices Black and Douglas dissented from the Court's holdings with respect to both the mailer and to the importer.

CONTEMPT

Two contempt cases touched on the obligation of a judge before whom the contempt is allegedly committed to recuse himself and have the contempt charges heard by another judge.

Mayberry v. Pennsylvania, 400 U.S. 455, 8 CrL 3065

A Pennsylvania criminal defendant who repeatedly insulted and villified the trial judge in the course of disrupting the courtroom proceedings was entitled to a public trial before another judge on the contempt charges, the Court held in one of the few unanimous criminal law decisions of this Term.

While vigorously condemning the antics of this defendant, who used "tactics taken from street brawls," Mr. Justice Douglas nevertheless concluded that, in view of the "marked personal feelings" that were "present on both sides," the Due Process Clause requires that the defendant be given a public trial "before a judge other than the one reviled by the contemnor."

Mr. Justice Douglas noted that "the arsenal of authority described in [Illinois v.] Allen, [397 U.S. 337, 7 CrL 3001] was available to the trial judge to keep order in the courtroom." The judge could have instantly held the defendant in contempt, excluded him from the courtroom, or otherwise insulated his "vulgarity from the courtroom."

Mr. Justice Black concurred with all of the opinion except the part indicating that the judge could have, without a jury, convicted the defendant of contempt simultaneously with the outburst.

Mr. Justice Harlan concurred in the reversal solely on the basis of the 22-year contempt sentence imposed by the judge who had been the victim of the abusive conduct. This sentence indicates a deprivation of due process Mr. Justice Harlan thought.

Johnson v. Mississippi, 403 U.S. 212, 9 CrL 3193

In a per curiam opinion, the Court held that a civil rights worker summarily convicted of contempt two years after the alleged contumacious conduct was entitled to reversal of his conviction. The alleged conduct was not personally observed by the presiding judge, and furthermore, the judge was one of the defendants in a successful civil rights suit filed by the defendant. The judge should have recused himself from hearing the contempt charge.

The Court also referred to In re Oliver, 332 U.S. 257, in which it held that if some of the essential elements of the offense are not personally observed by the judge, so that he has to depend on statements made by others for his knowledge about those elements, the Due Process Clause requires that the accused be accorded a fair hearing.

ABORTION — APPEALS

U.S. v. Vuitch, 402 U.S. 62, 9 Crl 3071

A District of Columbia abortion statute declared unconstitutional two years previously by a federal district court was given a saving construction by the Court. The statute prohibits abortions "unless necessary for preservation of the mother's life or health." This language, the Court held, is capable of the interpretation that it includes preservation of the mother's mental health as well as her physical health, and in fact, it has been so interpreted in the past. Thus, it is not void for vagueness and can be constitutionally applied to physicians. It requires the prosecution to prove that the abortion was unnecessary for the preservation of the mother's life or health.

The Court divided sharply in holding that a federal district court judgment that the invalidity of a District of Columbia criminal statute requires dismissal of an indictment brought thereunder is directly appealable to the U.S. Supreme Court under the Criminal Appeals Act, 18 U.S.C. Section 3731. The literal wording of the Act "plainly includes this statute even though it applies only to the District," Mr. Justice Black wrote for the majority. Even though the legislation is limited as to the place of its application, it is nevertheless a "statute" in the sense meant by Section 3731. The Act contains no language purporting to limit or qualify the statute.

Four justices dissented as to the Court's jurisdiction to entertain this case on direct appeal.

Tracing the development of the "question of overlap between the appellate routes available to the Government in criminal cases under the D.C. Code and 18 U.S.C. Section 3731," Mr. Justice Harlan concluded that the proper disposition of the case would be to vacate the district court judgment and remand the case for entry of a judgment from which the Government could take a

timely appeal to the U.S. Court of Appeals for the D.C. Circuit pursuant to the D.C. Code.

However, Justices Blackmun and Harlan, while disagreeing with the majority as to the jurisdiction point, agreed with the majority on the merits.

HABEAS CORPUS

Procunier v. Atchley, 400 U.S. 446, 8 CrL 3057

The failure of a federal habeas corpus petitioner to allege facts that would establish the involuntariness of his 1959 confession barred the grant of a new hearing on the question of voluntariness, the Court unanimously held, even though the California trial court did not comply with the procedures required by Jackson v. Denno, 378 U.S. 368, for determining the voluntariness of the confession.

The "confession" was not made to police, but to an insurance agent who visited the defendant while he was in jail awaiting murder charges. The agent was wired for sound, and tapes of the statement, as well as the agent's testimony, were introduced at trial.

In Jackson, Mr. Justice Stewart pointed out for the majority, the Court "did not jump from the premises that the procedures used to determine voluntariness were inadequate, to the conclusion that the petitioner was entitled to a new hearing." And, under the law predating Escobedo v. Illinois, 378 U.S. 478, and Miranda v. Arizona, 384 U.S. 4036, this "confession" was voluntary.

TRAVEL ACT — GAMBLING

Rewis v. U.S., 401 U.S. 803, 9 CrL 3055

Also unanimous was the Court's conclusion that the Travel Act, 18 U.S.C. 1952, was not violated by the mere operation of an illegal lottery frequented by out-of-state bettors, even though interstate travel by customers could have reasonably been foreseen.

STATUTES AND ORDINANCES

Two Ohio city ordinances limiting freedom on the sidewalk were declared unconstitutional.

Coates v. City of Cincinnati, 402 U.S. 611, 9 CrL 3181

A Cincinnati ordinance that forbids three or more persons to assemble on the sidewalks and "annoy" any "persons passing by" and that has not been narrowed by Ohio Supreme Court construction was held unconstitutionally vague and overbroad on its face.

Palmer v. City of Euclid, 402 U.S. 544, 9 CrL 3175

An ordinance punishing as a "suspicious person" anyone found abroad late at night without any lawful business who does not give a satisfactory account of himself was held by a per curiam Court to be unconstitutionally vague as applied to a defendant who discharged a passenger from his car at an apartment house, and then talked on an automobile telephone while his car was parked on the street.

EXTORTION

Perez v. U.S., 402 U.S. 146, 9 CrL 3091

The absence of proof of any connection between a loan shark's activities and interstate commerce was not fatal to his conviction under Title II of the Consumer Credit Protection Act of 1968, 18 U.S.C. (Supp. V) 891 et seq., the Court held; Title II's prohibition of extortion of credit transactions is a permissible exercise of congressional authority under the Commerce Clause.

PRESUMPTIONS

U.S. v. International Minerals & Chemicals Corp., 402 U.S. 558, 9 CrL 3177

The Court also held that the Government, in a prosecution for failing to label appropriately a corrosive liquid shipped in interstate commerce, need not prove knowledge of the regulation requiring such labeling, since the shipper of such inherently dangerous material must be presumed to be aware of regulations covering its transportation.

CIVIL RIGHTS ACTIONS

One way of lightening the federal judiciary's staggering workload is curtailing federal jurisdiction. The U.S. Supreme Court took a long stride toward that end by a series of decisions limiting federal intervention in state criminal matters. The impact on the Court's own workload was immediate: more than 20 pending cases were disposed of, or remanded for reconsideration, in light of the standards announced.

Most of those were cases in which federal district courts, usually three-judge, had declared state criminal statutes unconstitutional. The net result was to reduce the recently expanded role of the federal civil rights actions in criminal litigation.

Younger v. Harris, 401 U.S. 37, 8 CrL 3103

Dombrowski v. Pfister, 380 U.S. 479 (1965), the Court made clear, did not open the federal courts to every state defendant able to show that the statute under which he was being prosecuted was, on its face, overly broad or vague in violation of the First Amendment. Dombrowski had not eliminated the requirement that bad faith or harassment be shown.

Stressing "the fundamental policy against federal interference with state criminal prosecutions," the Court in Younger, with but one dissent, held that a federal district court may not enjoin a pending state prosecution unless the plaintiff can prove the existence of "irreparable injury" that is "both great and immediate." By "pending" state prosecutions, Mr. Justice Black, speaking for the Court, referred only to state proceedings initiated prior to the filing of the federal action.

The Court did not base its landmark holdings on the federal abstention doctrine or the anti-injunction statute, 28 U.S.C. 2283. Instead, these holdings rested on federal policy and fundamental principles of equity jurisdiction dictating when intervention in another court's proceedings is appropriate.

Specifically, the Court found certain types of injury not to constitute the requisite "irreparable injury." Federal intervention is no longer justified merely by "the cost, anxiety, and inconvenience of having to defend against a single criminal prosecution." Mr. Justice Black said that instead, "the threat to the plaintiff's federally protected rights must be one that cannot be eliminated by his defense against a single criminal prosecution."

Further elucidating the test for federal intervention, Mr. Justice Black held that in order to halt pending state prosecution, the plaintiff must show "bad faith, harassment, or any other unusual circumstance that would call for equitable relief." Moreover, the necessary "irreparable injury" is not established by the mere facial overbreadth and vagueness of a statute, which thus "chills" protected expressive activity.

This is directly contrary to what Dombrowski had said about the necessary type of "irreparable injury," but Mr. Justice Black's opinion labeled those statements mere dicta and expressly abandoned them. Many federal district courts, like the district court in Younger, had seized upon these statements in Dombrowski that federal courts in a First Amendment case may intervene, without any showing of bad faith or harassment prosecution, whenever a state statute is "on its face" vague or overbroad.

Mr. Justice Black emphasized the main reason for the long-standing public policy against federal court interference with state court proceedings. The basic doctrine of equity jurisprudence is that equity courts should not act, especially to restrain a criminal prosecution, if the moving party has an adequate remedy at law and therefore will not suffer irreparable injury if he is denied equitable relief.

Mr. Justice Stewart, joined by Mr. Justice Harlan, agreed with the result in the case, but was quick to give recognition to the areas into which the Court's holding did not necessarily extend. He noted that the Court did not reach any of the questions concerning the independent force of the federal anti-injunction statute, 28 U.S.C. Section 2283. And therefore it did not decide whether the word "injunction" in that section of the statute should be interpreted to include a declaratory judgment, or whether an injunction to stay proceedings in a state court is "expressly authorized" by Section 1 of the Civil Rights Act of 1871, 42 U.S.C. Section 1983.

In addition, these concurring Justices pointed out that, since the case involved a state criminal prosecution, the Court did not deal with the considerations that should govern a federal court asked to intervene in state civil proceedings; there, for various reasons, the balance might be struck differently. Also, they noted that the Court did not resolve the problems involved were a federal court asked to give injunctive or declaratory relief from future state criminal prosecutions.

Boyle v. Landry, 401 U.S. 77, 8 CrL 3109

In Boyle, seven groups of Civil Rights Act plaintiffs from Chicago who won the race to the courthouse and obtained federal injunctive relief against possible future prosecutions under an Illinois intimidation statute found that they had ultimately lost their case. In an opinion by Mr. Justice Black, the majority of the Court held that the plaintiffs had no standing, since they had not been prosecuted or even threatened with prosecution under that Illinois statute. In other words, there was no showing of the requisite irreparable injury; and as Mr. Justice Black put it, "The normal course of state criminal prosecutions cannot be disputed or blocked on the basis of charges which in the last analysis amount to nothing more than speculation about the future. The policy of a century and a half against interference by the federal courts with state law enforcement is not to be set aside on such flimsy allegations as those relied upon here."

These rulings on interference with pending state criminal prosecutions did not extend to that rare and ephemeral creature, the "threatened" prosecution. Rather, some of the plaintiffs were found not even to have been threatened.

Samuels v. Mackell, 401 U.S. 66, 8 CrL 3113

The same reasoning was applied in Samuels, with Mr. Justice Black again writing the majority opinion. Here the Supreme Court recognized the argument so often advanced by lower federal courts denying Civil Rights Act relief that for these purposes a federal declaratory judgment of a state statute's unconstitutionality is often every bit as damaging as a federal injunction. The Court held that "in cases where the state criminal prosecution was begun prior to the federal suit, the same equitable principles relevant to the propriety of an injunction must be taken into consideration by federal district courts in determining whether to issue a declaratory judgment, and that where an injunction would be impermissible under these principles, declaratory relief should ordinarily be denied as well."

The Court, however, expressed no opinion on the propriety of declaratory relief if, at the time the federal suit is begun, no state proceeding is pending.

Perez v. Ledesma, 401 U.S. 82, 8 CrL 3116

Mr. Justice Black also delivered the majority opinion in this case. And once again, the Court asserted that only in cases of proven harassment by state officials in bad faith without hope of getting a valid conviction and perhaps in other special circumstances where irreparable injury could be shown would federal injunctive relief against pending state prosecutions be proper. In this case, a three-judge court had, Mr. Justice Black found, improperly interfered with the state's criminal process by its order suppressing evidence during the course of a good-faith

obscenity prosecution and directing the return of all seized allegedly obscene materials. In a special concurring and dissenting opinion, Mr. Justice Brennan, joined by Mr. Justice White and Mr. Justice Marshall, commented that bad-faith harassment could take many forms including "arrests and prosecutions under valid statutes where there is no reasonable hope of obtaining conviction, * * * and a pattern of discriminatory enforcement designed to inhibit the exercise of federal rights." In addition, the Court held that it had no jurisdiction to review the state's appeal from a single judge's declaratory judgment that the local ordinance was unconstitutional, even though the three-judge court on which he had sat was of the same opinion.

The three Justices dissented only from the Court's holding that the judgment of the three-judge court was not properly before the Court for review. They concluded that "where no criminal prosecution involving the federal court parties is pending when federal jurisdiction attaches, declaratory relief determining the disputed constitutional issue will ordinarily be appropriate to carry out the purposes of the Federal Declaratory Judgment Act and to vindicate the great protections of the constitution."

Dyson v. Stein, 401 U.S. 200, 8 CrL 3134

Repeating the rule of Douglas v. City of Jeanette, 319 U.S. 57 (1943), a per curiam Court held that federal intervention affecting pending state criminal prosecutions, either by means of injunction or declaratory judgment, is proper only where irreparable injury is threatened.

In Dyson, the Court held that a three-judge federal district court improperly declared a Texas obscenity statute unconstitutional and enjoined a newspaper publisher's prosecution and any other prosecution under it in the absence of a finding of irreparable injury. The Court did stress, however, that the existence of such irreparable injury was a matter to be determined carefully under the facts of each case.

Mr. Justice Brennan, joined by Mr. Justice Marshall, concurred in the result using the same reasoning as in his separate opinion in Perez. Mr. Justice Douglas dissented, graphically describing the police conduct upon which the appellee rested his allegations of bad faith and harassment. His dissent contained vivid images of the two raids in the case which were "search-and-destroy missions in the Vietnamese sense of the phrase." Mr. Justice Douglas went on to clearly point out that the Texas obscenity statute was unconstitutional, and even though he realized that this question was not before the Court, he maintained that it was plain error and an end should be put to the "lawless" raids under the statute.

Mr. Justice Douglas stood firm in his position that "any regime of censorship over literature whether expressed in a criminal statute or an administrative procedure, is unconstitutional by reason of the command of the First Amendment." He emphasized that there was no clearer case justifying federal intervention to prevent a state criminal trial. In Dyson, only future prosecutions were sought to be enjoined, not pending ones. In addition, if Zwickler v. Koota, 389 U.S. 241 (1967), meant anything at all, it meant that the asked-for declaratory relief should also be granted.

Byrne v. Karalexis, 401 U.S. 216, 8 CrL 3132

In another decision involving obscenity, the Court, per curiam, deemed improper a federal district court's grant of injunctive relief against pending or future state obscenity prosecutions. The Court could not find that a movie exhibitor's First Amendment rights could not be adequately protected in a single state criminal prosecution for exhibiting an allegedly obscene film. The Court merely let Younger and the other companion cases decided that day also be the guide for deciding Byrne.

Mr. Justice Brennan, joined by Mr. Justice White and Mr. Justice Marshall, disagreed with the Court and referred to his opinion in Perez for his reasoning.

SELECTIVE SERVICE

Most of the Court's draft law cases this term were a disappointment to draft registrants. The Court rejected "selective objection," and post-induction order reopening, and declined to declare a right to counsel in draft board hearings by finding itself without jurisdiction to review a case involving that issue. It did, however, stop short of retracting the previous Term's broad construction of the "religious training and belief" requirement for conscientious objection. Welsh v. U.S., 398 U.S. 333, 7 CrL 3106.

Gillette v. U.S., 401 U.S. 437, 8 CrL 3155

The big decision of the Term in selective service law, and one which came to terms with a fundamental issue, was one in which the Court saw no statutory or constitutional bar to the denial of conscientious objector status to selective objectors —whose objection, even though religious and sincere, is limited to participation in a particular war. With only Mr. Justice Douglas dissenting, the Court rejected selective objection both as a ground for pre-induction exemption from the draft and as a ground for conscientious objector administrative discharge.

Mr. Justice Marshall's majority opinion in the combined cases of a draft registrant who was denied conscientious objector classification and an in-service claimant who sought federal habeas corpus after being denied an administrative conscientious objector discharge rejected several federal district court holdings that recognized conscientious objection to the Vietnam war alone and had held section 6(j) of the Military Selective Service Act of 1967 unconstitutional in its restriction of CO exemption to total objectors.

The Supreme Court majority refused to read section 6(j) as requiring recognition of selective objectors and found no First Amendment defect in the statute as narrowly construed. The majority explained that the Act's express exemption of those "conscientiously opposed to participation in war in any form" was meant to cover only those who oppose all shooting wars. It did not think that a subtle grammatical construction of this phrase could make it read as a selective objector's ticket to a conscription-free life.

The court found no support in the legislative history of the section or in logic itself for the construction urged by the Vietnam-only objectors. "Conscientious scruples relating to war and military service must amount to conscientious opposition to participating personally in any and all wars."

Nor did the majority have any difficulty with the First Amendment arguments. Exempting total objectors while requiring anti-Vietnam objectors to serve is neither an establishment of religion, an unjustifiable burden on the free exercise of Christian and other faiths which recognize the supremacy of individual conscience, nor an irrational discrimination between the two kinds of religious objectors. The selective-total distinction is supported by valid reasons —neutral in respect to religion —such as the need to insure a fair and uniform system for deciding who will and will not be forced to serve.

Mr. Justice Douglas in his dissent was persuaded by the selective objectors' constitutional arguments —although unimpressed by the statutory construction argument. It violates the First Amendment, he argued, to send a sincere conscientious objector of any kind into involuntary military service. Mr. Justice Black, without filing an opinion, stated that he agreed with the Court's statutory ruling and concurred in that part of its opinion.

Ehlert v. U.S., 402 U.S. 99, 9 CrL 3082

Taking what had very recently become the minority view among the federal circuits on what was known as the "post-induction order reopening" issue, a majority of the Supreme Court relegated registrants who raised their conscientious objection claims only after receipt of an induction order to the tender mercies of the Armed Services. The Army is an appropriate place for such late-blooming claims to be resolved by the method of application for administrative discharge as a conscientious objector and, failing that, habeas corpus.

In making this division of labor the majority, speaking through Mr. Justice Stewart, expressly relied on the Army's assurances that it has adequate procedures to deal with these objectors' claims just as fully and fairly as the Selective Service System would.

The majority held that the Army's readiness to hear conscientious objector claims and to employ objecting servicemen in "duties which involve minimum conflict with their asserted beliefs" while their release applications are pending so fully protects the applicant's rights under Section 6(j) of the 1967 Act that there is no need to require draft boards to hear any claims arising after receipt of the induction order. Therefore the applicable Selective Service regulation can properly be construed so as to bar the hearing of such late claims. The Court, the majority said, should defer to Selective Service's interpretation of its own rules.

Thus it makes no difference that the Act itself protects a true conscientious objector against being involuntarily subjected to combatant training and service. Even though the draft board does not have to reopen the registrant's I-A classification, the registrant's claim will eventually be heard, so he has no complaint.

The majority thus found it unnecessary to decide the central issue upon which the case had been argued and upon which the decisions of the lower federal courts had turned: whether, within the language of the regulation, the late and perhaps sudden "crystallization" of a legally acceptable conscientious objection is a "change in the registrant's status resulting from circumstances over which the registrant had no control" —and thus an event requiring a reopening of classification.

A dissent by Mr. Justice Douglas did address this central issue, and cited the experience of Saul of Tarsus on the road to Damascus as supporting the often-suspect credibility of late discoveries of religious objection. Quoting at length from accounts by conscientious objectors of their treatment in the Army, he was also very skeptical of the adequacy of Army procedures to treat objectors properly while their claims were pending and to permit decision on the nature of their religious objections with the kind of sensitiveness that draft boards are supposed to employ.

A dissent by Justices Brennan and Marshall objected that the majority had based its entire holding on the acceptance of Selective Service's interpretation of its own regulations and that no such interpretation existed.

Clay v. U.S., 403 U.S. 698, 9 CrL 3258

The old question of whether a person whose faith allows him to fight in a theocratic war can still be a pacifist was once again before the Supreme Court in the case of Black Muslim, boxing champion Muhammad Ali. In fact, the case seemed to fall so much within the already-established rules of Sicurella v. U.S., 348 U.S. 385, U.S. v. Seeger, 380 U.S. 163, and Welsh v. U.S., 398 U.S. 333, that commentators couldn't see any reason why the Court granted certiorari unless it was to cut back on Welsh. Ali himself raised many controversial legal issues in seeking review of his induction refusal conviction, but the Court restricted the grant of review to the conscientious objection issue.

But when the case reached the argument stage, the Government conceded the "religiousness" of Clay's Islam-based objection and relied instead on an argument that no member of the Court could buy —that willingness to take part in a Muslim holy war or jihad made Ali's objection "selective."

The Court's per curiam opinion reversing Ali's conviction left the selectivity question unanswered, for it found that of the three grounds stated by Selective Service in denying the CO claim —insincerity, secularity, and selectiveness —it was impossible to tell whether Selective Service relied on "selectivity" or the two clearly improper grounds of insincerity and secularity.

The Court held that the Government was indeed correct in conceding upon oral argument that Ali's objection was both sincere and religious. As for the effect of holy-war participation on "religiousness," it found that the case "falls squarely within the four corners of this Court's decision in Sicurella."

Mr. Justice Harlan concurred in the result on the ground that the Selective Service may have relied on an interpretation of the law as to sincerity and timeliness of assertion of the CO claim which would have been entirely erroneous. A concurrence by Mr. Justice Douglas emphasized his belief that all "just-war" believers, whether Muslim or Roman Catholic, should be treated as qualified conscientious objectors.

McGee v. U.S., 402 U.S. 479, 9 CrL 3168

In an opinion by Mr. Justice Marshall, the Court, with Mr. Justice Douglas again the only dissenter, decided that a registrant who announced his position of utter non-cooperation with the Selective Service System was properly held to the rule of waiver by failure to exhaust administrative remedies. Affirming his conviction of refusing induction, the majority held that his refusal to fill out Selective Service questionnaires and seek a personal appearance or appeal board review deprived him of the right to assert the defense of erroneous draft classification when he came to trial.

The registrant had at one time entered a graduate study program that might have qualified him under the applicable standards for a theological exemption, but the majority saw this as no bar to his conviction in the factual context of the case. The administrative exhaustion rule was properly applied here since this particular failure to exhaust administrative remedies jeopardizes the valid interest of the Selective Service System in performing its duties of classification.

Mr. Justice Douglas pointed out that every judge who had been involved with the case had agreed that this man was a conscientious objector. It seemed from all facts in the record that he would still qualify for CO status. In the dissenter's view of the facts the draft board defaulted on its administrative duties, not the registrant. The board acted lawlessly in refusing to consider this registrant's claim at the time when he was cooperating and asked to have it considered.

U.S. v. Weller, 401 U.S. 254, 8 CrL 3142

A case that might have resolved an important question in Selective Service procedural law —whether the right to counsel should apply to registrants' personal appearances before draft boards —was avoided as a majority of the Court found that it had no jurisdiction to hear the appeal. Again with only Mr. Justice Douglas dissenting, the majority in an opinion by Mr. Justice Stewart, construed the Criminal Appeals Act, 18 U.S.C. 3731, to foreclose review of decision in the registrant's favor by a federal district court trying him for refusal of induction.

The majority said that the district court's determination that the Military Selective Service Act of 1967 didn't authorize the Selective Service regulation prohibiting counsel at board hearings was not a construction of the regulation so inextricably intertwined with the statute that the district court's dismissal of the prosecution could be considered a "construction of statute" under the Criminal Appeals Act.

MILITARY CASES

Relford v. Commandant, 401 U.S. 355, 8 CrL 3146

Once again the Court found no need to decide a much-disputed issue —this time the retroactivity of the O'Callahan v. Parker, 395 U.S. 258, 5 CrL 3082, "service-connection" requirement for court-martial jurisdiction — as it upheld the military conviction of a soldier charged with kidnaping and raping two women on an Army base. The answer here was that entirely aside from retroactivity, the fact situation was in several ways distinguishable from O'Callahan's and presented a much stronger case for military jurisdiction.

The Court's unanimous opinion, written by Mr. Justice Blackmun, observed that O'Callahan, where there was not enough service connection to give the court-martial subject-matter jurisdiction over the serviceman's offense, had involved an off-base indecent assault on U.S. territory, against a civilian victim and triable in a civilian court, committed in peacetime while the serviceman defendant was on leave and out of uniform. All O'Callahan definitively held was that the mere fact of the accused's membership in the armed services was not enough, standing alone, to make military jurisdiction attach.

The present appellant, on the other hand, committed his crimes on base. Certainly an on-post offense of this type, which violates the security of persons or property on the base, is service-connected, the Court said, within the meaning of O'Callahan.

Schlanger v. Seamans, 401 U.S. 487, 8 CrL 3169

The intricate jurisdictional questions presented when a serviceman files habeas corpus against his military superiors came before the Supreme Court to a certain limited extent in the case of a disgruntled Air Force officer candidate. The holding, set forth in an opinion by Mr. Justice Douglas, was so tied to the unique fact situation of the case that it held few lessons for the many federal district courts now confronted with servicemen's habeas petitions.

A federal district court, the opinion said, lacks jurisdiction over an enlisted man's habeas claim when the defendant commanding officer neither resides in the court's judicial district nor is amenable to its process. Thus even though the petitioner serviceman found himself in Arizona on temporary duty orders he could not go to the district court nearest him, as his actual commanding officer was in Georgia and the officials above him in the chain of command were located in places other than Arizona. Although the commander of the Air Force ROTC program for Arizona State University was one of the defendants, the Court held that he was not a proper defendant, since he had no control over petitioner who had been kicked out of the AF ROTC program and activated as an enlisted man.

Mr. Justice Harlan concurred in the result, and Mr. Justice Stewart dissented, each without opinion.

1971–1972 Term

The 1971–72 Term's work by the Court in criminal law and related areas revealed a "balance" of views among the Justices so precarious that no decisional "trends" were discernible. However, the Court had never been more productive —or controversial. It firmly grasped several nettles of constitutional magnitude that had generated heated debate for decades —although the close division among the Justices sometimes produced unclear results. It used the Eighth Amendment to do away with the death penalty as presently applied. It finally decided whether a witness must be given transactional immunity before being compelled to testify; its decision was negative. Even petty offenders who face any incarceration at all are now entitled to counsel, and the President was held bound by the Fourth Amendment in authorizing electronic surveillance of domestic subversives.

Part of the controversy surrounding this Term was due not only to the close divisions on the Court and the results in some of its cases, but to the publicity that had attached to some of these cases even before they reached the Court. Nationally known antiwar activists, civil rights workers, domestic "subversives," and even two U.S. Senators were involved.

On the other hand, the Court quietly achieved clear majorities and even virtual unanimity in several decisions that were to directly affect far more individuals than the more famous cases. The criminal law revolution of the Sixties continued in such areas as the rights of parolees facing revocation, prisoners' rights, and the application of vagrancy and loitering laws that go back to Queen Elizabeth.

CAPITAL PUNISHMENT

Furman v. Georgia, 408 U.S. 238, 11 CrL 3231

No unifying reason supported the Court's 5–4 decision that the death penalty in its present form in the states is unconstitutional. The net result of the Court's decision, with each Justice writing his own opinion, was that the death penalty, as imposed within the discretion of the jury, violates the Eighth Amendment not becuase it is inherently intolerable, but because it is applied so rarely, "so wantonly and freakishly," that it serves no valid purpose and now constitutes cruel and unusual punishment.

Thus capital punishment in its present form was rendered "cruel and unusual" by the operation of what was intended to be, at the time of its introduction, an ameliorative feature of the criminal justice system —the jury's discretion to impose a lesser sentence.

Only Justices Brennan and Marshall would have held the death penalty unconstitutional per se. Mr. Justice Douglas refrained from reaching this ultimate question. He based his decision on the fact that capital punishment statutes are applied in a way that discriminates against the minorities and the poor, and on his conclusion that such discrimination is not compatible with the equal protection idea implicit in the ban on cruel and unusual punishment.

The "swing" votes were cast by Justices Stewart and White, neither of whom expressed outright opposition to the death penalty. Rather, they based their conclusions on the infrequency and manner of its imposition.

Ironically, perhaps the strongest declarations of personal belief against capital punishment came from Justices Burger and Blackmun, who thought, however, that it was not for the Court to do away with this form of punishment.

Mr. Justice Stewart acknowledged that Justices Brennan and Marshall presented a "strong" case in favor of the death penalty's unconstitutionality per se. But he rested his opinion on a far narrower basis: the Eighth and Fourteenth Amendments are violated by impositions of death under legal systems that permit capital punishment "to be so wantonly and freakishly imposed."

This case does not involve state or federal statutes that make death mandatory for certain offenses, Mr. Justice Stewart emphasized. Review of sentences imposed under these statutes would present the question whether a legislature could set automatic death as the penalty for certain offenses on the ground that society's interest in deterrence and retribution for such offenses "wholly outweighs" considerations of rehabilitation.

"On that score, I would say only that I cannot agree that retribution is a constitutionally impermissible ingredient in the imposition of punishment."

However, Mr. Justice Stewart continued, the death penalty is applied on such a random and capricious basis that its imposition has indeed become cruel and unusual. There is no legislative determination that death is necessary to deter crimes for which it is imposed. Few defendants incur it, while "a capriciously selected" handful do. "These death sentences are cruel and unusual in the same way that being struck by lightning is cruel and unusual."

Mr. Justice White's concurrence hinged on his observation that the death penalty is now so infrequently imposed that it no longer satisfies "any existing general need for retribution" or has any deterrent value. "A penalty with such negligible returns to the state would be patently excessive and cruel and unusual punishment violative of the Eight Amendment * * *. This point has been reached with respect to capital punishment, as it is presently administered * * * in these cases."

The policy of vesting juries with sentencing authority as a means of mitigating the harshness of the law and bringing community judgment to bear on the question of punishment "has so effectively achieved its aims that capital punishment within the confines of the statutes now before us has for all practical purposes run its course."

The fact that the death penalty is almost exclusively imposed upon the poor and the powerless led Mr. Justice Douglas to concur in striking down the death penalty as presently imposed. He expressly refrained, however, from going so far as to find it inherently unconstitutional.

"It would seem to be incontestable that the death penalty inflicted on one defendant is 'unusual' if it discriminates against him by reason of his race, religion, wealth, social position, or class, or if it is imposed under a procedure that gives room for the play of such prejudices," Mr. Justice Douglas wrote. "And there is evidence that the 1689 English Bill of Rights provision, that served as the model for the Cruel and Unusual Punishment Clause, 'was concerned primarily with selective or irregular application of harsh penalties * * *.'"

To Mr. Justice Douglas, the words of the Eighth Amendment, when read in light of the English proscription, "suggest that it is 'cruel and unusual' to apply the death penalty —or any other penalty —selectively to minorities * * * whom society is willing to see suffer though it would not countenance general application of the same penalty across the board."

Evidence is overwhelming that the death penalty is, in fact, applied in this way, Mr. Justice Douglas noted. "These discretionary statutes are unconstitutional in their operation. They are pregnant with discrimination and discrimination is an ingredient not compatible with the idea of equal protection of the laws that is implicit in the ban on 'cruel and unusual' punishments."

Mr. Justice Brennan was moved to declare capital punishment inherently unconstitutional by application of four basic principles by which severe punishment must be measured against the Cruel and Unusual Punishment Clause.

The primary principle, Mr. Justice Brennan stated, "is that a punishment must not be so severe as to be degrading to the dignity of human beings." Second, it must not be applied arbitrarily, and third, it "must not be unacceptable to contemporary society." Finally, the punishment must not be excessive; it must serve a penal purpose more effectively than a less severe punishment would.

Mr. Justice Brennan condemned, as an abdication of the judicial function, the dissenters' interpretation of the Clause only in light of the Framers' concern with torture and with what they would have found cruel and unusual at the time. What little evidence there is of the reason for its inclusion indicates that the Clause was intended to limit the legislative power to prescribe punishment.

It is impossible to know exactly what "cruel and unusual punishments" were at the time, Mr. Justice Brennan noted, but it is clear that the Framers did not intend to limit the Clause's application either to unspeakable atrocities or to evils that had been developed up to that point in history. Weems v. U.S., 217 U.S. 349 (1910) conclusively rejected this view. It was recognized in Weems that the restraint imposed on the legislature by the Clause must be expansive if individual freedoms and the rule of law were to be maintained. The Clause must be applied consistently with evolving standards of human dignity.

While the language of the Fifth Amendment itself makes it clear that the Framers "recognized the existence of what was then a common punishment," this does not mean that they intended to exempt it from the express prohibition of the Cruel and Unusual Punishment Clause. Thus, the death penalty is susceptible of examination under the Clause despite its mention elsewhere in the Constitution.

The primary principle by which a severe punishment must be measured —that it must not be so severe as to be degrading to human dignity —is based upon several factors. Pain is one such factor. But there are others; the true evil of barbaric torture techniques "is that they treat members of the human race as nonhumans, as objects to be toyed with and discarded." Some punishments —such as status punishment —are degrading simply because they are punishments. And, "a punishment may be degrading simply because of its enormity." Such was the case with expatriation, described in Trop v. Dulles, 356 U.S., 86 at 101, as "a punishment more primitive than torture."

Applying the first principle, Mr. Justice Brennan noted the uniqueness of the death penalty in "a society that so strongly affirms the sanctity of life * * * ." No other punishment has been so continuously and progressively restricted. No other punishment has been treated so differently from other forms of punishment by everyone directly concerned with it —including the accused. The only explanation for its uniqueness is its extreme severity, which renders it "unusual in its pain, in its finality, and in its enormity."

Mr. Justice Brennan continued: "The calculated killing of a human being by the state involves, by its very nature, a denial of the executed person's humanity." The uniqueness of the executed person's degradation stands in contrast to the punishment imposed upon a prisoner, who is not only allowed to live, but allowed to retain numerous legal rights, and above all, his membership in "the human family."

The death penalty also fails the second test, Mr. Justice Brennan concluded. It has been arbitrarily imposed.

The growing infrequency of its imposition is compelling evidence that it is no longer an ordinary punishment for any crime. The fact that it is inflicted in "a trivial number of the cases in which it is legally available" leads inescapably to the conclusion "that it is being inflicted arbitrarily. Indeed, it smacks of little more than a lottery system." And there is no reason to believe that it is being imposed with "informed selectivity."

The strong probability that an unusually severe and degrading punishment like death is being applied arbitrarily makes it likely that it is no longer accepted by contemporary society, Mr. Justice Brennan went on, and this likelihood is borne out by an examination of objective indicators of public opinion. Crimes punishable by death have progressively declined, and our concern for human dignity has not only led to the death penalty's removal as a public spectacle but has stimulated a search for more humane ways to impose it. Discretionary imposition, and outright abolition in nine states, are further indications "that our society seriously questions" its appropriateness.

Referring to Mr. Justice Marshall's treatment of the death penalty's history, Mr. Justice Brennan concluded that the battle against the death penalty has been fought on moral grounds and a history of the death penalty's decreasing use indicates that "it has proved progressively more troublesome to the national conscience. * * * Indeed, the likelihood is great that the punishment is tolerated only because of its disuse."

Finally, the principle that a severe punishment must not be excessive is applied by examining a severe punishment to determine if it is necessary. "The infliction of a severe punishment by the state cannot comport with human dignity when it is nothing more than a pointless infliction of suffering."

The death penalty's lack of demonstrated success in deterring capital crimes is a strong argument that it serves no penal purpose more effectively than a less severe punishment would. There is no evidence whatever that society's need for retribution must be satisfied by death rather than imprisonment. "Furthermore, it is certainly doubtful that the infliction of death by the state does in fact strengthen the community's moral code; if the deliberate extinguishment of human life has any effect at all, it more likely tends to lower our respect for life and brutalize our values."

Mr. Justice Marshall found no inconsistency between constitutional principles developed in prior cases dealing with different aspects of capital punishment and his conclusion that the death penalty is cruel and unusual punishment in the constitutional sense. Exhaustively reviewing cases involving cruel and unusual punishment claims, he found precedent for his way of dealing with the question in Wilkerson v. Utah, 99 U.S. 130 (1878), in which public execution by shooting was upheld. Wilkerson examined the history of the Utah territory and current writings on capital punishment, and compared this nation's practices with those of other countries. "It is apparent that the Court felt it could not dispose of the question simply by referring to traditional practices; instead, it felt bound to examine developing thoughts."

Another landmark of particular importance was Weems v. U.S. In this case "the Court made it plain * * * that excessive punishments were as objectionable as those which were inherently cruel."

A punishment permissible at one time may not be permissible today, Mr. Justice Marshall emphasized. And so it is with capital punishment. Establishing standards for his decision, Mr. Justice Marshall said that a punishment could be deemed cruel and unusual for any one of four reasons.

"First, there are certain punishments which inherently involve so much physical pain and suffering that civilized people cannot tolerate them —e.g., use of the rack, the thumbscrew, or other modes of torture."

Second, are "unusual" punishments —ones "previously unknown as penalties for a given offense."

"Third, a penalty may be cruel and unusual because it is excessive and serves no legislative purpose." This was the basis of the Court's decision not only in Weems, but in Robinson v. California, 370 U.S. 660, and Trop v. Dulles. The entire thrust of the Eighth Amendment, Mr. Justice Marshall emphasized, is against excess.

Finally, a punishment that is not excessive and does serve a valid legislative purpose may still be invalid "if popular sentiment abhors it." While no prior cases strike down a penalty on this ground, "the very notion of changing values requires that we recognize its existence."

Reviewing capital punishment's history in America, Mr. Justice Marshall pointed out that the death penalty was never as common in this country as it had been in Britain, and that by the early 19th century there were effective abolitionist movements. Even as early as the 17th century there was opposition to it.

The historical trend has been toward limiting or abolishing capital punishment, with some interruptions, particularly after wars. In the 1830s and 1840s states passed laws making imposition of the death sentence discretionary. By 1900, mandatory capital punishment had been almost completely eliminated. Michigan abolished capital punishment outright in 1846.

None of the six purposes conceivably served by capital punishment justify its retention, Mr. Justice Marshall concluded.

Retribution, "one of the most misunderstood [concepts] in all of our criminal jurisprudence," actually deals with the question of what justifies punishment, and not with why men punish. While the state may seek retribution against lawbreakers, punishment solely for the sake of retribution is not permissible under the Eighth Amendment.

Deterrence is offered as another justification for a criminal punishment, but the admittedly unsatisfactory empirical evidence that is available indicates that the death penalty has no effect on the murder rate. "Despite the fact that abolitionists have not proved nondeterrence beyond a reasonable doubt, they have succeeded in showing by clear and convincing evidence that capital punishment is not necessary as a deterrent to crime in our society. This is all that they must do."

Nor can capital punishment be justified because it forecloses the possibility of recidivism. Most murderers are first offenders, and they are extremely unlikely to commit other crimes, either in prison or upon release. As a means of preventing recidivism, capital punishment is clearly excessive.

No merit whatsoever can be attributed to the three remaining purposes underlying utilization of capital punishment —encouraging guilty pleas and confessions, eugenics, and reducing state expenditures.

While statistical evidence against the death penalty "is not convincing beyond all doubt," Mr. Justice Marshall acknowledged, "it is persuasive." It has been demonstrated that capital punishment has no rational basis. Further deference to the legislative branch is inconsistent with the Court's role as ultimate arbiter of the Constitution.

Even if it can be argued that capital punishment is not excessive, Mr. Justice Marshall concluded, "it nonetheless violates the Eighth Amendment because it is morally unacceptable to the people of the United States at this time in their history." While public opinion polls are somewhat helpful on this question, the real issue is not whether mere mention of capital punishment shocks the people's conscience and sense of justice, but whether people who are fully informed as to its purposes and liabilities would find it unacceptable. The question is what the American people would think of capital punishment "in the light of all the information presently available." And this information is damning.

For one thing, death sentences are imposed on a far higher proportion of Negroes than whites, and there is evidence that this is due in part, at least, to racial discrimination. A disproportionate number of men, as opposed to women, incur the death penalty, and the burden of capital punishment falls upon the poor, the ignorant, and the underprivileged. So long as the victims of capital punishment are members of the voiceless classes, their plight is ignored by the legislators. Finally, there is always the danger of an innocent man being put to death.

Concluding, Mr. Justice Marshall characterized the Court's blow against capital punishment as a major triumph of a free society.

While he made clear his own feelings that as a legislative matter the death penalty should be abolished or severely restricted, the Chief Justice thought that the result in this case seriously undermined the jury function in sentencing.

The Cruel and Unusual Punishment Clause was included in the Bill of Rights in response to objections against the lack of any constitutional ban on torture, the Chief Justice argued. Cases under the Eighth Amendment "are consistent with the tone of the ratifying debates" on this question. The Court's concern has been with the cruelty of the punishment imposed. "I do not suggest that the presence of the word 'unusual' in the Eighth Amendment is merely vestigial, having no relevance to the constitutionality of any punishment that might be devised." But in a case involving a punishment so well known to history, the outcome cannot correctly be tied to the term "unusual." This term "cannot be read as limiting the ban on 'cruel' punishments or as somehow expanding the meaning of the term 'cruel.' For this reason I am unpersuaded by the facile argument that since capital punishment has always been cruel in the everyday sense of the word, and has been unusual due to decreased use, it is, therefore, now 'cruel and unusual.' "

As it was to the other dissenters, it was clear to the Chief Justice that the Framers had "no thought whatever of the elimination of capital punishment." Nor, even in recent times, has the Supreme Court.

Of course, while the cruel and unusual punishment standard remains the same, its application can change. "The standard of extreme cruelty is not merely descriptive, but necessarily embodies a moral judgment." But it is not the Court's function to determine when "a shift in the weight of accepted social values" has rendered impermissibly cruel a certain form of punishment authorized by the legislatures. Previous cases construing the Clause have considered forms of punishment devised by penal authorities without legislative authorization. The presumption that the legislative judgment embodies a society's prevailing standards of decency can be negated only "by unambiguous and compelling evidence of legislative default." An examination of the indicators of the social conscience with respect to capital punishment, such as public opinion polls, and infrequent jury imposition of the death penalty, does not carry the argument that legislatures "have abandoned their essential barometric role with respect to community values."

The Chief Justice addressed himself in particular to the argument that the relatively rare jury imposition of the death sentence reflects a revulsion against the death penalty that would become law if only widely recognized. The characterization of juries that reject the death penalty as expressing civilized values, while painting juries that impose it as arbitrary and insensitive to prevailing standards of decency "is unsupported by known facts, and is inconsistent in principle with everything this Court has ever said about the functioning of juries in capital cases." Their selectivity in imposing death sentences "is properly viewed as a refinement on rather than as repudiation of the statutory authorization of that penalty." To assume that "only a random assortment of pariahs are sentenced to death is to cast doubt on the basic integrity of the jury system."

The Court's limited function in reviewing criminal punishments under the Eighth Amendment does not extend to determining whether it is necessary to achieve legitimate penal aims, the Chief Justice admonished. Weems v. U.S., 217 U.S. 349 (1910), is not to the contrary. There, the Court "was making an essentially moral judgment, not a dispassionate assessment of the need for the penalty."

Other reasons compel the conclusion that the necessity approach is outside Eighth Amendment purview. Both the moral question whether retribution is justifiable and the empirical question of capital punishment's deterrent value are locked in an impasse.

The actual scope of the Court's decision, the Chief Justice pointed out, is embodied in "the substantially similar concurring opinions" of Mr. Justice Stewart and Mr. Justice White. The infrequency of the death penalty's imposition is the critical factor in these opinions —and this factor, the Chief Justice submits, is treated not as evidence of society's abhorrence of capital punishment, "but as the earmark of a deteriorated sentencing system." Despite their nominal reliance on the Eighth Amendment, these opinions have no antecedent in death penalty cases. They make "essentially and exclusively a procedural and due process argument." And, the Chief Justice adds, this basis of decision "is plainly foreclosed as well as misplaced." McGautha v. California, 402 U.S. 183, 9 CrL 3109, 39 LW 4529, should govern here.

The Chief Justice then touched on legislative changes that would have to be made to allow the death penalty to survive in compliance with the result of this case.

It would be extremely difficult, he suggested, to set up any kind of discretionary system that would produce results different from the one heretofore in effect in the states. Legislative enactment of mandatory death penalties would provide an answer, but "if this is the only alternative * * * , I would have preferred that the Court opt for total abolition."

Emphasizing his personal abhorrence of the death penalty —which he made a matter of judicial record in several Eighth Circuit opinions —Mr. Justice Blackmun found much to commend in the argument that the time has come to take a great step forward and abolish capital punishment. "But it is a good argument and it makes sense only in a legislative and executive way and not as a judicial expedient."

Mr. Justice Blackmun expressed the fear that the key opinions of Mr. Justice Stewart and Mr. Justice White would encourage regressive legislation imposing mandatory death sentences. He also found it curious that none of the opinions for the majority refer to the misery occasioned by these petitioners' crimes.

Addressing himself to the contention that the death penalty is per se unconstitutional, Mr. Justice Powell made it clear that the "foundations of my disagreement with that broader thesis are equally applicable to each of the majority's opinions."

Mr. Justice Powell was particularly concerned with the effect of the majority's "collection of views" on the "root principles of stare decisis, federalism, judicial restraint, and —most importantly —separation of powers." The majority disregards the clear evidence that the Constitution and the Fourteenth Amendment posed no barriers to the death penalty, as well as "an unbroken line of precedent upholding the constitutionality of capital punishment." It encroaches upon the legislature's prerog-

ative of protecting the citizens by designating penalties, Mr. Justice Powell said. He emphasized actual acceptance of the death penalty in the Fifth Amendment by the same Framers who wrote the Eighth Amendment.

The several references to capital punishment in the Constitution do not foreclose consideration of whether capital punishment is cruel and unusual in a particular case, Mr. Justice Powell acknowledged, and they do not tie the Court to static interpretations of the essentially dynamic provisions of the Eighth and Fourteenth Amendments. The manner of the death penalty's imposition is clearly open to challenge, but it is clear that the penalty itself is constitutional.

The constitutionality of capital punishment has been both "assumed and asserted" by the Court on several occasions. Mr. Justice Powell referred to several cases, beginning with Wilkerson v. Utah, 99 U.S. 130 (1878), in which the Court reviewed the manner in which the death penalty was carried out. As recently as 1947 the Court expressly authorized imposition of the death penalty. Opinions in several other cases, most recently Witherspoon v. Illinois, 391 U.S. 510, 3 CrL 3109, and McGautha v. California have assumed the death penalty's constitutionality.

The petitioner's attempts to avoid the authority of these cases will not withstand analysis, Mr. Justice Powell continued. Their reliance upon several cases in which the Justices have recognized the dynamic nature of the prohibition against cruel and unusual punishment is based upon the correct view that "notions of what constitutes cruel and unusual punishment and due process do evolve." But their argument goes far beyond the case-by-case method of examining various means of punishment. "What they are saying in effect is that the evolutionary process has come suddenly to an end; that the ultimate wisdom as to the appropriateness of capital punishment under all circumstances, and for all future generations, has somehow been revealed."

Designation of punishment is a legislative function, and by dictating to the legislators of some 40 states on this question, the Court is making a particularly serious inroad. Mr. Justice Frankfurter's dissenting admonitions in Trop v. Dulles, 356 U.S. 86, are particularly apt here, Mr. Justice Powell maintained.

Nor was Mr. Justice Powell persuaded by the petitioners' "list of 'objective indicators' " that prevailing standards of human decency render capital punishment unconstitutional.

The petitioners have chosen to discount or ignore "the first indicator of the public 'attitude' —legislative judgments of the people's chosen representatives."

Reviewing various efforts to abolish or limit the death penalty, which have met with mixed results, Mr. Justice Powell concluded that their recent history "abundantly refutes the abolitionist position."

The jury is the "second and even more direct source of information reflecting the public's attitude toward capital punishment," Mr. Justice Powell said, and it is particularly noteworthy that during the 1960s juries returned more than 2,000 death sentences. While the percentage of cases in which the death penalty has been returned is debatable, it is clear that the death penalty is not unanimously repudiated and condemned. Furthermore, the annual rate of death sentences has remained relatively constant over the past 10 years.

The argument that the infrequency and discriminatory nature of capital punishment's imposition today has diffused public opposition to it implicitly concedes the unsoundness of the contention that modern civilized society rejects capital punishment. With respect to this argument, Mr. Justice Powell argued, the Court is being asked to decide a question based on a hypothetical assumption that may or may not be realistic. Mr. Justice Marshall's contention that the average citizen would find the penalty shocking were he aware of its disproportionate imposition on the underprivileged also calls for speculation.

The tragic fact that "the have-nots" in every society have always been subjected to greater pressure to commit crimes is not a constitutional argument under the Eighth and Fourteenth Amendments, Mr. Justice Powell said. The same argument could be made with respect to those sentenced to prison. The basic problem of the poor and underprivileged in this respect stems "from social and economic factors that have plagued humanity since the beginning of recorded history," and it is unrelated to the constitutional issues here.

The discriminatory impact argument would call for a reassessment of the "standards" aspect of McGautha v. California. It is difficult to see how the Court, having so recently upheld entrustment of the sentencing function to the jury, "can now hold the entire process constitutionally defective under the Eighth Amendment."

An Equal Protection Clause argument might well be made on the basis of racial discrimination in the imposition of this severe punishment, Mr. Justice Powell suggested. Maxwell v. Bishop, 398 F.2d 138 (CA 8 1968), vacated and remanded on other grounds, 398 U.S. 262 (1970), "does point the way to a means of raising the equal protection challenge that is more consonant with precedent and the Constitution's mandates than the several courses pursued by today's majority opinion."

Mr. Justice Powell found "no support * * * for the view that this Court may invalidate a category of penalties because we deem less severe penalties adequate to serve the ends of penology." And even if the Court "were free to question the justifications for the use of capital punishment," those attacking legislative judgment would bear a heavy burden.

Retribution, he continued, has not been rejected by the Court as a permissible basis for criminal punishment. Even a judge-imposed sentence has been upheld although clearly retributive. Williams v. New York, 337 U.S. 241 (1944). Retribution alone may seem unworthy, but its utility in a system of criminal justice has long been recognized.

As for capital punishment's deterrent value, the petitioners' arguments and evidence that it has none might have persuaded a legislative body. But the question is not a closed one, and they have not come close to showing legislative irrationality.

Mr. Justice Powell also examined the more limited question of the death penalty's alleged disproportionality to the offense of rape, and found it "quite impossible to declare the death sentence grossly excessive for all rapes."

Returning to "the overriding question in these cases," the Court's constitutional authority to abolish capital punishment "as heretofore known in this country," Mr. Justice Powell emphasized the serious disadvantages in constitutionally adjudicating such a great question. Legislative action is responsive to the democratic process, and to revision and change.

He concluded that "this is a classic case for the exercise of our oft-announced allegiance to judicial restraint. * * * It seems to me that the sweeping judicial action undertaken today reflects a basic lack of faith and confidence in the democratic process."

Mr. Justice Rehnquist dealt principally with the effect of this decision upon "the role of judicial review in a democratic society."

Because the courts have the last word as to the constitutionality of laws by virtue of their power to strike down legislation, this power must be exercised most sparingly. Judges, like other human beings, are susceptible to imposing their own views of goodness, truth, and justice upon others. Supreme Court Justices are different only in that they have the power to do so. For this reason, two centuries of precedent have counseled sparing exercise of that power.

Another reason for deferring to legislative judgment, Mr. Justice Rehnquist maintained, is the consequence of human error should the Court mistakenly strike down a law. The consequences of erring by letting a law stand are far less serious than the effect of striking it down, which is "to impose upon the nation the judicial fiat of a majority of a court of judges whose connection with the popular will is remote at best."

CORRECTIONS

Morrissey v. Brewer, 408 U.S. 471, 11 CrL 3324

While the Court's highly publicized death penalty opinions dealt with the "ultimate punishment" issue that has evoked national debate for at least a century and a half, it also made history with a virtually unanimous decision that the Due Process Clause entitles an accused parole violator to specific procedural safeguards in determining whether he should be returned to prison.

The Chief Justice announced that the Due Process Clause entitles a state parolee facing revocation to both a preliminary hearing to determine whether he actually violated parole and a final hearing to consider not only this fact question, but if there was a violation, what to do about it. The accused violator must have the opportunity to learn the case against him and present his own defense. If parole is revoked, he must be given the reason why. However, the Court, with only Mr. Justice Douglas disagreeing, expressly refrained from going so far as to hold that he had a right to counsel at such proceedings.

The Chief Justice outlined in some detail the protections to which due process entitles the accused violator who faces reincarceration. First, he is entitled to an informal preliminary hearing, as near as possible in time and place to the arrest. It is to be conducted by a hearing officer not involved in the case. The hearing officer is to keep an informal record of the evidence, and must determine whether there is probable cause to believe that the parolee has violated the terms of his parole.

The parolee must be given the opportunity to appear personally, to offer testimony and documentary evidence, and to confront any person who has given adverse information about him —unless the hearing officer determines that such a confrontation would subject the adverse witness to risk of harm. This hearing must, of course, be preceded by adequate notice to the parolee.

The actual revocation hearing must be held before a "neutral and detached" body, such as a traditional parole board. It must include all the protections provided by the preliminary hearing, plus written notice of the proceedings and charges. Furthermore, it is to be followed by written statements indicating the evidence relied upon and the reasons why parole has been revoked. At this hearing, the parolee must also be given the chance to present evidence in mitigation. Before announcing these requirements, the Chief Justice reviewed the parole system's place in the overall administration of criminal justice. "Rather than being an ad hoc exercise of clemency, parole is an established variation on imprisonment of convicted criminals. Its purpose is to help individuals reintegrate into society as constructive individuals as soon as they are able, without being confined for the full term of the sentence imposed. It also serves to alleviate the costs to society of keeping an individual in prison."

The Chief Justice noted the various restrictions on the parolee's freedom. These conditions both deter the parolee from behavior deemed dangerous to his rehabilitation and give the parole officer an opportunity to acquire information about the parolee and advise him.

However, the Chief Justice noted, "revocation of parole is not an unusual phenomenon, affecting only a few parolees. It has been estimated that about 35 to 45 percent of all parolees are subject to revocation and return to prison." And the loss of limited freedom involved here is sufficiently "grievous" to call for procedural protections.

The idea that the parolee is entitled to retain his liberty as long as he substantially abides by the conditions of his parole is central to the system. Thus, the first step in the revocation process must be a determination whether the terms of parole have, in fact, been violated. The preliminary hearing is designed to protect the parolee's rights at this stage.

A second step involves the decision whether or not to recommit the parolee if he has, in fact, violated the conditions of his release. "This part of the decision, too, depends on facts, and therefore it is important for the Board to know not only that some violation was committed but also to know accurately how many and how serious the violations were."

The Chief Justice further noted that, since the parolee often receives no credit for time "served" on parole if he is returned to prison, his return may constitute imprisonment for a substantial period.

The Court disclaimed any thought of creating "an inflexible structure for parole revocation procedure." It did not think that these "few basic requirements," which were to apply prospectively only, placed any great burden on state parole systems. Delaying tactics "and other abuses sometimes present in the traditional adversary trial situation" should be no threat.

Concurring in the result, Mr. Justice Brennan thought it clear under Goldberg v. Kelly, 397 U.S. 254, 38 LW 4223, that the parolee must be allowed to retain an attorney if he desires to do so. "The only question open under our precedents is whether counsel must be furnished the parolee if he is indigent."

Mr. Justice Douglas would hold that "the parolee should be entitled to counsel."

Younger v. Gilmore, 404 U.S. 15, 10 CrL 3002

In a two-paragraph per curiam opinion, the Court affirmed a ruling by a California federal district court that under the Fourteenth Amendment's Equal Protection Clause, the state must make available to indigent prisoners enough legal research material to insure that their access to legal advice and the courts is equal to that of more affluent prisoners. The Court also found that it had jurisdiction to entertain the state's appeal from the three-judge federal district court order granting this relief.

Haines v. Kerner, 404 U.S. 519, 10 CrL 3069

A cause of action under 42 U.S.C. Section 1983 was stated by the complaint of a 66-year-old Illinois prisoner that prison officials placed him in 15 days' solitary confinement, thus allegedly subjecting him to physical injury after he refused to discuss why he struck another inmate with a shovel. The Court announced this unanimous decision in a per curiam opinion. Mr. Justice Powell and Mr. Justice Rehnquist took no part in the case.

"Whatever may be the limits on the scope of inquiry of courts into the internal administration of prisons, allegations such as those asserted by petitioner, however inartfully pleaded, are sufficient to call for the opportunity to offer supporting evidence." This pro se complaint, held to less stringent standards than formal pleadings drafted by lawyers, makes enough of a showing to require a hearing.

Jackson v. Indiana, 406 U.S. 356, 11 CrL 3080

A deaf-mute Indiana defendant who was committed and confined as criminally insane after a determination that he was incompetent to stand trial cannot, consistent with the Due Process Clause, be confined indefinitely on this basis, the Court unanimously held. After commitment for a period that is reasonably necessary to determine the substantial probability that he will regain his competency, an incompetent defendant is entitled to either release or civil commitment proceedings. The criminal insanity statute under which this defendant was confined makes commitment easier than in civil cases, and release more difficult. It does not require that the defendant be afforded therapeutic care or treatment. Furthermore, a determination that reattainment of competency in the near future is likely will justify further incarceration only to the extent that progress toward recovery is shown.

Referring to the holding in Baxstrom v. Herold, 383 U.S. 107, that a state prisoner civilly committed at the end of his prison sentence was denied equal protection when deprived of a jury trial that other civilly confined persons would have received, Mr. Justice Blackmun, writing for the Court, concluded, "If criminal conviction and imposition of sentence are insufficient to justify less procedural and substantive protection against indefinite commitment than that generally available to all others, the mere filing of criminal charges surely cannot suffice."

The Court found singularly unpersuasive the state's argument that this defendant's detention was temporary. It had already gone on for four years. There was psychiatric testimony that chances of this deaf-mute improving his communicative skills or otherwise improving were rather dim. There was even less hope that he would be able to follow the proceedings against him.

Reviewing both federal and state procedures for dealing with incompetent defendants, the Court noted that few state courts appear to have addressed the problem. Considering the number of persons affected, the Court suggested that it was "remarkable that the substance of constitutional limitations on this power has not been more frequently litigated."

While it had no constitutional quarrel with an ex parte order committing a defendant for a period of observation to determine whether he is a defective delinquent, the Court held unanimously that there must be a rational limit to that confinement. Accordingly, the Court held that a defendant who was so committed under Maryland's Defective Delinquency Law six years ago following the imposition of a five-year sentence for the underlying crime, but who, because of his noncooperation, had never been evaluated, was denied due process and is entitled to immediate release.

It may be true, Mr. Justice Marshall, writing for the Court, acknowledged, that a temporary observation commitment need not be surrounded by the same procedural safeguards that must be attached to a finding of delinquency or a final commitment order. However, the duration of that confinement must be strictly limited. And if, as here, the practical effect of the order is permanent or indefinite commitment, the safeguards commensurate with a long-term confinement must be applied. While it did not set a strict time limit, the Court pointed out that the Maryland statute here sets a limit of six months.

The Court flatly rejected the state's contention that the continued confinement of the defendant here is analogous to punishment for civil contempt, arising as it did from his refusal to cooperate in the evaluation proceedings. If confinement is to rest on a theory of civil contempt, due process requires a hearing to determine whether he has in fact behaved in a manner that amounts to contempt.

Further, since the object of the entire procedure is to determine whether or not the defendant is a defective delinquent, and since civil contempt is coercive in nature, "there is no justification for confining on a civil contempt theory a person who lacks the present ability to comply."

Mr. Justice Douglas, concurring, saw a self-incrimination basis for the decision. He noted that the defendant's refusal to submit to questioning was based on his Fifth Amendment right to be silent; yet he remains confined without any finding that he has a propensity toward criminal activity and without any hope of having a hearing without surrender of his right against self-incrimination.

Murel v. Baltimore City Criminal Court, 407 U.S. 355, 11 CrL 3148

However, a more comprehensive challenge to Maryland's Defective Delinquency Law was not considered on its merits by the Court. The ineligibility of any petitioner for immediate relief from confinement under this statute, and the ongoing substantial revision of the state's commitment procedures, led the Court to decide that consideration of the challenge was inappropriate at the time. Thus, a previously granted writ of certiorari was dismissed as improvidently granted.

FIRST AMENDMENT

Branzburg v. Hayes, 408 U.S. 665, 11 CrL 3333

Newsmen fearing exposure of confidential sources nevertheless have no First Amendment exemption from the general duty to divulge to grand juries information either about the commission of crimes or their sources of information about possible criminal activity, the Court held.

A five-Justice majority, in an opinion by Mr. Justice White, rejected the contention that newsmen, subpoenaed to testify before grand juries, enjoy a privilege that, absent a government showing of compelling need, entitles them not to appear and not to answer questions about criminal activity they have observed or their sources of information about possible criminal activity. News gatherers are subject to the same obligation as other citizens, despite the incidental burden that being called to testify might place on news gathering.

The four dissenting Justices accused the majority of seriously damaging the First Amendment right of the public to the free flow of information.

Branzburg was a Kentucky reporter who wrote a story about a hashish-manufacturing operation and who refused to divulge to a county grand jury the names of those he observed conducting this operation. The second petitioner, Pappas, was a Rhode Island newsman-photographer who was admitted into Black Panther headquarters during a serious disturbance in New Bedford, Massachusetts. He refused to answer any grand jury questions about what had taken place while he was inside Panther headquarters.

The best known of the three petitioners was Earl Caldwell of the New York Times. Caldwell's unique rapport with the Black Panthers had enabled him to write extensively about that organization. He was subpoenaed before a federal grand jury investigating possible threats by various Panther functionaries against the President, as well as other possible criminal activity. The federal district court held that he was not required to reveal confidential associations, sources, or information received or maintained by him as a professional journalist during the course of his news-gathering activities, but it also held him in contempt for refusing to appear at all. Subsequently the district court, while repeating the protective provisions in its prior order, directed Caldwell to appear; he refused to do so and was found in contempt. The U.S. Court of Appeals for the Ninth Circuit reversed this contempt conviction and held that, absent compelling reasons for requiring his testimony, he was privileged to withhold it.

The newsmen, while not claiming an absolute privilege, insisted that the Government should have to show clearly a "compelling need" to obtain crime information; that the reporter has the information sought; and that it cannot otherwise be acquired.

But the First Amendment interests involved do not justify carving out such a drastic exception to the grand jury's authority to investigate criminal activity, Mr. Justice White emphasized. Various laws and even executive actions place incidental burdens on the media's news gathering. The press is not, under the prevailing view, even free to publish everything and anything it desires —as various libel cases decided by the Court demonstrate. Journalists do not have an unlimited right of travel for news-gathering purposes. Zemel v. Rusk, 381 U.S. 1 (1965). They are regularly excluded from grand jury proceedings and executive sessions of other official bodies.

In the 14 years since a special newsman's privilege was first asserted, state and lower federal courts have "almost uniformly rejected" the claim. Some states have provided statutory newsman's privileges of varying degree, but most have not. The prevailing view "is very much rooted in the ancient role of the grand jury * * * ."

The importance of the grand jury's law enforcement authority is enough "to override the consequential but uncertain burden on news gathering which is said to result from insisting that reporters, like other citizens, respond to relevant questions put to them in the course of a valid grand jury investigation * * * ."

The majority was careful to point out that its decision "involves no restraint on what newspapers may publish or on the type or quality of information reporters may seek to acquire, nor does it threaten the vast bulk of confidential relationships between reporters and their sources."

Nor did the assertion of the newsman's privilege fare any better with respect to situations where a source is not engaged in criminal conduct but merely has information suggesting illegal conduct by others. Assuming that there would be some adverse effect upon information-gathering from confidential sources who wish to remain anonymous, the majority could not "accept the argument that the public interest in possible future news about crime from undisclosed, unverified sources must take precedence over the public interest in pursuing and prosecuting those crimes reported to the press by informants and in thus deterring the commission of such crimes in the future."

The Court was also unconvinced "that a virtually impenetrable constitutional shield" should "protect a private system of informers operated by the press to report on criminal conduct * * * ." Police informers enjoy no such protection; the judiciary compels their disclosure when it is critical to the defense case.

Even if it is true that there is a greater need today for protection of confidential sources, recent developments purportedly creating such a need "are treacherous grounds for a far-reaching interpretation of the First Amendment fastening a nationwide rule on courts, grand juries, and prosecuting officials everywhere." Such sources as minority cultural and political groups and dissidents who are suspicious of the law and public officials will have nothing to fear as long as they are not engaged in criminal conduct. This case does not involve any Government abuse of authority.

In rejecting the argument that the Government should have to show "compelling need" before requiring reporters to testify, the Court strongly implied that the grand jury's law-enforcement responsibilities present a compelling need anyway.

The Court also rejected this "compelling need" rule as extremely difficult to administer. And, it would be necessary to categorize newsmen who qualified for the privilege as opposed to those who did not. Also, if newsmen are entitled to such a privilege, lecturers, political pollsters, novelists, academic researchers, and dramatists also have good claims.

The Court found "much force" in the view that the press has powerful weapons for protecting itself from harassment or substantial harm. And it called attention to the Attorney General's "Guidelines for Subpoenas to the

News Media," which represent "a major step in the direction petitioners desire to move."

Bad-faith harassment will not be tolerated, Mr. Justice White concluded; grand juries are subject to judicial control and the courts will not "forget that grand juries must operate within the limits of the First Amendment as well as the Fifth."

Concurring, Mr. Justice Powell emphasized "what seems to be the limited nature of the Court's holding." This decision does not mean that subpoenaed newsmen "are without constitutional rights with respect to the gathering of news or in safeguarding their sources." The majority was not, as suggested in the dissent, holding that authorities are free to use the news media as "an investigative arm of Government." The Court's record of solicitude for First Amendment freedoms "should be sufficient assurance against any such effort," even assuming that the press is incapable of self-protection.

The concluding portion of the majority opinion, Mr. Justice Powell assured, makes it clear that "no harassment of newsmen will be tolerated." A newsman who believes that a grand jury is not acting in good faith still has access to the courts on a motion to quash. Appropriate protective orders may still be entered. The balancing test between First Amendment freedoms and the interest of society in crime control awaits adjudication on the traditional case-by-case basis.

Mr. Justice Douglas was of the view that a reporter has an absolute First Amendment privilege, "absent his involvement in a crime," against appearing or testifying before a grand jury. He expressed dismay at the New York Times' "amazing position that First Amendment rights are to be balanced against other needs or conveniences of government." The majority's decision effectively permits Caldwell to be brought before the grand jury for the purpose of "exposing his political beliefs." Without complete First Amendment immunity, Mr. Justice Douglas maintained, publishers and editors "may be summoned to account for their criticism of the Government."

By holding that newsmen have no First Amendment right to protect their sources from grand jury inquiry, Mr. Justice Stewart wrote for himself and Justices Brennan and Marshall, the Court was inviting Government authorities to "undermine the historic independence of the press by attempting to annex the journalistic profession as an investigative arm of government." The effect of this, he warned, will be harmful to the administration of justice as well as the press.

The right to gather news is central to the First Amendment right to publish, Mr. Justice Stewart emphasized, and it implies a right to a confidential relationship between a reporter and his source. Inherent in this newsman-source relationship is the newsman's ability to maintain confidentiality. Informants are essential to a vigorous press, and many informants are in no position to have their identity disclosed. Unchecked Government power to disclose them deters these sources and deters publication of what they have to disclose. The Court's decision means that a public-spirited Government employee, for example, will be fearful of exposing corruption "because he will now know that he can be subsequently identified by use of compulsory process." The reporter will be faced with a choice between contempt and violating his profession's ethics.

Concrete evidence supports this view, Mr. Justice Stewart maintained. Impairment of the news flow cannot "be proven with scientific precision," as the Court seems to demand.

And the Court has never before demanded, as a prerequisite to forbidding acts that transgress on First Amendment rights, empirical proof demonstrating beyond doubt that First Amendment freedoms will be affected. All that is necessary is a rational connection between Government action and more than de minimus impairment of First Amendment activity.

Furthermore, the rule making everyone's evidence available to the grand jury has been limited not only by the Fourth and Fifth Amendments, but by common-law evidentiary privileges. The First Amendment protection of a confidential relationship clearly qualifies as a "real interest" to be protected against grand jury inquiry. The primary interest to be served by its protection is the free flow of information to the public.

The "compelling state interest" test applicable to attempted Government impairment of First Amendment freedoms has been developed in other contexts, and should apply here, Mr. Justice Stewart urged. The grand jury's function is no more important than the legislative function —which must yield to the First Amendment freedom of association unless the "compelling need" test is satisfied. And surely associational freedoms under the First Amendment are no more important than the public interest served by protecting a newsman's sources. Under this test, the Government must show the relevance of the information sought to a precisely defined objective of inquiry, that it is reasonable to think the witness has that information, and that the information can't be obtained in any way less destructive of First Amendment liberties.

To protect journalists' confidential relationships with news sources, Mr. Justice Stewart would have established an even more rigorous test. He would require a Government showing of probable cause to believe that the newsman has information that is clearly relevant to a specific probable violation of the law, that the information cannot be obtained by less intrusive alternative means, and that the Government has a compelling and overriding interest in the information.

The majority is highly misleading in its assurance that the reporter and news source need fear a grand jury subpoena only if the source is implicated in a crime or has relevant information about it, Mr. Justice Stewart argued. He pointed to the grand jury's extraordinarily broad powers and the weak standards of relevance and materiality that apply in its investigations. Furthermore, the Government may well have alternative means of obtaining the information it seeks from the reporter. By placing newsmen at the mercy of the grand jury subpoena, and discouraging them from developing news sources fearful of exposure, this decision may have the tragically paradoxical effect of drying up a valuable source of information for the Government as well as the public.

Considering the Caldwell case in particular, Mr. Justice Stewart concluded that the Government had not met the burden it should bear under the First Amendment.

SEARCH AND SEIZURE —GRAND JURIES

Gelbard v. U.S., 408 U.S. 41, 11 CrL 3196

The grand jury's need to gather information, sufficient to override any asserted newsman's privilege, could not prevail when based on questions obtained in violation of at least one Fourth Amendment right. A grand jury witness showing that Government questions are based on warrantless electronic eavesdropping gives him "just cause," under 18 U.S.C. 1826, to refuse to answer those questions. He has, as a defense to contempt charges, the ban imposed by 18 U.S.C. 2515, a provision of Title III of the Omnibus Crime Control Act, against grand jury use of warrantless wiretap products.

One of the cases that led to the Court's decision arose out of the refusal by alleged conspirators in the alleged "Harrisburg Nine" kidnap plot against presidential adviser Henry Kissinger to answer federal grand jury questions they claimed based on illegal electronic surveillance. Both witnesses, Sister Joques Egan and Anne Elizabeth Walsh, refused to testify, even after they received transactional immunity. The Government did not reply to their illegal interception allegations. The other case involved gamblers who faced questions admittedly based on wiretaps they challenged, without reply from the Government, as unconstitutional.

The 5–4 majority opinion, written by Mr. Justice Brennan, assumed for the purpose of decision that both cases involved questions based on surveillance in violation of Title III and that the witnesses' potential compelled testimony would be "disclosure" of illegally obtained information in violation of Title III. The Court concluded that the prohibition of Title III does constitute a defense to contempt charges.

The policy of Title III is plainly to protect individual privacy by strictly limiting the use of wiretapping and electronic surveillance, the majority said, and Congress simply cannot be understood to have sanctioned orders to produce evidence excluded from grand jury proceedings by Section 2515. To compel testimony from witnesses aggrieved in this manner would compound the statutorily proscribed invasion of their privacy.

Furthermore, 18 U.S.C. 3504, enacted as part of the Organized Crime Control Act of 1970, requires that in any grand jury proceeding, the claim of a "party aggrieved" that evidence is inadmissible because obtained by an illegal act or exploitation of such an act must be affirmed or denied by the opponent of the claim. This section parallels 2515 in its required procedures.

Nor is the Government persuasive in its argument that omission of grand jury proceedings from the suppression provision of 18 U.S.C. 2518(10)(a), which authorizes an aggrieved person to seek suppression of evidence derived from an intercepted communication, means that a grand jury witness cannot invoke Section 2515 as a defense.

This omission was apparently due to congressional concern that actual and potential defendants might hinder the return of indictments by use of suppression motions. Furthermore, suppression motions are not the means by which witnesses decide whether they may refuse to answer questions. Section 1826(a) embodies the usual procedure —a court order compelling testimony. "The asserted omission of grand jury proceedings from Section 2518(1)(a) may well reflect congressional acceptance of that procedure as adequate in these cases."

Although he joined in the majority opinion, Mr. Justice Douglas reiterated his belief that all wiretapping and bugging is unconstitutional and that the Fourth Amendment thus protects a grand jury witness from questions based on such surveillance regardless of any statutory refuge.

Concurring in the majority's opinion and judgment, Mr. Justice White agreed that "at least where the United States has intercepted communications without a warrant in circumstances where court approval was required, it is appropriate in construing and applying 28 U.S.C. 1826 not to require the grand jury witness to answer and hence further the plain policy of the wiretap statute." This unquestionably changes the law with respect to the rights of grand jury witnesses. However, in the event that the Government produces a court order for the interception and the witness nevertheless challenges the order's illegality, suppression hearings may not be appropriate. And in this situation, "the deterrent value of excluding the evidence will be marginal at best. It is well, therefore, that the Court has left this issue open for consideration by the district court on remand."

The four dissenters, in an opinion by Mr. Justice Rehnquist, accused the majority of reaching its conclusion "in utter disregard of the relevant legislative history, and quite without consideration of the sharp break which it represents" with traditional grand jury proceedings. The majority's construction, while supportable if only the language of Sections 2515 and 1826 is considered, is by no means compelled by that language, he maintained. And the presumptions on which the majority proceeds are so removed from the facts of the cases involved "as to virtually invite" its erroneous conclusion.

He agreed that Section 2515 prohibits the use of illegally obtained communications before grand juries. The true issue here, however, is whether the two statutes can be construed to require sweeping discovery "as a prelude to a full hearing on the issue of alleged unlawful surveillance * * * ."

Section 1826, Mr. Justice Rehnquist asserted, was an effort to treat the courts' authority to deal with recalcitrant grand jury witnesses separately from their general contempt power. This provision was designed to "codify the existing practice," and a review of federal cases dealing with recalcitrant witnesses demonstrates that protracted hearings at which witnesses have the right of discovery have never been a part of this practice. Before drastically expanding a grand jury witness' right of discovery, the Court "should require rather strong evidence" that this is what Congress intended.

The kind of hearing sought and obtained by these petitioners was not only unauthorized by law prior to the enactment of the 1968 Omnibus Crime Control Act, "but completely contrary to the ingrained principles which have long governed the functioning of the grand jury."

Mr. Justice Rehnquist noted that Section 2515's general prohibition against the use before grand juries of unlawfully intercepted communications apparently conflicts with Section 2518's omission of grand jury proceedings from those proceedings at which a suppression hearing must be held. The majority incorrectly resolved this conflict by holding that the witness must be entitled to such a hearing despite Section 2518's clear denial. A better construction, borne out by Title III's legislative history, is that the Act proscribes certain conduct but does not provide the hearing remedy with respect to grand jury proceedings. Grand jury witnesses do have other remedies —civil proceedings or the filing of a criminal complaint with respect to the illegal surveillance.

As for Section 3504(a)(1), it does not apply at all to the situation in which these petitioners find themselves. This Section was intended as a limitation on existing rights of criminal defendants, rather than as an enlargement. It was an effort to limit the effect of Alderman v. U.S., 394 U.S. 165, 4 CrL 3083.

SEARCH AND SEIZURE —ELECTRONIC EAVESDROPPING

U.S. v. U.S. District Court, 405 U.S. 443, 11 CrL 3131

A Presidential practice going back a quarter century — authorization of warrantless electronic surveillance in internal security matters —cannot constitutionally be extended to include activities of domestic "subversives." The Court, in an opinion by Mr. Justice Powell, reached this conclusion without a dissenting vote. Mr. Justice Rehnquist did not participate. "Fourth Amendment freedoms cannot properly be guaranteed if domestic security surveillances may be conducted solely within the discretion of the executive branch," Mr. Justice Powell wrote.

The surveillance in question, authorized by the Attorney General pursuant to authority delegated him by the President, involved a Michigan "White Panther" charged with the dynamite bombing of a CIA office. The Attorney General acknowledged that Government agents had overheard conversations in which this defendant had participated, but asserted that the eavesdrops were within the scope of the President's "internal security" power.

Upholding decisions of the Sixth Circuit and the U.S. District Court for Eastern Michigan that the surveillance violated the Fourth Amendment and that the Government must make full disclosure of the overheard conversations, the Court acknowledged that preservation of national security is the most basic function of government. But even when used for this purpose, electronic surveillance is a dangerous tool. And, given the historical "tendency of Government —however benevolent and benign its motives —to view with suspicion those who most fervently dispute its policies," this problem has First Amendment overtones as well.

As it did in Coolidge v. New Hampshire, 403 U.S. 443, 9 CrL 3208, the Court emphasized that the warrant requirement, with a few narrow and specific exceptions, is the determinant of Fourth Amendment "reasonableness." Title III of the 1968 Omnibus Crime Control Act, in citing specific standards for judicial authorization of electronic surveillance, did not purport to authorize the wiretaps involved here. It did nothing more than leave untouched whatever constitutional power the President may have, with or without a warrant, to eavesdrop electronically in national security cases.

While the Fourth Amendment is not absolute in its warrant requirement, the fundamental responsibility of the Government to protect domestic security simply does not demand that the executive branch be given this virtually unchecked power to employ electronic surveillance against its citizens. The executive branch of the Government, charged with enforcement of the laws, may yield too readily to pressures to obtain evidence at the expense of privacy and protected speech.

The Court gave "the most careful consideration" to the Government's contention that the judiciary has neither the expertise nor the resources for evaluating security problems nor the means of assuring secrecy in considering them. It noted the argument that considerations involved in national security cases differ from those in criminal cases. But these arguments do not make a case for departure from traditional Fourth Amendment standards. "We recognize, as we have before, the constitutional basis of the President's domestic security role, but we think it must be exercised in a manner compatible with the Fourth Amendment."

The Court was careful to emphasize that it expressed no opinion on "the issues which may be involved with respect to activities of foreign powers or their agents." Furthermore, the standards and procedures prescribed by Title III are not necessarily applicable to this case. A different kind of investigation and surveillance may be involved. The Court invited Congress to consider writing into the 1968 Act specific standards for judicial authorization of national security wiretaps.

Declining the Government's invitation to overrule Alderman, the Court approved the Alderman disclosures ordered by the courts below.

The Chief Justice concurred in the result.

Mr. Justice White would have affirmed the decision below on statutory grounds only. He maintained that the 1968 Act does carve out an exemption for national security wiretaps, but concluded that nothing alleged by the Attorney General brought this case within the Act's exemption. No clear and present danger to the Government has been shown.

Concurring, Mr. Justice Douglas emphasized that "more than our privacy is implicated. Also at stake is the reach of the Government's power to intimidate its critics."

Adams v. Williams, 407 U.S. 143, 11 CrL 3113

Compared to other Terms in recent years, the 1971 Term brought little Fourth Amendment news for the cop on the beat. But what news it had was mainly good.

When the Court approved the concept of stop and frisk, Terry v. Ohio, 39 U.S. 1, 3 CrL 3149, it said that the officer must have something specific to go on before acting. This year, the Court, as many lower courts had done, held that the officer can obtain this specific information by means other than his own observation.

A six-Justice majority ruled that readily verifiable information, supplied at 2:15 a.m. by a woman who had supplied the officer with information in the past, that the lone occupant of a nearby car in a high crime area had a gun in his waistband and narcotics in his possession gave the police officer sufficient cause to ask the occupant to get out of the vehicle. And, when the occupant rolled down his window instead, the officer was justified in reaching into the occupant's waistband to seize the gun.

To justify an officer's approaching and stopping the suspicious person, his information must simply have "sufficient indicia" of reliability, Mr. Justice Rehnquist wrote for the majority. This woman's tip did have strong indicia of reliability, even though it may not have given the officer probable cause to make an arrest. The officer knew the woman. She had approached him personally, and she would have been liable for making a false complaint had she been wrong.

Under Terry, an officer who makes a justified, forcible stop may, of course, frisk if he has reason to believe that the suspicious person is armed and dangerous. Here, the officer had good reason to fear for his safety, especially after the man rolled the window down instead of obeying his request to open the door. And, once the officer had found the gun precisely where the informant had predicted, he had probable cause to arrest the suspect for its possession. The proof of what the informer had said tended to corroborate her further report of narcotics, "and together with the surrounding circumstances certainly suggested no lawful explanation for possession of the gun."

Each of the three dissenters wrote an opinion. Mr. Justice Douglas, joined by Mr. Justice Marshall, noted his agreement with the views of Judge Friendly of the U.S. Court of Appeals for the Second Circuit, that the stop and frisk rationale should not apply to purely possessory offenses.

Mr. Justice Douglas further maintained that the problem for police in weapons possession cases is made difficult not by the Fourth Amendment but by the Second. If any Amendment is to be watered down, he suggested, "I would prefer to water down the Second rather than the Fourth Amendment."

Mr. Justice Brennan also adopted Judge Friendly's view that Terry was meant for serious cases of imminent danger or harm and not for the conventional case of possessory offenses. If Terry is to be thus extended, he maintained, it should be only where observation of the officer himself, or well-authenticated information, shows that criminal activities may be afoot.

Mr. Justice Marshall, joined by Mr. Justice Douglas, accused the majority of treating this case as if the warrantless search is the rule rather than the narrowly drawn exception.

Shadwick v. City of Tampa, 407 U.S. 345, 11 CrL 3146

On the same day that it reaffirmed the need for prior judicial approval of even those domestic "searches and seizures" where the President or the Attorney General acts in the interests of national security, the Court indicated that the Warrant Clause is flexible when it comes to the question of just what kind of judicial approval is needed. A unanimous Court approved of a warrant system that authorizes municipal court clerks disassociated from law enforcement to issue arrest warrants for breaches of city ordinances, even though the clerks need not be lawyers or judges and are appointed by an executive official.

Historically, the term "magistrate," frequently used by the Court to describe those who may issue warrants, has been broadly defined, Mr. Justice Powell pointed out in his opinion for the Court. The primary function of the "magistrate" or "judicial officer," as far as issuing warrants is concerned, is to assure "that a search and arrest will not proceed without probable cause to believe that a crime has been committed and that the person or place named in the warrant is involved in the crime. Thus an issuing magistrate must meet two tests. He must be neutral and detached, and he must be capable of determining whether probable cause exists for the requested arrest or search."

While a warrant issued by a prosecutorial officer clearly does not satisfy the "detached and neutral" requirement, Coolidge v. New Hampshire, 403 U.S. 443, 9 CrL 3208, there has been no showing that these court clerks, who work for judges, are affiliated with, or partial to, prosecutors or police. And appointment by the executive is hardly a disqualifying factor. After all, judges come by their jobs in a variety of ways, and many must be reappointed or reelected.

Furthermore, a law degree is no prerequisite to being entrusted with the responsibility of determining probable cause. "Grand juries daily determine probable cause prior to rendering indictments, and trial juries assess whether guilt is proved beyond a reasonable doubt."

The Court did not say whether these clerks may issue search warrants or act as judicial officers in cases involving more serious offenses. In U.S. v. U.S. District Court, decided the same day, the Court's opinion by Mr. Justice Powell, in discussing the general Fourth Amendment requirement of "prior judicial judgment," explained in footnote 18 that "the word judicial * * * connote[s] the traditional Fourth Amendment requirement of a neutral and detached magistrate." Federal wiretaps, of course, must be issued by a "judge of competent jurisdiction." 18 U.S.C. 2518(1).

U.S. v. Biswell, 406 U.S. 311, 11 CrL 3024

The authority granted by 18 U.S.C. 923 to inspect the premises of a dealer in firearms is not inconsistent with the Fourth Amendment, the Court held in an 8–1 decision. According to Mr. Justice White, writing for the majority, the importance of warrantless inspections to effective enforcement of the federal regulatory scheme makes the warrantless entry provision reasonable under the Fourth Amendment.

A gun dealer's privacy is not significantly invaded by this provison, the Court explained, for he has voluntarily entered the closely regulated field of firearms commerce. Although the search in Colonnade Catering Corp. v. U.S., 397 U.S. 72, 6 CrL 3063, was held unreasonable because the statute did not provide for a forcible entry in the event of illegal nonconsent, the reasonableness decision as to warrantless inspection of a licensee's premises was the same. Here, the majority noted, the dealer at first refused permission to enter but gave in when the Treasury Agent read him the statute.

To Mr. Justice Douglas, this case is within the rule of Colonnade Catering Corp. because it involves a warrant-less entry. Citing Bumper v. North Carolina, 391 U.S. 543, 3 CrL 3119, he argued that "forced" consent to such an entry is no consent at all. The dealer simply yielded to a claim of lawful break-in authority that the agent did not have.

Combs v. U.S., 408 U.S. 224, 11 CrL 3227

In a per curiam opinion, the Court held that the lack of a factual determination as to whether a bootlegging defendant, who had appealed his conviction on Fourth Amendment grounds after a joint trial with his nonap-pealing father, had a reasonable expectation of privacy with respect to his father's illegally searched premises that would demonstrate a basis for standing to attack the search, requires vacation of his conviction and a remand for such a determination.

SELF-INCRIMINATION

Kastigar v. U.S., 406 U.S. 441, 11 CrL 3045

Few constitutional issues have generated as much heated debate as the question whether a reluctant witness must be granted full transactional immunity from future prosecution before he may be compelled to waive his privilege against self-incrimination. This Term the Court at last provided a clear-cut answer, and the answer was "no." By a 5–2 vote, with Justices Brennan and Rehnquist not participating, the Court upheld a provision of the 1970 Organized Crime Control Act authorizing com-pelled testimony upon a grant of immunity from use of such testimony and use of any evidence derived from it. The Court disavowed as dictum the broad language in Counselman v. Hitchcock, 142 U.S. 547, implying that "absolute" immunity is required, and extended the reasoning of Murphy v. Waterfront Comm., 378 U.S. 52, which involved a state witness who feared federal prosecution based on his testimony.

Mr. Justice Powell, author of the majority opinion, pointed out that Counselman involved a federal statute granting mere "use" immunity. In holding that the grant of mere "use" immunity was not enough to protect the Fifth Amendment privilege, the Counselman Court declared that "a statutory enactment, to be valid, must afford absolute immunity against future prosecution for the offense to which the question relates." In response to this broad language, Congress drafted an immunity statute that afforded full transactional immunity. "This transactional immunity statute became the basic form for the numerous federal immunity statutes until 1970," when Congress enacted 18 U.S.C. 6002 and 6003, the statutes involved in this case. However, despite the broad language in Counselman, immunity from use and derivative use of compelled testimony is consistent with its conceptual basis, Mr. Justice Powell said.

The 1970 statute, Mr. Justice Powell emphasized, goes beyond the mere use immunity found inadequate in Counselman. Providing not merely immunity from use of the compelled testimony, but immunity from evidence derived directly or indirectly therefrom, it affords protection coextensive with the constitutional safeguard provided by the Fifth Amendment. This is all that is required of an immunity grant. "Transactional immunity, which accords full immunity from prosecution for the offense to which the compelled testimony relates, affords the witness considerably broader protection than does the Fifth Amendment privilege. The privilege has never been construed to mean that one who invokes it cannot subsequently be prosecuted."

The reasoning of Murphy v. Waterfront Comm. also leads to this conclusion, Mr. Justice Powell maintained. True, Murphy had been granted transactional immunity by New Jersey and New York, the states that sought to compel his testimony. But the Court held that he could not be compelled to testify "unless the compelled testimony and its fruits cannot be used in any manner by federal officials in connection with a criminal prosecution against him."

The scope of the privilege is the same whether invoked in a federal or a state jurisdiction, so "the Murphy conclusion that a prohibition on use and derivative use secures a witness' Fifth Amendment privilege against infringement by the Federal Government demonstrates that immunity from use and derivative use is coextensive with the scope of the privilege."

The use and derivative use immunity conferred by the 1970 law is rendered constitutionally adequate by the Government's heavy burden of proof, should it subsequently choose to prosecute the witness in connection with the matter about which he has testified, of establishing that its proposed evidence is in no way "tainted" by any reliance upon the compelled testimony. "This burden of proof, which we reaffirm as appropriate, is not limited to a negation of taint; rather, it imposes on the prosecution the affirmative duty to prove that the evidence it proposes to use is derived from a legitimate source wholly independent of the compelled testimony."

The majority also found the statue "analogous to the Fifth Amendment requirement in cases of coerced confessions."

Dismissed as without merit was the contention that no immunity statute can ever afford a lawful basis for compelling incriminatory testimony.

The two dissenters, Justices Douglas and Marshall, each wrote an opinion. Because his view that the Fifth Amendment requires transactional immunity has been set forth in previous opinions, Mr. Justice Douglas found it unnecessary to write at length. Murphy v. Waterfront Comm. is not applicable here, he maintained. Requiring transactional immunity between jurisdictions raises problems of federalism that do not apply "when the threat of prosecution is from the jurisdiction seeking to compel the testimony, which is the situation we faced in Counselman, and which we face today."

Counselman flatly required transactional immunity, Mr. Justice Douglas reiterated, and in this requirement it does not stand alone. Brown v. Walker, 161 U.S. 591; Albertson v. Subversive Activities Control Board, 382 U.S. 70.

Both Justices Douglas and Marshall maintained that it is futile to expect enforcement of the prohibition against use and derivative use of testimony. Mr. Justice Marshall could not agree that a total ban on use would be possible so long as the Government could convict on the basis of independent evidence. The burden on the Government will not, in fact, be a heavy one; it can be met "by mere assertion if the witness produces no contrary evidence." And even the good faith of the prosecutor, "the sole safeguard of the witness' rights," will not be enough to guarantee that evidence derived from use of the incriminating testimony does not creep into a prosecution case.

Contrary to the majority's assertion, Mr. Justice Marshall added, there is no relationship at all between a statutory grant of immunity and the "immunity" that is "inadvertently conferred by an unconstitutional interrogation." An immunity statute does not merely attempt to provide a remedy for past police misconduct; it "operates in advance of the event, and it authorizes —even encourages —interrogation which would otherwise be prohibited by the Fifth Amendment." It must remove the danger of incrimination completely and absolutely, and its application poses no threat to an otherwise valid conviction. It enables a prosecutor to decide whether to forego a prosecution in order to obtain testimony he could not otherwise acquire.

Zicarelli v. N.J. State Comm. of Investigation, 406 U.S. 472, 11 CrL 3055

The Court also upheld a New Jersey immunity statute compelling witnesses before a state criminal investigation commission to testify in return for use and derivative use immunity like that conferred by the federal statute approved in Kastigar. The Court found no constitutional flaw in the statute's limitation of immunity to "responsive" answers and "responsive" evidence provided by the witness. Statutory guidelines with respect to what is responsive are unnecessary, Mr. Justice Powell wrote for the majority. The term "responsive" has been construed by the New Jersey Supreme Court as protecting a "witness against answers and evidence he in good faith believed were demanded." "Responsive" is thus construed in terms of ordinary usage and not in the legal evidentiary sense. Furthermore, a witness before this commission is entitled to advance notice of the subject about which he will be questioned and is entitled to the assistance of counsel when he testifies.

This witness' claim that testimony sought by the commission would expose him to foreign prosecution was dismissed by the Court as without factual support. The witness offered magazine articles purportedly characterizing him as organized crime's chief internationalist, but even if this is so, Mr. Justice Powell said, none of the questions asked by the commission placed him in danger of disclosing information that might incriminate him under foreign law. His claim, unsubstantiated as it is, does not present a constitutional issue.

Again the vote was 5–2 with Justices Brennan and Rehnquist not participating. Justices Douglas and Marshall dissented for the reasons stated in their opinions in Kastigar.

Sarno v. Illinois Crime Investigating Comm., 406 U.S. 482, 11 CrL 3058

Again by 5–2 vote, the Court dismissed as improvidently granted, in light of Kastigar and Zicarelli, a writ of certiorari presenting the question whether procedures under an Illinois immunity statute concerning testimony before the state crime investigating commission properly assures witnesses that they are granted transactional immunity before allowing compulsion of self-incrimination testimony.

Brooks v. Tennessee, 406 U.S. 605, 11 CrL 3068

While the practice of requiring a testifying defendant to appear as the first defense witness has practical value and an historical basis, the U.S. Supreme Court acknowledged, its value can't offset its constitutional infirmities. The Court held that a Tennessee statute requiring a defendant who wishes to testify to do so before any other testimony for the defense is heard violates both the Fifth Amendment's Self-Incrimination Clause and the Fourteenth Amendment's Due Process Clause.

Five Justices agreed that the rule embodied in the Tennessee statute is an impermissible restriction on the defendant's right to remain silent unless he chooses to speak. Requiring him to appear first or not at all "casts a heavy burden on a defendant's otherwise unconditional right not to take the stand." While it recognized that there are dangers in allowing a defendant to wait before taking the stand, the Court noted that the adversary system "reposes judgment of the credibility of all witnesses in the jury." Pressuring the defendant to take the stand by foreclosing later testimony if he refuses is not a "constitutionally permissible means of insuring his honesty."

The Court also held that the statute violates due process by depriving the defendant of the "guiding hand" of counsel at every step in the proceedings against him. Requiring the accused and his lawyer to choose between silence and taking the stand without the opportunity to evaluate the actual worth of the testimony given by defense witnesses restricts the defense —particularly counsel —in planning the case.

Mr. Justice Stewart went along, but only on the due process ground.

The Chief Justice, joined in dissent by Mr. Justice Blackmun and Mr. Justice Rehnquist, saw this case as "an example of the Court confusing what it does not approve with the demands of the Constitution." He pointed out that the Constitution requires only that the defendant cannot be compelled to be a witness against himself; it does not forbid requiring him to choose between alternative routes to exercising that right.

Mr. Justice Rehnquist filed a separate dissent in which the Chief Justice and Mr. Justice Blackmun joined. He found it difficult to understand how, in view of the fact that the defendant here never took the stand, his right to remain silent was in any way infringed. Further, Mr. Justice Rehnquist found no case previously decided by the Court which "elevates the defense counsel to the role of impresario with respect to the decisions as to the order in which witnesses shall testify at trial."

CONGRESSIONAL IMMUNITY

Gravel v. U.S., 408 U.S. 606, 11 Crl 3361

Senator Mike Gravel's alleged arrangement for private publication of the Pentagon Papers, in no way essential to the deliberations of Congress, was not legislative activity protected by the Speech or Debate Clause, a sharply divided Court held. Although the Speech or Debate Clause has been extended beyond pure speech or debate, the requirement of legislative action remains. Hence, a Senate aide can be compelled to testify before a grand jury about this alleged publication arrangement.

However, when legislative activity is involved, the testimonial privilege provided by the Clause extends even to the agents and aides of members of Congress. Thus Leonard Rodberg, an aide to the Senator, cannot be compelled to answer grand jury questions about preparation of the Pentagon Papers for entry into the official record at a subcommittee session.

The heart of the Clause, Mr. Justice White wrote for the five-Justice majority, is speech or debate in either House. Insofar as the Clause is construed to reach other matters, they must be an integral part of the "deliberative and communicative process" by which members participate in committee and House proceedings with respect to the consideration, or passage or rejection, of proposed legislation or with respect to other matters that the Constitution places within the jurisdiction of either House.

It is clear, Mr. Justice White said, that the Speech or Debate Clause at least protects Senator Gravel from criminal or civil liability about events at the subcommittee hearing, as well as from questioning elsewhere than in the Senate about this hearing. And, while it is true that the Clause itself only mentions "Senators and Representatives," the privilege has not been narrowly applied. For one thing, it has been held to protect more than mere speech and debate; committee reports, resolutions, and the act of voting are also covered. "We have little doubt that we are neither exceeding our judicial powers nor mistakenly construing the Constitution by holding that the Speech or Debate Clause applies not only to a Member but also to his aides insofar as the conduct of the latter would be a protected legislative act if performed by the Member himself."

Dombrowski v. Eastland, 387 U.S. 82, which held that a subcommittee counsel was unprotected by the Clause for his activities in conspiring with state officials to carry out an illegal seizure of records sought by the subcommittee, is not to the contrary. It was held there that the Clause did not shield counsel from answering charges of conspiracy to violate constitutional rights of private parties. "Unlawful conduct of this kind the Speech or Debate Clause simply did not immunize." By placing beyond the Clause "a variety of services characteristically performed by aides for members of Congress, even though within the scope of their employment," the Dombrowski

Court prevented legislators from protecting others from the operation of the law.

On the other hand, Senator Gravel's alleged arrangement with Beacon Press, a private company, to publish the Pentagon Papers was not protected by the Clause. This alleged act went beyond the legislative sphere. It was not an integral part of the deliberative and communicative aspect of legislative activity. It was in no way essential to congressional deliberations. The grand jury's inquiry about possible criminal violations resulting from private publication does not threaten congressional integrity or independence. It must be remembered that Congressmen are not exempted from liability or process in criminal cases.

Nor was the aide protected by any nonconstitutional privilege. Just as the "executive privilege" does not shield executive officers from prosecution for criminal activity, so too is a legislative employee not shielded. Therefore, the court of appeal's protective order shielding the aide from testifying with respect to any act within the scope of his employment was too severe a restriction of the grand jury's inquiry. Absent Fifth Amendment objections, the majority held, the grand jury is entitled to question him about any arrangements by himself and the Senator with respect to republication or third-party conduct under valid investigation "as long as the questions do not implicate legislative action of the Senator." Furthermore, the grand jury is free to ask questions relevant to tracing the source of these highly classified documents.

Dissenting in part, Mr. Justice Stewart interpreted the majority's holding to mean "that the Speech or Debate Clause does not protect a congressman from being forced to testify before a grand jury about sources of information used in preparation for legislative acts." This issue was neither briefed nor argued, Mr. Justice Stewart maintained, and he was unable to join in its "summary resolution."

In holding that a congressman can be compelled to testify concerning the sources of information used by him in the performance of his duties if the inquiry "proves relevant to investigating possible third party crime," the Court opened the way for subpoena "by a vindictive Executive to testify about informants who have not committed crimes and who have no knowledge of crime." This compulsion is a distinct possibility in view of the virtual absence of judicially imposed limitations on the grand jury's investigatory powers. A balancing test is called for here, Mr. Justice Stewart maintained. Why shouldn't Congress itself be recognized as the proper institution in most situations to impose sanctions upon a member who withholds information about crime acquired in the course of his legislative duties?

Mr. Justice Douglas would have held that the Senator and his aides are completely insulated from grand jury inquiry concerning the Pentagon Papers and their Beacon Press publication, which was but another way of informing the public about secret executive acts with respect to the Vietnam War. Alternatively, he would have

afforded complete First Amendment protection to Beacon Press. This case, Mr. Justice Douglas maintained, presents various separation of power problems.

Mr. Justice Brennan, joined by Justices Douglas and Marshall, agreed that a congressman's immunity under the Speech and Debate Clause must be extended to his aides. But the majority reads the Clause far too narrowly, they maintained. In taking a "far too narrow view of the legislative function," the Court reaches the anomalous holding that Senator Gravel, who would have been protected by the Clause had he read the documents on the Senate floor or entered them in a Senate report, is left unprotected just because he sought to reach a broader audience. The legislator's duty to inform the public is at the heart of the democratic system. Moreover, in these times, communication between Congress and the electorate fosters badly needed confidence in the responsiveness of Government.

The dissenters accused the majority of accepting the executive's notion of what is "relative" to the legislative function. If Senator Gravel was wrong in asserting that the Vietnam War is relevant to his subcommittee's work, it is up to the Senate to deal with him.

The Court further encroaches on the legislative prerogative by allowing a grand jury to inquire into the source of documents received and made public by the Senator, Mr. Justice Brennan maintained. If a member of Congress can be required to make such revelations, it is up to his House alone to do it.

U.S. v. Brewster, 408 U.S. 501, 11 CrL 3304

A United States Senator is not protected by the Speech or Debate Clause from solicitation and acceptance of a bribe in return for his vote on legislation, the Court held. Writing for a six-Justice majority, the Chief Justice explained that the Clause only protects members of Congress from inquiry into their legislative acts or the motivation behind these acts, and a prosecution for taking a bribe does not require such an inquiry. Thus the Government was free to proceed with its prosecution of former Senator Daniel Brewster under 18 U.S.C. 201(c)(1) and 201(g).

U.S. v. Johnson, 383 U.S. 169, is distinguishable, the Chief Justice said. Representative Johnson was allegedly bribed to make a speech on the House floor. At trial, the Government questioned him about the speech, who wrote it, and its factual basis. The Court held that use at trial of the speech or the congressman's reason for making it violated the Speech or Debate Clause, but emphasized the limited nature of its holding.

Johnson stands as a unanimous holding for the proposition that a member of Congress can be criminally prosecuted as long as the Government's case does not rely on his legislative acts or motives. "A legislative act has consistently been defined as an act generally done in Congress in relation to the business before it. In sum, the Speech or Debate Clause prohibits inquiry only into those things generally said or done in the House in the performance of official duties and the motivation for those acts."

The wide range of activities in which congressmen engage that are merely related to their legislative responsibilities are not covered by the Clause. The Chief Justice pointed out that, in Johnson, seven counts involved his attempt to influence other congressmen, and the Court had noted approvingly that no argument was made that he couldn't be prosecuted for this activity.

The purpose of the Clause must be kept in mind, the Chief Justice admonished. It is to protect the integrity of the legislative process. To leave to Congress the responsibility for punishing criminal activities that are simply related to the legislative process is no remedy, either as far as the Constitution is concerned or as a practical matter. The dissenters' analogy to the English system, where Parliament is supreme and functions as the nation's highest tribunal, is inappropriate.

Also, the Court held that it had jurisdiction under the Criminal Appeals Act, 18 U.S.C. 3731, to consider the Government's appeal from dismissal of the indictment, which a district court found covered by the Clause. To dismiss the counts, the Chief Justice explained, the district court had to pass on the constitutionality of the statutes under which the Senator was indicted, insofar as they applied to this case.

Dissenting Justices Brennan and Douglas contended that the only issue in this case was whether the prohibitions of the Speech or Debate Clause could be "waived" by Congress through authorization in the form of a narrowly drawn bribery statute. The Government acknowledged that the Senator's activities were otherwise covered by the Clause, the dissenters maintained. The majority's holding goes against binding precedent. Most important, "it repudiates principles of legislative freedom developed over the past century in a line of cases culminating in Johnson."

The majority's separation of the money-taking from the act of voting is highly artificial, Mr. Justice Brennan argued. The same is true of the counts charging only a corrupt promise to vote a certain way. Proof of an agreement to be "influenced" in the performance of legislative acts by definition involves an inquiry into motives.

Furthermore, Justices Brennan and Douglas did not believe that Congress could "waive" its immunity by legislative enactment. They found unpersuasive all of the reasons in favor of the proposition that Congress itself is unable to deal with corrupt acts like those alleged here.

Mr. Justice White, joined by Justices Douglas and Brennan, maintained that the sole issue here is in what forum an allegedly corrupt legislator must be tried. The same infirmities present in the Johnson prosecution are present in the indictments brought under 18 U.S.C. 201 (g) and 201 (c)(1).

Mr. Justice White could see the possibility of the Executive intimidating a congressman by informing him of allegations that he has corruptly decided to vote a certain way and expressing the hope that the allegations are not true. "The realities of the American political system, of which the majority fails to take account, render particularly illusory a Speech or Debate Clause distinction between a promise to perform a legislative act and the act itself."

The effect of all this, Mr. Justice White maintained, is to hinder legislators' efforts to represent their constituents and supporters. Neither this case nor the statutes in question distinguish between payments for personal use and campaign funds. The line between personal and political use is most difficult to draw. Prosecutions for alleged abuses in this area are altogether different than ordinary criminal prosecutions for crimes that have no direct bearing whatsoever on how a member of Congress does his job. "The threat of prosecution for supposed missteps which are difficult to define and fall close to the line of what ordinarily is considered permissible, even necessary, conduct scarcely ensures that legislative independence which is the root of the Speech and Debate Clause."

LEGISLATIVE CONTEMPT

Groppi v. Leslie, 404 U.S. 496, 10 CrL 3065

Father James Groppi, the militant civil rights worker whose march on and invasion of the Wisconsin Assembly resulted in a contempt conviction by the Assembly and a two-year court battle between the priest and the legislature, emerged victorious in the end. A unanimous Supreme Court held that the Assembly denied Father Groppi due process of law by failing to provide him with notice and a hearing before sentencing him for conduct that had occurred two days previously. Father Groppi was readily available for such a hearing, the Chief Justice noted in his opinion for the Court.

This case did not present the occasion to define or delineate the rights of an alleged contemnor prior to a legislature's imposition of punishment. It was clear that this summary procedure was totally inadequate.

Even accepting for the sake of argument the state's contention that a legislature has the power to punish summarily, analogous to that of the courts, such power has rarely been exercised as it was here, two days after the alleged contempt. When a court acts immediately to punish the contempt, the contemnor is, of course, present.

RIGHT TO COUNSEL

Argersinger v. Hamlin, 407 U.S. 25, 11 CrL 3089

The Sixth Amendment forbids imposing a prison or jail sentence on any indigent who has not been afforded the right to counsel, the Court held. The label a state places on a particular crime has no significance.

Mr. Justice Douglas, writing for the Court, emphasized that the right to counsel is not analogous to the right of trial by jury, which is constitutionally available only to defendants who face more than six months' imprisonment. These two rights have different genealogies. At common law, accused misdemeanants actually had the right to counsel. And, while the Sixth Amendment has extended the right to counsel "beyond its common-law dimensions" by making counsel available as of right to all accused felons, nothing in its history or Supreme Court case law indicates that it was intended to restrict the counsel right in petty offense cases. Furthermore, other Sixth Amendment rights such as notice, confrontation, public trial, and compulsory process are available in all prosecutions, regardless of possible punishment.

The Court was unconvinced by the argument that the legal issues in petty offense cases are less complex than in cases involving more serious punishments. Plea negotiations raise problems that require the attention of a lawyer, and this is true of minor offense cases as well as more serious prosecutions. And, in view of the size and continued expansion of the legal profession, the Nation is well able to meet the increased demands for counsel that will result from this decision.

Mr. Justice Brennan, joined by Justices Douglas and Stewart, observed that law students "may provide an important source of legal representation for the indigent."

Concurring in the result, the Chief Justice acknowledged the burden that this decision would place on the states. Nevertheless, several factors make counsel a constitutional necessity for defendants facing incarceration. Any deprivation of liberty is a serious matter. Even a simple case may present issues that are beyond a layman's capability —especially when he is opposed by a lawyer. And an appeal based on an uncounselled trial record will hardly be of help.

This decision, the Chief Justice added, should hardly be a surprise to the legal profession, in view of the right-to-counsel recommendations of the American Bar Association's five-year-old Report on Standards Relating to Providing Defense Services.

Mr. Justice Powell, joined by Mr. Justice Rehnquist, concurred in the result. But he thought that due process considerations of fundamental fairness, rather than an inflexible rule based on possible imprisonment, should determine an indigent's right to counsel. Mr. Justice Powell fully agreed that the consequences of a misdemeanor conviction frequently cannot be dismissed as "petty" —even where incarceration is not involved. Severe consequences may also flow from convictions that don't lead to incarceration. On the other hand, not all petty offense trials are complex enough to put the unassisted defendant at a serious disadvantage. In many state cases, the judge is a layman and no lawyers are involved on either side.

The result in this case may not only lead to undue inflexibility in treating misdemeanor offenses, Mr. Justice Powell warned, but it may raise equal protection problems, especially in view of the varying, often arbitrarily drawn line between indigency and bare self-sufficiency.

The Court's assessment of the Nation's legal resources as a whole is also unrealistic, Mr. Justice Powell added.

Many lawyers are simply not available to handle these cases. Furthermore, lawyers are not evenly distributed. This decision will seriously strain community resources in many areas. Small communities, with no means of providing counsel in petty offense cases, may wind up with no credible means of enforcing their petty offense laws against indigents.

Kirby v. Illinois, 406 U.S. 682, 11 CrL 3072

The right to counsel at police-conducted lineups announced by U.S. v. Wade, 388 U.S. 218, is not as broad as most lower courts had assumed. Although Wade involved a post-indictment lineup, most federal and state courts had extended the counsel right to pre-indictment proceedings. Only "on-the-scene" showups held soon after commission or report of the offense were generally exempted from this requirement.

But, last Term the Supreme Court, by a 5–4 vote, held that the right to counsel did not apply to a police-arranged investigatory confrontation between victim and suspect held at the stationhouse two days after the crime and shortly after the suspect had been arrested, but before any formal charges had been brought.

Although only three other Justices joined unequivocally in Mr. Justice Stewart's lead opinion, the Court held that Wade does not require defense counsel at identification proceedings before the defendant has been "formally charged." Mr. Justice Stewart did not specify what was meant by "formal charges." However, his reasoning was consistent with his oft-expressed view that the right to counsel does not arise until a criminal proceeding enters the "critical stage," at which "the Government has committed itself to prosecute." In his opinion for the Court in Massiah v. U.S., 377 U.S. 201, and in his dissent in Escobedo v. Illinois, 378 U.S. 478, he referred to indictment as the beginning of the "critical stage" of a criminal case.

The Chief Justice, concurring in the opinion and holding, simply agreed "that the right to counsel attaches as soon as criminal charges are formally made against an accused and he becomes the subject of a 'criminal prosecution.'"

Mr. Justice Powell, concurring only in the result, stated his belief that the "per se exclusionary rule" of Wade and Gilbert v. California, 388 U.S. 263, should not be extended.

The right of an in-custody defendant to counsel before he may be interrogated, announced in Escobedo and amplified in Miranda v. Arizona, 384 U.S. 436, is not the primary right involved in such an interrogation, Mr. Justice Stewart explained. Miranda simply deemed counsel necessary to protect the privilege against self-incrimination. And Wade made it clear that self-incrimination is not involved in an identification proceeding. The right to counsel announced in Wade was based on the belief that a post-indictment lineup is a "critical stage" of a criminal prosecution at which counsel is required to assure fairness of the proceeding. Not until formal charges are announced does the adversary proceeding begin.

Citing Stovall v. Denno, 388 U.S. 293, Mr. Justice Stewart emphasized that abuse of the identification procedure during the investigatory stage of a case can still be remedied under the Due Process Clause of the Fifth or Fourteenth Amendments.

Mr. Justice Brennan, the author of the majority opinion in Wade, wrote a dissenting opinion on behalf of himself and Justices Douglas and Marshall. He noted that the purpose of the Wade-Gilbert rule was to protect the defendant's "most basic right" to have a fair trial at which witnesses against him might be meaningfully cross-examined. Nothing in Miranda or Escobedo links the counsel right only to the Fifth Amendment protection. Rather, the principle of Powell v. Alabama, 287 U.S. 45, requires scrutiny of any pretrial confrontation to determine whether the presence of counsel is necessary to preserve the right to a fair trial. Mr. Justice White, whose dissent in Wade and Gilbert complained that counsel was now required for all police-conducted identifications, now maintained that Wade and Gilbert "govern this case and compel reversal" of the conviction.

Adams v. Illinois, 405 U.S. 278, 10 CrL 3087

Five of the seven Justices participating agreed that Coleman v. Alabama, 399 U.S. 1, 7 CrL 3121, which held that state defendants have the right to counsel at sufficiently important preliminary hearings, does not apply to such hearings held before Coleman was decided. Mr. Justice Brennan, writing for himself and Justices Stewart and White, concluded that Coleman should not be accorded retroactivity; "the role of counsel at the preliminary hearing differs sufficiently from the role of counsel at trial in its impact on the integrity of the fact-finding process as to require the weighing of the probabilities of such infection against the element of prior justified reliance and the impact of retroactivity on the administration of justice."

The balance, these Justices concluded, is in favor of non-retroactivity. The old rule was widely relied upon by law enforcement officials and the courts, and retroactive application of the Coleman rule might seriously disrupt the administration of justice.

The Chief Justice, who dissented in Coleman, concurred in the result. He reiterated his belief that, while counsel should be provided at the preliminary hearing, it should not be a constitutional requirement. Mr. Justice Blackmun also concurred on the ground that Coleman was wrongly decided.

Mr. Justice Douglas, who was joined in dissent by Mr. Justice Marshall, argued that "even-handed justice requires either prospectivity only or complete retroactivity." He believed that the Court was minimizing the importance of the preliminary hearing. It was "somewhat anomalous" he suggested, to deem it important enough to be incorporated into the Fourteenth Amendment, "but

not fundamental enough to warrant application to the victims of previous unconstitutional conduct."

INDIGENTS

The far-reaching idea that an indigent must be afforded essentially the same resources available to an affluent defendant for the purposes of conducting his defense and challenging his conviction was implicit not only in Argersinger v. Hamlin, but in two cases involving the right of appealing or retried indigents to meaningful records of their trials. Furthermore, the defendant in one of these cases did not even face incarceration.

Mayer v. City of Chicago, 404 U.S. 189, 10 CrL 3003

The rule of Griffin v. Illinois, 351 U.S. 12, that indigent felons have the right to their trial records for purposes of appeal was extended to all indigent criminal defendants, even those charged with misdemeanors not punishable by imprisonment. There were no dissenters from the holding that the indigent misdemeanor defendant or petty offender must be afforded "a record of sufficient completeness to permit proper consideration of his claims."

This does not necessarily mean, Mr. Justice Brennan wrote for the Court, that the indigent must always be given a complete verbatim transcript. Suitable alternatives in an individual case might be a partial transcript, a "settled statement," or a stipulation of facts. However, when an indigent misdemeanant's grounds of appeal make out "a colorable need for a complete transcript," the state bears the burden of showing that some other alternative will suffice. The line between felony and misdemeanor cases, the Court emphasized, is an "unreasoned distinction forbidden by the Fourteenth Amendment."

The Chief Justice, concurring, observed that most criminal appeals do not turn on disputed fact situations, so that full verbatim transcripts will not be necessary in most appeals. The Chief Justice also stressed the need for some means of turning out transcripts with more speed and efficiency.

The Chief Justice, concurring, observed that most criminal appeals do not turn on disputed fact situations, so that full verbatim transcripts will not be necessary in most appeals. The Chief Justice also stressed the need for some means of turning out transcripts with more speed and efficiency.

Also concurring, Mr. Justice Blackmun wondered whether the defendant in this case, a medical student at the time he was convicted of disorderly conduct and interference with a police officer, was now able to pay for his own transcript; he had since become a doctor.

Britt v. North Carolina, 404 U.S. 226, 10 CrL 3007

The Court also made it clear that the Griffin rule extends to a case in which a retried defendant demonstrates the need for a transcript of the original trial to aid in his second-trial defense. However, five of the seven

Justices sitting were convinced that in this murder case, an alternative short of a transcript would have been adequate. This prosecution occurred in a small town. Counsel, judge, and the court reporter were the same at both trials. Defense counsel and the court reporter were friends, and the reporter could easily have been called to the stand, had counsel so requested, to read back his notes of the mistrial.

Dissenting Justices Douglas and Brennan maintained that a transcript would have been extremely useful here to a non-indigent retried defendant who could purchase it. The indigent was denied this beneficial tool by the sole reason of his poverty, the dissenters argued.

James v. Strange, 407 U.S. 128, 11 CrL 3109

On the same day that it expanded indigents' right to counsel to petty-offense cases, the Court unanimously held that the Equal Protection Clause is violated by a Kansas statute's provision for state recoupment of funds spent in defense of an indigent defendant. The recoupment procedures are the same as those for recovering a civil debt judgment, but indigents are denied all but one of the protective exemptions —the homestead exemption — available to other judgment debtors. The Court announced this decision without ruling on the general validity of statutes providing for state recoupment of funds spent for indigents' counsel fees.

Mr. Justice Powell, the Court's spokesman, pointed to the many crushing burdens imposed by this statute. Embodying "elements of punitiveness and discrimination," it not only denies equal protection, but raises barriers to rehabilitation.

BAIL —EQUAL PROTECTION

Schilb v. Kuebel, 404 U.S. 357, 10 CrL 3043

The Court divided 5–2 in upholding an Illinois bail reform statute that requires defendants who post ten percent of the bond amount in cash to pay one percent as cost of bail administration. These defendants are entitled to return of the ten percent posted, less the one percent charge, upon compliance with the terms of their bail. Defendants who post the full amount get it all back upon satisfaction of bail terms.

Mr. Justice Blackmun, writing for the majority, examined the statute's discrimination between three classes of bail defendants and found it constitutionally justifiable. One class consists of defendants who are released on personal recognizance and thus pay no fees. The reasonableness of the distinction between these defendants and those who must pay the one percent is obvious, the majority said.

The Court had more difficulty with the state's failure to exact any fees from defendants who are able to deposit the full amount of the bond in cash or property; the actual cost of administering this form of release is at least as great as with the ten percent depositors. However, Mr. Justice Blackmun concluded, the state does derive some

advantages from the full deposit which can rationally be considered as a fair exchange for the lack of fee. More important, there was no showing that this discrimination actually works against the poor. It was "by no means clear" that the ten percent deposit route is less attractive to the affluent defendant than the full-amount alternative. Nor are acquitted defendants denied due process by imposition of court costs; the majority found that the one percent is an administrative fee.

Concurring, Mr. Justice Marshall was unwilling to strike down as unfair a reform that rescues the ten percent depositor from the professional bail bondsman, who retains the full ten percent "premium."

Justices Stewart and Brennan could not accept as rational the distinction between the "ten percenters" and those released on personal recognizance. While those released without bond are "more worthy" of unsecured release, they are not more worthy of exemption from an administrative fee admittedly designed to cover cost of the system. Mr. Justice Douglas based his dissent on due process; he argued that imposing even a one percent charge on a defendant who is eventually acquitted violates the rudimentary concept of due process.

INTERROGATION

For more than 30 years, the trend of Supreme Court case law on confessions, culminating in the strict rules for custodial interrogation announced in Miranda v. Arizona, 384 U.S. 436, clearly ran in the defendant's favor. Now, the trend is running the other way. In the 1970–71 Term, the Court held that Miranda's exclusionary rule does not bar impeachment use of an otherwise reliable statement obtained in violation of its rules. In the 1971–72 Term, the Court turned its attention to the standard of proof by which an in-custody confession's voluntariness must be measured.

Lego v. Twomey, 404 U.S. 477, 10 CrL 3057

The Court held that a trial judge was entitled to admit a pre-Miranda confession that he was satisfied by a preponderance of the evidence was voluntary. Consistent with its tradition of dividing closely on questions concerning police-obtained confessions, the Court split 4–3 in rejecting the argument that voluntariness must be established beyond a reasonable doubt. The majority also held that once the trial judge makes the determination that a confession is voluntary, the defendant is not entitled to have the jury then consider his involuntariness claim anew.

A confession, Mr. Justice White pointed out on behalf of the majority, is not an element of the crime but an item of proof. Jackson v. Denno, 378 U.S. 368, which required a separate determination of voluntariness, did not set a burden of proof standard, but said that the defendant is entitled to a reliable and clear-cut determination of voluntariness. This means that voluntariness must be determined by a preponderance of evidence, although, "[o]f course, the states are free, pursuant to their own law, to adopt a higher standard."

Jackson v. Denno did not even suggest "that the Constitution requires submission of voluntariness claims to a jury as well as a judge," Mr. Justice White added.

Joined in dissent by Justices Douglas and Marshall, Mr. Justice Brennan maintained that under the Jackson rationale, preponderance of the evidence standard does not provide sufficient protection against the danger that an involuntary confession would be used. A confession is an extremely damaging item of evidence, and compelled self-incrimination is "alien to the American sense of justice." Thus, the dissenters would have required a finding beyond a reasonable doubt that the defendant "spoke of his own free will."

Milton v. Wainwright, 407 U.S. 371, 11 CrL 3153

Again dividing sharply, this time by a 5–4 vote, the Court held that any error in the admission of a 1958 murder defendant's incriminating post-indictment statement, elicited by a police officer who posed as his cellmate after defense counsel had advised him not to discuss the case with anyone, was rendered harmless by overwhelming evidence of guilt. The Chief Justice, writing for the majority, noted that this evidence included three properly admitted pre-indictment confessions that revealed essentially the same information as his statement to the undercover officer. The majority concluded that the jury at this defendant's trial would have reached the same result without hearing the officer's testimony.

Mr. Justice Stewart, writing for the four dissenters, accused the majority of turning its back on Powell v. Alabama, 287 U.S. 45. The courts below erroneously decided the case on the ground that Massiah v. U.S., 377 U.S. 201 (1964), does not apply retroactively. Massiah represented no new departure in the law, and did not alter accepted prosecutorial practices. Nor, if it were applied retroactively, would it threaten to disrupt the criminal justice system. Furthermore, the other inculpatory statements were all taken after intensive interrogation during an 18-day period of incommunicado detention. And the officer's statement about what the defendant had told him was referred to repeatedly by the prosecutor in his final argument.

STATUTES AND ORDINANCES

Papachristou v. City of Jacksonville, 405 U.S. 156, 10 CrL 3081

Whatever doubt about the constitutionality of vagrancy laws remained after Coates v. City of Cincinnati, 402 U.S. 611, 9 CrL 3181, and Palmer v. City of Euclid, 402 U.S. 544, 9 CrL 3175, was put to rest this Term by a unanimous Court as it struck down a typically vague Jacksonville, Florida ordinance. The ordinance punished, among other activities, "strolling around from place to place without any lawful purpose or object," habitual loafing, and living off the income of a wife while able to work.

Mr. Justice Douglas, for the Court, found this ordinance shot through with flaws. It fails to give a person of ordinary intelligence fair notice, he observed, and it encourages arbitrary arrests and convictions. It would punish various intra-family financial arrangements, and would forbid amenities of American life, such as aimless strolling, that have been extolled by Walt Whitman, Henry Thoreau, and Vachel Lindsay. This ordinance gives the police unfettered discretion to punish whatever activity comes within its all-inclusive and generalized list of "criminal" activities. By its vagueness, it permits investigative arrests based on mere suspicion of future criminality. It may well be used to compel those most often caught within its broad net "—poor people, nonconformists, dissenters, idlers —" to adhere to a life style deemed appropriate by the local police.

Mr. Justice Douglas made clear the implications of this opinion for vagrancy laws in general. "Vagrancy laws of the Jacksonville type teach that the scales of justice are so tipped that even-handed adminstration of the law is not possible."

Gooding v. Wilson, 405 U.S. 518, 10 CrL 3137

The Court also struck down as facially vague and overbroad a Georgia statute prohibiting use of "opprobrious words or abusive language" tending "to cause a breach of the peace." The statute had not been limited by the state courts to "fighting words" tending "to incite an immediate breach of the peace," Mr. Justice Brennan explained for the 5–2 majority. Georgia court decisions have applied this statute to utterances raising no likelihood of a violent response by the person addressed. Under Chaplinsky v. New Hampshire, 315 U.S. 568, which set forth the "fighting" words test, a narrower standard is required.

Dissenting, Mr. Justice Blackmun, joined by the Chief Justice, emphasized just what conduct was involved in this case. The defendant said to a police officer, who was attempting to restore access to a public building, "White son of a bitch, I'll kill you." To another officer, he said, "You son of a bitch, I choke you to death."

Any Georgia schoolboy, Mr. Justice Blackmun maintained, would consider these words within the purview of the state statute. The state, because of the way in which this statute has been interpreted in other cases, is now left without a valid statute to meet true "fighting words" language like that employed by this defendant. Decisions such as this one and Cohen v. California, 403 U.S. 15, 9 CrL 3189, render the holding in Chaplinsky a mere nullity.

In his own dissent, the Chief Justice found it remarkable that a statute could be voided on its face not because of its language, but because of the way the state courts have construed it in the distant past. Most of these state cases cited by the majority for their overbroad construction of the statute preceded Chaplinsky.

Smith v. Florida, 405 U.S. 172, 10 CrL 3086

The Court also vacated a Florida Supreme Court affirmance of a conviction under a state vagrancy statute that included within the term "vagrant" those persons who are found "wandering or strolling around from place to place without any lawful purpose or object." The case was remanded for reconsideration in light of Papachristou.

Eisenstadt v. Baird, 405 U.S. 438, 10 CrL 3111

A Massachusetts criminal statute prohibiting distribution of contraceptives to unmarried individuals except to prevent the spread of disease was struck down by the Court on equal protection grounds. Thus birth control advocate William Baird, who more than three years before had openly invited prosecution by exhibiting contraceptives to a college audience and handing a young woman a package of vaginal foam, was ultimately successful in his challenge to this statute. As a preliminary matter, the Court held that Baird, who was not a single person, a physician, or an authorized contraceptive's distributor, did have standing to assert the rights of unmarried persons denied access to contraceptives.

There is no rational ground for the legislative distinction between married and unmarried persons, Mr. Justice Brennan said in his four-Justice opinion for the Court. The deterrence of premarital sex cannot reasonably be regarded as the purpose of this law. It would be unreasonable to assume that the state has prescribed pregnancy as punishment for fornication, which is itself punishable under Massachusetts law. And, it is hard to believe that this statute, carrying a five-year penalty, was intended to partially deter fornication —a mere misdemeanor offense punishable by 90-day incarceration.

Mr. Justice Douglas joined in the Court's opinion, but viewed this as "a simple First Amendment case."

Concurring Justices White and Blackmun thought that the statute, as so far as it applies to potentially hazardous contraceptive devices like the pill, expressed a legitimate state interest in the health of its citizens. But they agreed that Baird was denied due process by his prosecution for giving the young lady a product that is widely available without prescription. There was no showing that a health hazard was involved or that the recipient was unmarried.

To the Chief Justice, dissenting, the only issue before the Court was the validity of the restriction on dispensing of medicinal substances —Baird, he maintained, had no standing to challenge the restriction against distribution to unmarried people.

The Chief Justice was critical of the "novel constitutional doctrine" that a state cannot regulate distribution of a substance without offering uncontroverted evidence supporting the classification or showing that the health hazard is so serious that it can be judicially noticed. The Chief Justice saw nothing in the Fourteenth Amendment or any other constitutional provision "which even vaguely

suggests that these medicinal forms of contraceptives must be available in the open market." Griswold v. Connecticut, 381 U.S. 479, which struck down a law prohibiting the use of contraceptives, is not applicable to this case, involving regulation of their distribution.

U.S. v. Bass, 404 U.S. 336, 10 CrL 3037

Disagreement over the significance of a comma that wasn't there divided the Court in holding that a previously convicted felon's conviction under Title VII of the Omnibus Crime Control Act of 1968 for receipt or possession of a firearm can't be sustained without proof that such receipt or possession had a nexus with interstate commerce. Section 1202 (a) of the Criminal Code provides for the conviction and punishment of any previously convicted felon "who receives, possesses, or transports in interstate commerce or affecting interstate commerce * * * any firearm * * *."

To the 5–2 majority, speaking through Mr. Justice Marshall, it would have been anomalous to hold that the absence of a comma after "transports" means that only transportation of a firearm, and not receipt or possession, must have a nexus with interstate commerce; virtually all transportation involves possession or receipt. While the statute is, under any interpretation, infelicitously worded, use of a comma after transportation would be considered discretionary by many grammarians. "When grammarians are divided, and surely where they are cheerfully tolerant, we will not attach significance to an omitted comma."

Furthermore, the majority said, it would vastly alter federal-state relations with respect to law enforcement. Such a drastic alteration is undesirable in the absence of a clear legislative mandate —which Congress did not provide here. Also, ambiguity in a criminal statute should be resolved in favor of lenity. Four of the seven Justices then sitting agreed that nexus can, however, be established with respect to receipt of a firearm if it is simply proved that the firearm has moved in interstate commerce. Mr. Justice Brennan saw no need to discuss this question.

Mr. Justice Blackmun, joined by the Chief Justice, maintained that the clear language of the statute supported the interpretation that the interstate nexus need not be shown with respect to mere possession or receipt. Mr. Justice Blackmun noted that four of the five U.S. courts of appeal that had passed on this question had so held. The punctuation is critical here, he maintained. "The structure of the vital language and its punctuation make it refer to one who receives, to one who possesses, and to one who transports in commerce." Furthermore, the purpose of the Act, as stated in 18 U.S.C. 1201, was clearly to forbid mere possession or receipt of a firearm by previously convicted felons, regardless of any connection with interstate commerce in a particular case.

Rabe v. Washington, 405 U.S. 313, 10 CrL 3095

The Court held, without dissent, that a theatre operator in a state obscenity conviction, based on his exhibition of an X-rated picture at an outdoor theatre whose screen was visible to passersby and nearby residents, denied the operator due process in view of the state obscenity statute's failure to give fair notice that the location of the exhibition was a vital element of the offense. The Court, in a per curiam opinion, emphasized the narrowness of its holding.

The Chief Justice and Mr. Justice Rehnquist concurred solely on lack-of-notice grounds; they did not doubt that a state may, with a properly drawn statute, prohibit the public display of explicit sexual activity.

SPEEDY TRIAL

Barker v. Wingo, 407 U.S. 514, 11 CrL 3174

For the first time, the Court squarely faced the question of just when a defendant has been denied his right to a speedy trial. It achieved unanimity in its conclusion that inflexible rules will not do. To set an inflexible time limit would be to indulge in judicial legislation. And the "demand-waiver" rule, which presumes that a defendant does not assert his speedy trial right until he actually demands it, is inconsistent with the presumption against waiver of rights.

Rather, Mr. Justice Powell wrote for the Court, a defendant's claim that he has been denied this right must be determined by a balancing test, in which four factors can be isolated: length of delay, reason for the delay, the defendant's assertion of the right or failure to assert it, and prejudice caused by the delay.

Applying this balancing test to the case before it, the Court concluded that a post-indictment delay of more than four years, although unjustified, did not prejudice a defendant who did not demand a speedy trial until three years after he was indicted, and who probably did not want to be tried until final disposition of his separately tried codefendant's case, which dragged through five trials.

The speedy trial right "is generically different" from any other constitutional right, Mr. Justice Powell observed. Society's interest in providing an accused with a speedy trial exists independently of, and frequently in opposition to, the defendant's own interests. Delay may well work to the defendant's advantage. Perhaps most important, the speedy trial right is more vague than other procedural rights. It also involves an "unsatisfactorily severe" remedy —outright dismissal of the prosecution.

Absolute time limits and the "demand-waiver" rule may well be due to the right's "slippery quality," Mr. Justice Powell noted. But, while the states are free to set reasonable fixed-time standards, the Supreme Court's function is not to prescribe procedures for the states to follow unless it is constitutionally necessary. And there is no constitutional basis for quantifying this right "into specific days or months." Furthermore, the "demand-waiver rule" —employed by the U.S. Court of Appeals for the Sixth Circuit in its refusal to consider all unchallenged pretrial delays —infringes on the right to "every reasonable presumption against waiver." It is not necessarily true that delay benefits the defendant; hence the need for a balancing test.

Each of the four factors involved in this balancing test must be weighed in light of the nature of the particular case, Mr. Justice Powell cautioned, and each factor itself involves several considerations. A longer delay must be permitted in a complex case than in a simple one. The weight to be given the Government's reason for delay will depend upon what that reason is. If delay is due to a Government effort to impede the defense, then, of course, it will weigh heavily against the Government. If the reason is neutral, such as crowded courts, it will still go against the Government, but less heavily. A valid reason —such as a missing prosecution witness —would "justify appropriate delay."

The defendant's claim of prejudice will be considered in light of his pretrial incarceration, if any; the anxiety or concern that he suffers; and, most serious, impairment of his defense occasioned by the delay. The interaction of these disadvantages must also be considered. The defendant's demand for a prompt trial will always weigh heavily in his favor, while a failure to assert the right will make it difficult for him to prove that he was denied it.

Justices Brennan and White, concurring, said that the conviction of the defendant in this case would not be so easily affirmed were it not so clear that he actually wanted his trial delayed as long as possible.

U.S. v. Marion, 404 U.S. 307, 10 CrL 3028

The argument that the Sixth Amendment's speedy trial guarantee applies to delays in bringing criminal charges, which had never significantly impressed any federal court of appeals, found no favor with a majority of the Supreme Court, as it reversed a federal district court decision dismissing a fraud indictment for undue pre-indictment delay. Mr. Justice White, writing for four of the seven Justices then sitting, found no Sixth Amendment safeguard against "the mere possibility" that pre-indictment delays will prejudice a criminal defendant; statutes of limitation already assure this protection. "Invocation of the speedy-trial provision * * * need not await indictment, information, or other formal charge, Mr. Justice White said, but until the time of arrest, the defendant suffers none of the evils sought to be avoided by this right.

The majority noted the Government's concession that the Fifth Amendment Due Process Clause would require purposeful pre-indictment delay caused substantial prejudice and was intended to do so. But, the question whether such violation has occurred must be decided on a case-by-case basis. It did not occur in this case; despite a 38-month delay between the end of the alleged fraud scheme and the indictment, the defendants made no showing of prejudice or intentional delay to gain advantage.

Justices Douglas, Brennan, and Marshall concurred in the result, but maintained that the speedy trial provision was meant to apply before arrest and indictment. Writing for the concurring Justices, Mr. Justice Douglas thought that the majority gave undue significance to the word "accused" in the Speedy Trial Clause. Nevertheless, he agreed that these defendants failed to show specific prejudice resulting from the delay in bringing criminal charges, and this was an extremely complex case.

JURIES

Johnson v. Louisiana, 406 U.S. 356, 11 CrL 3027; Apodaca v. Oregon, 406 U.S. 404, 11 CrL 3031

State juries need not return unanimous verdicts any more than they need consist of 12 members, the Court decided as it upheld, by a 5–4 vote, provisions in the Louisiana and Oregon constitutions that permit 12-man juries to convict by votes of 9–3 and 10–2 respectively.

In the Louisiana case, which involved a prosecution that predated application of the Sixth Amendment right of jury trial to the states, the Court held that the Due Process Clause does not mandate a unanimous verdict in order to give effect to the requirement that guilt be proved beyond a reasonable doubt. In the Oregon case, four Justices agreed that the unanimous verdict, while a historical and traditional fixture, does not rise to the level of a constitutional requirement. However, Mr. Justice Powell's swing vote, giving the Court a five-Justice majority, was based on his belief that a state jury trial need not be identical in every respect to the federal jury trial required by the Sixth Amendment. In his view, it is the Fourteenth Amendment, and not the Sixth, that imposes the jury-trial obligation on the states; thus the Sixth Amendment has no application to this case.

Mr. Justice White wrote the opinion for the Court in both cases. In the Louisiana case, he rejected the contention that a nine-juror finding of guilt beyond a reasonable doubt is in any way undermined by the failure of the remaining three jurors to reach the same conclusion. It is unlikely that the majority jurors would simply override their colleagues without listening to them. It is far more likely that reasoned arguments by jurors in favor of acquittal would either be answered or be persuasive enough to prevent conviction. Nor can it be said, that, under the Due Process Clause, a three-juror vote for acquittal impeaches the verdict of the "substantial majority" of nine.

Furthermore, the Court held, non-capital Louisiana defendants tried by a five-man jury —whose verdict must be unanimous —are not denied equal protection. There is a rational purpose behind the statutory scheme under which the seriousness of the crime determines the number of jurors who must be convinced of guilt beyond a reasonable doubt.

Mr. Justice Douglas, dissenting in both cases along with Justices Brennan and Marshall, pointed out that the Court had held long ago that the verdict in civil trials must be unanimous.

Mr. Justice Stewart wrote a dissent in each case. Joined in his Louisiana dissent by Justices Brennan and Marshall, he agreed that the Sixth Amendment's guarantee of trial by jury is not applicable because Duncan v. Louisiana, 391 U.S. 145, 3 CrL 3062, is not retroactive. But he was convinced that the Fourteenth Amendment alone clearly requires that if a state purports to grant a right of trial by jury, only unanimous juries can return a constitutionally valid verdict. In the Oregon case, however, he saw the only relevant question as that whether the Sixth Amendment guarantee of a trial by jury embraces the unanimity requirement. He would have held that it does.

Justices Brennan and Marshall each filed dissenting opinions in which the other joined. Mr. Justice Brennan said that when jury verdicts must be unanimous, no member of the jury may be ignored by the others; however, when less than unanimity is sufficient, consideration of minority views may become "nothing more than a matter of grace." Only a unanimous verdict indicates the right of all groups in this nation to participate in the criminal process.

Mr. Justice Marshall maintained that the Court's decision "cuts the heart out" of the defendant's jury right and his right to proof beyond a reasonable doubt. He thought it "utterly and obviously clear" that so long as the fact-finding tribunal "bears the label 'jury,' it will meet Sixth Amendment requirements as they are presently viewed by this Court." He was particularly distressed with the "cavalier treatment the Court gives to proof beyond a reasonable doubt." When three members of a jury are not convinced of guilt, "it does violence to language and to logic to say that the Government has proved the defendant's guilt beyond a reasonable doubt."

Peters v. Kiff, 407 U.S. 493, 11 CrL 3157

Racial discrimination in the jury selection process is per se harmful to the defendant, the Court held. Even a white defendant is entitled to habeas corpus relief from his state conviction if he can prove that Negroes —or any other identifiable class —have been systematically excluded either from the grand jury that indicted him or the petit jury that convicted him. And, the majority said, he is entitled to such relief even if unable to show that he was directly harmed by such exclusion.

Mr. Justice Marshall, writing the principal opinion for himself and Justices Douglas and Stewart, relied upon the Fourteenth Amendment's Due Process Clause. He pointed out that the exclusion of a discernible class from jury service injures not only those defendants who belong to the excluded class, but other defendants as well, "in that it destroys the possibility that the jury would reflect a representative cross-section of the community." Even if there was no showing of actual bias, due process is denied by circumstances that create the likelihood or appearance of bias.

It cannot be assumed that the exclusion of Negroes had relevance only for issues involving race, Mr. Justice Marshall said. "When any large and identifiable segment of the community is excluded from jury service, the effect is to remove from the jury room qualities of human nature and varieties of human experience the range of which is unknown and perhaps unknowable."

Justices White, Brennan, and Powell, concurring in the judgment, pointed out that 18 U.S.C. Section 243 prohibits racial discrimination in the jury selection process. These three Justices "would implement the strong statutory policy of Section 243, which reflects the central concern of the Fourteenth Amendment with racial discrimination, by permitting a petitioner to challenge his conviction on the grounds that Negroes were arbitrarily excluded from the grand jury that indicated him."

The Chief Justice, joined in dissent by Justices Blackmun and Rehnquist, pointed out that the defendant in this case was tried two years before Duncan v. Louisiana, 391 U.S. 145, 3 CrL 3062, at a time when he had no constitutional right to be tried before a jury at all.

Alexander v. Louisiana, 405 U.S. 625, 11 CrL 3001

Applying "settled principles," the Court unanimously voided the conviction of a Louisiana Negro who made a prima facie showing of racial bias in the selection of the grand jury that indicted him; the defendant showed that the all-white grand jury was selected from a parish population in which 21 percent of the adults were black. He further demonstrated that racial designations were obvious to the all-white jury commission throughout the selection process, during which the percentage of Negroes was progressively reduced.

The state offered nothing to refute this presumption except the testimony of the five white commissioners that they had made no conscious racial discrimination. Such self-serving avowals of impartiality have been enough to carry the burden —once shifted to the state —of disproving bias.

The Court refused, over protests of concurring Mr. Justice Douglas, to decide the defendant's claim that the alleged exclusion of women from the grand and petit juries violated his rights.

GUILTY PLEAS

Santobello v. New York, 404 U.S. 257, 10 CrL 3016

The Court had underscored in recent Terms the esteem to be accorded guilty plea negotiations as an integral part of the criminal justice system, emphasizing that, once a plea bargain has been struck, it is not to be lightly overturned —even in the face of defense claims of undue pressure.

Now the Court, in an opinion by the Chief Justice, emphasized the opposite side of the coin —that the prosecution's failure to carry out its part of a plea bargain

cannot go unrectified even if the prosecutorial breach arguably had no effect on the sentence imposed. The Court divided only as to what form the relief should take.

The majority held that a New York prosecutor's recommendation of a maximum sentence for a guilty-pleading gambler, which was an inadvertent breach of his predecessor's agreement not to recommend a sentence, requires that the state courts determine whether the defendant was entitled to withdraw his plea or simply be resentenced before another judge. This result is required, the majority held, even though the sentencing judge, who was not aware of the earlier prosecution promise, stated at the time he imposed the maximum sentence that he was not influenced by the prosecution recommendation.

Concurring, Mr. Justice Douglas offered a brief review of Supreme Court decisions concerning guilty pleas. He noted the importance of plea bargaining to the administration of justice both at the state and the federal levels.

Mr. Justice Marshall, writing for himself and Justices Brennan and Stewart, maintained that the defendant should be allowed to withdraw his plea and exercise his right to a trial if he so desires. "When a prosecutor breaks the bargain, he undercuts the basis for the waiver of constitutional rights implicit in the plea. This, it seems to me, provides the defendant ample justification for rescinding the plea."

Dukes v. Warden, 406 U.S. 250, 11 CrL 3017

The Court was unpersuaded by the claim of a narcotics defendant who reluctantly pleaded guilty that his lawyer's eloquence in defense of two codefendants in an unrelated matter before the same judge rendered his guilty plea involuntary. A 7–2 majority found no merit in his argument that the lawyer's disparaging remarks about him, made in defense of the two codefendants before the same judge who took his plea, reflected a fatal conflict of interest.

The majority, in an opinion by Mr. Justice Brennan, pointed out that the defendant was fully aware that his lawyer also represented the codefendants at the time he was hired. The record indicated that the judge carefully inquired about the defendant's mental state at the time of the plea. Furthermore, there was no evidence that the attorney's remarks had any effect on the quality of his representation of the defendant. The defendant had initially rejected a plea bargain made by this attorney, and then had agreed to essentially the same bargain when made by the attorney's partner.

Mr. Justice Stewart, concurring, maintained that the claim here "should be evaluated under the standards governing an act on a guilty plea made after judgment, not under the far different standards governing a motion to withdraw a plea made before judgment is pronounced." Mr. Justice Stewart did not think that Santobello v. New York applied here, and he agreed that the defendant's claim lacked merit.

Justices Marshall and Douglas, dissenting, emphasized the sharp conflict between lawyer and client over the decision to plead guilty. They were convinced that the lawyer had a "gross conflict of interest," which was ignored by the majority.

STATUTES AND ORDINANCES —PICKETING

Chicago Police Dept. v. Mosley, 408 U.S. 92, 11 CrL 3211

A Chicago ordinance forbidding all picketing except peaceful labor picketing within 150 feet of a school was held to violate the Equal Protection Clause by impermissibly distinguishing between two kinds of peaceful picketing on the basis of content. The ordinance, Mr. Justice Marshall explained for the Court, "describes impermissible picketing not in terms of time, place and manner, but in terms of subject matter." While, of course, preventing school disruption is a legitimate concern, the city itself has determined that peaceful labor picketing during school hours will not cause such disruption. Thus, it cannot, under the Equal Protection Clause, maintain that other picketing will do so simply because it is not related to labor matters.

Justices Blackmun and Rehnquist concurred in the result. The Chief Justice joined in the Court's opinion but pointed to various qualifications of the First Amendment right of free speech that have been recognized by the Court.

Grayned v. City of Rockford, 408 U.S. 104, 11 CrL 3215

Another Illinois ordinance prohibiting picketing near schools, virtually identical to the invalid ordinance in Mosley, was struck down by the Court. However, in the same case, the Court upheld an anti-noise ordinance also designed to protect schools from disruption. This law punished anyone who, on school grounds while school is in session, "shall willfully make or assist in the making of any noise or diversion which disturbs or tends to disturb the peace or good order of such school session or class thereof * * * ."

The ordinance narrowly passed the vagueness test. The Court extrapolated its language, never construed by Illinois courts, to mean that it forbids only deliberate noise or diversionary activity that is serious enough to actually disrupt school activities. Thus, Mr. Justice Marshall wrote in his opinion for the Court, it could not be used to punish "undesirables" or those engaged in activity that may simply be annoying.

Furthermore, the statute forbids no conduct that is constitutionally protected. Mr. Justice Marshall emphasized that it narrowly regulates activity so as to further a legitimate government function. It does not deny access to school grounds or buildings. It would not, Mr. Justice Marshall assumed, stop peaceful picketing. It does not give license to punish anyone because of what he is saying. Only noisy demonstrations incompatible with normal school activities come within its reach. While such activity may be all right at other times and places, it certainly may be prohibited next to a school while classes are in session.

Only Mr. Justice Douglas dissented with respect to the anti-noise ordinance. Examining the facts of the case, Mr. Justice Douglas concluded that the defendant had made no noise whatsoever, and that most of his picketers were students in the school. He also emphasized that the picketing related to an issue dealing with race.

SENTENCING

Colten v. Kentucky, 407 U.S. 104, 11 CrL 3102

A misdemeanor defendant who seeks a trial de novo in a court of record following his conviction in an inferior court is not constitutionally protected against a sentence that is harsher than the original sentence imposed by the inferior court. A seven-Justice majority of the Court concluded that the rule of North Carolina v. Pearce, 395 U.S. 711, 5 CrL 3119, barring unexplained harsher sentences upon retrial following a successful appeal, does not apply to Kentucky's two-tier trial system for petty offenses.

The constitutional impropriety of requiring a defendant to risk penalty for seeking a new trial, which underlay Pearce, is not present in the trial de novo arrangement, Mr. Justice White said for the majority. The possibility of vindictiveness is not present under this system. Unlike a successful appellant, the defendant who exercises his de novo trial right is retried on a clean slate before an entirely different court. Thus the Court upheld a $50 fine following the trial de novo of a defendant originally fined $10 for obstructing a policeman trying to make a valid traffic arrest.

On an entirely unrelated First Amendment question, the Court upheld the defendant's disorderly conduct conviction under a statute that would not punish bona fide attempts to exercise constitutional rights. This defendant had participated in an anti-war demonstration. But he interfered with the officer after the demonstration had ended. His activities were in no way related to the demonstration and were impeding traffic.

Dissenting from the Court's First Amendment holding, Mr. Justice Douglas maintained that the defendant was simply petitioning a representative of government for a redress of grievances.

Mr. Justice Marshall, also dissenting, urged that North Carolina v. Pearce should apply to the trial de novo. The deterrent effect of seeking recourse in a higher court is the same whether a defendant "appeals" or seeks a trial de novo, Mr. Justice Marshall maintained. The core problem, he suggested, is the second trial.

North Carolina v. Rice, 404 U.S. 244, 10 CrL 3013

The Court remanded, for "reconsideration of the question of mootness," a North Carolina defendant's challenge to his already served sentence following his jury trial de novo, that was harsher than the sentence he received following his original trial in an inferior court.

The U.S. Court of Appeals for the Fourth Circuit had granted him habeas corpus relief under North Carolina v. Pearce, 395 U.S. 711, 5 CrL 3119.

U.S. v. Tucker, 405 U.S. 443, 10 CrL 3053

A federal bank robbery defendant sentenced in 1953 to 25 years won reconsideration of his sentence as a divided Court, upholding a grant of postconviction relief by the U.S. Court of Appeals for the Ninth Circuit, observed that the trial judge might have imposed a different sentence had he known at the time that at least two of the defendant's prior convictions were invalid because they were obtained without the assistance of counsel.

Mr. Justice Stewart, writing for the majority, maintained that this sentence was not one imposed within the judge's informed discretion. Rather, it was "founded at least in part on misinformation of a constitutional magnitude."

Mr. Justice Blackmun, joined by the Chief Justice, dissented. He accused the majority of engaging in an "exercise in futility." The defendant admitted the conduct underlying the two invalid convictions, and it was more than likely, the dissenters thought, that the judge would have imposed the 25-year sentence regardless of the validity of the two convictions.

IMPEACHMENT

Loper v. Beto, 405 U.S. 473, 10 CrL 3122

A majority of the Court also held that a state court's impeachment use of a rape defendant's prior convictions, which were unconstitutionally obtained without legal representation, deprived him of due process —if their use influenced the outcome of the case. The case was, accordingly, remanded to the court of appeals for determination of this question.

While the Tucker case involved only that aspect of Burgett v. Texas, 389 U.S. 109, which prohibited use of an invalid prior conviction to enhance punishment, this case involved such use to support guilt. This decision, the majority maintained, is consistent with the rationale under which Gideon v. Wainwright, 372 U.S. 335 (1963), was given retroactive application.

Concurring in the result, Mr. Justice White emphasized that the defendant's conviction needn't necessarily be set aside. The factual questions as to whether the challenged priors were obtained without counsel or a valid waiver of counsel would be better answered by the court of appeals. Furthermore, there is the possibility that use of the old priors was harmless error.

The Chief Justice and Justices Blackmun, Powell, and Rehnquist all dissented. The Chief Justice and Mr. Justice Powell thought there was no basis for making Gideon v. Wainwright available to challenge use in a 1953 proceeding, of 1932, 1935, and 1940 convictions, obtained after trials at which the defendant may or may not have been represented by counsel at a time when he may or may not have been able to afford counsel.

Emphasizing the procedural posture of the case, Mr. Justice Rehnquist, joined by the other three dissenters, pointed to the insuperable difficulties that a Texas federal district court will face in trying to determine whether the Mississippi and Tennessee convictions, obtained 30 to 40 years ago, were, in fact, obtained in violation of Gideon. The habeas court did hear the petitioner's contentions about his asserted lack of representation at these trials. The court chose, as was its prerogative, to disbelieve him. The dissenters would have dismissed the writ of certiorari as improvidently granted, but on the merits, they would have affirmed the judgment below on the ground that the petitioner had not satisfactorily carried his burden of proof.

RIGHT OF CONFRONTATION

Schneble v. Florida, 405 U.S. 427, 10 CrL 3106

The Court held, 6–3, that a non-testifying Florida murder defendant convicted on the basis of his detailed confession was not prejudicially denied his right of confrontation by the admission into evidence of his non-testifying, jointly tried codefendant's out-of-court statement that corroborated certain details of the defendant's confession. The codefendant's statement also undermined the defendant's initial exculpatory out-of-court statement, which was admitted into evidence by way of a police officer's testimony.

The defendant's confession was the key to the prosecution's case, Mr. Justice Rehnquist emphasized for the majority. Without the confession, there could have been no conviction. Thus, admission of the codefendant's statement merely corroborating parts of this confession, which was itself overwhelming evidence of guilt, was harmless error at most. The majority refrained from saying whether this case did present a violation of Bruton v. U.S., 391 U.S. 123, 3 CrL 3085.

Mr. Justice Marshall, joined by Justices Douglas and Brennan, agreed that the confession was a critical element of the case, but they thought that it might very well have been involuntary. While this question was not within the grant of certiorari, it was important in that, without the confession, the defendant could not have been convicted. The dissenters thought it impossible to conclude that the evidence in this case was so "overwhelming" that the admission of the codefendant's statement made no difference.

Mancusi v. Stubbs, 408 U.S. 204, 11 CrL 3221

Use at a murder retrial of a key prosecution witness' first trial testimony, after it was learned that the witness had taken up permanent residence in Sweden and thus was unavailable to testify at the retrial, did not violate the Confrontation Clause, the Court held in an opinion by Mr. Justice Rehnquist. True, the defendant had obtained federal habeas corpus relief on the basis of an apparent per se rule, disapproved in Chambers v. Maroney, 399 U.S. 42, 7 CrL 3131, that late appointment of counsel at the first trial rendered his assistance ineffective. However, the record reveals that there was an adequate opportunity for cross-examination at the first trial, the majority concluded. Thus a court of appeals judgment granting habeas corpus relief was reversed.

Mr. Justice Marshall, dissenting, would have dismissed the writ as improvidently granted, but he also disagreed with the majority position on the merits. In his disagreement on the merits, he was joined by Mr. Justice Douglas.

FAIR TRIAL

Giglio v. U.S., 405 U.S. 150, 10 CrL 3080

A forgery defendant was found entitled to a new trial on the basis of newly discovered evidence that the Government failed to disclose an Assistant U.S. Attorney's promise to the defendant's coconspirator that, in exchange for the coconspirator's testimony, he would not be prosecuted. The unanimous Court, in an opinion by the Chief Justice, emphasized that an Assistant U.S. Attorney's promise is attributable to the Government even if he exceeded his authority in making it. Here, the coconspirator's testimony was almost the Government's entire case, and the jury was entitled to know about this agreement in view of its bearing on his credibility.

DISCOVERY

Moore v. Illinois, 408 U.S. 786, 11 CrL 3379

The discovery rule of Brady v. Maryland, 373 U.S. 830, barring state suppression of possibly exculpatory evidence, did not require disclosure of items that the defense in an Illinois murder trial did not specifically request in its discovery motion and that were not material in any way, a majority of the Court held. The defendant was not denied due process by the admission into evidence of a shotgun found in his possession, but which was not the shotgun used in the murder. Nor was he denied due process by the state's failure to disclose police investigatory work, not contained in the prosecutor's files, that turned up statements either tending to confuse the defendant with another man or indicating that the defendant was not at the scene of the crime. These statements did not impeach any positive identification testimony, and they were not otherwise material.

The majority, in an opinion by Mr. Justice Blackmun, emphasized as "the heart" of Brady's holding its condemnation of the suppression of materially favorable evidence requested by the defense.

Mr. Justice Marshall, joined in dissent by Justices Douglas, Stewart, and Powell, concurred only in the majority's act of voiding this defendant's death sentence under Furman v. Georgia, 11 CrL 3231. The dissenters found it obvious that both the statements were not merely material to the defense; "they were absolutely critical."

EQUAL PROTECTION

Humphrey v. Cady, 405 U.S. 504, 10 CrL 3132

The Court unanimously agreed that a Wisconsin misdemeanant who was committed under the state's Sex Crimes Act to the "sex deviate facilities" at the state prison for a period equaling the maximum sentence he could have incurred must be afforded an evidentiary hearing on his federal habeas corpus claim that, under the Equal Protection and Due Process Clauses, he was entitled to a jury trial before he could be recommitted under the Act for a five-year period. Also, assuming that mootness is not a problem, he is entitled to a hearing on his contention that he was denied due process by his commitment to the state prison rather than to a mental hospital, as he would have been had his commitment proceedings been brought under the Mental Health Act.

Persons committed under the Mental Health Act have the rights at their commitment hearings that the defendant claimed he was denied, and commitment under the two Acts involves some of the same considerations. Baxstrom v. Herold, 383 U.S. 107, might well control here.

The petitioner's equal protection claim will be even more persuasive, the Court said, if it turns out that he was denied these procedural rights by an arbitrary decision to seek his commitment under the Sex Crimes Act.

The Court also made it clear that a deliberate bypass of appropriate state remedies will not be presumed in the absence of a showing that failure to exhaust such remedies was the result of the petitioner's knowing and understanding decision, rather than decision or default of counsel.

EXHAUSTION OF STATE REMEDIES

Picard v. Connor, 404 U.S. 270, 10 CrL 3024

A federal habeas corpus petitioner's failure in the highest state court to assert his claim that the state's "John Doe" indictment procedures violated the Fourteenth Amendment's Equal Protection Clause constituted a failure to exhaust state remedies as required by 28 U.S.C. 2254 (b), with respect to that issue, the Court held, even though he had contended that the procedures did violate state law and the Fifth Amendment right to indictment, which he asserted, has been made applicable to the states by the Fourteenth Amendment.

Dissenting, Mr. Justice Douglas maintained "that in this case we carry the rule of exhaustion of state remedies too far."

MISCELLANEOUS

Duncan v. Tennessee, 405 U.S. 127, 10 CrL 3078

The interrelationship of double jeopardy questions and unchallenged rules of criminal pleading peculiar to Tennessee led the Court to dismiss certiorari as improvidently granted.

1972–1973 Term

Whether the Court's work is to be measured by the production of highly publicized bombshells or the far-ranging effect of less noted decisions, the 1972–1973 Term did not have the impact of the virtually inimitable 1971–72 Term, which made even the busiest years of the "Warren Court's" criminal law revolution seem tame by comparison.

Decisions producing bombshells this year did not affect law enforcement efforts aimed at crime in the streets or organized crime in the usualy sense. Rather, they dealt with controversial activities whose asserted criminality deeply divides American society. One such activity, the procuring of an abortion, was held to be a fundamental right of the woman and her doctor, and as such, outside the state's control until a late stage of pregnancy. Another kind of activity —distribution or exhibition of materials that are deemed obscene —was subjected to tighter state control than before.

While the abortion and obscenity decisions dominated the Term, the Court did have several significant things to say in other areas of the criminal law. It upheld the right of a grand jury to require witnesses to give voice and handwriting exemplars for identification purposes without a preliminary showing of Fourth Amendment reasonableness. A state, it was held, can establish that an individual voluntarily consented to a search without first having to show that he knew he could have withheld his consent. The Court approved the warrantless taking, prior to formal arrest, of evidence from beneath the fingernails of a suspect the police had probable cause to arrest. It upheld the holding of a photographic showup in the absence of counsel for the in-custody accused.

At the same time, the Court strengthened the trial rights of state defendants, in what Mr. Justice Rehnquist referred to in dissent as the "constitutionalization of the intricacies of the common law of evidence." A Mississippi rule barring a party from impeaching his own witness and excluding declarations against penal interest as inadmissible hearsay was deemed a due process violation. An Oregon notice of alibi statute denying a defendant reciprocal discovery with respect to the state's rebuttal plan suffered the same fate. And, for the third time in 41 years, a five-Justice majority held that the predisposition of a federal defendant, rather than the nature of the Government's inducement, remains the key to an entrapment defense.

ABORTION

The right of privacy included in the fundamental personal liberty protected by the Fourteenth Amendment's Due Process Clause bars any state interference, absent a compelling state interest, with the decision of a pregnant mother and her physician to terminate her pregnancy by abortion. This conclusion led a 7–2 majority of the Court, to strike down a Texas statute banning all abortions not necessary to save the mother's life. The Court also declared unconstitutional certain regulatory provisions of a 1968 Georgia statute patterned, like most other modern abortion laws, on the American Law Institute's Model Penal Code.

Roe v. Wade, 410 U.S. 113, 12 CrL 3099

For approximately the first trimester of a pregnancy, Mr. Justice Blackmun wrote for the majority, the state must leave the abortion decision "to the medical judgment of the woman's attending physician." From the end of this stage until the fetus becomes viable —that is, capable of existing outside the womb —the decision whether to abort is still primarily the mother's. At this time, however, the state has the authority to "regulate the abortion procedure in ways that are reasonably related to maternal health." Not until the fetus becomes viable does the state's interest "in the potentiality of human life" become compelling. At this point, the state may "regulate, and even proscribe, abortion except where it is necessary, in appropriate medical judgment, for the preservation of the life or health of the mother."

The Court found support for its rollback of state anti-abortion authority in history, current medical knowledge, and constitutional development of the privacy right.

Restrictive state abortion laws like the Texas statute are "of relatively recent vintage," Mr. Justice Blackmun observed in an historical survey that went back to antiquity. They find little support in the common law. Abortion before quickening was not an indictable common-law offense. Even post-quickening abortion was never conclusively established as a common-law crime. England did not have a criminal abortion statute until 1803, when abortion of a quickened fetus was made a capital offense. Lesser penalties were imposed for the felony of abortion before quickening. The quickening distinction disappeared, along with capital punishment of the offense, in 1837 and did not reappear until 1929. The trend since then has been toward liberalization.

Until the mid-19th century, the majority noted, American abortion law in all but a few states was derived from the English common law. Connecticut enacted the earliest abortion statute in 1828, but pre-quickening abortion was made a crime only in 1860. Not until after the Civil War did state legislatures generally begin to replace the common law with statutes. Most of these severely punished post-quickening abortions, but were lenient as to abortions induced during the pre-quickening stage. Most statutes eventually required actual necessity to save the mother's life. Not until the middle and late 19th century did the quickening distinction disappear. The degree of the offense and the penalties attached to it increased. By the end of the 1950s a large majority of the states banned abortion outright except to save or preserve the mother's life. But the recent trend toward liberalization has led to the adoption by about one-third of the states of less restrictive laws, most of them patterned after the American Law Institute Model Penal Code.

Mr. Justice Blackmun noted the shift in the American Medical Association's position, from adamant opposition except for the preservation of the mother's life to a position basically in conformity with that of the Model Penal Code. The views of the legal profession have undergone a similar shift; in 1972, the ABA House of Delegates voted to approve the Uniform Abortion Act. "It is thus apparent that at common law, at the time of the adoption of our Constitution, and throughout the major portion of the 19th century, abortion was viewed with less disfavor than under most American statutes currently in effect. Phrasing it another way, a woman enjoyed a substantially broader right to terminate a pregnancy than she does in most states today."

Two state interests might justify interference with the woman's decision to terminate her pregnancy, Mr. Justice Blackmun said. One is medical —the state's interest in protecting the mother. The other is the protection of prenatal life. The mother's right to determine whether she will bear a child or procure an abortion is fundamental, however, and the state can intervene only when its interests become compelling. The mother's right flows from the Court's long-time recognition that the Constitution protects "a right of personal privacy, by a guarantee of certain areas or zones or privacy * * * ." While this right is not explicitly mentioned in the Constitution, its roots have been found in the First, Fourth, and Fifth Amendments, "in the penumbras of the Bill of Rights; * * * in the Ninth Amendment, * * * or in the concept of ordered liberty guaranteed by the first section of the Fourteenth Amendment." Only personal rights can be deemed fundamental. But this right of privacy has been extended to various activities that are central to the family and other intimate relationships. This right "is broad enough to encompass a woman's decision whether or not to terminate her pregnancy." If denied it, she may suffer obvious physical and psychological harm —not to mention the distress to everyone concerned that results from the birth of an unwanted child.

However, Mr. Justice Blackmun continued, this right is not absolute; at some point the state's interests do become compelling. Medically, the state has "a definite interest in protecting the woman's own health and safety when an abortion is proposed at a late stage of pregnancy."

The question of the state's right to protect prenatal life was more difficult to resolve. The fetus is not a "person" within the meaning of the Fourteenth Amendment, the Court held. Other areas of the law have never recognized the fetus as a person "in the whole sense." There is no philosophical, medical, or scientific consensus as to when "life" begins. The view officially held by the Roman Catholic Church and shared by many non-Catholics is that life begins at conception. But this view has been seriously undermined by new data indicating that "conception" is a " 'process' over time, rather than a fixed event." However, the state's interest in preserving the life of the fetus does become compelling at the time the fetus is capable' "of meaningful life outside the mother's womb."

Concurring, Mr. Justice Stewart welcomed the Court's resurrection of the "substantive due process" doctrine that had purportedly been done away with ten years ago by Mr. Justice Black's opinion for the Court in Ferguson v. Skrupa, 372 U.S. 726. The abortion decision restores the Fourteenth Amendment's Due Process Clause to its rightful place as a barrier against state intrusion upon a broad range of personal freedoms encompassed within the term "liberty". This was implicit in Griswold v. Connecticut, 381 U.S. 479. "As so understood, Griswold stands as one in a long line of pre-Skrupa cases decided under the doctrine of substantive due process, and I now accept it as such."

Justices Rehnquist and White dissented vehemently. The liberty protected by the Fourteenth Amendment is not guaranteed absolutely, Mr. Justice Rehnquist pointed out, "but only against deprivation without due process of law." The traditional test "in the area of social and economic legislation is whether or not a law such as that challenged has a rational relation to a valid state objective." The abortion law clearly does, Mr. Justice Rehnquist said; the majority's attempt to ignore this interest recalls the judicial activism that reached its unhappy zenith in Lochner v. New York, 198 U.S. 45 (1905), and other decisions striking down economic and social welfare legislation. The Lochner standard "will inevitably require this Court to examine the legislative policies and pass on the wisdom of these policies in the very process of deciding whether a particular state interest put forward may or not be 'compelling.' "

The very fact that for a century or more states have restricted abortions refutes the argument that the asserted right to an abortion is "so rooted in the traditions and conscience of our people as to be ranked as fundamental." By the time the Fourteenth Amendment was adopted, Mr. Justice Rehnquist pointed out, "there were at least 36 laws enacted by state or territorial legislatures limiting abortion." Many of these laws are still in effect.

Mr. Justice Rehnquist also objected to the majority's striking down the Texas statute in toto, "even through the Court apparently concedes that at later periods of pregnancy Texas might impose these selfsame limitations on abortion."

Doe v. Bolton, 410 U.S. 179, 12 CrL 3118

The extent to which a woman's right to an abortion must remain unfettered was underscored by the Court in striking down key procedural provisions of Georgia's modern "therapeutic" abortion statute, patterned after an ALI Model Penal Code provision adopted by approximately one-fourth of the states.

Declared unconstitutional were the 1968 statute's prohibition of all abortions except those performed upon a Georgia resident by a physician in a hospital accredited by the Private Joint Committee on Accreditation of Hospitals, after approval by a hospital committee and the consensus of two other physicians. These restraints, Mr. Justice Blackmun explained, bear no rational relationship to the legitimate ends of the regulatory scheme.

Even the requirement that the operation take place in a hospital is not justified as to operations during the first trimester, the Court also held. Beyond that point, however, the state's interest in limiting the privacy right to protect the health of mothers does enter into the picture.

The residency requirement was found to violate the Privileges and Immunities Clause.

The Court did uphold the state's restriction of abortion operations to licensed physicians. It also rejected a vagueness claim against a provision conditioning the legality of an abortion on the doctor's use of his "best clinical judgment". This vagueness argument, Mr. Justice Blackmun said, was answered by the Court's decision in U.S. v. Vuitch, 402 U.S. 62, 9 CrL 3071.

In a concurrence that went to both majority opinions, the Chief Justice added that personally he would not strike down the requirement for certification by two physicians. While he would allow the states to regulate the performance of abortions, he agreed that they could not do so by requiring complex and burdensome administrative steps such as those involved here.

Mr. Justice Douglas, also concurring in both opinions, spelled out in some detail his view of the rights protected by the term "liberty" as used in the Fourteenth Amendment.

Joined by Mr. Justice Rehnquist, Mr. Justice White asserted, that at "the heart of the controversy in these cases are those recurring pregnancies that pose no danger whatever to the life and health of the mother but are nevertheless unwanted for any one of a variety of reasons —convenience, family planning, economics, dislike of children, the embarrassment of an illegitimacy, etc." The Court largely supports termination of pregnancy for these reasons, Mr. Justice White maintained, by simply fashioning and announcing "a constitutional right for pregnant mothers and, with scarcely any reason or

authority for its action," of investing "that right with sufficient substance to override most existing state abortion statutes." Noting the extremely broad consequences of the majority's decision, he termed it "an improvident and extravagant exercise of the power of judicial review which the Constitution extends to this Court."

OBSCENITY

Despite dissenting protests that it was attempting the impossible, the Court, in seven opinions by the Chief Justice, made a monumental effort to clear up years of confusion over what obscenity is and what constitutional standards govern state and federal attempts to clean it up.

For the first time in 16 years, since Roth v. U.S., 354 U.S. 476, a majority stood behind a new definition of obscenity. The same five Justices rejected any idea of a "national community" obscenity standard, and found no need for expert testimony as to material that is itself admitted into evidence. While forbidding warrantless seizures of alleged smut, the same majority permitted issuance of warrants without prior adversary hearings. Nor did they see any First Amendment bar to prohibition of obscene entertainment, even for adults only. And they upheld strict federal prohibitions against its transportation, even when private consumption is the goal. The four dissenting Justices accused the majority of countenancing serious threats to First Amendment freedoms.

Miller v. California, 413 U.S. 15, 13 CrL 3161

The Court, upholding a California obscenity statute, held that the First Amendment does not bar a state obscenity conviction for distribution of material that, in the judgment of the fact-finder, (a) the average person, applying contemporary community standards, would find, taken as a whole, appeals to the prurient interest, (b) depicts or describes in a patently offensive way sexual conduct that is specifically defined by state law, and (c) taken as a whole, lacks serious literary, artistic, political, or scientific value. The last part of the test replaced the "utterly without redeeming social value" criterion of Roth and Memoirs v. Massachusetts, 383 U.S. 413 (1966). Furthermore, the fact-finder's determination of whether the material appeals to "the prurient interest" or is "patently offensive" need not be based on "uniform national standards."

Underlying the Court's willingness to undertake anew the arduous task of developing an obscenity test, as well as the resolution of all the obscenity questions that followed, was one fundamental principle: the kind of sex-oriented material that fits this obscenity definition is something altogether different from the kind of expression that enjoys First Amendment protection. It is analogous to the physical pollution that results from other commercial enterprises and is just as susceptible to legislative control.

It follows from this, the Chief Justice emphasized, that the Court cannot, without abdicating its rightful constitutional role, withdraw from the obscenity thicket by taking an "anything goes" approach. It is true that the absence since Roth of a majority view on proper obscenity standards "has placed a strain on both state and federal courts." But the Court now offers concrete guidelines, and "no amount of 'fatigue' " justifies abdication.

The Chief Justice found no merit to the argument that continued regulation of obscenity will adversely affect the free flow of art and ideas. The 19th century era from Jefferson to Theodore Roosevelt, with its harsh Comstockian laws, was one of extraordinary intellectual vigor. It left a rich heritage in literature and science. Not every state regulation of commercial exploitation of sex harbors the threat of censorship and repression of political ideas.

The Court's refusal to require a single nationwide "community standard" for deciding, in a given prosecution, whether the material appeals to the prurient interest or is patently offensive rested on the Chief Justice's explanation that the United States is simply too big and diverse a country for such a broad resolution of what is essentially a question of fact.

Mr. Justice Brennan, joined by Justices Stewart and Marshall, maintained that the California statute here was overbroad under the approach he advocated in the next companion case, Paris Adult Theatre I v. Slaton. He took the position that no limitations can constitutionally be placed on the properly safeguarded distribution or exhibition of any kind of sexual material for enjoyment by consenting adults.

Also dissenting, Mr. Justice Douglas asserted that "[t]he Court has worked hard to define obscenity and concededly has failed." How, he wondered, could the "vague test" that the Court had "written into the Constitution" be used to "sustain convictions for the sale of an article prior to the time when some court has declared it to be obscene?"

Mr. Justice Douglas reiterated a position he and Mr. Justice Black had long taken, that the First Amendment, without exception, absolutely forbids any regulation of speech. There are simply no constitutional guidelines for deciding what is and is not obscene. The question of obscenity is one of "taste and standards of literature," and any attempt to regulate such standards results in censorship —which should only be "done by constitutional amendment after full debate by the people."

Furthermore, there is no "captive audience" problem in obscenity cases, Mr. Justice Douglas pointed out. "The idea that the First Amendment permits Government to ban publications that are 'offensive' to some people puts an ominous gloss on freedom of the press."

Paris Adult Theatre I v. Slaton, 413 U.S. 49, 13 CrL 3171

Exhibition of obscene films is not protected, even when conducted in an "adult theatre" that effectively restricts films to consenting adults, without "pandering" or obtrusive advertising, the Court went on to hold. The constitutional right of privacy that protects an individ-

ual's consumption of obscenity in his own home does not extend to such exhibitions.

An equally significant holding was that the prosecution need not introduce expert testimony as to whether material, that is itself placed in evidence, meets components of the constitutional test for obscenity.

The Court expressly approved the Georgia civil procedure employed in this case. By seeking an injunction to forbid the showing of allegedly obscene films or other materials, the authorities give the exhibitor or purveyor "the best possible notice, prior to any criminal indictments, as to whether the materials are unprotected by the First Amendment and are subject to state regulation."

The asserted right to commercially show or distribute obscene material even to consenting adults was found inferior to the state's legitimate long-range interests in its regulation. These interests include protection of the quality of life "and the total community environment, the tone of commerce in the great city centers, and, possibly, the public safety itself." All of these are valid interests even aside from an "arguable correlation between obscene material and crime." Even in the absence of scientific data on the extent, if any, to which exposure to obscene materials adversely affects individuals or society, state regulation of obscenity does not infringe upon any constitutionally protected right. The legislatures are not forbidden to make the rational assumption that they do have a valid interest. Unprovable assumptions underlie much lawful state regulation of commercial and business affairs. Legislative and administrative efforts to protect the physical environment from pollution and to protect natural resources are also based on imponderables. "The sum of experience, including that of the past two decades, affords an ample basis for legislatures to conclude that a sensitive, key relationship of human existence, central to family life, community welfare, and the development of human personality, can be debased and distorted by crass commercial exploitation of sex."

The Court also emphasized the difference, for purposes of the right of privacy, between the private home and a commercial enterprise. Stanley v. Georgia, 394 U.S. 557, was decided on a narrow basis, the Chief Justice noted. Nor did he think that the regulatory legislation involved here was an attempt to control the minds or thoughts of those who patronize theatres.

Mr. Justice Brennan's dissent from this decision was the most exhaustive of all the obscenity decisions. He was joined by Justices Stewart and Marshall.

Convinced that the question of obscenity simply does not admit of resolution by "stable and manageable standards," Mr. Justice Brennan asserted that stability in this area of the law is impossible "without jeopardizing fundamental First Amendment values". This case involved suppression of materials shown only to consenting adults, Mr. Justice Brennan noted. He traced the history of what he termed the Court's futile efforts to come to grips with constitutional problems posed by attempted regulation of obscenity. The attempt to separate all forms of sexually explicit expression into two categories —one subject to governmental suppression and the other beyond the reach of government regulation —has simply failed. The meaning of such concepts as "prurient interest," "patent offensiveness," and "serious literary value" that must form the constitutional boundary between protected and unprotected material "necessarily varies with the experience, outlet, and even idiosyncracies of the person defining them." Furthermore, obscenity is a function of the circumstances of its dissemination. The nature of the subject matter makes case-by-case obscenity determinations unavoidable. The vagueness of the statutes raises several distinct problems. First, persons engaged in the type of conduct that may be proscribed are not given adequate notice. Such persons can only guess as to whether their conduct is covered by a criminal statute and as to whether it falls within the constitutionally permissible reach of the statute. This uncertainty, in turn, has a chilling effect on the exercise of First Amendment rights.

A more subtle set of problems arises. Institutional stress inevitably results from the excessive vagueness of the line separating protected speech from unprotected speech. Almost every adjudicated case is marginal, and presents a constitutional question of exceptional difficulty. This leads to a huge volume of cases each of which must be separately adjudicated, cluttering the dockets. Another consequence is reliance on per curiam reversals or denials of certiorari, "a practice which conceals the rationale of decisions and gives at least the appearance of arbitrary action by this Court."

No alternative except withdrawal from the obscenity thicket is satisfactory, Mr. Justice Brennan concluded. Clarity could be obtained only by "drawing a line that resolves all doubts in favor of state power and against the guarantees of the First Amendment." A formula making obscenity enforcement predictable would certainly give fair notice and regularity. But it "would be appallingly overbroad, permitting the suppression of a vast range of literary, scientific, and artistic masterpieces." The second alternative, that taken by the majority, "still leaves in this Court the responsibility of determining in each case whether the materials are protected by the First Amendment."

Reduction of the role of the judiciary in determining obscenity might alleviate institutional stress, but it would offer no cure for the other vagueness vices.

Mr. Justice Brennan also asserted that the approach of Justices Black and Douglas —that the First Amendment bars suppression of any sexually oriented expression — deprives the states of their legitimate authority to protect juveniles and unwilling adults from exposure to such material. "I would hold, therefore, that at least in the absence of distribution to juveniles or obtrusive exposure to unconsenting adults, the First and Fourteenth Amendments prohibit the state and federal governments from attempting wholly to suppress sexually oriented

materials on the basis of their allegedly 'obscene' contents."

Kaplan v. California, 413 U.S. 115, 13 CrL 3194

The fact that a book has no pictures does not protect it from a finding that it is obscene, the same five-Justice majority held. Accordingly, the Court sustained a bookseller's conviction for distributing "Suite 69," a virtually plotless book made up entirely of repetitive, clinically descriptive sexual episodes of every conceivable kind. The fact that a book does, and should, "have a preferred place in our hierarchy of values," is nonetheless qualified by its contents. The Chief Justice once more emphasized the authority of the states to act without the benefit of conclusive empirical data as to the effect of the matter regulated.

U.S. v. Orito, 413 U.S. 139, 13 CrL 3159

The same considerations behind the go-ahead it gave the states to regulate exhibition of obscene films in an "adult theatre" led the majority to conclude that the zone of constitutionally protected privacy encompassing the possession of obscenity in one's home does not extend to transportation of obscene materials, in violation of 18 U.S.C. 1462, by a passenger on a common carrier even though he intended this material for private use. Such regulation could reasonably be based "on a legislatively common risk of ultimate exposure to juveniles or to the public and the harm that exposure could cause."

Mr. Justice Douglas maintained that under Stanley v. Georgia, 394 U.S. 557, 5 CrL 3019, it is "too obvious for argument" that one who reads obscene material on common carriers is just as protected as one who enjoys it in his home. Justices Brennan, Stewart, and Marshall rested on Mr. Justice Brennan's dissents in the Miller and Paris Adult Theatre cases.

U.S. v. 12 200-Ft Reels of Super 8mm Film, 413 U.S. 123, 13 CrL 3197

Congressional authority to regulate obscenity extends to a ban on the importation of obscene material, even if the importation is for the individual importer's private use and possession in his home, the same five-Justice majority also held. Restriction of imports rests on different considerations of constitutional law than do domestic regulations, the Chief Justice noted. And the right under Stanley v. Georgia, 394 U.S. 557, 5 CrL 3019, to privately enjoy obscenity does not include its importation for such a purpose. Rather, Stanley marks a line of demarcation, and importing obscenity is beyond that line.

Mr. Justice Douglas attacked the decision as permitting Government censorship that would appall the authors of the First Amendment. At the time the Amendment was adopted, Mr. Justice Douglas noted, two classics in pornography —"The Toast" and "Fanny Hill" had been published for four decades virtually without molestation.

Heller v. New York, 413 U.S. 483, 13 CrL 3240

An adversary hearing is not a prerequisite to the warrant-authorized seizure of a single copy of film for evidentiary use in an exhibitor's criminal obscenity trial, the majority held. However, the seizure must be hedged with certain safeguards. These include issuance of a warrant after a determination of probable obscenity by a neutral magistrate, and the availability of a prompt subsequent adversary hearing on the obscenity issue.

The Court also suggested that copying the seized film be permitted if necessary to continue exhibition during the legal proceedings. The four dissenters did not express any opinion on the seizure question.

Roaden v. Kentucky, 413 U.S. 496, 13 CrL 3243

While the seizure of books and films need not be preceded by an adversary hearing, it must not be warrantless, the Court admonished. Furthermore, a higher standard of Fourth Amendment "reasonableness" applies to any seizure that has the effect of a prior restraint on expression.

The concurrence by Justices Brennan, Stewart, and Marshall expressed the view that the obscenity statute involved in this case was unconstitutionally overbroad. Mr. Justice Douglas would have reversed the conviction for the same reason.

ENTRAPMENT

U.S. v. Russell, 411 U.S. 423, 13 CrL 3055

For the third time in 41 years, a five-Justice majority of the Court held that the key to an entrapment defense in a federal prosecution is the predisposition of the defendant rather than the nature of the Government's inducement. Mr. Justice Rehnquist, the majority's spokesman, went on to reject the argument that the entrapment defense should be elevated to constitutional status. A defense analogy to the exclusionary rule that applies to illegal searches and seizures and improperly obtained confessions broke down over the fact that the Government did not violate any independent constitutional right of the defendant, a manufacturer of illegal drugs, by supplying him with a chemical that is legal to possess but difficult to obtain.

The Court did not, however, rule out the possibility that sufficiently outrageous Government behavior could immunize a defendant from prosecution regardless of his predisposition. In the event of shocking Government conduct, in violation of fundamental fairness, the Due Process Clause might require an entrapment finding.

Infiltration is the only viable means of combating illicit drug production, which is a continuing process, Mr. Justice Rehnquist said. And it is not desirable to immunize someone "fully committed" to criminal enterprise just because the Government's inducement might have seduced a hypothetical individual who was not so predisposed.

Several recent lower federal court decisions barring prosecution because of what they thought was "overzea-lous law enforcement did not intend to 'give the federal judiciary a chancellor's foot' veto over law enforcement practices of which" they "did not approve," Mr. Justice Rehnquist added.

In view of its conclusion that the entrapment defense is not one of constitutional dimension, the majority noted that "Congress may address itself to the question and adopt any substantive definition of the defense that it may find desirable."

A dissenting opinion by Justices Douglas and Brennan, the only members of the current Court who participated in the more recent prior entrapment case, Sherman v. U.S., 356 U.S. 369 (1958), made it clear that their views on the issue had not changed.

Writing for himself and Justices Brennan and Marshall, Mr. Justice Stewart, who joined the Court only months after Sherman was decided, thought that the "objective" approach to entrapment advanced by the concurrences in Sorrells and Sherman "is the only one truly consistent with the underlying rationale of the defense."

The purpose of the entrapment defense "cannot be to protect persons 'who are otherwise innocent,' " Mr. Justice Stewart said. "Rather it must be to prohibit unlawful governmental activity in instigating crime."

The "subjective" entrapment test adhered to by the majority permits the admission of all kinds of otherwise inadmissible hearsay evidence that would be inadmissible in any other context. Furthermore, and more important, it makes the permissibility of given police conduct depend upon the particular defendant's past record and propensities.

Under the "objective" test, Mr. Justice Stewart noted, it is the trial judge, and not the jury, that decides the entrapment issue.

SEARCHES AND SEIZURES

The general trend toward easing Fourth Amendment restrictions on law enforcement officials continued this Term, most notably in the area of consent searches. Only on the question of "roving" border searches did the Court disapprove of activities by law enforcement officials of any kind.

Schneckloth v. Bustamonte, 412 U.S. 218, 13 CrL 3107

Evidence obtained by a consent search in a non-custodial setting can be admitted without a showing that the person who consented knew he could withhold permission, six Justices agreed. The voluntariness of a consent to a search, Mr. Justice Stewart said for the majority, is to be determined from "the totality of all the circumstances." The Court held that "the state of a defendant's knowledge is only one factor to be taken into account in assessing the voluntariness of a consent." Thus, there is no need that Miranda-like warnings be given to the person whose consent is asked.

If the burden to show that a consenting defendant knew of his right to refuse were placed on the prosecution, Mr. Justice Stewart said, the defendant could   keep the fruits of the search out of evidence "by simply failing to testify that he in fact knew he could refuse to consent." And to require that a cumbersome warning be given at the time consent is requested would unduly burden police investigations. It would frustrate society's interests in crime-solving and in avoiding accusations against the innocent.

The reasoning of Miranda v. Arizona, 384 U.S. 436, that one cannot waive a right one is unaware of, was distinguished by an observation that Miranda's special rules were called for by the "inherently coercive situation of custodial interrogation."

Although the Court rejected the Miranda waiver test, it went back to pre-Miranda confession cases for an analysis of "voluntariness." The "totality of the circumstances" test developed in this line of cases takes into account "both characteristics of the accused and the details of the interrogation."

The consent in the case before the Court was obtained under congenial circumstances from the driver of the car in which the defendant was riding. In fact, the driver offered to assist the officer in making the search.

The Court's prior holdings "do not reflect on critical demand for a knowing and intelligent waiver in every situation where a person has failed to invoke a constitutional protection," Mr. Justice Stewart emphasized. The "knowing and intelligent waiver" reasoning of Johnson v. Zerbst, 304 U.S. 458, applies to waivers in the courtroom of procedural rights that are necessary to preserve a fair trial. The Fourth Amendment's protections and the Exclusionary Rule protecting them are quite different from these rights; they have nothing to do with promoting the fair ascertainment of truth at trial.

The majority found its conclusion consistent with its previous consent cases, from Amos v. U.S., 225 U.S. 298, and Davis v. U.S., 328 U.S. 582, to Coolidge v. New Hampshire, 403 U.S. 443, CrL 3208.

Mr. Justice Powell, joined by the Chief Justice and Mr. Justice Rehnquist, agreed with the majority's conclusion as to the consent issue, but would have gone on to hold that federal habeas corpus is unavailable to a state prisoner for the purposes of raising a Fourth Amendment claim. Federal habeas, he said, "should be confined solely to the question of whether the petitioner was provided a fair opportunity to raise and have adjudicated the question in state courts."

Dissenting, Mr. Justice Marshall thought it "curious" that one can choose to relinquish a constitutional right without knowing that he has the alternative of refusing to do so. He accused the majority of misstating the true issue in the case, which was "whether a simple statement of consent to search, without more, should be sufficient to permit the police to search and thus act as relinquishment of [the consentor's] constitutional right to exclude the police."

The pre-Miranda voluntariness standard for confessions involves issues altogether different from those raised in a consent search, Mr. Justice Marshall maintained.

Those cases dealt with compulsion, while consent is "a subtly different concept to which different standards have been applied in the past." Freedom from coercion is a substantive right, while consent is a mechanism by which otherwise applicable substantive requirements may be avoided. Consent searches are permitted not because of law enforcement exigencies, but "because we permit our citizens to choose whether or not they wish to exercise their constitutional rights." Mr. Justice Marshall could not understand why consent could not be taken to mean a "knowing choice," or how "a decision made without knowledge of available alternatives can be treated as a choice at all." The burden should be on the Government to see that a subject knew of his rights; this is the clear import of previous consent cases, such as Johnson v. U.S., 333 U.S. 10, and see 391 U.S. 43. The effect of this holding, Mr. Justice Marshall said, was to confine Fourth Amendment protections against searches without probable cause "to the sophisticated, the knowledgeable, and, I might add, the few."

Mr. Justice Brennan was unable to comprehend how a citizen can meaningfully waive a right he doesn't know he has.

Mr. Justice Douglas, also dissenting, wondered why the Court couldn't have allowed the case to be remanded for a substantive factual hearing as to whether or not the defendant knew he had the right to refuse consent.

Cupp v. Murphy, 412 U.S. 291, 13 CrL 3129

Weaving a connecting thread through Terry v. Ohio, 392 U.S. 1, and Chimel v. California, 395 U.S. 752, 5 CrL 3131, the Court approved the warrantless investigative seizure of a murder suspect whom the police had probable cause to arrest. With two dissenting voters, it also upheld the subsequent scraping of his fingernails for "highly evanescent" evidence that he had throttled his wife. The suspect's nails were forcibly scraped after he refused to consent to a scraping and started rubbing his hands together in an apparent effort to destroy the evidence. Three courts reviewing this case, the majority asserted, had found that the police had probable cause to arrest the suspect at the time he was seized and his fingernails scraped.

Mr. Justice Stewart, writing for the majority, held that the detention of the suspect against his will was a seizure, and the scraping was clearly a search. This was so even though he was not under formal arrest, had come to the station voluntarily, and was allowed to leave after his nails were scraped. But the probable cause factor made this case distinguishable from Davis v. Mississippi, 394 U.S. 721, 5 CrL 3038, which condemned dragnet investigative seizures to obtain identification evidence. Furthermore, the highly destructible nature of the evidence added to the justification for the limited intrusion upon the defendant's privacy.

The Court explicitly refrained from "that a full Chimel search would have been justified in this case without a formal arrest and without a warrant," adding that "the respondent was not subjected to such a search." Rather, it described the nail-scraping as the kind of brief though severe intrusion involved in Terry. However, it applied one of Chimel's justifications for a warrantless search incident to arrest —prevention of evidence destruction.

Mr. Justice Marshall, concurring, thought that the detention and scrapings were permissible under Terry's stop and frisk doctrine; "if the police had done more than take fingernail scrapings, I would be inclined to hold the search illegal."

Mr. Justice Blackmun and the Chief Justice concurred, with the understanding that the Court's restricted holding was limited to those cases where no arrest has been made. Mr. Justice Powell, joined by the Chief Justice and Mr. Justice Rehnquist, also concurred. But he restated his reservations about federal habeas review of state searches and seizures.

Mr. Justice Douglas, dissenting in part, agreed with the majority that the police were justified in detaining the defendant, but only for the purpose of obtaining a search warrant. The issue of probable cause had not, in fact, been determined, he argued. He further contended that the seizure in this case was "on all fours with Davis v. Mississippi," and that this search produced evidence protected by the Fifth Amendment.

Mr. Justice Brennan agreed with Mr. Justice Douglas that the question of probable cause was still open.

Almeida-Sanchez v. U.S., 413 U.S. 266, 13 CrL 3206

Although the law enforcement agencies charged with preserving the integrity of the Nation's boundaries have broad search and seizure powers, the U.S. Supreme Court reminded them that their powers are still subject to some Fourth Amendment limitations. A 5–4 majority concluded that the Border Patrol's practice of conducting random warrantless searches of automobiles and other conveyances unrelated to border crossings but within a reasonable distance from the border, violates the Fourth Amendment.

Recognizing the difficult and important task Border Patrol agents must perform, Mr. Justice Stewart's opinion for the majority nevertheless found no justification for searches of this type. The Court's most recent administrative search decisions, were of no help, as the searches there were of regulated businesses. Here, however, there was no assurance that the individual search was within the proper scope of the Border Patrol's scrutiny. Nor could the searches be upheld under any of the Court's automobile search decisions.

Mr. Justice Powell, concurring, agreed that the administrative search cases cannot be fairly read to cover cases of this type. "One who merely travels in regions near the borders of the country can hardly be thought to have submitted to inspections in exchange for a special perquisite." He did, however, add that "on appropriate facts," and with advance judicial approval, the Government could "satisfy the probably cause requirement for a roving search in a border area without possessing information about particular automobiles."

Mr. Justice White, joined in dissent by the Chief Justice, Mr. Justice Blackmun, and Mr. Justice Rehnquist, noted the well-established judgment of Congress that, for the purposes of enforcing the immigration laws, it is reasonable to treat the exterior boundaries of the country as a zone, not a line. There are recurring circumstances in which the search of vehicular traffic away from the border itself, without a warrant and without probable cause, may be reasonable. The Court has traditionally been willing to apply the Fourth Amendment's broad reasonableness standard to situations in which strict probable cause or warrant requirements would not permit a balancing of the public interest against individual rights. The Court has been particularly sensitive to the reasonableness standard "where authorizing statutes permitted the challenged searches."

Brown v. U.S., 411 U.S. 223, 13 CrL 3023

A defendant's standing to seek suppression of evidence on Fourth Amendment grounds may well hinge not only on the facts of the case, the Court indicated, but on the nature of the offense charged. A unanimous Court denied Fourth Amendment standing to two federal stolen-goods defendants who had no possessory interest in the premises searched, were not on the premises during the search, and were not charged with an offense that includes as an essential element possession at the time of the search.

The defendants, the Chief Justice pointed out in his opinion for the Court, were faced with neither the danger of self-incrimination nor the possibility that the prosecution could contradict itself by alleging possession as an element of the offense while denying sufficient possession to challenge the search.

The Court expressly left unresolved the question of whether Simmons v. U.S., 390 U.S. 377, which forbade use at trial of a defendant's suppression-hearing testimony, has rendered obsolete the "automatic standing" rule announced in Jones v. U.S., 362 U.S. 257, with respect to defendants who are present at the seizure and are charged with crimes in which "possession * * * at the time of * * * seizure [is] a critical part of the Government's case." The opinion by the Chief Justice did raise the possibility, however, that this doctrine's days are numbered: "[t]he self-incrimination dilemma, so central to the Jones decision, can no longer occur under the prevailing interpretation of the Constitution."

The Court was also unanimous in finding harmless the admission of the jointly tried defendants' statements incriminating each other in violation of Bruton v. U.S., 391 U.S. 123.

Cady v. Dombrowski, 413 U.S. 433, 13 CrL 3231

Leaving unresolved many of the thorniest Constitutional problems police face in making warrantless automobile searches, the Court did offer some guidance with a 5–4 decision upholding the warrantless search of a wrecked car belonging to an in-custody defendant, a drunken out-of-state police officer. The Court made clear the advantages — in warrantless car-search situations — that are enjoyed by police departments able to claim that they have a standard search or inventory policy. This search was made pursuant to a standard policy aimed at securing weapons. The vehicle had been towed to a private, unguarded lot several miles from the police station.

Since the car was to be left in an unguarded lot, the police sent an officer out to search the trunk to see if he could locate the weapon that they believed the defendant was required by law to carry. In the process of searching for the weapon, the local officer found blood-stained evidence.

When the officer made the search, he had no reason to believe that the officer was involved in anything more serious than drunken driving. Time was of the essence, and, this being a small town, it would have been difficult to post a guard at the vehicle pending the obtaining of a warrant. "The fact that the protection of the public might, in the abstract, have been accomplished by a 'less intrusive' means does not, by itself, render the search unreasonable," Mr. Justice Rehnquist wrote for the majority.

Dissenting Justice Brennan, joined by Justices Douglas, Stewart, and Marshall, contended that nothing in the Court's prior decisions supported either the reasoning or the result reached by the majority. The search could not be sustained under the automobile exception to the Fourth Amendment warrant requirement; there was no reasonable likelihood that the automobile would or could have been moved once it had been towed to its final location. Nor could it be justified as a search incident to arrest; it was too remote in time and place. Finally, the search could not be justified under the plain view doctrine, which could be invoked only if the search for the gun were constitutional.

U.S. v. Ash, 413 U.S. 300, 13 CrL 3217

An examination of recent Sixth Amendment developments led the Court to conclude that the risks inherent in the use of photographic displays are not "so pernicious" that an extraordinary system of safeguards is required. Accordingly, by a 6–3 vote, it held that the right to counsel does not apply to a pretrial photo display to witnesses, even with respect to indicted, in-custody defendants.

Mr. Justice Blackmun writing for the majority, studied those parts of criminal prosecutions deemed to be "critical stages" and concluded that photographic displays are not. A photographic showing can be easily reconstructed at trial, and if the defendant himself is not present, it cannot be realistically classified as a confrontation.

Mr. Justice Stewart, concurring in the judgment, noted that a photographic identification is quite different from a lineup. There are substantially fewer possibilities of

impermissible suggestion when photographs are used, and any unfair inferences can readily be reconstructed at trial.

Mr. Justice Brennan, joined in dissent by Justices Douglas and Marshall, contended that the majority's decision "marks simply another step towards the complete evisceration of the fundamental constitutional principles" established in U.S. v. Wade, 388 U.S. 218, and its companion cases.

Mr. Justice Brennan accused the majority of overlooking the fundamental premise underlying all of the Court's Sixth Amendment decisions: A critical stage of the prosecution is one at which the presence of counsel is necessary to protect the fairness of the trial itself.

GRAND JURIES

Neither the Fourth nor the Fifth Amendment offers a federal grand jury witness any shelter from an order compelling him to provide voice or handwriting samples, the Court held. The Court also declared that the Government need not make any preliminary showing of reasonableness before it is entitled to a court order for such samples. As long as the samples are sought for their physical characteristics, rather than informational content, the witness must comply or face contempt charges.

U.S. v. Dionisio, 410 U.S. 1, 12 CrL 3083

A gambling suspect ordered to produce samples of his voice for comparison with voices on certain recordings lost out on both his Fourth and Fifth Amendment claims.

Mr. Justice Stewart, writing for a 7–2 majority on the Fifth Amendment question, noted that it has long been held that the compelled display of identifiable physical characteristics infringes no interest protected by the privilege against compulsory self-incrimination." There is nothing testimonial about such evidence.

The Fourth Amendment holding, decided by a 6–3 majority, was two-fold. First, applying the "seizure" criteria of Schmerber v. California, 384 U.S. 757, Terry v. Ohio, 392 U.S. 1, and related cases, the majority concluded that a grand jury subpoena is not a "seizure" within the meaning of the Fourth Amendment. Although imposing a duty that may be "onerous" at times, it does not entail the loss of liberty or other oppressive attributes of a law enforcement seizure. Second, a person has no more reasonable expectation of privacy with respect to voice or handwriting samples than he does with respect to other physical attributes such as eyes, hair and facial features. Thus the Government need not make any showing of Fourth Amendment "reasonableness" before obtaining a court order to compel the production of voice or handwriting samples.

Mr. Justice Brennan agreed that the witness had no Fifth Amendment claim. But he added, while the reasonableness requirement does not apply to a grand jury subpoena compelling appearance to testify, it does cover an order compelling a grand jury witness who has been subpoenaed in order to produce voice or handwriting samples. In this case, reasonableness cannot be presumed and must be shown affirmatively.

Justices Douglas and Marshall dissented on both the Fifth and Fourth Amendment points.

Mr. Justice Douglas argued that this decision made the grand jury nothing more than an agent of the prosecution.

Mr. Justice Marshall found the Wade-Gilbert declaration that the Fifth Amendment privilege is limited to testimonial evidence "at odds at what I have always understood to be the function of the privilege." The Government should not be able to compel a man to give evidence that could not be obtained without his cooperation. The privilege as stated is not restricted to testimonial evidence. To give it this crabbed construction is to go against the broad reading it received in Boyd v. U.S., 116 U.S. 616. Mr. Justice Marshall traced the steps by which the Court over the years has, improperly in his view, cut back on the scope of the privilege.

Mr. Justice Marshall also questioned the ease with which the majority reached its decision that subpoenas don't give rise to seizures. Investigative seizures by police are covered by the Fourth Amendment, and the grand jury's subpoena here was no less an intrusive official act. A subpoena duces tecum is covered by the Fourth Amendment, and the Amendment's protections clearly go beyond documents. The majority's characterization of a grand jury subpoena as less inconvenient or embarrassing than a police stop will not hold up.

U.S. v. Mara, 410 U.S. 19, 12 CrL 3089

The same considerations that kept grand jury demands for voice exemplars outside the scope of the Fourth and Fifth Amendments were applied by the Court to handwriting exemplars. "Indeed," Mr. Justice Stewart wrote, "this case lacks even the aspects of an expansive investigation that the Court of Appeals found significant in Dionisio."

All three dissenting opinions in Dionisio were directed to this case as well.

FAIR TRIAL

Taken as a group, the Court's decisions on the trial rights of state defendants promise to have a significant effect on the conduct of state prosecutions.

Chambers v. Mississippi, 410 U.S. 284, 12 CrL 3150

Two widely approved common-law rules of evidence were thrown into serious question by the Court's holding that they were unconstitutionally applied against a Mississippi murder defendant. The case was characterized by weak prosecution facts and by strong defense testimony that was kept from the jury. Mr. Justice Powell's opinion for the Court held that the defendant's right to present evidence in his own defense was denied by Mississippi's refusal to treat declarations against penal interest as exceptions to the hearsay rule as its application

of the "voucher rule" that a party cannot impeach his own witness.

"We establish no new principles of constitutional law," the majority concluded. The denial of a fair trial in this case rose to the level of Fourteenth Amendment due process deprivation. But even with its caveat that it intended "no diminution of respect" for state evidentiary rules, the opinion provided for the first time a basis for constitutional attack on them.

In dealing with the so-called "voucher rule," the Court construed for the first time the Sixth Amendment Confrontation Clause's phrase "witnesses against him." Rather than limiting the phrase to mean only witnesses who directly incriminate a defendant, the Court interpreted it to include a witness whose testimony or nontestimony damages the defense in any way. The defense at trial asked to have a witness declared "adverse," but the trial court refused on the ground that the witness' testimony didn't directly incriminate the defendant.

Whatever validity the so-called voucher rule "may have once enjoyed" and may still enjoy in civil cases, Mr. Justice Powell declared, it bears little relationship, to the "realities" of a criminal trial in which "defendants are rarely able to select their witnesses." That difficulty is especially apparent in this case, where the defendant waited vainly in hopes that the state would call the witness as its own.

Finding a second abuse that contributed to the cumulative due process violation, the Court held that "the hearsay rule may not be applied mechanistically to defeat the ends of justice" by keeping out evidence, inadmissible under state law, that would tend to prove innocence. The defendant, the Court says, was improperly kept from placing on the stand several individuals who would have testified that the witness told them he had committed the homicide.

Refusing to treat as sacred the rule that a declaration against penal interest is still inadmissible hearsay, the Court required a strong state showing of good reasons for application of a rule that keeps out exculpatory testimony.

The Court also held that the Mississippi Supreme Court's failure to consider a constitutional question raised by the defendant did not foreclose its own review of the issue. Concurring, Mr. Justice White noted that normally the Court would treat a state appellate court's silence on such an issue as meaning that it was not properly raised there. But this practice is not a rigid one, and a deviation from it was proper here, Mr. Justice White agreed.

Dissenting on this jurisdictional question, Mr. Justice Rehnquist stated that "[w]ere I to reach the merits in this case, I would have considerable difficulty in subscribing to the Court's further constitutionalization of the intricacies of the common law of evidence." He did not reach the merits, however; reviewing the petitioner's constitutional arguments, the Court was exceeding the limits of its jurisdiction under 28 U.S.C. 1257(3). This provision has been interpreted to require that a constitutional issue be raised in "due time," Mr. Justice

Rehnquist said. That most assuredly was not done here. Not until his motion for a new trial did the petitioner's counsel even hint "that his previous evidentiary objection had constitutional basis."

Tacon v. Arizona, 410 U.S. 351, 12 CrL 3159

In another state case raising a fair trial question, however, the Court dismissed the writ of a certiorari as improvidently granted. The constitutional issue before the U.S. Supreme Court was the protection of a defendant being tried in absentia. Post-argument examination of the record itself led the Court to hold that the supposed constitutional issue not only had been ignored by the Arizona Supreme Court, but actually had not been raised by the petitioner below.

Wardius v. Oregon, 412 U.S. 470, 13 CrL 3141

Deciding the question that it expressly left open in Williams v. Florida, 399 U.S. 78, 7 CrL 3143, the Court held, without a dissent, that a state notice-of-alibi statute's failure to give the defendant reciprocal discovery rights with respect to the prosecution's planned rebuttal is a violation of the Fourteenth Amendment's Due Process Clause. An Oregon defendant who was convicted after a trial at which he was forbidden to offer his alibi defense because of failure to comply with the statute was entitled to reversal of his conviction.

Notice of alibi rules represent a salutary development, Mr. Justice Marshall noted on behalf of the Court. They are removing one of the "poker game" characteristics of criminal trials. Although the Due Process Clause says little about discovery, "it does speak to the balance of forces between the accused and his accuser." The notice rule upheld in Williams v. Florida struck such a balance, but the Oregon law did not. The unfairness in the way it operated was compounded by the fact that Oregon grants no discovery rights to criminal defendants at all, not even bills of particulars. "More significantly," the state was not required to reveal the names and addresses of the witnesses planned for use in rebutting the alibi defense.

Without suggesting that the Due Process Clause requires the state to adopt discovery provisions, the Court did "hold that in the absence of a strong showing of state interest to the contrary, discovery must be a two-way street. * * * It is fundamentally unfair to require a defendant to divulge the details of his own case while at the same time subjecting him to the hazard of surprise concerning refutation of the very pieces of evidence which he disclosed to the State."

These principles were not contested by the state, which argued against reversal of the conviction on the narrow ground that this defendant had not complied with the statute at trial. But this failure did not preclude relief, the Court said. The mere fact that the state might have added into the statute a reciprocal discovery requirement was not enough to save this conviction.

The Chief Justice concurred in the result. Also concurring in the result, Mr. Justice Douglas would have reversed the conviction for the reasons stated by Mr. Justice Black in his dissent in Williams v. Florida.

Ham v. South Carolina, 409 U.S. 524, 12 CrL 3078

A young, bearded, politically active Negro was entitled, under the Fourteenth Amendment Due Process Clause, to have veniremen at his South Carolina marijuana possession trial interrogated specifically about racial bias, the Court held. The judge's general questions on voir dire about bias in general were not enough.

However, a majority of the Court added in an opinion by Mr. Justice Rehnquist, the defendant was not constitutionally entitled to an inquiry about bias against bearded people. While inquiry as to racial prejudice is based on firmly established precedent, the judge's refusal to ask about beards "does not reach the level of a constitutional violation."

The Court also found the record inadequate to determine the merits of the petitioner's allegation that he was prejudiced by pretrial publicity.

Mr. Justice Douglas took issue with the majority on the beard question. Beard growth can, he maintained, seriously prejudice an individual in the eyes of many.

Dissenting in part, Mr. Justice Marshall could not agree "that the judge acted properly in totally foreclosing other reasonable and relevant avenues of inquiry as to possible prejudice." The propounded questions about beards were obviously relevant, Mr. Justice Marshall asserted, and permitting them to be asked would not have seriously taxed the court's resources.

Ward v. Village of Monroeville, 409 U.S. 57, 12 CrL 3007

An Ohio mayor's lucrative traffic court that generated a considerable portion of the village revenue was deemed by the Court to violate a motorist's due process right to a trial before an impartial tribunal. The Court distinguished an earlier case upholding a mayor's court by noting that the mayor here had broad executive authority with much responsibility for the village's finances. In Dugan v. Ohio, 277 U.S. 61, (1920), his function was primarily judicial.

Nor did it matter that offenders are entitled to a trial de novo before a regular court if unsatisfied. The constitutional right must be satisfied in the first instance.

Dissenting Justices White and Rehnquist maintained that the due process issue should be decided on "a case-to-case basis" rather than by this "prophylactic, per se rule."

FAIR TRIAL —CONFESSIONS

Swenson v. Stidham, 409 U.S. 224, 12 CrL 3043

While Jackson v. Denno, 378 U.S. 368, requires that a confession whose voluntariness has been questioned must be evaluated after a separate hearing, it does not absolutely require that such a hearing precede the confession's admission at trial, a unanimous Court indicated. Accordingly, the Court held that a state prisoner who was afforded a full and adequate evidentiary hearing on the voluntariness of his confession following his motion to vacate the sentence after conviction was not entitled to a new trial even if the judge at his trial failed to comply with Jackson.

Jackson requires that the state provide the defendant an error-free judicial determination of the voluntariness of the confession —"error-free in that the determination was procedurally adequate and substantively acceptable under the Due Process Clause." Here, Mr. Justice White pointed out in his opinion for the Court, the Missouri courts provided him with such a hearing even though it came after the trial.

"This, of course, does not end the matter. A state prisoner is free to resort to federal habeas corpus with the claim that, contrary to a state court's judgment, his confession was involuntary and inadmissible as a matter of law. Neither the district court nor the court of appeals reached this issue."

SELF-INCRIMINATION

Couch v. U.S., 409 U.S. 322, 12 CrL 3051

A taxpayer's assertion of her privilege against self-incrimination was found ineffective against an IRS subpoena directing her accountant to turn over business records going back several years. The Seven-Justice majority also refused to recognize "an expectation of protected privacy or confidentiality" arising from the accountant-client relationship.

Mr. Justice Powell, writing for the majority, first pointed out that there was no personal compulsion against the taxpayer. The subpoena was directed against her accountant, an independent contractor. Second, the taxpayer had turned over her business records to the accountant every year for 13 years so that he could prepare her income tax returns. Thus, although she retained her proprietary interest in the records, she had relinquished her possessory interest in them. Her reliance upon Boyd v. U.S., 116 U.S. 616, was misplaced. There, the person who successfully claimed the privilege not only owned the records, but possessed them as well.

The majority pointed out that neither federal nor state law has recognized an accountant-client privilege. Nor did it find justification for such a privilege where records relevant to income tax returns are involved in a criminal investigation or prosecution.

Mr. Justice Brennan, concurring, joined the majority on the understanding that its opinion "does not establish a per se rule defeating a claim of Fifth Amendment privilege whenever the documents in question are not in the possession of the person claiming the privilege."

Mr. Justice Douglas, dissenting, accused the majority of ignoring the "interplay" of the fundamental values protected by the Fourth and Fifth Amendments.

His dissent closely scrutinized Boyd v. U.S. and the relationship, in cases such as Boyd and the present one, between the Fourth and Fifth Amendments. Both Amendments are concerned with the expectation of privacy, and he would have remanded the case for consideration in light of criteria derived from that expectation. Here, he thought, the majority created a "bright line" rule that no constitutional protection is violated by enforcing a summons for paper not in the owner's possession and then blurred that line by suggesting that a temporary relinquishment of possession presents a different case.

SPEEDY TRIAL

Strunk v. U.S., 412 U.S. 434, 13 CrL 3139

Flexibility was the essence of the test announced by the Court in Barker v. Wingo, 407 U.S. 514, 11 CrL 3174, for determining whether a defendant has been denied his Sixth Amendment right to a speedy trial. But dismissal of the indictment is the only remedy for a violation of this right, the Chief Justice now made clear. His opinion was supported by a unanimous Court.

Explaining that "such severe remedies are not unique in the application of constitutional standards," the Court reversed a Seventh Circuit decision that denied a federal defendant the "harsh remedy" of dismissal. On an explicit finding that his Sixth Amendment right had been denied, the Seventh Circuit simply reassessed the sentence and reduced it by the number of days of improper pretrial delay found attributable to the Government.

"In light of the policies which underlie the right to a speedy trial, dismissal must remain * * * 'the only possible remedy,' " the Chief Justice emphasized. This prisoner did not testify at his Dyer Act trial, and offered no defense witnesses. However, as Baker points out, one of the principal considerations underlying the Sixth Amendment right is the need to hold a trial before defense witnesses, as well as prosecution witnesses, disappear.

The Chief Justice did not focus on the way in which pretrial delay can sabotage a defense. He concentrated instead on the suffering inherent in pretrial delay.

DOUBLE JEOPARDY

Illinois v. Sommerville, 410 U.S. 458, 12 CrL 3169

An Illinois trial judge acted out of manifest necessity in declaring a mistrial, over defense objection, after the jury had been empaneled and the prosecution discovered that the indictment failed to allege a material element of the crime, a 5–4 majority held. Illinois law forbids amending an indictment. Thus the retrial did not violate the Fifth Amendment's Double Jeopardy Clause.

The interest of a defendant in having his fate determined by the jury first empaneled is weighty, Mr. Justice Rehnquist acknowledged on behalf of the majority. But the prosecution should not have been required to proceed to a verdict which would be overturned on appeal. Downum v. U.S., 372 U.S. 734, said that jeopardy attaches when the jury is empaneled. But the conclusion that jeopardy has attached "begins, rather than ends, the inquiry as to whether the Double Jeopardy Clause bars retrial." The crucial question is whether the declaration of a mistrial was required by a manifest necessity or the ends of public justice. Here, it was.

Mr. Justice White, joined in dissent by Justices Douglas and Justice Brennan, argued that Downum and U.S. v. Jorn, 400 U.S. 470, 8 CrL 3071, forbade the result reached here. These cases underwrote the independent right of the defendant to have a verdict by the initial jury.

Mr. Justice Marshall, in a separate dissenting opinion, accused the majority of eviscerating the rationale of Jorn and Downum, which "appeared to give judges some guidance in determining what constituted 'manifest necessity' for declaring a mistrial, over a defendant's objection. Today, the Court seems to revert to a totally unstructured analysis of such cases."

Robinson v. Neil, 409 U.S. 505, 12 CrL 3071

There is more than one way to turn back the constitutional clock, the U.S. Supreme Court indicated en route to a unanimous holding that Waller v. Florida, 397 U.S. 387, 7 CrL 3017, which abolished the dual sovereignty theory with respect to successive city and state prosecutions, is fully retroactive.

Writing for the Court, Mr. Justice Rehnquist observed, "[w]e do not believe that this case readily lends itself to the analysis established in Linkletter [v. Walker, 381 U.S. 618]. The Linkletter guidelines seem to be geared for application to rules affecting the integrity of the fact finding process, not to double jeopardy issues that decide whether the process should even take place.

Accordingly, the Court vacated the attempted murder conviction of a Tennessee defendant who, allegedly for the same offense, had previously been convicted of assault and battery under a city ordinance. The Court refused to grant an outright reversal; there remained unanswered a question as to whether the state and municipal prosecutions were actually for the same offense.

Mr. Justice Brennan, joined in concurring opinion by Justices Douglas and Marshall, would have reversed the court of appeals decision outright. He would have done so on the basis of the "transactional" theory set forth in his dissent in Ashe v. Swenson, 397 U.S. 436, 7 CrL 3020.

Chaffin v. Stynchombe, 412 U.S. 17, 13 CrL 3093

North Carolina v. Pearce, 395 U.S. 711, 5 CrL 3119, which forbade judges to impose unexplained harsher retrial sentences on defendants who successfully appeal their convictions, does not apply with the same force to jury-imposed sentences, a 5–4 majority decided. Jury-imposed harsher sentences on retrial do not violate the Double Jeopardy Clause and do not offend the Fourteenth Amendment Due Process Clause so long as the jury is not informed of the prior sentence and the second sentence is not otherwise shown to be a product of vindictiveness. Nor does the possibility that the retrial jury might impose a stiffer sentence on a successfully appealing defendant impose an impermissible burden on the defendant's exercise of his right to appeal.

Mr. Justice Powell, writing for the majority, explained that Pearce was premised upon the need to guard against vindictiveness in the resentencing process. However, the possibility of a stiffer sentence upon retrial following reversal of a former conviction is a recognized concomitant of the retrial process. When a jury does the sentencing after a properly controlled retrial at which it is unaware of the first conviction, the danger of vindictiveness is so remote that there is no Double Jeopardy or Due Process violation.

Mr. Justice Douglas dissented for the reasons he stated in Moon v. Maryland, 398 U.S. 319, 7 CrL 3101.

Mr. Justice Stewart, joined in his dissent by Mr. Justice Brennan, asserted that there is a real danger of vindictiveness even where the jury is imposing a sentence. The danger of vindictiveness in those cases comes from the judge and the prosecutor, who might, by their actions, influence the jury to impose a stiffer sentence.

Mr. Justice Marshall, also dissenting, accused the majority of taking inconsistent positions by recognizing that a jury can violate the Constitution when it gives the defendant a more severe sentence to punish him for successfully taking an appeal, yet refusing to apply the North Carolina v. Pearce restrictions. "[O]nly when the possibility of vindictiveness can confidently be said to be de minimis can Pearce be distinguished." And this can be done only by asking juries questions that will tend to inform them of the initial conviction. Other efforts to achieve the controlled retrial described by the majority will also run into trouble. Application of Pearce limitations would be the best solution, and would not infringe upon any state interest.

Michigan v. Payne, 412 U.S. 47, 13 CrL 3087

The same day that it refused to extend North Carolina v. Pearce to jury-imposed sentences upon retrial following a successful appeal, the Court also held that "the due process holding * * * of * * * Pearce * * * is non-retroactive." A majority of the Court pointed out in opinion by Mr. Justice Powell that the rule of Pearce is prophylactic. Therefore, the Court reversed a Michigan Supreme Court decision, announced after Pearce, that afforded relief to a defendant whose pre-Pearce resentencing was neither factually vindictive nor supported by the kind of reason-statement that Pearce requires.

Applying the now-traditional retroactivity test of Stovall v. Denno, 388 U.S. 293, 1 CrL 3102 (1967), the majority noted that the purpose of the rule announced by Pearce has nothing to do with fair determination of guilt or innocence. It does involve questions touching on the integrity of the judicial process. However, its safeguards are so analogous to those of Miranda v. Arizona, 384 U.S. 436 that they should receive the same prospective treatment. Retrospective application of either Pearce or

Miranda would "occasion windfall benefits for some defendants who have suffered no constitutional deprivation." Also, neither decision conferred a new constitutional right. Each was aimed at better protecting an existing one.

Mr. Justice Marshall, dissenting, questioned the entire Stovall mode of analysis. He argued that "principled adjudication requires the Court to abandon the charade of carefully balancing countervailing considerations when deciding the question of retroactivity." Whenever a case doesn't deal with fundamental subject-matter jurisdiction and does not announce a rule that is central to the process of determining guilt or innocence, the holding has been subject to the Stovall analysis and invariably held non-retroactive. Thus, he said, the Court was not really applying a balancing test under Stovall. The only relevant test has been the determination of which general class a case falls into.

Finally, in a section of the dissent to which Mr. Justice Stewart also subscribed, Mr. Justice Marshall noted that the Pearce rule is related to "integrity of the judicial process, and not to the limitations placed by the Constitution on police behavior."

Mr. Justice Douglas again dissented for reasons stated in his dissent in Moon v. Maryland.

SENTENCING

Bradley v. U.S., 410 U.S. 605, 12 CrL 3198

Prosecution includes sentencing as well as conviction, the Court observed as it held that a defendant convicted of violating the law repealed by the 1970 Comprehensive Drug Act, 21 U.S.C. 801, 8 CrL 3105, and sentenced after the Act took effect, could not benefit from the more lenient sentencing provision of the 1970 Act. The 8–1 majority noted that the 1970 Act's saving clause specifically provides that pending prosecutions were not to be affected by the new law.

Mr. Justice Marshall, writing for the majority, rejected the defendant's argument that the word "prosecution" contained in the saving clause must be given its "everyday meaning," which would lead to the conclusion that the prosecution is over once the conviction is obtained. That position is not consistent with Congress' intent to use familiar legal expressions in their familiar legal sense. Thus, prosecution clearly implies a begining and an end, and a final judgment means sentence. The prosecution terminates only when the sentence is imposed. Accordingly, these defendants, who were convicted five days after the 1970 Act took effect, must be sentenced under the more stringent mandatory-minimum, no probation, no-parole provisions of the earlier Act.

Mr. Justice Douglas, dissenting, believed that the correct interpretation of the word "prosecution" as used in the saving clause of the 1970 Act was that the prosecution ended with conviction.

HABEAS CORPUS

The remedy of federal habeas corpus for state prisoners was expanded in several respects this Term.

Hensley v. Municipal Court, 411 U.S. 345, 13 CrL 3041

The restraints still imposed on a convicted California defendant whose release on recognizance was continued after an unsuccessful state appeal, so that he could pursue federal habeas, constituted "custody" within the meaning of the federal habeas corpus statute, a sharply divided Court held. Thus the Court, in an opinion by Mr. Justice Brennan, allowed the federal habeas petitioner to proceed in federal court without going through the procedure of ending his release, being jailed by state authorities on a misdemeanor charge, and then bringing his federal habeas petition.

The finding of custody in this unique case doesn't necessarily apply to all releases on recognizance, the majority cautioned. Under California law, this petitioner was required to appear whenever and wherever ordered by court or magistrate. He was under a constant threat of summary revocation of his release. He was subjected to re-arrest for failure to appear as agreed, and willful failure to appear was itself a criminal offense.

Mr. Justice Blackmun concurred in the result, for reasons of stare decisis, but observed that "the Court has wandered a long way down the road in expanding traditional notions of habeas corpus."

Mr. Justice Rehnquist, joined by the Chief Justice and Mr. Justice Powell, dissented. "The Court apparently feels, like Faust, that it has in its previous decisions, already made its bargain with the devil, and it does not shy from this final step in the re-writing of the statute." This petitioner, who for over three years had been allowed to travel outside the state of California, was hardly in "custody."

Neil v. Biggers, 409 U.S. 188, 12 CrL 3037

The question whether the federal courts can entertain habeas corpus applications from prisoners whose state convictions have been affirmed on direct appeal by an evenly divided U.S. Supreme Court was settled in favor of the prisoners. Reviewing a grant of habeas relief to a Tennessee rape defendant who was identified in a suggestive showup, the Court held that the federal habeas corpus statute's exclusion from jurisdiction of cases "actually adjudicated" by the Court, 28 U.S.C. 2244(c), doesn't apply to the mere automatic result of the Court's inability to agree.

The prisoner lost on the merits, however, despite his success before the Federal district court and the court of appeals. Mr. Justice Powell's majority opinion deemed inapplicable the Court's "rule of practice" against re-examining the concurrent fact-findings of two lower federal courts. This case was one in which the constitutional significance of the facts, rather than the facts themselves, were in dispute. The relevant facts, the majority pointed out, were all contained in a state trial record that was just as available to the Supreme Court as it was to the lower federal courts. Examining this record, the majority held that the unnecessarily suggestive showup did not, under the totality of the circumstances, render the victim's in-court identification unnecessarily suggestive.

This identification predated Stovall v. Denno, 388 U.S. 293, and the majority carefully skirted the question whether Stovall means that unnecessarily suggestive identification procedures bar outright in-court identifications based upon these procedures.

Bearing in mind that it was only the Stovall opinion that gave state courts and law enforcement authorities any incentive to build a record sufficient to establish non-suggestiveness, the majority, in determining reliability of the identification, applied a different "totality of the circumstances" test from the "totality" rule that Stovall itself set up. The evidence of suggestiveness was addressed to the jury, the majority says, and the jury apparently found the identification reliable. Weighing all the factors, the majority found no substantial likelihood of misidentification.

Mr. Justice Brennan, joined in his partial dissent by Justices Douglas and Stewart, pointed out that the district court below fully and conscientiously assessed the "totality of the circumstances," as did the Sixth Circuit, 448 F.2d 91, 95, 9 CrL 2497. The dissenters saw no reason under these circumstances to depart from the "two-court rule," an indispensable time saver for the U.S. Supreme Court. It made no difference, they maintained, that the lower courts' findings of fact were based upon the state court record. The majority, they said, had done more than "merely assay constitutional significance." There had been a de novo inquiry.

Braden v. Kentucky 30th Judicial Circuit Court, 410 U.S. 484, 12 CrL 3179

A state prisoner who is under another state's detainer can enforce his right under Smith v. Hooey, 393 U.S. 374, 4 CrL 3077, to a speedy trial by habeas corpus in the federal courts of the state that issued the detainer, a majority of the Court held. Thus resolved was the anomalous situation in which an Alabama prisoner had found himself under the Fifth Circuit rule that habeas enforcement of such a right had to be brought in the federal courts of Kentucky, and the Sixth Circuit rule that it had to be brought against the detainer-holding authority in Alabama.

The Alabama prisoner, who plainly was in custody, didn't have to be physically present within the Kentucky federal district to fulfill the requisites of jurisdiction and venue there, the Supreme Court majority said. His custodians, the Kentucky officials who refused to bring him speedily to trial, were present within the district and amenable to federal process there, and that is all that matters.

Moreover, the majority said, this petitioner had exhausted as many state remedies as federal constitutional law requires, even though he had not yet been brought to trial by Kentucky.

Mr. Justice Blackmun concurred in the result. He offered the comment that the law has certainly come a long way since the early development of the Great Writ.

Mr. Justice Rehnquist dissented. He was joined by the Chief Justice and Mr. Justice Powell. He pointed out the fact acknowledged by the majority, that the present opinion at least in part overrules Ahrens v. Clark, 335 U.S. 188 (1948). The majority ignores part of the legislative history of the present federal habeas corpus statute, he added.

POST-CONVICTION RELIEF

Tollett v. Henderson, 411 U.S. 258, 13 CrL 3034

State grand jury discrimination can't ordinarily be challenged by federal habeas corpus after a guilty plea is entered upon advice of counsel, Mr. Justice Rehnquist said on behalf of a six-Justice majority. Observing that the only exception would be for cases in which the defendant's legal representation didn't meet the "range of competent advice" standard of McMann v. Richardson, 397 U.S. 759, 7 CrL 3055, the majority refused relief to a Tennessee black who was convicted in 1948 without being told that he had a right to challenge the grand jury selection, and who waited for many years to assert this claim.

This "competent advice" test, and not the "knowing and intelligent waiver" standard of Johnson v. Zerbst, 304 U.S. 458 (1939), governs when a guilty plea is involved, the majority explained. A previous violation of constitutional rights is not automatically ground for relief.

Mr. Justice Marshall, joined by Justices Douglas and Brennan, accused the majority of disregarding Johnson v. Zerbst. He did not see why counsel should not be responsible for putting every possible pretrial constitutional defense before a defendant. Such defenses are likely to be few.

Davis v. U.S., 411 U.S. 233, 13 CrL 3026

In a case similar to Tollett v. Henderson but involving a federal defendant, the same majority held, again in an opinion by Mr. Justice Rehnquist, that Fed. R. Crim. P. 12(b), requiring that defects in the indictment be raised before trial, governs a 28 U.S.C. 2255 post-conviction motion alleging such a defect. Post-conviction relief was thus denied to a defendant who waited until three years after conviction to challenge the grand jury selection process in his case.

Rule 12 treats as waived those objections not made before trial, but it allows a federal district judge to entertain later challenges upon a showing of "good cause." The majority saw no abuse of discretion in the refusal of the district judge here to find "good cause" and waive the deadline.

The three dissenters in Tollett were no happier with this result. Rule 12, Mr. Justice Marshall said, should not bar a habeas or 2244 petitioner from claiming grand jury discrimination, so long as he can show that this failure to make the claim before trial was not a knowing and intelligent waiver of the Johnson v. Zerbst variety.

LaVallee v. Delle Rose, 410 U.S. 690, 12 CrL 4187

A sharply divided Court summarily reversed a Second Circuit decision that upheld a grant of federal habeas release to a New York murder convict. The four dissenters decided not to invoke the "rule of four" and have the case argued orally. The majority held that the federal district judge was wrong in holding that a 1963 statecourt voluntariness finding under the "totality of the circumstances" test didn't sufficiently articulate whether the state judge believed the defendant and whether he was applying the proper constitutional standard.

Under the Federal Habeas Corpus Statute, 28 U.S.C. 2254(d), the factual holdings of the state court in constitutional questions are to be presumed correct. Townsend v. Sain, 372 U.S. 293 (1963), says that "the district judge may in the ordinary case in which there has been no articulation, properly assume that the state trier of fact applied correct standards of federal law to the facts * * *."

The majority also looked at the evidence that came before the state tribunal and held it to have been far more likely that the state judge disbelieved the defendant's "third degree" story than that he applied an improper constitutional standard to believed allegations.

Dissenting Justice Marshall, joined by Justices Douglas, Brennan and Stewart, charged that the majority misconstrued the "may" in Townsend to mean "must." A district judge not only has the discretion to refuse to assume correctness of unexplained state court findings, but also, according to the dissenters, has a third option in probing those findings. When assessing the voluntariness of a confession, even under Miranda requirements, he could find that the state courts applied the wrong standard, or that they made a factual error he has no power to disturb —but he also might find that correct standards were wrongly applied to the facts of the case.

Also, they said, the majority disregards the possibility that the state court might have believed some of the defendant's allegations and rejected others.

Fontaine v. U.S., 411 U.S. 213, 13 CrL 4001

The fact that the requirements of Fed.R.Crim.P. 11 have been met does not absolutely bar a guilty-pleading federal defendant from possible post-conviction relief, the Court held in an 8–1 per curiam decision.

True, a defendant whose plea is taken in compliance with Rule 11 "may not ordinarily" repudiate his statements to the sentencing judge. But the exercise of Rule 11, "like any procedural mechanism, * * * is neither always perfect nor uniformly invulnerable to subsequent challenge calling for an opportunity to prove the allegations." The record in this case did not permit the statutorily required assurance that under no circum-

stances could the facts warrant relief under 28 U.S.C. 2255. Thus, the petitioner was entitled to hearing.

Mr. Justice White dissented without opinion.

FIRST AMENDMENT

California v. La Rue, 409 U.S. 109, 12 CrL 3027

In a decision that boded ill for those who like to mix their liquor and naked women, a divided Court upheld the constitutionality of California liquor regulations barring the sale of liquor by the drink in bars that offer live or filmed sex shows —even though some of these shows would not be obscene.

The majority, in an opinion by Mr. Justice Rehnquist, pointed out that the challenged regulations "come to us not in the context of censoring a dramatic performance in a theatre, but rather in a context of licensing bars and nightclubs to sell liquor by the drink." The Twenty-First Amendment confers "something more than the normal state authority over public health, welfare, and morals."

While the regulations on their face might proscribe some forms of visual presentation that would not be found obscene under existing standards, states may proscribe expression, consisting in part of "action" or "conduct," that has an illegal objective.

The regulations were based on fact-finding that uncovered not only evidence of audience-participation in the performers' sexual activities, but various sex crimes on or around the premises of topless-bottomless establishments.

Mr. Justice Stewart, in his concurrence, explains that First and Fourteenth Amendment limitations upon state activities were not involved here.

Dissenting, Mr. Justice Douglas argued that the district court should have abstained from giving a constitutional ruling until the general provisions of the rules were given particularized meaning.

Also dissenting, Mr. Justice Brennan feared that this decision leaves the state free to use the Twenty-first Amendment and the liquor licensing powers as a means of deliberate inhibition of protected, "even if distasteful," forms of expression.

Mr. Justice Marshall asserted that the regulations were unconstitutionally overbroad. "These regulations create a system of per se rules to be applied regardless of context."

Also, Mr. Justice Marshall did not see how the Twenty-First Amendment, which speaks of importation of liquor, enables the states to do what the First Amendment would otherwise forbid.

CORRECTIONS

The current prison and corrections law revolution, helped along somewhat by the Court in recent years, was left primarily to the lower federal courts during the 1972–73 Term. Besides a decision dealing with federal relief avenues available to prisoners undergoing prison disciplinary measures, the Court concerned itself primarily with clarifying Morrissey v. Brewer, 408 U.S. 471, 11 CrL

3324 its landmark decision setting forth in detail the due process rights of state parolees facing revocation.

Gagnon v. Scarpelli, 411 U.S. 778, 13 CrL 3081

The Court answered two critical questions that it left open in Morrissey v. Brewer. Probationers facing possible revocation are on the same footing as parolees similarly situated. And with but one dissenting vote, the Court went on to hold that neither probationers nor parolees are entitled to counsel as a matter of right at revocation hearings. Rather, the parole authority may appoint counsel on a case-by-case basis when it determines that legal assistance may be necessary as matter of fundamental fairness.

Mr. Justice Powell, writing for the Court, noted that there were extremely good arguments on both sides of the counsel question. In most cases counsel is constitutionally unnecessary and may even be undesirable. However, there may be cases where counsel is necessary, such as where the probationer or parolee makes a counsel request based on a timely and colorable claim that he has not committed the alleged violation upon which the revocation proceeding is based or that even if the violation is a matter of public record or is uncontested there are substantial reasons that justify or mitigate it. Further, in passing on a request for the appointment of counsel, the responsible agency should consider, especially in doubtful cases, whether the probationer appears to be capable of speaking effectively for himself. "In every case in which a request for counsel at a preliminary or final hearing is refused, the grounds for refusal should be stated succinctly in the record."

Accordingly, the Court held that a Wisconsin probationer whose freedom was revoked without a hearing after he was caught in the act of a burglary was now entitled to a hearing. And, because he raised a claim regarding his admission of guilt, the department of probation was directed to reexamine his request for counsel.

Mr. Justice Douglas' dissent went only to the facts of this case. He stated his belief that due process requires the appointment of counsel in this case because of the claim that the probationer's confession was made under coercion. In Morrissey, Mr. Justice Douglas' partial dissent called for the right of counsel at the final revocation hearing.

Preiser v. Rodriquez, 411 U.S. 475, 13 CrL 3065

Habeas corpus, and not the 1871 Civil Rights Act, 42 U.S.C. 1983, is the appropriate route for prisoners seeking to challenge disciplinary actions depriving them of good time credit. Such prisoners are challenging the fact or duration of their confinement, and the relief they seek is simply a release therefrom, and that is the very "heart of habeas corpus." Mr. Justice Stewart, writing for a six-Justice majority, offered a lengthy history of the writ in support of this conclusion.

The Court found it plain from the history and function of the federal habeas statute, 28 U.S.C. 2241–2245 that it was meant to be the sole federal remedy for obtaining absolute release from confinement. The later and more specific 1948 amendments to the habeas statute clearly take precedence over the earlier and more general ones of Section 1983. True, Civil Rights Act relief is available to challenge conditions of confinement, even though it overlaps habeas in that regard. Wilwording v. Swenson, 404 U.S. 249, 10 CrL 4085, did hold that state prisoners' complaints about prison conditions are cognizable in either kind of action.

Challenges to conditions of confinement however, are different from attacks on length of confinement. The same comity reasons that make Civil Rights Act relief unavailable to obtain release from an unconstitutional state conviction sentence apply here. Premature federal interference with state prison-disciplinary administrative action is as damaging as premature interference with state court action.

A lengthy dissent by Mr. Justice Brennan, joined by Justices Douglas and Marshall, regarded these cases as indistinguishable from Wilwording, and criticized "the Court's newfound and essentially ethereal" concept of habeas corpus. Placing a prisoner in solitary — a "condition of confinement" that the Court in Haines v. Kerner, 405 U.S. 519, 10 CrL 3069, held was reachable by a 1983 action —usually has the effect of also lengthening the duration of confinement. The dissenters sympathized with the majority effort to see that the exhaustion requirement of the federal habeas statute is not abused by frivolous overuse of the Civil Rights Act, but they suggested other ways of preventing this.

McGinnis v. Royster, 410 U.S. 263, 12 CrL 3143

New York's legitimate interest in having an opportunity to evaluate a state prisoner's conduct and rehabilitative progress, coupled with the lack of serious rehabilitative programs in county jails, justified a statutory scheme that denied convicted felons good time credit for time spent in county jails pending imposition of sentence or transfer to state prison, the Court held. Convicted felons who were free on bail or recognizance pending sentence or transfer were entitled to such credit.

Mr. Justice Powell stressed that the Court did not wish to inhibit state experimental classification. He concluded that the distinction here served a legitimate, articulated state purpose. The state did have a legitimate interest in not foisting convicted and unrehabilitated criminals back on society.

Dissenting Justice Douglas, joined by Mr. Justice Marshall, asserted that "the discrimination in the present case is a statutory one levelled against those too poor to raise bail and unable to obtain release on personal recognizance." No state policy justifies this "deep seated, inequity," Mr. Justice Douglas maintained.

FEDERAL LIABILITY

Logue v. U.S., 412 U.S. 521, 13 CrL 3144

Without a dissenting vote, the Court concluded that the Federal Government is not liable, under the Federal Tort Claims Act, to federal prisoners in local "contract" jails. When the United States contracts with a local jail for the care and custody of federal prisoners, the jail is a "contractor" and not a "federal agency" within the meaning of the Act —which makes the U.S. liable only for the acts of "federal agency" employees. The Act, at 28 U.S.C. 2671, specifically excludes "any contractor with the United States" from the definition of "federal agencies," for the acts of which the United States has consented to be suable in tort.

The Court found itself unable to abandon the distinction, for purposes of liability, between federal employees and the employer of contractors with the Federal Government. Whatever may be the better view, Mr. Justice Rehnquist said on the Court's behalf, Congress has made its intent clear.

Nor could the Court accept yet another alternative contention that the local sheriff's deputies and guards, because they "acted on behalf of a federal agency in an official capacity," might be Federal Government employees without being federal agency employees.

However, the Court remanded for consideration of Government liability for the possibly negligent acts of the U.S. marshal who put the suicidal federal detainee in the Texas jail and did not arrange for his constant supervision. Justices Stewart and Marshall joined in the majority's opinion "upon the understanding that, upon remand, the Court of Appeals' consideration of [the marshal's] negligence will not be limited to his alleged failure to make 'specific arrangements * * * for constant surveillance of the prisoner.'"

CIVIL RIGHTS ACTIONS

Gilligan v. Morgan, 413 U.S. 1, 13 CrL 3202

A five-Justice majority held that a complaint brought by individuals who were students at Kent State University at the time of the fatal National Guard shootings in 1970 seeking judicial review and continued judicial surveillance of training, arming, and orders of the Guard did not present a justiciable question. The relief sought embraced an area of responsibility explicitly vested in Congress by Article I Section 8 Clause 16 of the Constitution.

Justices Douglas, Brennan, Stewart, and Marshall, convinced that the case was now moot, dissented. Justices Blackmun and Powell would have agreed that the controversy was now moot except for the continuing surveillance of Guard activities sought by the complainants. The concurring Justices noted that the complaint was based upon a single, isolated and tragic incident. The complaint, they said contained nothing suggesting that specific injury was apt to be suffered in the future as a result of the practices they challenged.

City of Kenosha v. Bruno, 412 U.S. 507, 13 CrL 3139

A city is not a "person," as defined by 42 U.S.C. 1983, the Court held and thus is not subject to a federal district court seeking injunctive relief from the city's refusal to renew liquor licenses.

District of Columbia v. Carter, 409 U.S. 418, 12 CrL 3064

All the Justices agreed that suit does not lie under 42 U.S.C. 1983 for deprivation of federal civil rights in the District of Columbia by D.C. police. The District is not a "state or territory" within the meaning of Section 1983, Mr. Justice Brennan pointed out on behalf of the unanimous Court.

PRESUMPTIONS

Barnes v. U.S., 412 U.S. 837, 13 CrL 3153

An examination of the presumptions and inferences it has considered in recent years led a divided Court to conclude that a federal trial court properly invoked the classic stolen goods presumption in the case of a defendant who forged and cashed stolen Treasury checks. The 6–3 majority found proper the trial judge's instruction that the defendant's unexplained possession of recently stolen Treasury checks was a circumstance from which the jury could find beyond a reasonable doubt that he knew they were stolen. The charge was supported by evidence establishing beyond a reasonable doubt that the defendant possessed checks payable to persons he did not know. The evidence furnished no plausible explanation for possession consistent with innocent behavior.

Mr. Justice Powell, writing for the majority, explained that the teaching of Gainey v. U.S., 380 U.S. 63; Romano v. U.S., 382 U.S. 136; Leary v. U.S. 395 U.S. 6, 5 CrL 3053; and Turner v. U.S., 396 U.S. 398, 6 CrL 3042, is that due process is afforded by a statutory inference, which satisfied the reasonable doubt standard as well as a more-likely-than-not standard. In view of the evidence underlying the instruction here, which had an impressive historical basis, the jury was entitled to find beyond a reasonable doubt that the defendant knew the checks were stolen.

In a footnote, the majority noted that the defendant had received identical concurrent sentences on all counts. "[A]lthough affirmance of petitioner's conviction of two of the six counts carrying identical concurrent sentences does not moot the issues he raised pertaining to the remaining counts, Benton v. Maryland, 395 U.S. 784 (1969), we decline as a discretionary matter to reach these issues."

Mr. Justice Douglas, dissenting, noted that an essential element of the crime was the defendant's knowledge that the checks in question were stolen from the mail. Without the mail element, there was no federal offense. And there was no evidence, he contended, that this defendant knew the checks had been stolen from the mail.

Mr. Justice Brennan, who was joined in dissent by Mr. Justice Marshall, contended that the trial court erred in instructing the jury that it could infer knowledge of theft from unexplained possession.

PERJURY

Bronston v. U.S., 409 U.S. 352, 12 CrL 3061

A unanimous Court, in an opinion by the Chief Justice, held that the federal perjury statute, 18 U.S.C. 6121, does not make punishable a witness' answer which, while literally true, was unresponsive to the question asked, was arguably untrue by negative implication, and may well have been intended to evade. It was quite likely that his answer did not reflect his "true belief." But the real truth could have been elicited by a single additional question had counsel been sufficiently alert. Furthermore, the Chief Justice pointed out, it is not uncommon, under the stress of interrogation, for even the most earnest witness to give answers that are not entirely responsive. It is unlikely that the drastic sanction of perjury was intended to cure such a testimonial mishap. A holding otherwise would put undue strains on the adversary testimonial system.

TRAVEL ACT

Erlenbaugh v. U.S., 409 U.S. 239, 12 CrL 3047

Unwilling to read two sections of the Travel Act as one, a unanimous Court held that the shipment of a "scratch sheet" in interstate commerce violated the statute even though the second section specifically exempts newspapers. Writing for the Court, Mr. Justice Marshall said that 18 U.S.C. 1953 was not in pari materia with Section 1952, and the exemption 1953 grants does not apply to 1952.

True, Section 1952 and 1953 are both part of the same comprehensive federal legislative effort to assist local authorities dealing with organized criminal activity. But the two statutes play different roles in achieving this goal. Section 1953 has a narrow, specific function while Section 1952 is much broader in scope.

MILITARY JURISDICTION —RETROACTIVITY

Gosa v. Mayden, 413 U.S. 665, 13 CrL 3248

Although a majority of the Court denied relief to two court-martialed servicemen who sought retroactive application of O'Callahan v. Parker, 395 U.S. 258, 5 CrL 3082, which limited the jurisdiction of military tribunals to "service-connected" offenses, O'Callahan's retroactivity apparently remained an open question. Four justices agreed that O'Callahan does not meet the retroactivity criteria of Stovall v. Denno, 388 U.S. 293. Four other Justices, two of whom believed O'Callahan was wrongly decided and should be overturned, argued that it nontheless should be applied retroactively. Mr. Justice Douglas thought that one of the cases should be set for re-argument on the question whether the jurisdiction of the court-martial, since it was not contested at the time, has become res judicata.

Mr. Justice Blackmun, writing for himself, the Chief Justice, and Justices White and Powell, concluded that the validity of convictions by military tribunals, now said to have exercised jurisdiction inappropriately over nonservice-connected offenses, is not sufficiently in doubt to require reversal of all such convictions rendered since 1916, when Congress provided for military trial for civilian offenses committed by servicemen. Also, this case was not one concerned with the integrity of the fact-finding process but rather with its forum.

Accordingly, a Fifth Circuit decision, holding O'Callahan to be prospective only, was upheld, and with it the 1966 court-martial conviction of an airman who, while on authorized leave, raped a civilian. However, a Second Circuit decision, applying O'Callahan retroactively to the 1944 court-martial conviction of an AWOL sailor who stole a civilian's car, was reversed.

Justices Stewart and Rehnquist, while unhappy with O'Callahan, said that until or unless it is overruled, it must be given retroactive application. The 1944 court-martial conviction is not subject to O'Callahan restrictions, however; it involved a serviceman who deserted his post and then stole a car during a time of Congressionally declared war. Thus it was a service-connected offense.

Mr. Justice Douglas, concurring in part, agreed with Justices Stewart and Rehnquist that the auto theft was service-connected. But, he said, the 1966 conviction should be set for reargument to determine whether res judicata controls its disposition.

Mr. Justice Marshall, joined in full by Mr. Justice Brennan and in part by Mr. Justice Stewart, argued that O'Callahan may only be read as a decision dealing with the constitutional limits of the military's adjudicatory power. Thus, it raised a jurisdictional question.

EQUAL PROTECTION —FEDERAL JURISDICTION

Keeble v. U.S., 412 U.S. 205, 13 CrL 3103

An 1885 federal statute, originally meant to assure that American Indians who murder other Indians are punished other than with relatives' private vengeance, was never meant to require absolute denial of a lesser included offense instruction to an Indian defendant. The Court divided in reaching this result as it overruled the Eighth Circuit's standing interpretation of the Major Crimes Act, 18 U.S.C. 1153, a statute that mandates trial in federal district court of major felonies perpetrated by red men on reservations or in federal territory.

The Court reversed the aggravated assault conviction of a federally tried Indian who unsuccessfully sought an instruction on simple assault, a crime not listed as federally triable by the 1885 statute. The Eighth Circuit thought that no instruction on simple assault was proper, since that offense couldn't be tried in federal district court.

But the majority, in an opinion by Mr. Justice Brennan, noted the Act's express provision that Indians charged under it are to be tried in the same manner as others accused of "committing any of the above crimes within the exclusive jurisdiction of the United States." Congress surely did not intend to deny to Indians the benefits "available to any non-Indian charged with the same offense."

Justice Stewart, joined by Justices Powell and Rehnquist, thought that the Court's holding "would be correct only if the lesser included offense were one over which.the federal court had jurisdiction."

WITNESSES

Hurtado v. U.S., 410 U.S. 578, 12 CrL 3197

In one of its first opinions ever on the matter of involuntarily incarcerated material witnesses, the Court, without addressing any of the constitutional questions raised by such detention, interpreted the federal witness-compensation statute to require that a witness incarcerated under Fed. R. Crim. P. 46 (b) be compensated at a rate of $21 per day of "attendance upon" a court that is in session during the proceeding for which he has been detained. He is entitled to this sum even if he is not physically present in the courtroom. However, remuneration for other days of confinement is only $1 per day.

The Court was not persuaded by the incarcerated witnesses' constitutional argument that their pretrial detention at the compensation rate of only $1 per day constituted a "taking" without compensation under the Fifth Amendment. Every citizen or alien has the duty to attend a trial for purposes of testifying, Mr. Justice Stewart observed, so it is not a "taking" when the Government demands it. Since both indigent witnesses who are incarcerated because they cannot make bond, and those who await their hour upon the stand in some place other than a jail, will receive the same compensation, there is no equal protection issue.

Agreeing with much of what the majority had to say, Mr. Justice Brennan rejected its conclusion with respect to the time a witness is held in custody prior to inception of the proceeding.

Mr. Justice Douglas argued that all of the indigent petitioners in this case had been subjected to unjustifiable discrimination.

TRAVEL ACT

U.S. v. Enmons, 410 U.S. 396, 12 CrL 3161

Over the dissents of Mr. Justice Douglas, the Chief Justice, and Justices Powell and Rehnquist, the Court held that striking labor union members' violence, readily punishable under state law, in furtherance of legitimate collective bargaining objectives did not violate the Hobbs Act, 18 U.S.C. 1951.

TAX EVASION

U.S. v. Bishop, 412 U.S. 346, 13 CrL 3134

With Mr. Justice Douglas the lone dissenter, the Court held that the element of willfulness necessary to support the misdemeanor conviction under 26 U.S.C. 7207 of a taxpayer who "willfully delivers or discloses" to the Internal Revenue Service any return or document "known to him to be fraudulent or to be false as to any material matter" is the same element necessary to support a Section 7206 (1) felony conviction of a taxpayer who "willfully makes and subscribes any return" under the penalties of perjury, "which he does not believe to be true and correct as to every material matter."

1973–1974 Term

When the U.S. Supreme Court finally ended its extended 1973–74 Term by holding that the President's claim of executive privilege with respect to his confidential communications must yield to the search for truth in a criminal prosecution, it established the Term as one of the most significant in history. Even before the decision in U.S. v. Nixon, however, the 1973–74 Term had made a considerable impact on several areas of the criminal justice system.

Scrutinizing prison disciplinary proceedings and interview regulations, the Court continued its trend in recent years of strengthening the due process rights of convicts whose freedom or privileges are threatened by administrative action. However, the rollback of Fourth Amendment protections gained momentum. The Court reversed four different federal court of appeal decisions as it strengthened the authority of police officers to engage in warrantless searches. It also refused to extend the Fourth Amendment exclusionary rule to grant jury proceedings. But at the same time the Government was severely penalized for its failure to comply with the letter and spirit of the federal electronic eavesdropping law.

EXECUTIVE PRIVILEGE

U.S. v. Nixon; Nixon v. U.S., 418 U.S. 683, 15 CrL 3329

Probably no other decision in the U.S. Supreme Court's history has had a more dramatic immediate impact than its holding that the Constitution did not shield President Nixon from the Special Prosecutor's subpoena for tapes of key presidential conversations in the Watergate coverup. But the significance of the Chief Justice's opinion for a unanimous Court goes far beyond its catalytic role in the President's resignation 15 days later. While affirming that the President has a strong privilege of confidentiality with respect to high-level conversations, the Court held that this privilege must yield to the legitimate demands of judicial process during the course of a federal criminal prosecution.

However, this holding was tempered by several references to the fact that the President had no claim here of any need to protect military or diplomatic secrets.

The importance of the criminal justice interests at stake in this case —the "Watergate coverup" prosecution of former top-level officials in the Nixon Administration — was underscored by the swiftness with which the Court acted. Its decision came precisely two months after the Special Prosecutor, having obtained a trial court order enforcing his subpoena, filed a petition for certiorari in advance of appellate court judgment. The effect of the Supreme Court's decision was to compel production of the taped conversations for in-camera inspection.

In reaching its decision, the Court flatly rejected the claim that, under the separation of powers doctrine, a presidential assertion of executive privilege is beyond judicial review. The Court had never before defined the specific scope of judicial power to enforce a subpoena for confidential communications, and the interpretation by any branch of Government of its powers "is due great respect from" the other branches. However, the Chief Justice pointed out, the Court has consistently and unequivocally reaffirmed the holding of Marbury v. Madison, 1 Cranch 137 (1803), that "it is emphatically the province and duty of the judicial department to say what the law is." Having "consistently exercised the power to construe and delineate claims under express powers," it follows "that the Court has authority to interpret claims with respect to powers alleged to derive from enumerated powers."

After reaffirming its authority to review the President's assertion of privilege, the Court went on to hold that, at least absent a claim of need to protect military or diplomatic secrets, the privilege was not absolute. The separation of powers doctrine did not support him, for "the separate powers were not intended to operate with absolute independence. * * * To read the Art. II powers * * * as providing an absolute privilege against a subpoena essential to enforcement of criminal statutes on no more than a generalized claim of the public interest in confidentiality of nonmilitary and nondiplomatic discussions would upset the constitutional balance of 'a workable government' and gravely impair the role of the courts under Art. III."

And the court did not see how, "[a]bsent a claim of need to protect military, diplomatic or sensitive national security secrets * * * even the very important interest in confidentiality of presidential communications is significantly diminished by production of such materials for court will be obliged to provide."

Balancing the claim of privilege against the needs of judicial process in a criminal prosecution, the Court concluded that the President's claim was outweighed by the "fundamental and comprehensive" need "to develop all relevant facts in the adversary system."

The traditional privileges against giving evidence — such construed, for they are in derogation of the search for truth." The President's claim in this case was not based on the ground that the conversations sought "are military or diplomatic secrets. As to these areas of Art. II duties the courts have traditionally shown the utmost deference to presidential responsibilities. * * * No case of the Court, however, has extended this high degree of deference to a President's interest in confidentiality."

To be balanced against this privilege, which is nowhere explicitly mentioned in the Constitution, are the explicit Sixth Amendment rights of a defendant to confrontation and compulsory process, and the Fifth Amendment right to due process. The Court concluded "that when the ground for asserting privilege as to subpoenaed materials sought for use in a criminal trial is based only on the generalized interest in confidentiality, it cannot prevail over the fundamental demands of due process of law in the fair administration of criminal justice. The generalized assertion of privilege must yield to the demonstrated, specific need for evidence in a pending criminal trial."

Before reaching the privilege issue, the Court found that the district court's enforcement order was appealable. The traditional contempt avenue to appeal was "peculiarly inappropriate due to the unique setting in which the question rises," the Court observed. The President should not be required to disobey the court order merely to obtain review of his constitutional claims, and a trial court should not be required to cite the President for contempt.

The Court also held, contrary to the President's argument, that this controversy was justiciable. It was not merely a dispute between a "subordinate and a superior of the same executive branch and hence not subject to judicial resolution." The Special Prosecutor had received a valid delegation of prosecutorial authority from the Attorney General, who has statutory responsibility under Art. II, Para. 2 to conduct the Government's criminal litigation. The Attorney General had promulgated regulations giving the Special Prosecutor explicit power, in seeking evidence he believes relevant, to contest a claim of executive privilege. Under McCardy v. Shaughnessy, 347 U.S. 260, this regulation had the force of law until amended or revoked.

The Special Prosecutor had also satisfied the requirements of Fed.R.Crim.P. 17(c). He had established the relevancy and admissibility of the specific conversations he sought, and the district court did not abuse its discretion in enforcing the subpoena. It was also clear that the materials sought were not available from any other source, and that their examination and processing should not await the trial itself.

The Court dismissed as improvidently granted the question of whether the President could properly be named as an unindicted co-conspirator by the grand jury that had indicted the defendants in this case.

SEARCH AND SEIZURE

Reversing federal appellate court judgments in two traffic arrest cases, a 6–3 majority of the Court held that a law enforcement officer's authority, incident to a lawful arrest, to make a full search of the person he is taking into custody requires no justification beyond the fact of the custodial arrest itself. The Court squarely rejected the view that a full search of an arrested person is justified only for reasons of safety and securing evidence of the offense. It thus found the "limited search" rationale of Terry v. Ohio, 392 U.S. 1, inapplicable to custodial arrests for offenses, such as traffic violations, that involve no evidence other than the fact of the illegal act.

U.S. v. Robinson, 414 U.S. 218, 14 CrL 3043

In the first of these cases, the majority held admissible heroin that was discovered by an officer during his thorough search of a traffic offender being taken into custody for a violation carrying a mandatory minimum jail term, a mandatory minimum fine, or both. The search, carried out pursuant to standard District of Columbia "field arrest" procedures, was not motivated by any fear on the officer's part. Nor did the officer have reason to believe that there was further evidence of crime on the offender's person. And his search went beyond the person —to an examination of the contents of a crumpled cigarette package found in a pocket of the offender's coat.

Mr. Justice Rehnquist drew a distinction between the scope of the area that may be searched incident to an arrest —a question frequently considered by the Supreme Court —and the search of the arrested person —the validity of which "has remained virtually unchallenged until the present case." An officer's authority to search the arrested person has been consistently reaffirmed by the Court in its numerous opinions concerning the permissible area of searches incident to arrest. The Court has spoken "not simply in terms of an exception to the warrant requirement, but in terms of an affirmative authority to search * * *." True, these statements "affirming the existence of an unqualified authority to search incident to a lawful arrest are dicta," the majority acknowledged. But the few early state court decisions on the question "tend to support the broad statement of the authority to search incident to arrest found in successive decisions of this Court, rather than the restrictive one which was applied by the court of appeals in this case." The scarcity of case law prior to the Supreme Court's first recognition of searches incident to arrest in Weeks v. U.S., 232 U.S. 383 (1914), was "doubtless due in part to the fact that the issue was well settled."

In disagreeing with the court of appeals determination that a search incident to a traffic arrest should be limited to a Terry-type pat-down for possible weapons, the majority emphasized that "the authority for a search incident to a lawful arrest rests quite as much on the need to disarm the suspect in order to take him into custody as it does on the need to preserve evidence on his person for later use at trial. The standards traditionally governing a search incident to a lawful arrest are not, therefore, commuted to the stricter Terry standards by the absence of probable fruits or further evidence of the particular crime for which the arrest is made."

Mr. Justice Powell's concurrence emphasized what he found to be the essential premise of these decisions: "[T]he custodial arrest is the significant intrusion of state power into the privacy of one's person. If the arrest is lawful, the privacy interest guarded by the Fourth Amendment is subordinated to the legitimate and over-riding governmental concern."

Dissenting Justice Marshall, joined by Justices Douglas and Brennan, accused the majority of turning its back on fundamental Fourth Amendment principles. The consti-tutional validity of a warrantless search can only be decided in the concrete factual context of each case; the majority was wrong in announcing a rule that gave police blanket authority to search without a warrant. It is the responsibility of a detached magistrate rather than a law enforcement officer to determine the reasonableness of any given search.

The majority, Mr. Justice Marshall said, simply ignored the wealth of state and lower federal court decisions specifically disapproving of searches of traffic offenders that go beyond the need to secure the safety of the arresting officer. And the suggestion that the intrusion brought about by the arrest renders unnecessary protec-tion against examination of the arrested person's effects "was expressly rejected by the Court in Chimel [v. California, 395 U.S. 752]."

Although he explored in considerable detail the differences between the search incident to a traffic arrest and the kind of pat-down approved in Terry v. Ohio, Mr. Justice Marshall found it unnecessary to determine whether the "stop and frisk" approach was appropriate for traffic-arrest searches. The search in this case involved more than a mere search of the person; it extended beyond the person to the crumpled package, and the search of the package was not justified by any reason whatsoever.

Gustafson v. Florida, 414 U.S. 260, 14 CrL 3056

The majority also upheld a warrantless search of a college student who was found driving without his operator's permit on his person. The search yielded a cigarette box, and the officer found marijuana inside the box. Although the officer had lawfully arrested the student for failure to have his license in his possession, he took the youth into custody "in order to transport him to the stationhouse for further inquiry." Unlike the officer in the Robinson case, the Florida officer was not required to take the violator into custody. But the absence of a departmental policy was not determinative; it was sufficient that the officer had probable cause to arrest the petitioner and that he lawfully effectuated the arrest and placed the petitioner in custody."

Mr. Justice Stewart, concurring, observed "that a persuasive claim might have been made in this case that the custodial arrest of the petitioner for a minor traffic offense violated his rights under the Fourth and Fourteenth Amendments." But validity of the custodial

arrest having been conceded, "it follows that the incidental search of his person was also constitutionally valid."

Justices Marshall, Douglas, and Brennan dissented for the reasons stated in Mr. Justice Marshall's opinion in Robinson.

U.S. v. Edwards, 415 U.S. 800, 14 CrL 3147

The Court divided 5–4 in another opinion simulta-neously explicating and expanding the authority of law enforcement officers to make warrantless searches "inci-dent" to arrest. The majority, in an opinion by Mr. Justice White, dealt yet another blow to the idea that the police must take advantage of every opportunity to get a search warrant as it upheld the warrantless seizure of clothing worn by a jailed suspect whose arrest had taken place about eight hours earlier. The seizure was still within the scope of "incidence" to arrest; it was not, as the U.S. Court of Appeals for the Sixth Circuit had held below, a search "after the administrative process and mechanics of the arrest had come to a halt."

The arrest took place at 11 p.m., and the officers had reasonable cause to believe that the clothing of defendant, who had been charged with attempting to break into a post office, contained paint particles. The police were not able to buy replacement clothing for the suspect until the next morning, so it was reasonable for them to wait until they had the new clothing.

The police had custody of the clothing as well as the suspect anyway, Mr. Justice White pointed out, and they could have searched for the evidence they sought without removing the clothing from either the suspect or the cell. Furthermore, the inapplicability of the Warrant Clause to this kind of search does not leave the police free to engage in unreasonable searches of recently arrested prisoners.

Mr. Justice Stewart, joined in dissent by Justices Douglas, Brennan, and Marshall, urged that a search "incident" to arrest must be "substantially contempora-neous with the arrest." These clothes were taken to obtain evidence, so this was no "routine exchange of civilian clothes for jail garb." The police had ample time to seek a warrant, Mr. Justice Stewart pointed out; thus the considerations specifically justifying warrantless arrests were absent here. The majority's position here —that the relevant question is not the opportunity to procure a warrant but the overall reasonableness of the search — was explicitly rejected in Chimel v. California, 395 U.S. 752.

Cardwell v. Lewis, 417 U.S. 583, 15 CrL 3163

The Court's latest effort to shed light on the Fourth Amendment problems inherent in warrantless automobile searches came to nothing. Dividing so sharply that no majority emerged on the car seizure and "search" question in this case, the Court reversed a grant of federal habeas corpus relief to an Ohio murder defendant whose automobile was seized, without a warrant, from a public parking lot and examined the next day for tire and exterior paint matchups.

The Court divided 4–4 on the legality of the warrantless seizure and inspection; the swing vote was cast by Mr. Justice Powell, who stood by his position in Schneckloth v. Bustamonte, 412 U.S. 218, 13 CrL 3107, that federal habeas review of Fourth Amendment claims should be limited to the question of adequate review at the state level. Mr. Justice Blackmun, spokesman for the four-Justice plurality that explicitly found no Fourth Amendment violation here, flatly stated that a person "has a lesser expectation of privacy in a motor vehicle because its function is transportation and it seldom serves as one's residence or as the respository of person effects." Of course, "[t]his is not to say that no part of the interior of an automobile has Fourth Amendment protection; the exercise of a desire to be mobile does not, of course, waive one's right to be free of unreasonable government intrusion."

Chambers v. Maroney, 399 U.S. 42, 7 CrL 3133, was also deemed applicable. Both the car here and the vehicle in Chambers were immobilized once they had been seized, Mr. Justice Blackmun pointed out. And, at the time the car in this case was seized, there was a real threat of its removal.

Mr. Justice Stewart, speaking for the four dissenters, focused upon the seizure of the car and emphasized that it was not covered by any of the established exceptions to the warrant requirement. Mobility is the traditional justification for warrantless vehicle searches, he stressed, not the mere fact that the subject of the seizure is an automobile.

U.S. v. Calandra, 414 U.S. 338, 14 CrL 3061

The purpose of the Fourth Amendment exclusionary Rule is to deter official wrongdoing rather than "to safeguard * * * a personal constitutional right of the party aggrieved," a six-Justice majority emphasized as it refused to extend the rule to grand jury questions based on illegally seized evidence. The witness who sought to invoke the rule had first claimed his Fifth Amendment privilege against self-incrimination, and turned to the Fourth Amendment only after the Government sought immunity for him.

The historic and integral role of the grand jury in insuring effective law enforcement would be compromised by introduction of the exclusionary rule into its proceedings, Mr. Justice Powell explained on behalf of the majority; proceedings would very likely get bogged down with suppression motions by witnesses. While a grand jury's investigative powers, particularly its powers of subpoena, are limited by constitutional protections as well as by statutory and common law privileges, justification for the exclusionary rule is strongest in a proceeding where conviction may result from unlawful Government conduct. And illegally obtained evidence used by a grand jury still could not be used at a subsequent trial.

The majority's attitude toward the exclusionary rule was lukewarm; it "is thought to be an important method of effectuating the Fourth Amendment. But it does not follow," Mr. Justice Powell went on, "that the Fourth Amendment requires adoption of every proposal that might deter police misconduct. * * * Whatever deterrence of police misconduct may result from the exclusion of illegally seized evidence from criminal trials, it is unrealistic to assume that application of the rule to grand jury proceedings would significantly further that goal."

In a footnote, Mr. Justice Powell, referring to the frequently-cited article by Dallin Oaks, Studying the Exclusionary Rule in Search and Seizure, 37 U.Chi.-L.Rev. 665 (1970), noted "some disagreement as to the practical efficacy of the exclusionary rule * * *. We have no occasion in the present case to consider the extent of the rule's efficacy in criminal trials."

Mr. Justice Brennan, writing for himself and Justices Douglas and Marshall, accused the majority of downgrading the exclusionary rule by ignoring its "twin goals of enabling the judiciary to avoid the taint of partnership in official lawlessness and of assuring the people * * * that the government would not profit from its lawless behavior, thus minimizing the risk of seriously undermining popular trust in government." This case, the dissenters maintained, is controlled by Silverthorne Lumber v. U.S., 251 U.S. 385 (1920).

The dissenters also pointed out that the Fourth Amendment rights violated in this case were those of the witness himself.

In leaving ajar "the only courtroom door remaining open to evidence secured by official lawlessness,'" Mr. Justice Brennan, quoting from Mapp v. Ohio, 367 U.S. at 654–55, said that Mr. Justice Powell's opinion left him "with the uneasy feeling that a majority of my colleagues have positioned themselves to reopen the door still further and abandon altogether the exclusionary rule in search and seizure cases."

U.S. v. Matlock, 415 U.S. 164, 14 CrL 3108

Having long approved the use of hearsay to establish probable cause, both in affidavits for warrants and at pretrial suppression hearings, the Court made it clear that the usual rules of evidence excluding hearsay from trial are not necessarily a bar to the use of hearsay at pretrial suppression hearings for purposes other than establishing probable cause.

Reversing the U.S. Court of Appeals for the Seventh Circuit, a six-Justice majority held that a federal district judge determining the validity of a third-party consent should have taken into account police testimony as to what the consenting party had said about her relationship with the defendant.

While reminding the courts below "that the rules of evidence normally applicable in criminal trials do not operate with full force at hearings before the judge to determine the admissibility of evidence," the majority, in an opinion by Mr. Justice White, was not so clear as to when, if ever, these rules do apply to such proceedings. In this case, the Court considered the reliability of the hearsay statements.

Among the factors making the woman's statements reliable were their consistency with each other and their corroboration by other evidence. Furthermore, her revelation that she and the defendant lived together out of wedlock was a declaration against penal interest. Also, she testified on the defendant's behalf at the suppression hearing, and so was available for cross-examination.

The authority of a third party to consent, the Court said, "does not rest upon the law of property, with its attendant historical and legal refinements, * * * but on mutual use of the property by persons generally having joint access or control for most purposes," so that all "have assumed the risk that one of their numbers might permit the common area to be searched."

While inclined to believe that "the Government sustained its burden of proving" the legal sufficiency of the consent "by the preponderance of the evidence," the majority remanded the case with instructions to the court of appeals to have the district court reconsider the sufficiency of the evidence in light of this decision and opinion.

Dissenting, Mr. Justice Douglas would have relied on the district court's finding that there were no exigent circumstances excusing the officers' failure to secure a warrant.

Justices Brennan and Marshall, noting their dissents in Schneckloth v. Bustamonte, 412 U.S. 218, 13 CrL 3107, renewed their objections to finding a valid consent without a showing that the consenting party knew of the right to refuse.

Gooding v. U.S., 416 U.S. 430, 15 CrL 3019

Once federal officers have established probable cause for a warrant to search for controlled substances under 21 U.S.C. 879, a majority of the Court held, there is no need for a further showing to justify executing the warrant at night. Mr. Justice Rehnquist, writing for a 6–3 majority, explained that the statutory language, while not crystal clear, requires only a showing that the contraband is likely to be on the property or person to be searched at the time the warrant is to be executed.

While legislative history is silent on this question, Section 879's companion provisions speak of making it easier to enforce the 1970 Comprehensive Drug Control Act. Thus it would make no sense to interpret this provision as requiring an additional showing to justify nighttime execution of warrants.

The majority also held that where an Assistant U.S. Attorney, citing violations of federal narcotics laws, asks a U.S. magistrate for a search warrant to be executed in the District of Columbia by D.C. police, the execution of that warrant is governed by Section 879 rather than the D.C. Code. The operative facts in this case "strongly indicate that the standard for issuance of a warrant should

be governed by the nationwide federal legislation enacted by Congress —that is 21 U.S.C. 879(a) —rather than by the local D.C. laws."

Dissenting Justice Douglas, joined by Justices Brennan and Marshall, pointed out that the D.C. Code provision in question here was passed after the federal law. Furthermore, 60 percent of the warrants issued in the District of Columbia are for narcotics, and if Congress had intended to exempt federal narcotic search warrants from the protections of unnecessary nighttime searches, it would have done so.

In a separate dissent, Mr. Justice Marshall, joined by Justice Douglas and Brennan, accused the majority of analyzing Section 879 in a vacuum "totally oblivious" to such important constitutional considerations as the protection of individual privacy. The dissenters maintained that some additional justification for authorizing a search over and above the ordinary showing of probable cause must be made.

ELECTRONIC EAVESDROPPING

U.S. v. Giordano, 416 U.S. 505, 15 CrL 3033

Resolving a question that had generated much litigation in the lower federal courts and considerable embarassment for the Justice Department, a unanimous Court concluded that 18 U.S.C. 2516(1) means exactly what it says —only the Attorney General or an Assistant Attorney General specially designated by him can approve a request to apply for a wiretap. The Court, in an opinion by Mr. Justice White, pointed out that Congress was so concerned with limiting electronic eavesdropping authority that suppression is the only appropriate remedy for noncompliance with Sec. 2516(1).

The legislative history of the wiretap provisions in the 1968 Omnibus Crime Act, 18 U.S.C. 2510 et seq., plainly indicates Congress' desire to vest the approval authority in few and highly identifiable officials within the Justice Department. It is also clear, Mr. Justice White said, that Section 2516 overrides 28 U.S.C. 510, which authorizes the Attorney General to delegate any of his functions to others within the department.

Accordingly, a wiretap order, the application for which was approved by the Attorney General's executive assistant, was unlawful. Thus noncompliance with Sec. 2516 rendered the resulting wiretap unlawful within the meaning of Section 2518(10)(a), and subject to suppression under 18 U.S.C. 2515. This illegality also fatally tainted any extensions of the original order.

Mr. Justice Powell took issue with this last point. Writing for himself, the Chief Justice and Justices Blackmun and Rehnquist, he argued that the extensions in this case rested only in part on the invalid wiretap order and were not marred by the authorization defect.

U.S. v. Chavez, 416 U.S. 562, 15 CrL 3050

The Justice Department fared better in a second electronic surveillance case as a majority of the Court held that, while misidentification of the official who did approve a request to apply for a wiretap violates 18 U.S.C. 2518(4)(d), it is not so serious that evidence obtained from the wiretap must be suppressed. Again writing for the majority, Mr. Justice White pointed out that here the application named the Assistant Attorney General as the person who, acting under Section 2516, approved the request when in fact it had been approved by the Attorney General himself.

There is little doubt, the Court acknowledged, that the purpose of Section 2518(4)(d) is an important one —to make clear who is responsible for approving an application. However, "the misidentification of the officer authorizing the wiretap application did not affect the fulfillment of any of the reviewing or approval functions required by Congress * * *."

Mr. Justice Douglas, joined in dissent by Justices Brennan, Stewart, and Marshall, could not agree that Title III, fairly read, authorizes the courts to pick and choose which provisions are to be considered serious enough to require suppression as a remedy for non-compliance.

INTERROGATION

Michigan v. Tucker, 417 U.S. 433, 15 CrL 3145

Although it declined an invitation by the State of Michigan to overrule Miranda v. Arizona, 384 U.S. 436, a majority of the Court found a distinction between substantive violations of a defendant's Fifth Amendment rights and mere failure of interrogating officers to satisfy all of the Miranda requirements. Accordingly, the testimony of a witness whose name police got from a rape defendant during a pre-Miranda interrogation was properly admitted at the defendant's post-Miranda trial.

Finding no violation of the defendant's Fifth Amendment privilege against compulsory self-incrimination, the majority, in an opinion by Mr. Justice Rehnquist, concluded that the prophylactic rules announced in Miranda did not require suppression of the witness' testimony despite the fact that the interrogation, which took place two months before Miranda was announced, was not preceded by advice about the defendant's right to appointed counsel. The police did ask the defendant whether he wanted an attorney and whether he understood his rights; they also advised him that anything he said could later be used against him in court. He said that he did not want an attorney and that he did understand his rights. He then said that he had been with the witness the night of the rape, but the witness actually weakened his alibi, and testified against him.

The privilege against self-incrimination has been given a broad scope where there has been genuine compulsion of testimony, Mr. Justice Rehnquist noted. But the evidence that resulted from this defendant's interrogation was not a statement by him at all. Rather, it was the testimony of a third party who was not subjected to any custodial pressures. And the reliability of this testimony "was subject to the normal testing process of an adversary trial."

Mr. Justice Brennan, joined by Mr. Justice Marshall, concurred in the reversal of the Sixth Circuit's grant of federal habeas relief, but for apparently different reasons. He would have confined the reach of Johnson v. New Jersey, 384 U.S. 719, which makes Miranda applicable to all cases in which the trial was commenced after the date of the Miranda decision, to those cases in which the direct statements of the accused made during a pre-Miranda interrogation were introduced at his post-Miranda trial. "If Miranda is applicable to all to the fruits of statements made without proper warnings, I would limit its effect to those cases in which the fruit was obtained as a result of post-Miranda interrogation." Mr. Justice Rehnquist replied in a footnote that the issue raised in this case was not present in Miranda; even if Miranda were made fully retroactive it would not resolve this issue. Mr. Justice Brennan, he said, would "determine in the present case the retroactivity of a holding the Court has yet to make."

Mr. Justice Stewart, concurring, added "only that I could also join in Mr. Justice Brennan's concurrence. For it seems to me that despite differences in phraseology, and despite the disclaimers of their respective authors, the Court opinion and that of Mr. Justice Brennan proceed along virtually parallel lines, give or take a couple of argumentative footnotes."

Mr. Justice White concurred for reasons stated in his dissent in Miranda. He reiterated his view that Miranda is an ill-conceived opinion without constitutional justification. At any rate he was against extending its prophylactic scope to bar the testimony of third persons even though they may have been identified by means of statements that are themselves inadmissible under Miranda.

Mr. Justice Douglas, dissenting, asserted that in Miranda the Court held the requirements of warnings and waiver of rights to be fundamental to the protection of the Fifth Amendment privilege. Thus the Miranda requirements are not simply guidelines, but constitutional standards. Further, the testimony of the witness in this case was no less a fruit of unconstitutional police action than were the photographs in Silverthorne Lumber Co. v. U.S., 251 U.S. 385, or the narcotics in Wong Sun v. U.S., 371 U.S. 471. As for Mr. Justice Brennan's retroactivity basis, Mr. Justice Douglas pointed out that Miranda himself had been interrogated three years before this defendant.

PRISONS

The Court came squarely to grips this Term with several of the major issues that have come to the fore in the "prison law revolution".

Wolff v. McDonnell, 418 U.S. 539, 15 CrL 3304

Unanimously dispelling any doubt that the Fourteenth Amendment's Due Process Clause protects state prisoners facing loss of good-time credit or punitive confinement, the Court divided over the extent of this protection.

The majority, in an opinion by Mr. Justice White, reversed a holding by the U.S. Court of Appeals for the Eighth Circuit that the full panoply of protections announced for parolees and probationers in Morrissey v. Brewer, 408 U.S. 471, 11 CrL 3324, and Gagnon v. Scarpelli, 411 U.S. 778, 13 CrL 3081, should generally apply to prison disciplinary proceedings at which inmates face such serious deprivations. Justices Douglas, Marshall, and Brennan would have extended to prisoners the procedural safeguards spelled out in Morrissey and Gagnon.

Prisoners facing solitary confinement or the loss of good-time credit must be given written notice of the alleged infraction at least 24 hours prior to the hearing; they must also be afforded a written statement as to the evidence relied upon and the reasons for any disciplinary action taken. However, the majority found no unqualified right to call witnesses and present documentary evidence, and refused to extend either the right of confrontation or the right to counsel to such proceedings. But for cases where an inmate is illiterate or the charges are particularly complex, the majority did suggest allowing assistance from another inmate.

While the Court's discussion of these safeguards was in the context of good-time credits, Mr. Justice White stated in a footnote that "it would be difficult for the purposes of procedural due process to distinguish between the procedures that are required where good-time is forfeited and those that must be extended when solitary confinement is at issue." However, he disclaimed any suggestion that the required due process procedures "would also be required for the imposition of lesser penalties such as the loss of privileges."

The interests of a prisoner in his good-time credits must be balanced against the special needs of prison administration, the majority emphasized. "For the prison inmate, the deprivation of good-time is not the same immediate disaster that the revocation of parole is for the parolee." Such deprivation could postpone the date of parole eligibility and extend maximum time to be served, but it might not, for good-time credit may be restored. And even if it is not restored, the actual date of parole may not be affected.

However, the majority made it clear that the state interests were the determining factor in deciding how far procedural safeguards should go at this time —when there is so much diversity, and experimentation, in the administration of the nation's prisons. Crucial here was the nature of prison society itself —including the unwritten code of behavior among prisoners themselves. Retaliation against inmates who make complaints or furnish evidence against a disciplined inmate is a real possibility, "and the basic and unavoidable task of providing reasonable personal safety for guards and inmates may be at stake, to say nothing of the impact of disciplinary confrontations and the resulting escalation of personal antagonisms on the important aims of the correctional process." The proceedings themselves may play a major role in the institutional goal of rehabilitation, and it would be most unwise to encase disciplinary procedures "in an inflexible constitutional straitjacket." And the insertion of counsel into such proceedings would tend to give them "a more adversary cast" and tend to reduce their rehabilitative utility.

The majority also refused to rule that a three-person disciplinary board consisting entirely of high ranking prison officials was insufficiently impartial. The procedures under which this committee operates are such that there is no hazard of arbitrary decisionmaking in violation of due process.

These present limitations on due process safeguards, Mr. Justice White emphasized, are "not graven in stone." Changes in circumstances in the future may well require further "consideration and reflection of this Court."

The majority also reversed a court of appeals holding that due process requirements for prison disciplinary proceedings must be applied retroactively.

No constitutional violation was found in the prison practice of opening, in the inmate's presence, incoming attorney mail —where less intrusive means of examining such mail for contraband have not proved satisfactory. The Court condemned as unworkable a court of appeals approach requiring that doubt as to whether a letter actually was from an attorney could be settled by a "simple telephone call".

The Court was in unanimous agreement that the due process right to legal assistance in the preparation of habeas corpus petitions, Johnson v. Avery, 393 U.S. 483, applies to the preparation of Civil Rights Act suits. The Court further found that Preiser v. Rodriquez, 411 U.S. 475, 13 CrL 3065, was no bar to an inmate's suit under 42 U.S.C. 1983 for relief from an unconstitutional deprivation of good-time credit that does not challenge the fact or duration of his confinement.

Mr. Justice Douglas would have applied "full" due process safeguards to an inmate threatened with any substantial deprivation of liberty within the prison. The right to produce witnesses and confront adverse witnesses "ought always to be available absent any special overriding considerations," he maintained. And these decisions should not "be left to the unchecked and unreviewable discretion of the Prison Disciplinary Board." The danger of retribution, he emphasized, "exists in every adversary proceeding." On the issue of mail receipt by prisoners, he adhered to the views of himself and Mr. Justice Marshall in Procunier v. Martinez, 15 CrL 3009.

While joining the Court's holdings as to the right to assistance in filing a civil rights action and with the result of the holding with respect to mail inspection, Mr. Justice Marshall, joined by Mr. Justice Brennan, asserted that the limited due process protections were of little utility absent "any enforceable constitutional right to the procedural tools essential to the presentation of any meaningful defense * * *." Justices Marshall and Brennan would also have extended the rights to call witnesses and to confront and cross-examine adverse witnesses.

Mr. Justice Marshall took particular issue with what he regarded as the majority's failure to treat the rights of confrontation and cross-examination as fundamental. These rights, he asserted, are particularly fundamental in a proceeding that will most likely turn on a question of fact. And the need to keep the identity of informers confidential "will exist only in a small percentage of disciplinary cases" —the complaining party is almost invariably a correctional officer. The majority's opinion, he asserted, does not even go as far as a substantial majority of the states have already gone in protecting inmates facing discipline.

Procunier v. Martinez, 416 U.S. 396, 15 CrL 3009

The Court was also unanimous in affirming a federal district court decision that struck down a broad mail censorship rule for California prisons. A six-Justice majority, in an opinion by Mr. Justice Powell, found no need to reach the issue of prisoners' First Amendment rights to correspond. Rather, its decision rested on the narrower and more settled basis of the First Amendment rights of the free citizens with whom the prisoners correspond.

Mr. Justice Powell noted the "array of disparate approaches" that the lower federal courts had taken with respect to prison censorship of inmate mail. This state of uncertainty had resulted in haphazard and inconsistent protection for First Amendment rights, made it impossible for correctional officers to anticipate what is required of them, and invited repetitive, piecemeal litigation. By focusing on the First Amendment rights of free citizens to correspond with inmates rather than grappling with the difficult and relatively novel question of the fundamental rights retained by prisoners, the Court was able to find guidance in its decisions "dealing with the general problem of incidental restrictions on First Amendment liberties imposed in furtherance of legitimate governmental activities."

The legitimate governmental interests at stake here are the preservation of order and discipline within the prison system —and, of course, rehabilitation of the prisoners. Prison mail censorship is justified only if practiced to protect one or more of these interests, and "the limitation of First Amendment freedoms must be no greater than is necessary or essential to the protection of" these interests. The Court gave as an example the Federal Bureau of Prisons policy which permits rejection of incoming or outgoing correspondence that might violate postal regulations, or that discusses criminal activities or enables an inmate to conduct a business.

The Court agreed with the district court that an inmate is entitled to notification "of the rejection of a letter written by or addressed to him, that the author of that letter be given a reasonable opportunity to protest that decision, and that complaints be referred to a prison

official other than the person who originally disapproved the correspondence."

Mr. Justice Marshall, joined by Mr. Justice Brennan and in part by Mr. Justice Douglas, would have reached the First Amendment rights of inmates independently of their correspondents' rights. The concurring Justices would have held that "prison authorities may not read inmate mail as a matter of course." Prisoners are "entitled to use the mails as a medium of free expression * * * as a constitutionally guaranteed right," Mr. Justice Marshall asserted. While applying the same "substantial governmental interest" test as the majority, he found no justification for a "blanket policy of reading all prison mail." No rehabilitative purpose is served by such indirect censorship, and other less intrusive means are available for preventing smuggling. Nor is a generalized fear of escape plans by mail enough to permit general reading of prison correspondence.

A separate concurrence by Mr. Justice Douglas, joined by Justices Brennan and Marshall, emphasized that prisoners are entitled to all constitutional rights except those that have been curtailed in procedures satisfying all due process requirements. Mr. Justice Douglas explained that he would incorporate free speech rights into the Fourteenth Amendment not only through the Due Process Clause but also as one of the privileges and immunities of all citizens.

The Court likewise affirmed the district court's refusal to abstain in the mail-censorship dispute, holding that the mere possibility of a state appellate decision against the regulations doesn't require federal abstention.

The Court also held that under Johnson v. Avery, 393 U.S. 483, the state could not forbid the use by attorneys of law students and other paralegal workers for prisoner interviewing purposes. Agreeing with the district court, the Court held that the California administrative rules restricting legal visits to members of the bar and state-licensed private investigators imposed an unconstitutional burden on the inmates' right of access to the courts, a right protected by the Fourteenth Amendment's Due Process Clause. Furthermore, these rules arbitrarily discriminated between law students employed by private attorneys and those participating in public programs — who are permitted to visit prisoners.

Pell v. Procunier; Procunier v. Hillery, 417 U.S. 817, 15 CrL 3202

While the Court was able to strike down California's broad regulations permitting prison mail censorship without reaching the question of prisoners' First Amendment rights, it did examine these rights in another context —that of interviews sought by the news media with specific prisoners.

The right of prison inmates to free speech does not include the right to be individually designated for interview by representatives of news media, a six-Justice majority held. A five-Justice majority also held that the news media have no free press right to interview specifically designated inmates.

At issue in two of these cases was a recently promulgated California Department of Corrections regulation providing that "[p]ress and other media interviews with specific inmates will not be permitted." Both individual newspeople seeking such interviews and individual prisoners designated by the reporters sought injunctive and declaratory relief under 42 U.S.C. 1983.

The majority's holding that the prisoners had no First Amendment right to individualized interviews was based not only on the legitimate correctional interests behind the regulation, but on the inmates' alternative means of communication with the outside world. The Court's opinion in Procunier v. Martinez, the majority noted, affirmed the rights of generally unmolested prison correspondence, and inmates retain the right to receive visits from family, friends, and clergy. A newsperson coming within one of these categories would not be excluded.

Deterrence of crime, rehabilitation of offenders, and — to all other corrections goals" —the internal security of the institutions themselves are all served by this regulation, Mr. Justice Stewart said in his opinion for the majority. In fact, this particular regulation came about as a response to a violent prison episode that authorities felt was at least partially attributable to the previous policy permitting such interviews. Prisoners who get such interviews, it was found, gained disproportionate notoriety and influence among other inmates, and seriously eroded institutional effectiveness.

The majority also found no First Amendment right on the part of the media sufficient to overcome the strong governmental interests protected by this regulation. Mr. Justice Stewart noted at the outset that "this regulation is not part of an attempt by the State to conceal the conditions in its prisons or to frustrate the press' investigation and reporting of those conditions. Indeed, * * * both the press and the general public are accorded full opportunities to observe prison conditions." Public prison tours are regularly conducted. But even beyond this, newsmen are permitted to visit both maximum and minimum security areas and to conduct random interviews with prisoners, and they may sit in on prison program meetings. "In short," Mr. Justice Stewart said, "members of the press enjoy access to California prisons that is not available to other members of the public." After discussing the First Amendment newsgathering right explicated in Branzburg v. Hayes, 408 U.S. 665, 11 CrL 3333, the majority noted that "[t]he First and Fourteenth amendments bar government from interfering in any way with a free press. The Constitution does not, however, require government to accord the press special access to information not shared by members of the public generally."

While journalists are free, of course, to seek out sources not available to the public generally, there is no support for the proposition that the government has an affirmative duty to make such sources specially available to them.

Saxbe v. The Washington Post Co., 417 U.S. 843, 15 CrL 3210

A Federal Bureau of Prisons ban on individualized press interviews at medium and maximum security institutions also passed First Amendment muster. The Bureau of Prisons' inmate visitation policies and its policies with respect to media access "do not differ significantly from the California policies," Mr. Justice Stewart pointed out. The Court reversed judgments of the lower federal courts in this case decreeing "a selective policy whereby prison officials could deny interviews likely to lead to disciplinary problems." While noting the judgment of prison officials that such a policy would exacerbate the problems it was designed to solve, the Court based its decision on the ground that the present visitation policy does not infringe on any First Amendment news gathering right.

Mr. Justice Powell agreed in Pell that inmates have no constitutional right to demand interviews. However, he argued that the absolute ban "against prisoner-press interviews impermissibly restrains the ability of the press to perform its constitutionally established function of informing the people on the conduct of their Government." Joined by Justices Brennan and Marshall in Saxbe, he would have required prison authorities to develop procedures which would protect the public's right to gather information through the agency of the media.

Mr. Justice Douglas, joined by Justices Brennan and Marshall, dissented in both cases. The regulations are overbroad, he argued, and prison authorities should have to make a case-by-case determination. He found unpersuasive the majority's answer to the newsmen that they have no special access privilege. Freedom of the press belongs to the general public and is impaired if access to information is denied.

MILITARY

Parker v. Levy, 417 U.S. 733, 15 CrL 3183

Stressing the differences between military and civilian societies, a 5–3 majority of the Court held that military code limitations on expression must be subjected to less stringent vagueness and overbreadth tests than those applied to statutes limiting expression in civilian society. The majority's new standard for due process vagueness challenges to the military code was identical to the standard for criminal statutes regulating economic affairs: a defendant cannot claim vagueness if he could have reasonably understood that his contemplated conduct was proscribed. And the extension of standing in First Amendment cases to challenge a statute for overbreadth does not apply to the military. Applying these standards, the Court upheld Articles 133 and 134 of the Uniform Code of Military Justice, which prohibit "conduct unbecoming an officer and gentleman" and "disorder and neglect to the prejudice of good order and discipline in the armed forces."

The Articles had been declared unconstitutional for vagueness and overbreadth by the U.S. Court of Appeals for the Third Circuit in the case of ex-Captain Howard Levy, who was court-martialed for refusing to train Special Forces personnel as ordered and for making "intemperate, contemptuous, and disrespectful" public statements relating to the Vietnam War. These statements included exhortations to blacks to refuse to go to Vietnam and to refuse to fight if sent. Levy also characterized Special Forces personnel as liars, thieves and murders.

"This Court has long recognized that the military is, by necessity, a specialized society separate from civilian society," Mr. Justice Rehnquist observed in his opinion for the majority. "We have also recognized that the military has, again by necessity, developed laws and traditions of its own during its long history." Because the military's primary responsibility is to fight or be ready to fight, it has developed what the Court, in Martin v. Mott, 12 Wheat. 19 (1827), described as "the customary military law" or "general usage of the military service." Enforcement of these customs and usages has been approved by the Court "from the early days of the Nation," and during the nineteenth century, the Court repeatedly recognized "that the longstanding customs and usages of the services impart accepted meaning to the seemingly imprecise standards of Arts. 133 and 134." These differences between civilian and military authority come through clearly in the Uniform Code, which regulates many areas of military life that are left unregulated in the civilian sphere. The Code is administered differently than a civilian criminal code; the military attempts to advise soldiers of its contents, and proceedings and sanctions for minor offenses are more civil in nature than criminal.

The broad reach of the Articles' literal language has been narrowed by military court construction, Mr. Justice Rehnquist noted. And, while there is a sizeable area in which their application is uncertain under existing case law, even this area may be supplied further content — "by less formalized custom and usage." The Articles clearly apply to a "substantial range of conduct without vagueness or imprecision," and Levy's conduct, as the Court of Appeals recognized, squarely falls within that range.

True, the Court has invalidated, under the Fifth and Fourteenth Amendment Due Process Clauses, statutes and ordinances containing no standard of proscribed conduct whatever, Mr. Justice Rehnquist acknowledged. But Levy did have fair notice that his published statements urging blacks to disobey orders violated both Articles, and Supreme Court decisions lend no support to the Court of Appeal's conclusion that he had standing to challenge their vagueness as they might hypothetically be applied to other conduct —a conclusion that may stem from a blending of the vagueness and overbreadth doctrines. While the vagueness doctrine may require more

precision in drafting legislation that regulates civilian expression, the First Amendment does not forbid a more relaxed standard of review for military restrictions on expression, and the test applied to criminal statutes regulating economic affairs is the proper one here.

As for the overbreadth issue, the nature of the military requires that its members be accorded a different application of First Amendment protections than civilians. "The fundamental necessity for obedience, and the consequent necessity for imposition of discipline, may render permissible within the military that which would be constitutionally impermissible outside it. Doctrines of First Amendment overbreadth * * * are not exempt from the operation of these principles." The "weighty countervailing policies" permitting extension of standing in First Amendment cases to persons whose conduct is clearly proscribed by the challenged statute "must be accorded a good deal less weight in the military context." Thus, since the Articles were constitutionally applied to him, Captain Levy had no standing to challenge them.

Mr. Justice Stewart, joined in dissent by Justices Douglas and Brennan, disagreed that the Articles have been clarified very much. He noted that the so-called limiting constructions have sanctioned the use of the Articles for widely disparate conduct, while the examples listed in the Manual for Courts-Martial are neither exclusive nor proscribed beyond doubt, in view of the Court of Military Appeals' refusal in several cases to uphold convictions based on certain of these examples.

A fundamental difference of opinion is underscored by the dissenters' view that, while in times past, professional military men might have clearly understood them, a draftee such as Levy cannot be expected to absorb "the arcane meaning of the General Articles." Mr. Justice Blackmun, concurring with the majority and joined by the Chief Justice, read this language as the acceptance of relativistic notions of right and wrong. He said that "times have not changed in the area of moral precepts," and that the concepts of right and wrong which underpinned the 1642 ancestor of the Articles are viable today.

In a separate dissent, Mr. Justice Douglas noted that this was the first case the Court had heard on the First Amendment rights of the military. While recognizing that "the power to draft an army includes . . . the power to curtail considerably the 'liberty' of the people who make it up," he argued that Congress did not intend to make any exceptions to the First Amendment in passing Articles 133 and 134.

Secretary of Navy v. Avrech, 418 U.S. 676, 15 CrL 3325

On the heels of its decision in Parker v. Levy, a six-Justice majority, in a per curiam opinion, upheld another court martial conviction for violation of UCMJ Article 134. The Court cited Parker as the sole basis for its decision.

The serviceman was convicted of attempting to publish a statement disloyal to the United States to members of the Armed Forces with the intent to promote disloyalty.

He challenged the conviction in the U.S. District Court for the District of Columbia, claiming that Article 134 was unconstitutionally vague and overbroad on its face and as applied and asserting jurisdiction under 5 U.S.C. 701–706, 28 U.S.C. 1331, and 28 U.S.C. 1362. The District Court denied relief, but the Court of Appeals reversed, holding Article 134 unconstitutionally vague. The Supreme Court reversed the Court of Appeals judgment, but declined to reach the "difficult" issue of whether the district court had jurisdiction over the case. "We believe that even the most diligent and zealous advocate could find his ardor somewhat dampened in arguing a jurisdictional issue where the decision on the merits is thus foreordained."

Mr. Justice Stewart concurred on the ground that the Parker decision, with which he disagreed, controlled the substantive issue here.

Mr. Justice Douglas dissented, characterizing this case and Parker as "backward steps measured by the standards of an open society."

Noting that the Court of Appeals resolved the serviceman's claims as to only one of the three provisions he attacked, Justices Marshall and Brennan would have remanded for Court of Appeals consideration of the remaining claims in light of Parker.

FIRST AMENDMENT —FLAG ABUSE

Smith v. Goguen, 415 U.S. 566, 14 CrL 3135

While "nothing prevents a legislature from defining with substantial specificity what constitutes forbidden treatment of United States flags," Mr. Justice Powell said on behalf of a five-Justice majority, a Massachusetts ban on "contemptuous" treatment is, at least absent narrowing judicial construction, unconstitutionally vague. Thus, although it sidestepped the decision by the U.S. Court of Appeals for the First Circuit that this law's overbreadth violated the First Amendment, the Court came a step closer to resolving the basic constitutional controversy over flag desecration that had been thrust upon it several times in recent years. The Massachusetts contempt provision was, like most state flag statutes, similar to the Uniform Flag Act of 1917. The Court noted that the federal flag desecration statute, on the other hand, was intended to reach only acts that physically desecrate the flag, "and has been so read by the lower courts, which have upheld it against vagueness challenges."

The primary vagueness flaw in the Massachusetts statute was its failure to provide minimal guidelines for its enforcement. The law rendered punishable "[w]hoever publicly mutilates, tramples upon, defaces or treats contemptuously the flag of the United States * * * whether such flag is public or private property * * *." It was devoid of narrowing state court interpretation at the time the defendant in this case was prosecuted for wearing a flag sewn to his hip pocket. This was a defect that the U.S. Supreme Court could not, of course cure, and without such narrowing construction, the "treats con-

temptuously" language in the statute allowed "policemen, prosecutors, and juries to pursue their personal predilections. Legislatures may not so abdicate their responsibilities for setting the standards of the criminal law."

The statute was vague for another reason —it failed to give the offender notice as to just what is contemptuous conduct. "[C]asual treatment of the flag in many contexts has become a widespread contemporary phenomenon," Mr. Justice Powell pointed out. While many careless or casual uses of the flag constituting nonceremonial treatment may be viewed as contemptuous by many people, it can hardly be said that every informal use of the flag is criminal conduct. "The statutory language under which Goguen was charged * * * fails to draw reasonably clear lines between the kinds of nonceremonial treatment that are criminal and those that are not."

A belated exhaustion-of-remedies argument put forth by the Commonwealth, premised on the claim that this flag-wearer was a "hard-core" violator, did not impress the Court at all —even aside from the fact that it failed "to take the full measure of Goguen's efforts to mount a vagueness attack in the state courts." For the statute's contempt provision was impermissibly vague even as applied to this defendant. This was not merely a statute of uncertain application; it had no ascertainable standard for defining contemptuous conduct at all. "This absence of any ascertainable standard for inclusion and exclusion is precisely what offends the Due Process Clause."

The Commonwealth fared no better with its various efforts to defend the contempt provision on the merits of the vagueness question. Neither the statute's narrow subject matter —"actual" flags of the United States —nor the highest state court's restriction of its scope to intentional contempt, could overcome its central flaw — the absence of any standard for defining "contemptuous treatment." And the assertion that the statute's first six words added specificity to the "treats contemptuously" phrase carried no weight at all —this defendant was convicted under the general phrase alone. And the Court found no support in the record or state case law for the claim that state authorities have shown themselves ready to interpret the statute narrowly.

Certain areas of human conduct, the majority acknowledged, are not amenable to precise legislative standards. But this is not so in the area of flag contempt. "Indeed, because display of the flag is so common and takes so many forms, changing from one generation to another and often difficult to distinguish in principle, a legislature should define with some care the flag behavior it intends to outlaw."

Mr. Justice White concurred in the result, but on First Amendment grounds. He could not agree that the statute was vague as applied to this defendant; both the record and the defendant's own argument left no doubt that he knew he was showing contempt for the flag. And if the statute was not vague as to his conduct, "it is irrelevant that it may be vague in other contexts with respect to other conduct."

As for the First Amendment issue, Mr. Justice White "would not question those statutes which proscribe mutilation, defacement or burning of the flag or which otherwise protect its physical integrity, without regard to whether such conduct might provoke violence. Neither would I find it beyond congressional power, or that of state legislatures, to forbid attaching to or putting on the flag any words, symbols or advertisements. All of these objects, whatever their nature, are foreign to the flag, change its physical character, and interfere with its design and function. There would seem to be little question about the power of Congress to forbid the mutilation of the Lincoln Memorial or to prevent overlaying it with words or other objects. The flag is itself a monument, subject to similar protection." However, this defendant was not convicted of attacking the flag's physical integrity. "[T]he jury must affirm that Goguen not only wore the flag on the seat of his pants but also that the act —and hence Goguen himself —was contemptuous of the flag. To convict on this basis is to punish for communicating ideas about the flag unacceptable to the controlling majority in the legislature." Any conviction under the "treats contemptuously" provision of the statute would suffer from the same infirmity, Mr. Justice White concluded.

Mr. Justice Blackmun, joined by the Chief Justice, urged in his dissent that the statute was not vague; that the Massachusetts courts had sufficiently narrowed it by requiring physical acts against an actual flag, and that this defendant did harm the flag's integrity.

Mr. Justice Rehnquist, also joined in dissent by the Chief Justice, found the statute free of unconstitutional vagueness for the same reasons given by Justice White. But he would have sustained it against First Amendment attack as well. This statute, he maintained, met the inseparable tests of serving a substantial governmental interest and of collaterally suppressing expression no more than was essential to protect that interest. "The significance of the flag, and the deep emotional feelings it arouses in a large part of our citizenry, cannot be fully expressed in the two dimensions of a lawyer's brief or of a judicial opinion," he asserted. "But if the Government may create private proprietary interests in written work and in musical and theatrical performances by virtue of copyright laws, I see no reason why it may not * * * create a similar governmental interest in the flag by prohibiting even those who have purchased the physical object from impairing its physical integrity." This defendant, Mr. Justice Rehnquist emphasized, was "quite free to express verbally whatever views it was he was seeking to express by wearing a flag sewn to his pants * * *."

Spence v. Washington, 418 U.S. 405, 15 CrL 3263

The Court did reach the First Amendment question in another flag case, but was unable to reach a definitive holding. In a per curiam opinion, a plurality of four Justices held that a Washington state statute forbidding "improper use of the flag" was unconstitutional as applied to a college student who, to protest the then-recent Cambodian invasion and Kent State killings, displayed an inverted flag on which a peace symbol was superimposed.

The plurality declared that such use of the flag is "closely analogous to the manner in which flags have always been used to convey ideas" and is protected under the First Amendment. Moreover, the context in which this student used the flag gave meaning to the symbol he invoked, and "it would have been difficult for the great majority of citizens to miss the drift of appellant's point at the time that he made it." He clearly intended to convey a particularized message, and the state's undefined interest in "preserving the national flag as an unalloyed symbol of our country" was not sufficient to overcome the protected character of this message.

On a more mundane level, the plurality noted that neither the flag nor the property where it was displayed was Government-owned. Nor did the low-key protest threaten a breach of the peace.

Mr. Justice Douglas concurred for the reasons set forth in a recent Iowa case, State v. Kool, 212 NW.2d 518. However, the plurality considered the analysis in the Kool case similar to its own.

Mr. Justice Blackmun concurred only in the result.

Mr. Justice Rehnquist, joined in dissent by the Chief Justice and Mr. Justice White, challenged the plurality's analysis of the state's interest, which, he said, lies in preserving the flag as a symbol of nationhood and unity. Whether a particular flag is damaged or not and whether it is publicly or privately owned are irrelevant issues, because "it is the character, not the cloth, of the flag which the state seeks to protect."

FIRST AMENDMENT —OBSCENITY

The Court's work in the obscenity area was confined this Term to tying up loose ends left in the wake of its prodigious efforts last Term in Miller v. California, 413 U.S. 15, 13 CrL 3161, and Miller's companion cases.

Jenkins v. Georgia, 418 U.S. 153, 15 CrL 3259

It may be art to the New Yorker or even the Atlantan, but if it's smut to the citizens of Albany (Georgia), then it's smut. Unless, of course, an appellate court decides it's not smut.

Thus, while a five-Justice majority went beyond its holding in Miller, that no "national" community standard need be recognized in an obscenity prosecution, to emphasize that a local jury need not "be instructed * * * to apply the standards of a hypothetical statewide community," the Court unanimously reversed an Albany theatre owner's conviction for exhibiting "Carnal Knowledge."

On the "community standards" question, Mr. Justice Rehnquist, writing for the majority, made it clear that the states have considerable latitude in defining obscenity offenses; they "may choose to define an obscenity offense in terms of 'contemporary community standards' as defined in Miller without further specification, as was done here," or they "may choose to define the standards in more precise geographic terms," as was done by California in Miller.

This does not mean, however, that the local juries applying the standards of the community from which they come are immune from appellate review. Miller, the majority pointed out, specifically contemplated that First Amendment values would be "adequately protected by the ultimate power of appellate courts to conduct an independent review of constitutional claims when necessary." The Georgia Supreme Court majority, in affirming the manager's conviction, overlooked this safeguard. And the U.S. Supreme Court's own viewing of "Carnal Knowledge" satisfied it that this film was altogether different from the kind of flick that is obscene under the Miller test. "While the subject matter of the picture is, in a broader sense, sex, and there are scenes in which sexual conduct including "ultimate sexual acts' is to be understood to be taking place, the camera does not focus on the bodies of the actors at such times. There is no exhibition whatever of the actors' genitals, lewd or otherwise, during these scenes. There are occasional scenes of nudity, but nudity alone is not enough to make material legally obscene under the Miller standards."

Mr. Justice Brennan, joined by Justices Stewart and Marshall, concurred in the reversal of the conviction, but stood by his contention in Miller that attempted judicial regulation of obscenity is a hopeless task.

Mr. Justice Douglas also concurred in the reversal, reiterating his view that any ban on obscenity is constitutionally prohibited.

Hamling v. U.S., 418 U.S. 87, 15 CrL 3239

Obscenity defendants whose convictions were on appeal at the time Miller v. California, 413 U.S. 15, 13 CrL 3161, was decided must receive the benefit of any favorable constitutional ruling announced therein, a divided Court concluded. However, the 5–4 majority found those benefits of no help to a group of pornographers who were convicted under 18 U.S.C. 1461 for mailing an obscene brochure advertising a very spicy "illustrated version" of the report of the President's Commission on Obscenity and Pornography.

En route to its affirmance of the convictions, the Court, in an opinion by Mr. Justice Rehnquist, reached a number of significant conclusions. First, the statute involved, 18 U.S.C. 1461, which the Court directly upheld in Roth v. U.S., 354 U.S. 476, and by implication in U.S. v. Reidel, 402 U.S. 351, 9 CrL 3103, was found to be neither vague nor overbroad when evaluated in light of the Miller standards.

Turning its attention to the question of which "contemporary community standards" are to be considered by federal juries, the majority decided that such juries are entitled to apply the community standards of the vicinage from which they are drawn. However, the trial judge is free to assist them by admitting evidence of standards existing in places outside the district. The trial

judge's instructions in this case, that the jury should apply the community standards of the "nation as a whole," did not require reversal in the absence of a showing that they materially affected the jury's deliberations to the defendant's prejudice. Nor did the judge abuse his discretion by refusing to admit comparable materials that were readily available for purchase in the community. He had allowed extensive expert testimony on the question of obscenity.

Resolving a conflict among the circuits, the majority concluded that a trial judge's failure to comply with Fed.R.Crim.P. 30's requirement that a defendant be given an opportunity to object, out of the jury's presence, to portions of the jury instructions does not require reversal. The better approach to such problems is to examine the prejudice, if any, to the defendant.

Mr. Justice Douglas, dissenting, argued that "[i]f officials may constitutionally report on obscenity, I see nothing in the First Amendment that allows us to bar the use of a glossary factually to illustrate what the Report discusses."

Mr. Justice Brennan, joined in dissent by Justices Stewart and Marshall, maintained that even assuming the Government may constitutionally regulate the distribution of sexually oriented materials, it may not totally suppress them. He also challenged the decision to let juries draw on their own communities in determining what is or is not obscene.

CONTEMPT

Codispoti v. Pennsylvania, 418 U.S. 506, 15 CrL 3289; Taylor v. Hayes, 418 U.S. 488, 15 CrL 3294

In a pair of opinions on contempt charges arising out of disruptive conduct at criminal trials, the Court posed a crucial tactical decision for a trial judge faced with an obstreperous defendant or attorney who is not likely to stop at just one contemptuous act. As a result of the Court's decisions in these cases, significant differences in the rights of the contemnor will flow from the judge's decision whether to punish each act of contempt as it occurs or to accumulate these citations and punish at the end of the trial. The Court's major constitutional holding had to do with the right of direct contempt defendants to trial by jury.

The same right to trial by jury that is available to indirect contempt defendants, Bloom v. Illinois, 391 U.S. 194, was extended to any direct contempt defendant whose sentence following a single proceeding is more than six months.

In the Codispoti case, involving the same disrupted trial that led to the U.S. Supreme Court's decision in Mayberry v. Pennsylvania, 400 U.S. 455, 8 CrL 3065, five Justices rejected the argument that, regardless of the punishment actually imposed, a contemnor is entitled to a jury trial whenever a strong possibility exists that he will face a substantial term of imprisonment upon conviction. The fixed dividing line between petty and serious offenses depends upon the sentence actually imposed, Mr. Justice

White emphasized on behalf of the five Justices, who also agreed that when a judge postpones until after trial a contempt conviction of an accused or his lawyer for several or more acts of contempt, "there is no justification for dispensing with the ordinary rudiments of due process." This is so even where, as here, the defendant is convicted of contempt by a judge other than the one who presided over the trial.

Four Justices joined in the part of Mr. Justice White's opinion holding that a judge does not, however, exhaust his power to convict summarily at the time of the contempt itself even if the punishment the judge imposes in this fashion for separate contempts equals or exceeds six months. However, since the four dissenters would not have found any right at all to jury trial in the case of a direct contempt, it was clear that repeated acts of contempt can still be punished on the spot with sentences totalling more than six months. Mr. Justice Marshall disagreed with the view that any "overriding need" to maintain order in the courtroom justifies this practice.

Dissenting Justice Blackmun, joined by the Chief Justice and Justices Stewart and Rehnquist, emphasized that this direct contempt case was clearly distinguishable from Bloom v. Illinois, in which an attorney was punished for out of court contempt that differed little from the run of the mill criminal offense. However, with an in-court contempt such as this, and with all the details clearly on the record, the dissenters were "at a loss * * * to see the role a jury is to perform. * * * The determination of whether basically undisputed facts constitute a direct criminal contempt is a particularly inappropriate task for the jury. Before today, this determination has always been the exclusive province of the court, not the jury, and never before has this Court required a jury trial in a case involving a direct contempt."

In the Taylor case, the Court reversed eight separate contempt convictions imposed after trial upon a Kentucky lawyer for his conduct during the course of a trial at which he defended a black murder defendant. Although all the Justices except Mr. Justice Marshall agreed that petty contempts, like other petty offenses, may be tried without a jury so long as the actual sentence is not more than six months, the Court held that the lawyer was entitled to notice and some kind of a hearing. Thus he was entitled to reversal of his convictions and vacation of his six-month sentence —which had originally totalled more than four years. This was so even though the trial judge had given the defendant the opportunity to respond to most of the contempt charges at the time he announced them during the course of trial. Under the reasoning of Groppi v. Leslie, 404 U. S. 496, "before an attorney is finally adjudicated in contempt and sentenced after trial for conduct during trial, he should have reasonable notice of the specific charges and opportunity to be heard in his own behalf. This is not to say, however, that a full-scale trial is appropriate. * * * But the contemnor might at least urge, for example, that the behavior at issue was not

contempt but the acceptable conduct of an attorney representing his client; or, he might present matters in mitigation or otherwise attempt to make amends with the court."

Also, eight Justices agreed that if this lawyer were to be retried for his alleged contempts, his retrial should not be before the same judge who imposed the original contempt sentences. While the lawyer's conduct was not the kind of personal attack that took place in Mayberry v. Pennsylvania, the judge did become embroiled in a running controversy with the lawyer, and his mounting exasperation had become increasingly clear.

The trial court's reduction to six months of the four and one half years that the original contempt sentences, consecutively applied, had totalled was seen by Mr. Justice Marshall as a transparent effort to deny him a jury trial.

Mr. Justice Rehnquist, joined in his dissent in both cases by the Chief Justice, accused the Court of climaxing "a recent trend of constitutional innovation which virtually emasculates this historic power of a trial judge. If the holdings in this area were the product of any new historical insight into the meaning of the Fourteenth Amendment, or if indeed they could be regarded as a desirable progression towards a reign of light and law, even though of dubious constitutional ancestry, there would be less occasion for concern." But the only consistent thread running through the majority's hodge podge of legal doctrine "is this Court's inveterate propensity to second-guess the trial judge." The Taylor decision, he claimed, overlooks past precedent. In Codispoti, a case whose longevity entitles it to a chapter in Dickens' Bleak House, the defendants were initially tried for contempt before the decisions extending the 6-month rule to the states were handed down. Joined by the Chief Justice, he concluded that the defendants should not have the benefit of those cases, Duncan v. Louisiana, 391 U.S. 145, and Bloom v. Illinois.

SELF-INCRIMINATION

Bellis v. U.S., 417 U.S. 85, 15 CrL 3111

A member of a dissolved three-person law partnership was properly held in contempt for refusing to deliver the partnership books in response to a grand jury subpoena, the Court declared. Mr. Justice Marshall's opinion for an eight-Justice majority explained that the Fifth Amendment privilege is limited to protection of "the natural individual from compulsory incrimination through his own testimony or personal records." The partnership had a separate "institutional identity," and the subpoenaed lawyer held the records in a representative capacity and not a personal one. This is true, the majority said, even though the partnership was small, and apparently had not articles of incorporation.

It is true that the privilege does apply to the business records of a sole proprietor or sole practitioner, and may still apply to the family-owned small partnership or to partners who had a special relationship of confidentiality before their formal association. But "no artificial organization may utilize the personal privilege."

Individual privacy, the majority said, was the purpose behind the protection of business records in such cases as Boyd v. U.S., 116 U.S. 616 (1886), even though the subpoena in that case was in fact directed to a partnership. A line of cases going back to Wilson v. U.S., 221 U.S. 361 (1911) has distinguished between corporate records and the private papers involved in Boyd. These decisions have established that an individual's privilege does not protect him against production of records he holds in a representative capacity, "even if these records might incriminate him personally." And the Fifth Amendment's "protection of an individual's 'right to a private enclave where he may lead a private life' " does not extend "to the financial records of an organized collective entity."

Mr. Justice Douglas, in a lone dissent, urged that the individual lawyer was obviously the target of the criminal investigation here. Common sense, he asserted, requires that the privilege protect him. The records he holds are his own, both in law and in fact. Had he been in solo practice, his privilege would now protect him. Mr. Justice Douglas was "unable to perceive why he should be held to have forfeited that constitutional right by joining with two others in a partnership."

Lefkowitz v. Turley, 414 U.S. 70, 14 CrL 3031

The Court was unanimous in holding that a New York statute which bars anyone who refuses to waive immunity in a grand jury investigation from doing any public contracting for a five-year period violates the Fifth Amendment. The threat of public-contract debarment compels incriminating testimony, Mr. Justice White's opinion explained, by pressuring a person to give evidence that can be used against him in a future criminal prosecution. This case, the Court asserted, is controlled by the policeman cases, Gardner v. Broderick, 392 U.S. 273, and Garrity v. New Jersey, 385 U.S. 493. "The waiver sought by the state, under threat of loss of contracts, would have been no less compelled than a direct request for the testimony without resort to the waiver device. A waiver secured under threat of substantial economic sanction cannot be termed voluntary."

The state interest in regulating the business of public contracting is of course strong, but it can easily be vindicated if the state is willing to immunize the witness. When that public interest is balanced against the strong interest in preserving Fifth Amendment rights, immunity is little enough to ask. The simple answer to the state interest argument is that "the price for incriminating answers from third-party witnesses is sufficient immunity to satisfy the imperatives of the Fifth Amendment * * * ."

To the state argument that public contractors unlike state employees, do not depend entirely upon the state for their livelihood and that a five-year debarment threat is not therefore a compulsion, the Court replied, "[w]e fail to see a difference of constitutional magnitude * * * ."

Justices Brennan, Douglas and Marshall refused to join in the majority's dicta that "use immunity," if offered, would have answered all Fifth Amendment objections.

RIGHT TO COUNSEL —REIMBURSEMENT

Fuller v. Oregon, 417 U.S. 40, 15 CrL 3103

A carefully drafted Oregon statute requiring convicted indigent defendants to repay their defense costs if they subsequently become able to do so without "manifest hardship" is constitutional, a majority of the Court decided. The statute neither invidiously discriminates against those defendants who are convicted, nor does it place an undue burden upon their exercise of the right to counsel.

Although the statute did not require repayment by those indigents who were acquitted or whose cases otherwise were terminated prior to conviction, Mr. Justice Stewart, writing for the majority, did not see this as constituting invidious discrimination of the type condemned in James v. Strange, 407 U.S. 128, 11 CrL 3109. A defendant whose trial ends without conviction or whose conviction is overturned on appeal has been seriously imposed upon by society without any demonstration that he is criminally culpable. Oregon can surely decide with objective rationality, Mr. Justice Stewart said, that when a defendant has been forced to submit to criminal prosecution which does not end in conviction, he will be freed of any potential liability to reimburse the state for the costs of his defense.

Nor does the statute place an impermissible burden on the defendant's right to counsel or "chill" his exercise of that right, the majority concluded. "The fact that an indigent who accepts state-appointed legal representation knows that he might some day be required to repay the costs of these services in no way affects his eligibility to obtain counsel." The Oregon statute is carefully designed to insure that only those who actually become able to reimburse the state will ever be required to do so and then only if it would not work a "manifest hardship" upon them.

Mr. Justice Douglas, concurring in the result, argued that the equal protection claim was not properly preserved below and was therefore not properly before the Court. However, in view of the manner in which the statute had been stringently narrowed by Oregon courts, he concurred in the judgment.

Mr. Justice Marshall, joined in dissent by Mr. Justice Brennan, asserted that the statute discriminated between indigent defendants and other civil judgment debtors. This kind of discrimination was condemned in James v. Strange, Mr. Justice Brennan said. He was especially disturbed by the fact that repayment of costs can be made, as it was in this case, a condition of the defendant's probation. Thus, a defendant could conceivably be sent to jail for failing to pay a civil debt.

RIGHT TO COUNSEL —APPEAL

Ross v. Moffitt, 417 U.S. 600, 15 CrL 3168

Stressing the significant differences between the trial and appellate processes, a majority of the Court concluded that the Fourteenth Amendment does not require states to provide indigents counsel for discretionary appeals to state or federal courts. Neither the Due Process nor the Equal Protection Clause requires such an extension of the Douglas v. California, 372 U.S. 353, right to counsel on appeal, Mr. Justice Rehnquist, writing for a 6–3 majority, explained. The mere fact an appeal has been provided "does not automatically mean that a State then acts unfairly by refusing to provide counsel to indigent defendants at every state of the way." Unfairness results only if indigents are singled out by the state and denied meaningful access to that system because of their poverty. What must be kept in mind is that an attorney at trial serves as a shield to protect the defendant from being haled into court by the state and stripped of his presumption of innocence, while on appeal, he acts as a sword to upset a prior determination of guilt. "This difference is significant for, while no one would agree that the State may simply dispense with the trial stage of proceedings without a criminal defendant's consent, it is clear that the State need not provide any appeal at all." McKane v. Durston, 153 U.S. 684.

With respect to the equal protection question, the majority said that the state's duty is not to duplicate the legal arsenal available to a well-heeled criminal defendant, but only to assure the indigent defendant the opportunity to present his claims fairly in the context of the state's appellate process.

There is also a significant difference between the source of the right to seek discretionary review on the state level and the source of the right to seek certiorari in the U.S. Supreme Court. With that in mind, and in view of the Court's consistent policy of denying applications for appointment of counsel by persons seeking jurisdictional statements or petitions for cert before it, the majority thought it would be odd to read the Fourteenth Amendment as imposing such a requirement on the states.

Mr. Justice Douglas, joined by Justices Brennan and Marshall, argued that the right announced in Douglas v. California was founded on concepts of fairness and equality. The right to discretionary review is a substantial one where a lawyer can be of significant assistance to an indigent defendant. It only makes sense, he said, that the same concepts of fairness and equality which require counsel in a first appeal of right, require counsel in other subsequent discretionary appeals.

Mr. Justice Douglas found himself in agreement with the unanimous opinion of the U.S. Court of Appeals in this case.

FAIR TRIAL —WITNESSES

Cupp v. Naughten, 414 U.S. 141, 14 CrL 3037

The Court continued this Term its increasingly close scrutiny in recent years of established state trial procedures, e.g., Chambers v. Mississippi, 410 U.S. 284, 12 CrL 3150, and Wardius v. Oregon, 412 U.S. 470, 13 CrL 3141. But a six-Justice majority, emphasizing that the Fourteenth Amendment does not forbid every state practice that is of doubtful wisdom or desirability, found no due process denial in an Oregon jury instruction, given at the trial of a silent defendant who presented no witnesses, that every witness "is presumed to speak the truth." The instruction included the caveat that this presumption may be overcome by the nature of manner of the testimony, by credibility factors or contradictory evidence, "or by a presumption."

Following the "well established proposition that a single instruction to a jury * * * must be viewed in the context of the overall charge," Mr. Justice Rehnquist, speaking for the majority, pointed out that this jury was twice instructed, fully and explicitly, on the presumption of the defendant's innocence and the state's burden of proving his guilt beyond a reasonable doubt.

It cannot be said, the majority concluded, that the due process requirement of proof of guilt beyond a reasonable doubt was violated here. The jury "remained free to exercise its collective judgment to reject what it did not find trustworthy or plausible. Furthermore, by acknowledging that a witness could be discredited by his own manner or words, the instruction freed [the defendant] from any undue pressure to take the witness stand himself or to call witnesses under the belief that only positive testimony could engender disbelief of the State's witnesses."

True, Mr. Justice Rehnquist acknowledged, federal courts of appeal are virtually unanimous in their disapproval of such presumption of truth instructions. But this disapproval has been expressed in these courts' exercise of their supervisory powers. Absent a showing that the instruction violates some right guaranteed by the Fourteenth Amendment, neither substantial unanimity among federal courts of appeals nor even "universal condemnation" is enough to render it unconstitutional. Thus the U.S. Court of Appeals for the Ninth Circuit erred in granting this defendant habeas corpus relief.

Dissenting Justice Brennan, joined by Justices Douglas and Marshall, asserted that "the charge permitted the jury to convict even though the evidence may have failed to establish [the defendant's] guilt beyond a reasonable doubt, and therefore denied respondent due process of law." The state's case rested almost entirely upon the testimony of two eyewitnesses and two police officers, and, in view of the defendant's failure to call witnesses or testify himself, "the practical effect of the court's instructions was to convert the State's burden of proving guilt beyond a reasonable doubt to proving guilt by a preponderance of the evidence."

This charge, Mr. Justice Brennan further maintained, permitted the prosecution the benefit of the mere probability that the witnesses told the truth. The jurors were directed in effect, to ignore doubts that they might have entertained concerning the credibility of these witnesses.

FAIR TRIAL —FORCED WAIVER

U.S. v. Kahan, 415 U.S. 239, 14 CrL 4195

The principle of Simmons v. U.S., 390 U.S. 377, that one can't be forced to waive one constitutional right in order to assert another, is not one of broad application, a majority of the Court indicated. With a "Cf." citation to Harris v. New York, 401 U.S. 222, 8 CrL 3139, and the observation that "the protective shield of Simmons is not to be converted into a license for false representations on the issue of indigency * * *", a per curiam majority upheld the perjury conviction of a federal bribery defendant for stating that he had no funds to employ counsel when in fact he had $27,000 in four Totten trusts.

"Even assuming that the Simmons principle was appropriately extended to Sixth Amendment claims," the majority said, it is important that here, the incriminating component of the statements in question derives not from their content, but from the perjurer's knowledge of their falsity. Thus the perjurer had no Sixth Amendment right to protect.

Justices Douglas and Brennan, dissenting, could not see "how testimony protective of Sixth Amendment rights is on a lower level" than that given to protect Fourth Amendment rights. As for the mere nonexistence of the Sixth Amendment right, the dissenters say it was not exactly beyond doubt that the money in question was within the defendant's actual reach. Nor did there appear facts about what obligations there may have been against his available money.

Moreover, the dissenting Justices said, indigency and the right to appointed counsel are legal concepts that a layman might well get wrong, and should not be responsible for determining in the legal sense before being able to speak on the subject.

Also dissenting, Mr. Justice Marshall would have sought a different solution, whereby willful perjury can still be prosecuted, but damaging truthful statements are barred from later use.

RIGHT OF CONFRONTATION

Davis v. Alaska, 415 U.S. 308, 14 CrL 3117

An Alaska trial judge misread the scales of justice when he issued a protective order that forbade a larceny defendant to cross-examine a key prosecution witness about the witness' status as a juvenile probationer, a 7–2 majority of the Court held in an opinion by the Chief Justice. In denying the defendant this crucial opportunity to prove that the youth's status might have caused him to be biased and prejudiced his identification, the court denied him his right of confrontation. The juvenile was on probation following an adjudication of delinquency based on burglaries in which he was involved.

The state's interest in protecting the anonymity of juvenile offenders was, in this case, outweighed by the defendant's right of confrontation, the Chief Justice explained. Although the majority was not willing to speculate as to whether the jury would have accepted the defense attorney's line of reasoning, the defendant nevertheless should have had the opportunity to present it.

Mr. Justice Stewart, concurring, emphasized "that the Court neither holds nor suggests that the Constitution confers a right in every case to impeach the general credibility of a witness through cross-examination about his past delinquency adjudications or criminal convictions."

Mr. Justice White, joined in dissent by Mr. Justice Rehnquist, argued that there was no constitutional principle at stake here. Rather, the dissenters said, this is merely a typical instance of a trial court exercising its discretion to limit or control cross-examination. The majority, they asserted, is merely second-guessing state courts and inviting federal review of every ruling made by a state trial judge who believes cross-examination has gone far enough.

APPEAL —HARSHER CHARGE

Blackledge v. Perry, 417 U.S. 21, 15 CrL 3097

Bringing a felony charge against an assault defendant after he has exercised his right to seek a trial de novo following his misdemeanor conviction violates the Fourteenth Amendment Due Process Clause, the Court held. In upping the charge this way, the prosecutor is penalizing him for exercising his statutory right to appeal. Resting its decision on due process grounds, the Court found it unnecessary to reach any double jeopardy question presented by this practice.

Mr. Justice Stewart, writing for the 8–1 majority, emphasized that North Carolina v. Pearce, 395 U.S. 711, 5 CrL 3119, and its progeny do not condemn all possible increased punishment upon retrial after appeal, but only those resulting from possible vindictiveness. And the danger of vindictiveness is great here. This is not a case of a judge imposing a harsher sentence, as it was in Pearce and in Colten v. Kentucky, 407 U.S. 104, 11 CrL 3102, or of a stiffer penalty imposed by a jury which had never heard of the original trial, as it was in Chaffin v. Stynchombe, 412 U.S. 17, 13 CrL 3093. Rather, the charge was increased dramatically —and it was the same prosecutor who pressed each of these charges. Discouragement of appeals in this manner —a tactic that is obviously in the prosecutor's interest —cannot be countenanced. And it is not necessary that "actual retaliatory motivation * * * exist." There was no evidence of such motive here. But the defendant must be left free of "apprehension that the State will retaliate * * *."

A 7–2 majority of the Court also concluded that defendant's guilty plea to the felony charge did not bar him from raising constitutional claims by means of a federal habeas proceeding. His challenge here went to the power of the state to charge him at all.

Mr. Justice Rehnquist, dissenting, viewed the majority's rationale as a double jeopardy argument dressed in due process language. Joined by Mr. Justice Powell, he also accused the majority of making a major departure from Tollett v. Henderson, 411 U.S. 258, 13 CrL 3034. The great majority of defendants, as well as prosecutors, have a great interest in the finality of guilty pleas, and if that finality can be swept away as easily as it is in this case, prosecutors will have a reduced incentive to bargain.

At most, there was a violation of Pearce standards here, and the proper remedy is resentencing.

POST-CONVICTION RELIEF

Donnelly v. De Christoforo, 416 U.S. 637, 15 CrL 3062

Stressing the "necessarily imprecise constitutional line" between state prosecutorial errors serious enough to merit federal habeas relief and those that are not, a majority of the Court held that habeas was not appropriate for a Massachusetts prosecutor's improper intimation during closing argument that the defendant had been ready to plead guilty. This remark, "but one moment in an extended trial and * * * followed by specific disapproving instructions," did not render the accused's trial "so fundamentally unfair as to deny him due process."

Thus the Court, by a 6–3 vote, reversed a decision by the U.S. Court of Appeals for the First Circuit ordering habeas corpus relief. But Justices Stewart and White joined the majority only because they felt bound by the Court's "rule of four" in granting review to decide the case on its merits; they agreed with dissenting Justice Douglas that, since no new principle of law was presented, the First Circuit's decision should have been left undisturbed in the first place.

The prosecutorial remark was an observation that "I quite frankly think that they hope you find him guilty of something a little less than first-degree murder." Coming after the mid-trial announcement of a codefendant's second-degree murder guilty plea, the remark seemed to the First Circuit to carry a potential for misleading the jury to believe that the defendant had unsuccessfully attempted a plea-bargain. But Mr. Justice Rehnquist, writing for the Supreme Court majority, pointed out that five Massachusetts Supreme Judicial Court Justices "and at least one federal judge have all confessed difficulty in making this speculative connection." This remark, made in the midst of a lengthy closing argument, was not the kind of serious prosecutorial misconduct that has been held in cases such as Miller v. Pate, 386 U.S. 1, and Brady v. Maryland, 373 U.S. 83, to violate due process.

Mr. Justice Douglas maintained in his dissent that the remark was an attempt to interject the inadmissible fact of a withdrawn attempt to plead guilty, and rises to the level of a due process violation. The aspect of his opinion in which Justices Brennan and Marshall joined and with which Justices Stewart and White agreed, was the conclusion that certiorari should not have been granted. He saw no reason to overturn the decision of "responsible federal judges who know the Federal Constitution as well as we do." Only grants or denials of habeas corpus relief that amount to "egregious" error should lead to a grant of certiorari, he asserted.

Davis v. U.S., 417 U.S. 333, 15 CrL 3134

The "law of the case" doctrine can't be used to cut off the right of a federal prisoner seeking post-conviction relief under 18 U.S.C. 2255 to argue new federal case law that came down after his conviction was affirmed, an eight-Justice majority held. Remanding a Ninth Circuit decision that upheld on "law of the case" grounds a district court's summary dismissal of a 2255 motion, the Court held that a Draft Act defendant was entitled to the benefit of a Ninth Circuit panel decision which postdated and squarely disagreed with the panel decision that upheld his conviction on direct appeal.

The majority saw no merit in a Government contention that Section 2255 relief is restricted to constitutional claims. The statute itself speaks of sentences in violation of "the laws of the United States," and the legislative history of Section 2255 shows clearly that it was intended to assume the full scope of federal habeas corpus — changing only the customary forum for such collateral attacks on federal convictions.

Justice Powell did not dispute the majority's reasoning on these two points, but he agreed with the original Ninth Circuit opinion on direct appeal that Gutknecht v. U.S., 396 U.S. 395, 6 CrL 3023, did not invalidate the delinquency induction order the petitioner here was convicted of disobeying. Thus he dissented from the majority's reversal of the Ninth Circuit's judgment.

Mr. Justice Rehnquist, dissenting, urged that nonconstitutional Section 2255 attacks on federal convictions should not be allowed. At least, he said, the matter is very much in doubt and it should not be assumed that Section 2255 can be invoked to raise non-constitutional issues of federal case law. He agreed with the "many decisions of lower federal courts" that have "at least implicitly limited collateral relief to claims of constitutional stature." To allow federal prisoners to invoke every new panel opinion as "new law," even after their direct appeals have been decided on these issues, will invite chaos. Furthermore, the petitioner merely touched on this issue in his Court of Appeals brief. It would have been preferable to give the Court of Appeals an opportunity on remand to fully consider it.

Wingo v. Wedding, 418 U.S. 461, 15 CrL 3281

Federal magistrates have no authority to hold evidentiary hearings in habeas corpus cases, a seven-Justice majority of the Court held as it struck down a local court rule purporting to give full-time magistrates this authority. Not only are district judges personnally required to conduct such hearings under 28 U.S.C. 2243, but magistrates are specifically precluded by 28 U.S.C. 636 (b) 3 from conducting proceedings of this type.

The legislative history of the Federal Magistrates Act convinced the majority that Congress intended to retain the exclusive policy of Section 2243, particularly in view of the careful way in which the scope of permissible assignments was limited by the language of Section 636 (b) of the Act.

Mr. Justice Brennan, the majority spokesman, concluded that the invalidity of the local rule was not cured by its provision allowing either party in a habeas proceeding to obtain de novo consideration by the district judge of the tape-recorded testimony of witnesses at the hearing.

The Chief Justice, joined by Mr. Justice White in dissent, asserted that the majority's holding was contrary to the purposes of the federal Magistrates Act and to the conclusions of the four federal circuits which have considered this issue. Citing a discussion of this very subject during Senate hearings on this legislation, the Chief Justice maintained that permission for magistrates to conduct habeas evidentiary hearings was clearly intended and that this interpretation would be consistent with the time-saving objectives of the Act.

SENTENCING —YOUTH CORRECTIONS ACT

Dorzynski v. U.S., 418 U.S. 424, 15 CrL 3270

The Court was unanimous in holding that the Youth Corrections Act requires a federal judge sentencing a youthful offender under other applicable penal statutes to first make an explicit finding that the offender would not benefit from treatment under the Act. Five Justices agreed that this finding need not be supported with a statement of reasons as to why the judge chose to sentence outside the Act.

The Act, intended to broaden the scope of sentencing discretion to include the alternatives of treatment or of probation for youthful offenders, was not aimed at limiting traditional judicial discretion in imposing sentence, the Chief Justice emphasized in his opinion for the Court. However, limited review is available if there has been no exercise of discretion at all. So an explicit "no benefit" finding will make clear the judge's awareness of the Act and his determination that it is not appropriate for the defendant before him.

Four Justices —Marshall, Douglas, Brennan and Stewart —urged that as construed by the Court, the "no benefit" finding was no finding at all. The Act was meant to set up sentencing under it as a preferred alternative, Mr. Justice Marshall maintained. In view of this, and since the Act explicitly requires the judge to make a finding, traditional sentencing discretion is limited. All courts of appeal except one have agreed that this is so. Furthermore, a statement of reasons would serve a number of other important policies, including rationalization of the sentencing process and reduction of disparities. It might also help corrections authorities in deciding how to handle the offender, and aid defense counsel in making sure that the sentence is not based on factual inaccuracies in the judge's sentencing material. Such an approach, limited to this Act, would not be the wholesale departure from traditional sentencing doctrines that the majority thinks it would be, Mr. Justice Marshall asserted.

Warden v. Marrero, 417 U.S. 653, 15 CrL 3177

Six Justices agreed that both the General Saving Clause, 1 U.S.C. 109, and the Saving Clause included in the Comprehensive Drug Abuse Prevention and Control Act of 1970, bar parole consideration for a narcotics offender sentenced under the now-repealed 26 U.S.C. 7237 (c), which precluded eligibility. This is so, Mr. Justice Brennan wrote on behalf of the majority, even though the offender would have been eligible if sentenced after the 1970 Act's effective date. Thus the Court answered the question it had expressly reserved in Bradley v. U.S., 410 U.S. 605, 12 CrL 3198. Parole eligibility under the 1970 Drug Act is determined at the time of sentence, and Bradley held that ineligibility for early parole was part of the "prosecution" saved by the 1970 Drug Act's saving clause.

In concluding that the General Saving Clause also bars the Board of Parole from considering parole for a defendant sentenced prior to the effective date of the 1970 Act, Mr. Justice Brennan's opinion for the majority interpreted the legislative history of the original no-parole provision as meaning that the provision was to be treated as part of the "punishment" for the narcotics offenses for which a respondent was convicted. The clause has been held to bar application of ameliorative sentencing laws replacing harsher ones that were in force at the time of the commission of an offense.

Mr. Justice Blackmun, joined in dissent by Justices Douglas and Marshall, did not consider parole eligibility as a penalty within the meaning of the General Saving statute. Furthermore, in passing the 1970 Drug Act, Congress explicitly rejected the concept of parole uneligibility, and congressional intent is crucial here.

FIRST AMENDMENT

Lewis v. City of New Orleans, 415 U.S. 130, 14 CrL 3097

The Louisiana Supreme Court's reconsideration on remand from the U. S. Supreme Court of a New Orleans breach of the peace ordinance failed to save the ordinance when it reached the U. S. Supreme Court a second time. The ordinance made it unlawful to "wantonly * * * curse or revile or to use obscene or opprobrious language toward or with reference to any member of the city police while in the actual performance of his duties." The state Supreme Court on remand did not refine or narrow these words, Mr. Justice Brennan said on behalf of a five-Justice majority, but took the position that the ordinance as written was narrowed to the necessary "fighting words" that fall outside the First Amendment under the doctrine announced in Chaplinsky v. New Hampshire, 315 U. S. 568, and reaffirmed in Gooding v. Wilson, 405 U. S. 518, 10 CrL 3137, 40 LW 4329. As authoritatively constructed by the Louisiana Supreme Court, the statute is still susceptible of application to speech that is protected despite its vulgarity or offensiveness.

Concurring in the result, Mr. Justice Powell emphasized that words may or may not be "fighting words" depending upon the circumstances in which they are spoken. It was highly unlikely in this case —involving a confrontation between a middle aged woman and an officer —that they would have precipitated physical violence. This ordinance, Mr. Justice Powell said, "confers on police a virtually unrestrained power to arrest and charge persons with a violation."

This case represents another example of the extremes to which the Court has allowed itself to be manipulated in First Amendment cases, Mr. Justice Blackmun maintained. Joined in dissent by the Chief Justice and Mr. Justice Rehnquist, he asserted that the overbreadth and vagueness doctrines are being invoked indiscriminately, regardless of the facts that each case presents. The Court has gone far beyond what was anticipated by the opinion in Chaplinsky v. New Hampshire. In fact, Mr. Justice Blackmun emphasized, there was a fight between the officer and the defendant in this case.

Inherent in the rubber-stamp use of the overbreadth and vagueness doctrines, Mr. Justice Blackmun warned, "is a judicial-legislative confrontation. The more frequent our intervention, which of late has been unrestrained, the more we usurp the prerogative of democratic government."

CIVIL RIGHTS ACTIONS

Steffel v. Thompson, 415 U.S. 452, 14 CrL 3123

The ban imposed by Younger v. Harris, 401 U.S. 37, 8 CrL 3103 and Samuels v. Mackell, 401 U.S. 66, 8 CrL 3113, on federal declaratory relief during a pending prosecution won't be extended to threatened prosecution, the Court held unanimously as it permitted an antiwar leafletter's declaratory suit to proceed. When no prosecution is pending, the considerations of equity, comity, and federalism underlying Younger and Samuels have little vitality.

Mr. Justice Brennan's opinion for the Court emphasized that except for the narrow purposes of Younger and Samuels, civil rights declaratory judgments are not to be equated with injunctive relief. Also, it did not matter that this plaintiff's attack on the statute's constitutionality was only "as applied" rather than facial.

The Court also reversed the holding that the leafletter, who alleged only that the stipulated state threat of prosecution kept him from returning to the shopping center where he had been distributing his leaflets, presented no actual case or controversy. However, the Court said, a remand hearing would be necessary to determine if there had been the kind of "end to the Viet Nam war that would end the actual controversy."

Mr. Justice Brennan emphasized that equating threatened prosecution with pending prosecution for Younger purposes would constitute an exhaustion requirement similar to that for habeas petitions for all civil rights litigation.

A brief concurrence by Mr. Justice Stewart and the Chief Justice reemphasized the limitations of Boyle v. Landry, 401 U.S. 77, 8 CrL 3104, on resort to federal litigation by those who haven't shown even a threat. Not everyone who feels a "chilling effect" from the mere existence of a state statute that might be unconstitutional has a right to enter the federal courts, Mr. Justice Stewart emphasized.

Mr. Justice Rehnquist, in a concurrence joined by the Chief Justice, expressed doubt that federal declaratory judgments obtained while actual prosecution is merely threatened should continue to have effect in the actual event of a prosecution against the plaintiff. A federal declaratory judgment cannot be used to support a federal injunction, Mr. Justice Rehnquist emphasized. Nor can it have res judicata effect as to the constitutional issue in the state prosecution.

Replying to Mr. Justice Rehnquist, Mr. Justice White would, at least for the present time, anticipate that a federal declaratory judgment should have res judicata effect in a state criminal prosecution. He was also persuaded, for the time being at least, that the constitutional decision embodied in a declaratory judgment can be enforced by federal injunction, for he saw no reason why a federal plaintiff should be restricted to reliance on the weaker shield of res judicata.

Allee v. Medrano, 416 U.S. 802, 15 CrL 3079

The Court also refused to extend to pending state injunctive proceedings the Younger principle requiring a special showing of extraordinary circumstances for 1871 Civil Rights Act relief when a state prosecution is pending. Mr. Justice Douglas' opinion for the Court affirmed a three-judge federal court's injunction against Texas Rangers' harassment and intimidation of farm labor organizers in an eight-year-old case.

Such three-judge court relief is appropriate even when harassment takes place under a valid statute, the majority said. The three-judge court may do so in conjunction with its examination of a constitutional challenge to other statutes. However, the part of the district court decree that declared five Texas statutes unconstitutional was remanded, for three of these statutes had since been replaced by narrower laws. Absent pending prosecutions under the superseded statutes, that part of the case would be moot. If there are such prosecutions, than a Younger v. Harris determination of bad faith prosecution must be made, Mr. Justice Douglas said. As for the two unrepealed statutes, the same contingent determinations of pending prosecution and bad faith were contemplated by the remand. But absent such pending prosecutions, the Court said, there still might be a live controversy presented by the threat of prosecution as reaffirmed in Steffel v. Thompson.

The Chief Justice, joined by Justices White and Rehnquist, concurred in the remand, but not in the reasoning that went with it, and dissented from the affirmance of the injunction against police misconduct. Younger v. Harris does apply, the dissenters asserted, and the facts did not satisfy its requirements.

O'Shea v. Littleton, 414 U.S. 488, 14 CrL 3085

Construing the case or controversy requirement of Article III of the U.S. Constitution, the Supreme Court, this Term, rejected the class action attempt of 17 black and two white residents of Cairo, Illinois to enjoin two local judges from engaging in bond, sentencing, and jury fee practices allegedly designed to deter civil rights protests. Specifically, the Court held that the activists' failure to allege specific individual injury to themselves required the dismissal of their complaint. "Accepting that they are deeply involved in a program to eliminate racial discrimination * * * and that tensions are high, we are nonetheless unable to conclude that the case or controversy requirement is satisfied by general assertions or inferences that in the course of their activities [these activists] will be prosecuted for violating valid criminal laws."

Moreover, even if a case or controversy existed, the Court concluded, equitable relief would be inappropriate since the activists established neither a likelihood of substantial and immediate irreparable injury nor the inadequacy of their remedy at law. Additionally, recognition of the need for a proper balance and the concurrent operation of federal and state courts counsels restraint in the issuance of injunctions against state officers engaged in administration of the state's criminal laws in the absence of a showing of irreparable injury and immediate harm.

In dissent, Mr. Justice Douglas, joined by Justices Brennan and Marshall, complained that "the one crucial issue on which the Court makes this case turn * * * was never argued." In the view of the dissenters, the allegations of the complaint support the likelihood that the complainants and members of their class will be brought before the defendant judges and be subjected to the alleged discriminatory practices. Hence, an Article III case or controversy is clearly presented.

Spomer v. Littleton, 414 U.S. 514, 14 CrL 3093

In a companion case, decided the same day, the Court unanimously refused to pass on the merits of a civil rights class action by the same activists against the then State's

Attorney individually and in his official capacity, charging him with certain purposeful racially discriminatory practices under color of the Constitution and the Civil Rights Acts, 42 U.S.C. Secs. 1981–1983, 1985. In the district court, the complaint was dismissed for lack of jurisdiction to grant injunctive relief, after which the court of appeals reversed, holding that the prosecutor's quasi-judicial immunity from injunctive proscription was not absolute, and inasmuch as the activists' remedies at law were inadequate, injunctive relief might be available if the activists were able to prove their claims.

Thereafter, the successor State's Attorney was substituted as party in the petition for certiorari filed with the Supreme Court. This substitution, according to Mr. Justice White, the Court's spokesman, requires vacation of the court of appeals decision and remand to that court to determine whether, in absence of allegations of wrongful conduct on the part of the successor State's Attorney, the dispute is moot. To Mr. Justice White it was apparent that there was nothing in the record upon which to firmly base a conclusion that a concrete controversy between the successor State's Attorney and the activists was presented to the Court for resolution. No allegations in the complaint cited any conduct of the successor as the basis for equitable or any other relief. Moreover, he was not named as a defendant in the complaint at all and he never appeared before either the district court or the court of appeals. "The injunctive relief requested against [the] former State's Attorney * * * moreover, is based upon an alleged practice of willfull and malicious racial discrimination evidenced by enumerated instances in which [he] favored white persons and disfavored Negroes. The wrongful conduct charged in the complaint is personal to [him], despite the fact that he was also sued in his then capacity as State's Attorney. * * * No charge is made in the complaint that the policy of the office of State's Attorney is to follow the intentional practices alleged, apart from the allegation that * * * the incumbent at the time, was then continuing the practices he had previously followed."

FIRST AMENDMENT —OBSCENITY

Speight v. Slaton, 415 U.S. 333, 14 CrL 3122

A three-judge federal district court's judgment refusing to enjoin state proceedings brought under a Georgia obscenity statute to close down a bookstore was vacated and remanded by a unanimous Court for reconsideration in light of an intervening Georgia Supreme Court declaration, in a similar case, that the applicable statute was unconstitutional as applied to close down a bookstore merely because some of its stock had been held judicially obscene.

CIVIL RIGHTS ACT PROSECUTIONS

Anderson v. U.S., 417 U.S. 211, 15 CrL 3119

Evidence that election officials, in an attempt to elect local candidates, conspired to cast false votes both for those candidates and for federal candidates running on the same "slate" was deemed sufficient by a majority of the Court to support their conviction under 18 U.S.C. Sec. 241, which makes it unlawful to conspire to injure any citizen in the free exercise of any right or privilege secured by the Constitution or laws of the United States. In so ruling, the Court, in a seven-Justice opinion by Mr. Justice Marshall, avoided any decision on whether Section 241 encompasses conspiracies to cast fraudulent votes in state and local elections.

The officials had argued that statements made by some of them after the federal election results where made final were hearsay and inadmissible since the conspiracy was not in progress at the time they were made. The statements were not hearsay, the Court explained; they were not offered to prove the truth of the matter asserted. Rather, they were introduced to prove that the officials, who made the statements at an election contest hearing challenging the local election results, had perjured themselves at the hearing.

The Court characterized the fact that the officials did not intend to influence the outcome of the federal election as irrelevant. "The specific intent required under Section 241 is not the intent to change the outcome of a federal election, but rather the intent to have false votes cast and thereby to injure the right of all voters in a federal election to express their choice of a candidate and to have their expressions of choice given full value and effect."

Mr. Justice Douglas, joined by Mr. Justice Brennan, disagreed with the majority. In failing to decide whether a conspiracy to cast false votes for candidates for state and local, as opposed to federal, office is unlawful under Section 241, the majority "avoids the issues squarely presented by petitioners and by the decision of the Court of Appeals," the dissenters asserted. After reviewing the legislative history of Section 241, Mr. Justice Douglas concludes that it "does not reach conspiracies to abscond with state elections, absent the element of racial discrimination."

EQUAL PROTECTION

Marshall v. U.S., 414 U.S. 417, 14 CrL 3077

Resolving a conflict among the federal courts of appeal, a six-Justice majority, in an opinion by the Chief Justice, found no denial of equal protection in the Narcotic Addict Rehabilitation Act's exclusion from eligibility for rehabilitative treatment of addicts with two or more prior felony convictions. NARA treatment, an alternative to simple penal incarceration, carries with it comparatively lenient sentencing possibilities.

The concept of equal protection as embodied in the Fifth Amendment's Due Process Clause does not require that all persons be dealt with identically, but simply that there must be some rational basis for statutory distinctions, the Chief Justice pointed out. The right to treatment cannot be considered a "fundamental" constitutional right, and this classification is not a suspect one.

It is clear, the majority said, that the two-felonies exclusion rule was aimed at excluding from NARA treatment those less likely to be rehabilitated by such treatment, and those with a history of serious crimes. Congress could rationally assume that addicts who were two-time felons were less likely to benefit from rehabilitation and thus would pose a greater threat to society upon release. This is an area fraught with medical and scientific uncertainties and legislative options in enacting an experimental treatment program such as this must be especially broad.

Mr. Justice Marshall, joined by Justices Douglas and Brennan, accused the majority of such deference to Congress that it was permitting the Equal Protection Clause to be emasculated. The two-felonies rule does not serve the legislative end of providing special treatment to those most likely to be rehabilitated; an addict with two prior felonies based upon addict-related offenses may be excluded while a recently-addicted defendant with a criminal record unrelated to any drug habit would be eligible. Furthermore, almost all addicts are "hardened criminals" in the sense that they must frequently commit crime to support their habits —and satisfaction of the habit itself involves the daily offense of possession.

The Act's "broad and arbitrary exclusion" cannot be justified on the ground that the program, now in its seventh year, is experimental, the dissenters said. Also, punishment of activities arising out of a disease like drug addiction raises Eighth Amendment problems.

Richardson v. Ramirez, 418 U.S. 24, 15 Crl 3220

California's disenfranchisement of convicted felons who have completed their sentences and paroles is not violative of the Equal Protection Clause of the Fourteenth Amendment, according to a 6–3 Court. A "compelling state interest" is not necessary to support such disenfranchisement, the Court explained, since it is expressly permitted by the Fourteenth Amendment.

The Court rested its decision on Section 2 of the Fourteenth Amendment. Section 2 imposes a sanction of reduced representation upon states which deny eligible citizens their right to vote, but exempts from this sanction a state's exclusion of persons who have participated "in rebellion or other crime * * * ." Section 1 of the Amendment —the Equal Protection Clause —could not have been meant "to bar outright a form of disenfranchisement which was expressly exempted from the less drastic sanction of reduced representation."

Mr. Justice Marshall, joined by Mr. Justice Brennan and in part by Mr. Justice Douglas, urged that the California Supreme Court's judgment invalidating the law rested on an adequate and independent state ground, and thus was not properly before the Court. Justices Marshall and Brennan also felt that no case or controversy was present, and dissented on the merits as well.

DUE PROCESS —FORFEITURE

Calero-Toledo v. Pearson Yacht Leasing Co., 416 U.S. 663, 15 CrL 3067

In a decision that could have significant implications for the business of renting vehicles and vessels, the Court found no due process violation in the forfeiture, pursuant to a Puerto Rican statute, of a concededly innocent owner-lessor's yacht that was used by a lessee to transport contraband. Mr. Justice Brennan, writing for a 7–2 majority, explained that, in the absence of a showing by the corporate owner that it did everything it could to insure that the vessel was not used illegally, the public interest in deterring such activity overrides the owner's property interest here.

Tracing the history of forfeiture back to its common-law origins, the majority noted that the owner's innocence has "almost uniformly been rejected as a defense." However, the door was left slightly ajar —for a case in which an owner could prove not only that he was uninvolved in and unaware of the wrongful activity, but also that he had done "all that reasonably could be expected" to prevent such use.

Nor was the owner constitutionally entitled to preseizure notice and hearing; postponement of a hearing was justified both by the public interest in preventing illicit use of the property against which the Government proceeds, and by exigent circumstances —the yacht could easily have been moved to another jurisdiction.

By an 8–1 vote, with Mr. Justice Douglas dissenting, the Court concluded that the forfeiture statute's failure to provide either notice or a hearing prior to seizure of the property to be forfeited does not deny the owner due process. The Court was unanimous in deciding that for purposes of the Three-Judge Court Act, 28 U.S.C. 2281, Puerto Rico's statutes are "state statutes."

Justices White and Powell, joining in the Court's opinion, added the observation that other situations besides the presence of important public interests could justify dispensing with preseizure hearings.

Justices Douglas and Stewart maintained that forfeiture of property belonging to an innocent and non-negligent owner violates due process. "If the yacht had been notoriously used in smuggling drugs, those who claim forfeiture might have equity on their side," Mr. Justice Douglas acknowledged. "But no such showing was made, and so far as we know only one marijuana cigarette was found on the yacht."

MAIL FRAUD

U.S. v. Maze, 414 U.S. 395, 14 CrL 3070

The Court held that the federal mail fraud statute, 18 U.S.C. 1341, which punishes use of the mails for "the purpose of executing * * * or attempting" to execute a scheme to defraud, does not cover a scheme that uses the mails only after the fraud has been perpetrated. A five-four majority, in an opinion by Mr. Justice Rehnquist, found no violation of the statute by a fraudulent credit card user whose scheme to defraud reached fruition when he obtained motel services by using the card. There is no indication that his scheme, a two-week cross country spending spree with a roommate's credit card, depended on the motels' use of the mails to send invoices to the bank, or the bank's use of the mails to bill the card's owner. "Indeed, from his point of view, he probably would have preferred to have the invoices misplaced by the various motel personnel and never mailed at all." Rather than serve any purpose, the mailings in this case actually increased the probability that he would be caught.

Pointing to Congress' recent enactment of the Truth-in-Lending Act, 15 U.S.C. Sec. 1644, which prohibits use of a fraudulently obtained credit card in a "transaction affecting" interstate commerce, the majority suggested that the mail fraud statute could have been worded so as to require only that the mails be in fact used. But Congress did not draft so broad a statute.

The Chief Justice and Justices Brennan, White and Blackmun dissented. Writing on behalf of all four dissenters, Mr. Justice White accused the majority of taking an unnecessarily restricted approach to the statute by selectively seizing on language from previous decisions construing it. Regardless of the point at which the defendant's scheme stopped, from a legal standpoint his use of the card was merely the first step in actually defrauding the bank that had issued the card. Furthermore, the delay caused by the time-consuming process of sending credit card invoices by mail served to conceal the scheme while it was still in progress.

The dissenters were also fearful of the long-term ramifications of this decision, which would make it unduly awkward to crack down on this burgeoning form of criminal activity. This single credit-card fraud will have to be dealt with on a state-by-state basis, by each state in which the crooked traveller used the card.

The Chief Justice, joined by Mr. Justice White, noted that the mail fraud statute has traditionally been used by the Government as a first line of defense for a new form of fraud until specific legislation can be enacted to deal with the problem. This decision, he hoped, will be limited to the narrow facts of this case, and he pointed out that the Court of Appeals whose judgment was affirmed was careful to state that it was not holding that the fraudulent use of a credit card can never constitute a violation of the mail fraud statute.

FIREARMS

Huddelston v. U.S., 415 U.S. 814, 14 CrL 3151.

Eight Justices agreed that a false statement on a federal firearms questionnaire made while redeeming a firearm from a pawn shop whose owner is a federally licensed firearm's dealer is punishable under 18 U.S.C. Sec. 922 (a) (6), which prohibits the making of a false statement "in connection with the acquisition * * * from any * * * licensed dealer" that is "intended or likely to deceive such * * * dealer * * * with respect to any fact material to the lawfulness of the sale or other disposition of such firearms * * *."

To Mr. Justice Douglas, the lone dissenter, this case presented a statutory ambiguity that should be resolved in favor of the defendant.

Table of Cases Cited
(Alphabetical)

Table of Cases Cited

(By Subject Classification*)

* *These subject classifications are not exhaustive. Each case is listed under only one subject classification, regardless of the number of issues it may involve.*

184